THE ECONOMIC DEVELOPMENT
OF FRANCE AND GERMANY
1815–1914

THE
ECONOMIC DEVELOPMENT
OF
FRANCE AND GERMANY
1815–1914

BY

J. H. CLAPHAM

FOURTH EDITION

CAMBRIDGE
AT THE UNIVERSITY PRESS
1968

Published by the Syndics of the Cambridge University Press
Bentley House, P.O. Box 92, 200 Euston Road, London, N.W. 1
American Branch: 32 East 57th Street, New York, N.Y. 10022

Standard Book Number:
521 04664 5 clothbound
521 09150 0 paperback

First edition 1921
Second edition 1923
Third edition 1928
Fourth edition 1936
Reprinted 1945 1948 1951
1955 1961 1963
1966 1968

Printed in Great Britain
at the University Printing House, Cambridge
(Brooke Crutchley, University Printer)

PREFACE

A great deal of important work bearing on some of the topics dealt with in this short survey has appeared since the third edition was published in 1928. This has made a few changes necessary, especially in Chapter I. It is a pleasure to acknowledge my debt to my friend Professor Marc Bloch and his colleague Professor Lefebvre, whose work has so vividly illuminated French agrarian history. For fresh light on Germany I owe most to Herr Franz Schnabel's recent *Deutsche Geschichte im Neunzehnten Jahrhundert*. The text of the book has, I hope, been improved in a number of small ways; but I have not been obliged to modify my general conclusions, although if I were writing it now for the first time I might alter the balance a little.

J. H. CLAPHAM

King's College,
May 16, 1936

CONTENTS

	PAGE
INTRODUCTION	1
§ 1. The year 1815 as an economic starting-point . . .	1

CH. I. RURAL LIFE AND AGRICULTURE IN FRANCE BEFORE THE RAILWAY AGE 6–28
§ 2. The framework of rural life 6
§ 3. Revolutionary legislation: the free use of land: commons and common rights 10
§ 4. Revolutionary legislation: tenures 13
§ 5. Revolutionary legislation: changes in land ownership . 18
§ 6. Changes in agriculture: new crops: cattle: implements . 21

CH. II. GERMAN RURAL CONDITIONS BEFORE THE RAILWAY AGE 29–52
§ 7. The framework of rural life 29
§ 8. The German peasantry 37
§ 9. Peasant emancipation 41
§ 10. Agricultural progress 47

CH. III. INDUSTRIAL CONDITIONS IN FRANCE, 1815– 1848 53–81
§ 11. The slow industrialisation of France 53
§ 12. The French coal position 56
§ 13. French metallurgy 58
§ 14. French textile industries 63
§ 15. New industries and processes 69
§ 16. Protective tariffs 71
§ 17. The industrial wage earners 75

CH. IV. INDUSTRIAL CONDITIONS IN GERMANY, 1815– 1848 82–103
§ 18. Medieval survivals 82
§ 19. Slow growth of modern industry 85
§ 20. German metallurgy 89
§ 21. German textile industries 92
§ 22. By-industries 95
§ 23. The Zollverein 96
§ 24. Industries with a future 101

CH. V. COMMUNICATIONS AND COMMERCE IN WESTERN EUROPE BEFORE THE RAILWAY AGE . 104–120
§ 25. Roads and canals in France 104
§ 26. Roads in Germany 107
§ 27. River transport, steam, and overseas trade . . . 109
§ 28. The staple articles of international trade 113
§ 29. Commercial organisation 116

PAGE

Ch. VI. MONEY BANKING AND INVESTMENT, 1815–1848 121–139

§ 30. The wars and finance 121
§ 31. Currency systems 123
§ 32. Development of banking systems 125
§ 33. Joint stock companies 130
§ 34. The investment habit 132
§ 35. Growing interdependence of nations: crises . . . 135
§ 36. The purchasing power of money 138

Ch. VII. THE MAKING OF THE FIRST RAILWAY AND
TELEGRAPH NETWORK, 1830–1869 . 140–157

§ 37. Belgian railways 140
§ 38. French railways 143
§ 39. German railways 150
§ 40. The telegraph 156

Ch. VIII. RURAL FRANCE, 1848–1914 158–194

§ 41. The turning point in rural history 158
§ 42. Constant elements in rural life 160
§ 43. Rural emigrants and immigrants 167
§ 44. Machinery 170
§ 45. Specialised agriculture 173
§ 46. Increase of produce 174
§ 47. Agriculture and tariffs 178
§ 48. Cooperation 183
§ 49. Labour movements 189
§ 50. Agriculture and capitalism 192

Ch. IX. RURAL GERMANY, 1848–1914 195–231

§ 51. Emancipation concluded 195
§ 52. Land-holding classes 198
§ 53. Forest, common, and common field 200
§ 54. The rural labour problem 204
§ 55. Agriculture and tariffs 209
§ 56. Technical progress 214
§ 57. Cooperation 221
§ 58. Home colonisation 227
§ 59. The Polish problem 229

Ch. X. INDUSTRY INDUSTRIAL POLICY AND LABOUR
IN FRANCE, 1848–1914 232–277

§ 60. Checks to industrialism 232
§ 61. Coal, iron and steel 235
§ 62. Shipbuilding 243
§ 63. Cotton 245
§ 64. Other textiles 249
§ 65. Chemical and electrical industries 256

CONTENTS

PAGE

§ 66. Industrial concentration 257
§ 67. Commercial policy 260
§ 68. The Labour Movement to 1870 265
§ 69. The Labour Movement from 1871 270

Ch. XI. INDUSTRY INDUSTRIAL POLICY AND LABOUR
IN GERMANY, 1848–1914 278–338
§ 70. The coming of industrialism 278
§ 71. Coal 280
§ 72. Iron, steel and machinery 283
§ 73. Flax and wool 289
§ 74. Cotton and silk 295
§ 75. Outwork industries 299
§ 76. Chemical and electrical industries 303
§ 77. The Kartells 309
§ 78. Commercial policy 314
§ 79. Labour conditions and policy, 1840–1869 322
§ 80. Labour in Imperial Germany 328
§ 81. Social legislation 333

Ch. XII. COMMUNICATIONS COMMERCE AND COM-
MERCIAL ORGANISATION IN THE RAIL-
WAY AGE 339–375
§ 82. Growth of railways 339
§ 83. Railway policy—France 340
§ 84. Railway policy—Belgium 344
§ 85. Railway policy—Germany 345
§ 86. Policy of roads and waterways 349
§ 87. Shipping 355
§ 88. Dependence on foreign trade 359
§ 89. Telegraph and telephone 362
§ 90. The commercial classes 364
§ 91. Shops, markets and fairs 366
§ 92. Exchanges and dealings in futures 371

Ch. XIII. MONEY BANKING AND INVESTMENT . 876–401
§ 93. The precious metals 376
§ 94. Gold and trade 381
§ 95. The banks: France 385
§ 96. The banks: Germany 389
§ 97. Joint stock companies 895
§ 98. Their international influence 400

EPILOGUE 402–407
§ 99. The wealth of the common man: 1815 and 1914 . . 402

INDEX 409

MAPS

I. France, Agrarian . . . . . AT END

II. German Empire, Agrarian . . . ,,

III. France, Industrial . . . . ,,

IV. German Empire, Industrial . . . ,,

INTRODUCTION

§ 1. No one is ever likely to doubt the political unity of the hundred years from 1815 to 1914. The dates are true starting and finishing points for a great age. In economic history starting and finishing points are always hard to find. But it seems likely that 1914 will remain a recognised finishing point. And though the fall of Napoleon, as an isolated episode, was only of second rate importance in the economic sphere, it marked the end of an age which had witnessed economic events, both destructive and creative, of the very first order. The mere cessation of wars which have been almost continuous for over twenty years is in itself an economic event of some magnitude. In 1815 the significance of peace was increased by the very unusual economic position in which the continent at that time stood in relation to England.

"From 1500 to 1850 the great social question of the day in Europe was the peasant question[1]." For this question the French Revolution had offered a solution which Napoleon endorsed. The revolutionary land settlement stood throughout the nineteenth century and stands to-day. In that settlement much was destroyed; something was created; and, though the peasant went on tilling his land almost exactly as his fathers had tilled it, there were real changes in the daily life of this representative common man of Western Europe. He was his own master as he had never been before. By example and the sword France had commended her settlement of the peasant question to her neighbours. She was not the first peasant country to attempt a final solution. Some of her smaller neighbours were before her. Some rulers of great states had made beginnings. (See *post*, § 9.) But her Revolution opened the last phase of the peasant problem in the West. From her revolutionary land settlement, through peasant emancipation in Prussia, to the emancipation of the

[1] Gustav Schmoller, *Volkswirthschaftslehre*, II, 520.

Russian serfs, and even to the modern land legislation for Ireland, there is a continuous historic chain. That settlement also completed her "unity and indivisibility." Not until after 1789, it is said, were the German speaking peasants of Alsace proud to be Frenchmen.

In the sphere of industry the revolutionary age was less decisive for France and the continent, because equally important questions were not ripe for settlement. What is called capitalism had long existed in Western Europe. In one or other of its forms, agrarian commercial or industrial, it is as old as civilisation. Only in the dark ages, after the fall of Rome, and later on the outskirts of civilised peoples could a society really ignorant of capitalism be found. By the eighteenth century industrial capitalism, the youngest of the three forms, was at least known all over Europe. The employer controlling capital, the life-long wage earner, the dealer who stands between producer and consumer, were all familiar types in France and Italy and Switzerland; though they became rarer with every day's march northeastward towards the outskirts of civilisation in Russia. But the life-long wage earners of industry were a minority in every continental country, and a tiny minority in most. Where they existed they were usually either outworkers or what might be called workshop hands, not factory hands. Their characteristic grievances, hopes and ambitions lay in the subconscious regions of national life. There they were working; but the nations were hardly aware of them.

The revolutionary legislators, individualists almost to a man, had only one common and keen desire for industry—to rid those who directed it from surviving medieval restrictions and the excesses of official control. They abolished the half decayed gilds and cut down state interference. But problems of the wage contract hardly interested them. These unfamiliar problems, when forced upon them, were handled with the prejudices and assumptions natural at the time to men who had never worked for wages, not with the imaginative sympathy extended to those problems of the land which had been for so long before the world of thought. Yet the early revolutionary labour policy, if so it may be called, marks a definite if not a decisive stage in the economic history of France, and of the adjacent continental countries which came under French influence in the Napoleonic age. It cleared the ground for the industrial growths of the nineteenth century. The unsympathetic rulings of revolutionary legislators on the grievances and hopes of industrial wage earners were given precision and permanence in Napoleon's Codes. (See *post*, § 17.) This in its turn gave precision to the hopes and grievances. French town workmen became self-conscious in hostility to the law; just as the English wage earners became self-conscious in hostility to the law administered by Napoleon's enemy. There was the added sore in France that fraternity and equality had been proclaimed and then hidden away. If French political history from 1789 to 1815 had run a different course, the labour history of the nineteenth century might have done so too.

The essentials of commerce were less affected by the revolutionary and Napoleonic age than were those of industry. Trade no doubt was diverted wholesale, and traders enriched or ruined in ranks, by British sea power and Napoleon's furious reactions against it. But when the artificial circumstance of war ended, commercial methods, staple branches of trade, the extent to which continental nations were dependent on commerce, and the nature of that dependence, reverted to something very like late eighteenth century conditions. Commerce was more capitalistic, more modern, more mature and so less easily altered in 1789 than either industry or rural life. It sprang back towards the old position when stress was removed. Only after many years, and under the pressure of immensely powerful new forces, were some of its essentials modified. A merchant of even the late nineteenth century would have been less out of place in an eighteenth century counting house than a late nineteenth century manufacturer or peasant would have been if moved back to his appropriate eighteenth century position.

Whatever its defects, the Congress of Vienna at least inaugurated a period of ninety-nine years in which Western Europe was free from long and devastating wars. That of 1870–1 was short and cannot be called devastating, when compared with those of any other century. It did not divert the course of civilisation; cripple or destroy great industries; completely ruin populous cities; throw wide stretches of land out of cultivation; or impose a fearful strain on the population of the combatants. The great wars of other centuries have done some or all of these things. Recovery from them has often been a matter not of years but of decades and generations. And between 1815 and 1914 the short, bitter, struggle of 1870-1 stands alone. Compared with the wars of other centuries those of 1859 and 1866, for instance, were hardly campaigns—just battles. The crops were trampled at Solferino or Sadowa—not much more. The Crimean War was fought *en champ clos*, like a tournament, and that far to the east.

About the year Napoleon was born, there had begun in England that familiar transformation of manufacturing methods which gave its character to the industrial history of the nineteenth century. Continental Europe knew a little about it before 1789; but technical knowledge spread slowly, even in time of peace, during the eighteenth century. Before the transformation had gone far in England—steam was first used to drive a cotton mill in 1785—war came down like a curtain between her and the continent. Although her mechanical knowledge leaked out during the wars and the one short interval of peace (Mar. 1802–May, 1803), she did her best to keep a monopoly of it; and with some success. Constant warfare distracted the continent from economic development. The entire absence of war on English soil, her special geographical advantages, and her vast colonial and commercial acquisitions enabled her to maintain her lead during the peace.

The opening years of the long peace of the nineteenth century, for so history will regard it when the ages are put in due perspective, saw this accumulated and accumulating English mechanical knowledge available for the continent. Official English attempts to retain a monopoly of it soon broke down. Never before had the close of a period of wars coincided with the unloosing of new economic forces on such a scale. The long peace gave these forces free play. They tended to draw the nations together. And the nations were more willing to play the part of good Europeans—at least in economic matters—than at any time since the fall of Rome.

Approximately coincident with the peace was the beginning of an increase in European population for which there was again no precedent. Many causes were at work, all the chief of which were life-saving not life-creating, though the break-down of old customary restrictions on early marriage may have created some "extra" life. Peace itself saved much life; improved communications kept famine away; above all, improved medical and sanitary knowledge dealt with small-pox and scurvy and ague and then with cholera and the risks of childbirth. In short, Malthus' positive checks were being lifted and his preventive check was not at work except perhaps in France. In France only was the growth of population at first relatively and later absolutely slow; yet the French population grew from 27,500,000 in 1801 to 36,500,000 in 1860, taking the same area at the two dates; and from 36,200,000 in 1871 to nearly 39,700,000 in 1913 on a reduced area. The increase from 1871 to 1913, regarded by contemporaries as most unnaturally slow, would have been rapid in many earlier, less peaceful, and less healthy ages.

All the economic forces which were at work in Western Europe during the long peace can be illustrated in French and German history. That history must be put into a European, and in its later phases an international, setting if it is to be thoroughly understood. Some attempt to do this is made, so far as space permits, in the chapters which follow.

CHAPTER I

RURAL LIFE AND AGRICULTURE IN FRANCE
BEFORE THE RAILWAY AGE

§ 2. A French scholar writing, just after the middle of the nineteenth century, about the medieval agriculture of a progressive French province, called his readers' attention to "the stationary state in which our agriculture has remained during nearly eight centuries. Almost all the methods which we shall describe," he said, "are practised by our cultivators to-day; so that a thirteenth century peasant would visit many of our farms without much astonishment[1]." If six centuries did so little to change the fundamentals of rural life, it is not to be expected that even the years of revolution and war from 1789 to 1815 would accomplish very much. True, a great deal of land changed hands. The determination of the men of 1789 to abolish feudalism had widespread and definite results. This abolition cleared the field for the operation of new forces, as the nineteenth century ran its course. But since the Revolution was concerned more with legal and proprietary relationships than with the material foundations on which those relationships rest; and since, even on the legal side, it was more destructive than creative; what was changed sometimes seems curiously small compared with what endured from the past.

Soil, climate, the course of ancient settlements, and the force of tradition among a peasantry mostly ignorant and generally ill-governed, had settled the conditions of rural life. No economic force had come into play, before 1815, strong enough to transform them. France had never undergone a change comparable with that inclosure movement which was in course of completion at this very time in England. There were, before the Revolution, inclosed districts; even whole provinces in which inclosed fields predominated; but to the amazement of the English traveller, accustomed to connect inclosure with improvement, in France that connection was not found. "The

---

[1] Léopold Delisle, *La classe agricole...en Normandie au moyen âge*, p. xl.

marvellous folly," wrote Arthur Young, "is that, in nine-tenths of the inclosures of France, the system of management is precisely the same as in the open fields." That was in 1794; but it would have been almost as true forty or fifty years later. The fact, which the Englishman did not realise, was that inclosed fields in France were generally not the recent work of improving landlords, but were inherited, with the system of management, from a remote past.

Across a broad belt of northern and north-eastern France, including nearly a third of the country, an open-field system closely related to that of medieval England had once prevailed. It was still the framework of all agricultural affairs, though its primitive uniformity had been considerably modified since the Middle Ages. But south of a line drawn roughly from the eastern base of the Cotentin peninsula to the Swiss frontier north of Geneva this was not so. The Breton promontory, the western coast, the valleys of the Loire and the Garonne, the central French highlands, the Alpine and Pyrenean slopes, and the Mediterranean coast lands, had never—so far as is known—been given over to the typically northern open-field system. But the system was found in patches south of the line just described —a result, as some have argued, of ancient settlement by Teutonic Goths, Vandals, and Burgundians[1].

In the far south, beyond the Cevennes, there had been inherited from classical times an old tried agriculture, well suited to local conditions, not capable of complete transformation, and in fact hardly requiring it. This was the agriculture of wheat, olives, fruits and vines, the agriculture too which had long known how to raise artificial meadows of clover, lucerne and sanfoin by the aid of irrigation. The arable fields mostly lay open, though vineyards oliveyards and orchards were walled. Villages were compact, solidly built, defensible, townlets rather than hamlets.

In the Alpine and Pyrenean departments there was an agriculture dictated by the dominant physical conditions and showing the characteristics of a mountain land; the scanty arable fields of the valley bottom and the lower slopes; the

---

[1] Few hold this opinion now. It was that of Meitzen. See below, p. 35, n. 1.

stretches of communal forest and the high common pastures reaching to the snows; villages and hamlets where room could be found for them; meadows irrigated from the abundant snow waters; and an economic life which, under whatever legal forms, was necessarily communal and relatively free. The lower valleys of the western Pyrenees, where these conditions were merging into those of the plain, were famous even before the Revolution for their free peasantry and their agriculture excellently adapted to the physical environment—"many small properties...every appearance of rural happiness...the country mostly inclosed, and much of it with thorn hedges, admirably trained and kept neatly clipped."

From this scene of rural happiness the transition was rapid and complete to the vast as yet unreclaimed stretches of the *landes* of the Biscay coast—sand, heath, and bog, league upon league. Northward again the rich valley of the Garonne, whose agriculture was commercial and modern even in the thirteenth century, remained what it always had been, "one of the most fertile vales in Europe...the hills covered with the most productive vineyards...the towns frequent and opulent; the whole country an incessant village," that is to say densely covered with hamlets and farmsteads. The crops were endlessly varied and the fertile soil of the vale itself was given no rest. But if the great vale maintained its traditions, so did the adjacent country, along the roads that ran north-eastward and northward towards the heart or over the spurs of the central highlands of Auvergne, the roads to Clermont, Limoges and Angoulême, and so down the northern slopes to Nevers, Tours, Angers and the north. A land of hamlets rather than of villages and a land, very largely, of inclosed fields; but a land also of relatively poor soil. "Where inferior soils demand something...of exertion, there is here, as in all other parts of France, an immediate blank; a fallow is the only resource." That is Arthur Young in 1794. More than sixty years later a French writer, speaking of the southern slopes, explained that the "traditional rotation of crops was the biennial, wheat and then fallow, which comes to us from the Romans[1]"; and that Berri, on the northern slopes, was agri-

[1] L. G. de Lavergne, *L'Economie rurale de la France*, 2nd ed. 1861, p. 316.

culturally what it had been in the seventeenth century—and no doubt much earlier.

The open-field region of the north, like the open-field districts of England, was a land of true villages rather than of hamlets. Round each village lay its three great fields, and in the fields were the scattered holdings of the cultivators, again just as in England before the inclosures. There were rights of pasture on the stubble and on the common, and rights or customs of wood cutting in whatever woodland there might be. Here and there, before the Revolution, the system had been broken into, especially in the Ile de France and in Picardy—the modern departments of Oise, Aisne and Somme—where a certain number of big farmsteads had been created on large compact holdings outside the villages. In some cases commons had disappeared. Right against Paris and the other large towns of the north, the fields had been broken up into market gardens at a very early date.

Owing to a more kindly climate, the vine played a part in the agriculture even of northern France which it had never played in England; so the open fields had long been associated with vineyards, and there was less need for barley growing than in lands further north. But, for arable farming, the open fields predominated. "They have travelled with me more or less all the way from Orleans," Arthur Young wrote at Valenciennes in 1794. So it was twenty years later, when their characteristic features were accurately described for various points in this open-field belt, in an agrarian survey ordered by Napoleon[1].

The open-field belt ended, on the north-west, with the heights of Artois, overlooking the Flemish flats. It swept round the Scheldt basin and extended through eastern Belgium away into Germany. (See *post*, §7.) Throughout it the old three-course crop rotation survived—winter corn, spring corn, fallow—though in a few districts, especially in the rich levels of Alsace, more intensive cultivation prevailed. North of the line Valenciennes, Douai, Hazebrouck lay Flanders—French and Belgian—the northern home of that scientific rotation of crops which England borrowed, and then gave back to France during the nineteenth

[1] *La Statistique Agricole de* 1814 (officially published, 1914).

century. The land, cut up into holdings and fields by ditch and
hedge, was tilled with infinite patience and skill, as it had been
for centuries, to supply food and raw material for the crowded
and frequent cities of the plain. It was here that Arthur Young,
wearied of the three-course rotation with "some variations but
of no consequence" all the way from Orleans, found that a
common course of husbandry was "wheat—and after it turnips
the same year; oats; clover; wheat; hemp; wheat; flax; coleseed;
wheat; beans; wheat," in an eleven-year cycle. An agriculture
so intelligent might be improved, but did not require transformation.

§ 3. Stress has been laid so far on those permanent aspects
of French agriculture which the Revolution hardly touched,
because it was more concerned with legal and proprietary
relationships than with the economic foundations upon which
those relationships rest. But in two important ways at least the
revolutionary settlement had affected those foundations and had
influenced agriculture itself, as distinguished from rights over
agricultural land and agricultural persons. In the first place
formal permission had been given to everyone to cultivate as he
pleased. The government of the old *régime* had for centuries
been anxious about the food problem, about the supply of the
capital, the great towns, and the infertile districts in years of
bad harvest. Everything possible had been done to keep up the
production of grain in every province. As late as 1747, for
example, an edict appeared forbidding the increase of vineyards
without official permission; and the edict was not allowed to
remain a dead letter. Since the traditional rotations of crops—
the two-course rotation of the south and the three-course
rotation of the north—had grain supplies primarily in view, for
they went back to early times when transport was imperfect and
each locality was necessarily self-sufficing, government influence
had generally been thrown into the scales in their favour. Any
variation in cropping which seemed to threaten the local supplies
of cereals had been discouraged. Government regulated not
only the rotation of crops but also everything connected with
grain, from sowing to market. It was not to be hoarded or
wasted; its price was carefully supervised. But the revolutionary

politicians were opposed to all this; and accordingly a law of Sept. 28, 1791 had set every proprietor free to cultivate as he pleased, to store up his crops if he wished, and to sell them as he liked. In the first generation he generally went on cultivating as his father had declared unto him; but at least a window had been opened through which the breath of change might blow.

Secondly, the legislation of the Revolution had taken direct notice of commons and common rights. The problems of commons and common rights varied greatly with the various geographical and agricultural regions of France. The most universal and the most essential type of common was the common woodland. In the Alpine zone and in all the highlands there were also very extensive common pastures, generally of good quality. Great stretches of barren heathy common, not at all of good quality, were particularly numerous in the west, from the Biscay *landes* to Brittany and the Channel coast; and similar common waste was to be found in many other provinces. It was in the open-field belt of the north, as already suggested, that the problem of common was most acute. In this belt, besides rights over woodland and waste, there had always existed those rights of grazing over the stubble of the open fields, in fact over all land in the commune not inclosed or sown, which in most northern countries, and particularly in England, had proved a serious obstacle to agricultural improvement. Outside the open-field belt, these rights were naturally not found in inclosed districts; nor were they at all general in districts, such as the far south, where many of the arable fields lay open. One reason for this was that the southern cultivator had learnt to provide fodder from irrigated meadows. Another was that he had never kept a heavy stock of cattle.

Under the feudal maxim of *nulle terre sans seigneur*[1], prerevolutionary law had generally assumed that all commons belonged to the lord and that all rights over them were enjoyed by his grace; though even in the seventeenth century there were legists who argued, with an eye on Roman Law, that the rights had been there before the lord. The prevalent doctrine was so essentially feudal that the men of 1789 were bound to attack it.

---

[1] The maxim of the north; that of the south was *Nul seigneur sans titre.*

Force was given to their attack by the teaching of agricultural reformers that commons and common rights were obstacles to improvement, and by the fact that in the model agriculture of Flanders they had died out centuries earlier. Moreover the wretched condition of many commons had popularised the policy of division and cultivation, both among large landowners and among peasants. As a result considerable stretches of land had been won from the waste for tillage between 1766 and 1789.

From the first the revolutionary assemblies took the view that commons belonged to the commune and that common rights were not grounded in the lord's grace. In 1792 a further step was taken. By a law of Aug. 14 in that year the division of all commons, except common woodlands, was made obligatory. But this was far too drastic and encroached too much on that communal self-government, which was one of the earliest products of the Revolution, to be successful. Within a year division was made optional. Results naturally varied. But in the north considerable areas of common were cut up among the peasants or sold, not always wisely, by the communal authorities between 1792 and 1795. In the metropolitan area commons almost vanished. A law of 1795 held up the work of division, and in 1803 the government of the consulate stopped it altogether, at the same time confirming the divisions and sales which had already been made. The partition of communal forests remained illegal throughout, though the communes were empowered to revise the rights of user and, if necessary, to levy a toll which was to go towards the maintenance of the wood-lands and the general expenses of the commune.

About one-tenth of France remained in common ownership in 1815; but the figure does not in any way indicate the position in the true agricultural districts. Most of the French commons consisted in the woods and mountain pastures of the Alps, the Pyrenees, the Vosges and the Jura. There were whole depart-ments in the north-west where commons were almost unknown.

With the legislative attack on commons there naturally went an attack on the much more harmful common grazing rights over arable land. But these rights were difficult to deal with. It is true that the peasant's newly acquired freedom to till his

land as he pleased struck a blow at them in principle. Under the
old open-field routine, when everyone grew the same crops, the
stubbles were thrown open to the beasts on a given day; but if
variations in the course of cropping were introduced this was
no longer possible. For these reasons *vaine pâture* gradually
declined during the nineteenth century[1]. But in the early years
with which this chapter deals, when the old rotations and the
old customs had been little altered, it still survived widely
though complaints of its harmful working were constant. It was,
for example, in full vigour so near Paris as the arrondissement of
Rambouillet in 1812, "although," as was officially reported,
"there was no good cultivator who would not vote for the
abolition of a right, which is as injurious to the rotation of crops
and the abolition of fallows as to the prosperity of sheep rearing."
"Often," the reporter continued, "two and even three shep-
herds arrive almost at the same moment in a field recently
reaped to feed their flocks. Each hustles his sheep with his
dogs to get there first; and, in the end, the two latest arrived
have tired their flocks to no purpose, for they have to go elsewhere[2]."

§ 4. It is not necessary to describe here all those remnants of
feudal and manorial subjection from which the Revolution had
freed the French peasantry; nor is it necessary to go far into
the difficult inquiry as to how many of the pre-revolutionary
peasants might be classified as proprietors. In strict law the
merest handful were what in England would be called free
holders. But very many, perhaps so many as 40 per cent., were
proprietors for most practical purposes, and were even so
described in official documents, although above them was a lord
who was regarded as the ultimate "owner" of the land[3].

Below the handful whose right of absolute ownership would
hardly have been challenged by the most captious feudal lawyer
were a great number who held land by paying an ancient fixed
quit-rent, or *cens*. The most favoured among them might owe
cens and nothing else but a fixed payment, akin to the fine in

---

[1] It did not die out, as stated in earlier editions. It still exists.
[2] *La Statistique Agricole de* 1814, pp. 507–8.
[3] The question and the literature are reviewed in Lefebvre, *Les paysans;
Cahiers de la Révn. Franç.* 1934.

English copyhold tenure, made when land subject to *cens* changed hands at death. As *cens* and fine had usually been fixed generations or even centuries back, and as the purchasing power of money had steadily fallen, the burden was singularly tolerable. Such men might for most purposes be treated as proprietors. Less favoured people might hold their land subject to an uncertain fine, which the lord's agent could screw up on a suitable occasion, or to galling and burdensome personal obligations, hated for their own sake and as relics of serfdom. At the very bottom of the land-holding peasantry came a small group of so-called *mainmortables*, who owed some manual service to their lord, and could not sell their land or even bequeath it except to children of their own, resident with them on that land. In the theory of the law they were bound to the soil. In fact however devices were known by which *mainmortables* became priests and even lawyers. These survivals of the medieval serf had been most numerous in the north-east—Franche Comté and Lorraine.

The Revolution had swept away together serfdom and *cens*; so that many landlords had found themselves in the position of that baron of Provence whom Arthur Young met in 1789—"an enormous sufferer by the revolution; a great extent of country, which belonged in absolute right to his ancestors, was formerly granted for quit-rents, *cens*, and other feudal payments, so that there is no comparison between the lands retained and those thus granted by his family." *Mainmortables* and *cens* payers alike had mounted into the ranks of proprietors, and not even the restored Bourbons dared challenge their position. The French peasant proprietor of the nineteenth century had good reason to look back with reverence to 1789. His gain had been of the tangible kind that he very well understood.

There were however important types of tenure which the Revolution had to some extent modified but by no means transformed. First, *métayage*, tenure by a sharing of the crops between landowner and cultivator; the landlord's share being generally one-half, but sometimes a third or even possibly two-thirds, in cases where he had furnished an extra large part of the working capital—some part he always furnished. Arthur Young had the idea that seven-eighths of the land of France was held on some variant of this tenure; but he certainly exaggerated. Indeed the figure clashes with his own estimate of the land held by peasant proprietors. Three-eighths or a half would probably be nearer the mark, though any estimate is at best guess-work. His account of the distribution of *métayage* is more trustworthy. He describes it as "pervading every part of Sologne"—across the Loire, south of Orleans—"Berri, La Marche, Limosin, Anjou, Bourgogne, Bourbonnois, Nevernois, Auvergne, etc.," in short the central highlands and the lands adjacent to them, especially on the north and west. He adds that it is found in, but evidently in his opinion does not thoroughly pervade, Brittany, Maine, Provence "and all the southern counties." He notes it in other places; but it was certainly not characteristic of any part of that open-field area which coincided with the basins of the Seine and its tributaries.

The Revolution had not touched the general principle of this share-tenancy. If the *métayer* had owed his lord feudal dues, if he was bound to grind his corn at the manorial mill or press his grapes in the manorial winepress, as he generally was, the obligation was removed, though probably not the habit. But the share-tenancy itself came to be treated as a free contract worthy of a free Frenchman. The proceeding was somewhat illogical, in view of the abolition of the much less onerous *cens*, but was in one way justified; because, whereas an absentee lord could draw *cens* for ever, making no returns of any sort, the lord of a *métayer* could not get his share of the produce without contributing his share of working capital—half the cattle and half the seed always; sometimes a share in the cost of implements; very generally half the taxes, and sometimes even, as in parts of Guienne, the whole.

However great or small the justification, *métayage* came unchanged, though stripped of some feudal adjuncts, through the tumult of the Revolution of 1789, to be formally examined and appraised by John Stuart Mill in his *Principles of Political Economy* a year before the Revolution of 1848.

If *métayage* was allowed to survive, the case for tenant farming was unanswerable. In fact its right to existence was not challenged at any stage of the Revolution. The farmer who hired land for a rent in money or corn was by no means unknown in eighteenth century France. He predominated in some important districts and was found occasionally in all. The districts where tenant farming predominated were Picardy, Artois, parts of Flanders and Normandy, the Ile de France and the Pays de Beauce; or in terms of departments, parts of the Nord, Pas de Calais, Somme, Aisne, Oise, Calvados, Eure, Eure-et-Loir, Loir-et-Cher and Loiret; or in terms of economic areas, the country which had been the main granary of Paris for centuries, and so had developed a more commercial system of agriculture. These farmers of the north-west before the Revolution were usually not to be distinguished from the rank and file of the other cultivators, from the point of view of ordinary well being. In some ways they were worse off than the *métayers*. The landlord usually paid half the *métayer's* taxes; but the farmer bore all his own burdens. He was bound by his lease to improve his land, to practise prescribed rotations of crops, to maintain ditches and fences where the country was inclosed. And as very often he was a farmer not from choice but from compulsion, because he was forced to hire scraps of land to get a living, having no land or not enough land of his own, his position was far from enviable. Moreover in the second half of the eighteenth century there had been a steady pressure on him from above to extract more rent, with the result that he was often among the most wretched of the peasantry. It must not be supposed that he held what in modern England would be called a farm. The land which he rented was most often some scrap or scraps in the open fields, or in inclosed country the smallest of small holdings. Here is an illustration. From Picardy, the modern department of the Somme, the Intendant reported to the government of Louis XVI that "farms were exceedingly minute; that farmers paid what they owed usually in grain; and as a result there was only just enough corn left to feed them[1]."

The French farmer class did however contain a small section comparable with those capitalist tenant farmers who were rising into such importance in England, in connection with the inclosures of the eighteenth and early nineteenth centuries. A few

---

[1] Loutchisky, *L'état des classes agricoles en France*, etc., p. 82.

French landlords had thrown farm to farm and had let the consolidated holdings to men of substance, who were in a position to pay considerable and regular money rents. But the possibilities of so doing had been limited by the very short supply of men of substance in rural France. Only in one district and on one class of land had this large farming of the English type become really common; though it is heard of elsewhere. The district included parts of Picardy (Somme), Artois (Pas de Calais) and the Ile de France (Oise and Aisne). The class of land was the land of the Church, which covered a large area in those parts, lands of the Abbey of Corbie on the Somme, of the Abbey of St Jean of Amiens, of the Abbey of Vauclerc near Laon and so on. About a half of these ecclesiastical lands were laid out in real farms, as an Englishman would have called them, and let to *gros fermiers*. Their substantial farm buildings, or it may be nineteenth century buildings on the same sites, became familiar to many Englishmen during the years 1914–18. Even in these districts however it is doubtful whether more than twenty per cent. of the land was farmed *à l'Anglaise*. Some middle-class landowners of the district had imitated the ecclesiastics; but the nobility, almost without exception, let out their land in scraps to wretched little working farmers from the lower ranks of the peasantry.

In principle the changes of the Revolution affected farming no more than they affected *métayage*. The readjustment of taxes, the abolition of tithe, the reform of the game laws, all eased the small farmer's lot. If custom or the terms of his lease had subjected him to any obligations which might be described as feudal, the Revolution removed the burden. But the revolutionary statesmen, who were enthusiastic individualists and believers in the freedom of contract, had never legislated in the interests of farmers as a class. The farming lease was modern; it was in no sense feudal; therefore it might remain and the farmer might improve the terms of it if he could, like any other free man, by equal bargaining.

There remains one more section of the rural population whose status was not affected in principle by the Revolution—the labourers. The men who did rural work for wages were a mixed class. But the class contained few absolutely landless and property-less individuals of the type familiar in the United Kingdom. Normally, a man worked for wages because his land, or his father's land, was inadequate for the support of the family. That land might be a very tiny scrap; it might be held by rent, share-tenancy, *cens* or more or less servile tenure; but it was there. The more peasant holdings there were in any province, the less room there was for a landless class. Some wage earners had land enough to keep them from absolute want. If they could not give time to it, their wives and children could. And there was a continual passage from the group which lived mainly on wages to the group which lived mainly by the land. A young man would take service, save some money, and then start on a little holding as farmer or *métayer*. Another, whose holding no longer sufficed for his family needs, would go out as a day labourer, as a harvester, or perhaps as an unskilled hand in a neighbouring town. In just a few provinces there was a considerable percentage of landless men in the labourer class. The percentage was particularly high in parts of Flanders and Normandy and in the neighbourhood of Versailles. It was fairly high in Burgundy. But as a rule it was low. Even for the large farm district north of Paris it has been estimated that about forty per cent. of the labourers had land enough to keep them from destitution; and of the rest almost all had some sort of garden, with perhaps a scrap of field attached. The surest proof of the general position is furnished by the widespread complaints of the larger proprietors, that the existence of peasant property led to idleness and prevented them from getting all the labour that their estates required.

The Revolution which had bettered the position of the land-holding peasant had really done nothing for the rural labourers as a class—sometimes less than nothing, for where commons were cut up they lost their old access to them.

§ 5. In approaching the way in which land had changed hands between 1789 and 1815, it must be clearly stated that the question has as yet been imperfectly examined. Probably the materials for a thorough examination do not exist. Note, at the outset, that there was nothing comparable with that sharing up of large stretches of noble or church land among the peasantry which has been witnessed in contemporary Russia. Neither the French nobility nor the French ecclesiastics did much cultivation of their estates in the eighteenth century; therefore there was not much land to share. The great nobles had gone to town and let out their estates to middlemen. The middlemen did not cultivate, but sublet to cultivators of all sorts. As a rule the greater estates were not compact stretches of territory. They were rather bundles of rights over a great number of scattered holdings. These holdings, being already occupied by peasants or farmers, could not be cut up. A great lord might quite well have no land in hand at all; though he drew a large income from rents and *cens* and other dues. Like Arthur Young's friend in Provence, if his *cens* vanished a large part of his estate went with it. Even if the estate happened to be continuous the situation was not different; there were *cens* payers, *métayers*, or farmers already on it. The landlord who had anything in the nature of an English home-farm was the exception. If he did keep a farm in hand, the chances were all against his cultivating it himself. In Normandy Arthur Young was shocked to find *métayers* "where they should least of all be looked for, on the farms which gentlemen keep in their own hands." "The consequence is," he added, "that every gentleman's farm must be precisely the worst cultivated in the neighbourhood"; for he had a low opinion of *métayage*. The fact was that, all over France, the smaller resident gentry were generally lords of *métayers*; and since *métayage* was not touched by legislation, and the smaller gentry came through the Revolution rather better than the great, many of them remained lords of *métayers* in 1815.

What happened was that very extensive estates, the property of royal princes, emigrant nobles, and above all of the Church, became national property and were put up for sale or exchanged for the notorious *assignats*, the paper money issued on the security of the confiscated Church land[1]. In so far as these estates had consisted merely in rights to receive *cens*, or other feudal payments, they melted away, so to speak, in the hands of the state. But there remained a great deal of farmed land

---

[1] The Church however owned not more than 5–10 per cent. of France.

and land let on a share-tenancy, with woodlands and wastes which had been definitely in private ownership and so did not pass to the communes. The problem which has never been solved statistically is—what shares of these lands came, firstly, into the hands of the peasantry, secondly, into those of a new class of landlords or, thirdly, came back at the Restoration to the original owners or their representatives? Probably the second and third shares were greater than the first.

At the Restoration there were still large stocks of confiscated emigrants' estates, which had never been sold or granted away by Napoleon. These were restored, although the demand of the returned emigrants that their old properties should be re-established in their entirety could never be granted. But it was open to them to buy. Moreover agents acting on their behalf had occasionally bought for them in their absence. Exiles who had made their peace with Napoleon had enjoyed earlier opportunities of recovering part of their lost lands. What with repurchase and regrant, it is believed that by 1820 the old nobility had made good about a half of its losses.

For the Church lands and the lay lands which were sold away from their original owners, the problem is both more complex and more obscure; but probably not much went to the smaller peasantry. The gamblers in *assignats* and land speculators of 1790-9 were no doubt drawn from all classes; but the majority were *bourgeois*—millers, brewers, parliamentary deputies, lawyers, and those people skilled in the handling of estates who had acted as middlemen for the nobility and the Church. In the metropolitan area land was bought freely by the *bourgeoisie*, in the strictest sense of the term. Where considerable purchases by cultivators are met with, the purchasers are inevitably fairly substantial persons; and such persons, as has been seen, were rare[1]. Some of the large farmers on ecclesiastical land took the opportunity to become owners, when their land came on the market; but the most that the small man could hope for was the addition of another fragment to his

---

[1] The latest summary, by M. Bloch, *Les caractères originaux de l'histoire rurale française*, 1931, agrees with these conclusions; but notes that in some districts "beaucoup de modestes paysans...acquirent eux aussi des parcelles...des manouvriers même." p. 247.

holding, if he found himself in a position to overbid the local or outside moneyed man. If he were exceptionally lucky or exceptionally able he probably became a little landlord himself; for there were always hard pressed cultivators ready to relieve the smallest landlord of the burden of personal labour.

To the original purchasers of confiscated lands were added, under the Empire, the new Napoleonic aristocracy who were endowed from the remaining reserves of national property. They too were for the most part *ex-bourgeois*—self-made soldiers become marshals, Jacobin lawyers dubbed barons, unfrocked priests turned into counts. All these new landowners merely stepped into the places of the old, so far as the reformed law would permit. They shared the cost of plough-oxen with *métayers* in the south. They gave leases to farmers in the north. It may fairly be assumed, though statistical evidence is not forthcoming, that their advent encouraged tenant farming as an alternative to *métayage*. Tenant farming was more suited to the urban traditions in which most of them had been reared. And the disappearance of *métayage* from the north, which was almost complete just after the middle of the nineteenth century, must have begun early; since such movements take time. Arthur Young had found it well known, though not predominant, in Normandy, Maine, Champagne, the Ile de France, and other northern provinces. Its early decline is registered once or twice in the reports of 1814. For example, there used to be share-tenancy before 1789 in Normandy, even in the cider orchards. The owner got half the "big" cider and the *métayer* all the "little." But "to-day when one knows that a thing has value one prefers to take none of the risks of agriculture and to assure to oneself a more fixed and uniform income; so every day landowners give up this method of tenure in favour of a money rent on the usual terms." No doubt the same motives were at work elsewhere.

All things considered, this fresh influx of bourgeois landowners is the most significant outcome of the revolutionary land settlement.

§ 6. Small as were the changes in agriculture itself which occurred between 1789 and 1815, and slowly as these changes extended in the generation which followed the wars, it must not be supposed that French agriculture was absolutely stationary. The way was being prepared for more radical transformations later in the nineteenth century; and to contemporaries, familiar with the immobility of the old order, changes of no great magnitude seemed radical enough. One thing at any rate in the countryside would have amazed the medieval peasant, even early in the century and still more towards 1850. That was the potato. It is difficult for the modern mind to realise that until almost the end of the eighteenth century the food problem in Europe had to be faced without potatoes, or that French menus contained no *pommes frites*. The old French government, when called upon to handle food scarcity, as it constantly was, made its calculations always and of necessity in terms of corn. In the south the olive, in the central highlands the chestnut, and everywhere various sorts of pulses and green vegetables entered into the people's dietary; but it is hardly an exaggeration to say that the typical peasant lived by bread alone.

How long the potato had been known in France is a matter of no importance. Its use was vigorously advocated in the reign of Louis XVI by Turgot and by one Parmentier; but the food history of the early years of the Revolution shows that they had not yet converted their countrymen. Arthur Young found potatoes many and good about Saverne in Alsace, many and bad in parts of Lorraine, many also in the Dauphiné; elsewhere very few. In most places he was told "that the people would not touch them; experiments had been made by gentlemen, with a view to introducing them for the poor, but no efforts could do it." Apparently it was not possible for him to quote potato prices at all in his section on the prices of provisions; at any rate he did not make the attempt.

It is evident that, in the twenty years which succeeded Young's travels, efforts to popularise potato growing met with some success, though the peasants' dislike only gave way slowly. The reports of 1812–14 already quoted furnish valuable, though unfortunately incomplete, evidence on the point. From the mountainous parts of Provence (Department of the Basses Alpes) it was reported that "potatoes being recognised as an article of prime necessity for the nourishment of all kinds of beasts and for that of man, especially in seasons of dear corn, their cultivation is carried on with the utmost care." In another hilly district of the south, the Department of the Tarn, the potato "though only introduced a few years ago, has made and is still making great progress....The population of the mountain cantons lives on nothing but potatoes and chestnuts for six months in the year." A poor diet, but at least better than chestnuts only. In the Department of the Rhone "potato growing, which was very little known before the Revolution, has greatly extended because of the safe market for them in Lyons and of their use for cattle food on the land." On the other side of the country, at Parthenay, west of Poitiers, where their introduction was equally recent, potatoes were taking the place of rye and even of wheat, but only it appears *pour les malheureux*. In Brittany, again a poor province, "it is consoling to see their cultivation spreading from day to day." The Mayor of Runan, reporting to the Sub-Prefect, said he had spoken much "of their inappreciable advantages, especially in certain circumstances"—famine years it may be assumed. At Bar-sur-Seine, in Champagne, potatoes were "good, much grown and a great assistance." But from a Norman arrondissement it was reported that the cultivators "attached little importance to this crop": they grew a few in their vegetable gardens but hardly ever in the fields.

Apparently the potato was not yet quite respectable. Beasts, *les malheureux*, hungry mountaineers and the Lyons proletariat are the chief consumers enumerated. But from this time onwards it made progress in all districts, except the lowlands of the south, where the climate was not entirely suitable to its growth, where also there were important rivals in onions and garlic.

The officials who reported to the Imperial Government seldom omitted to point out that potatoes were grown, either on spare pasture land newly broken up, or on the fallows between corn crops. In either case they were "a net addition to the supply of foodstuffs." To add to the supply of foodstuffs and to get rid of the wasteful medieval inheritance of fallowing,

2   CEC

under which half the arable land in the south and one-third of it in the north lay idle yearly, were of course the main ends of all agricultural reform. Potatoes, turnips, clover or other green crops on the fallow meant extra food for beast and man. "Perhaps the culture of turnips, as practised in England, is, of all others the greatest desideratum in the tillage of France," Arthur Young wrote. The French government had realised this even in his day; but the steps hitherto taken by government, the chief of which was distributing the seed, he had reason to believe "failed entirely." The failure was not fully rectified later. No successes with turnips were reported in 1814; and right down to the middle of the nineteenth century the turnip husbandry only made slow progress. It was not taken up at all in a great number of departments.

More successful were the efforts to extend the use of artificial meadows, clover, sainfoin and lucerne. The latter were both old French crops, as their names testify, but their spread had been very slow. Lucerne was being introduced in the open fields of the north before the Revolution; and in that area at least progress continued, gathering momentum as the years went on, but perceptible even before 1820. The 1814 reports mention recent developments in various districts. Close to Paris, for example, the introduction of artificial meadows had led to a many course rotation of crops not unlike that of Flanders— wheat, rye, barley, oats, lucerne, clover, sainfoin, fallow. This rotation had become almost universal in Seine-et-Oise and was inserted in farmers' leases. It is probable that, thanks to such innovations, fallow had been reduced in the north-west by more than a third before the Revolution of 1848. Like the potato, this curtailment of fallowing would have astonished the medieval peasant had he returned to a progressive province. But he could have visited many provinces, especially in the west and south-west, without any disquieting amazement.

French agriculture no doubt benefited from the intelligent oversight of Napoleon's prefects; still more perhaps because landlords and nobility, old and new, unlike those of the previous century, learnt to take their full share in agricultural development. It is only fair to add that the prefects carried on a tradition from the *ancien régime*, only with better knowledge, and that spirited landlords were not completely unknown before 1789.

It was in the reign of Louis XVI, for example, that the Spanish merino sheep were formally introduced into France; but they remained a curiosity in Young's time. He "was assured by very respectable manufacturers," in the Norman woollen district, "that not one fleece" of pure Spanish wool had ever been produced in France. The best wool came from Roussillon, where the sheep were naturally half Spanish, but not true merinos. The royal stud-farm at Rambouillet, founded in 1786, only began to produce results about the time of the Restoration. By that date the work of spreading improved breeds had been taken over from government by the landowners. No less a person than Lafayette, in his long retirement from politics between 1801 and 1830, managed to popularise the merino in the land between Paris and Rheims, the country of the Marne and the Ourcq. The year 1825 is the reputed date of the introduction of the first pure-bred Durham shorthorns into France, again by the enterprise of a country gentleman. Following the lead of England, careful breeding methods were applied to native French races of animals, such as the Percheron horse and to some of the noble strains of cattle from which sprang the draught-oxen of the south.

Government gave the initial impetus to the greatest agricultural innovation of the early nineteenth century—the introduction of the sugar beet. Men of learning had indicated its possibilities in the eighteenth century, but it was the pressure of the English blockade which made government act. England mocked this sugar substitute and her caricaturists drew pictures of Napoleon's infant heir chewing a beetroot unhappily, while the nurses said, "Suck, dear, suck; your father says it's sugar." It really was sugar. The task of growing it was undertaken mainly in the big farm country north of Paris and in Flanders. There was much to be learnt, as the crop if not well handled is exhausting. But the Flemish farmers, followed closely by those of the Pas de Calais and the Somme, who were borrowing Flemish methods, overcame the difficulties. When the sugar had been extracted the beet pulp was a valuable cattle food; so that the crop added greatly to the wealth of the districts in which it was grown. But the districts were small and the total French output of refined sugar rarely exceeded 50,000 tons a year before 1850, as compared with a minimum output of nearly 600,000 tons in the twentieth century.

Another specialised branch of rural industry, much encouraged by many governments, also made striking progress after the peace. This was the mulberry and silk-worm industry of the lower Rhone valley. The output of silk, which between 1789 and 1815 had at best remained stationary and is believed to have declined, was approximately quadrupled between 1815 and 1850. Unfortunately the ground gained was lost owing to disease among the silk-worms, in the fifties.

There was very little change in the implements with which the peasant worked during these years. He clung to his hoe, his long shafted spade, and that short scythe, the *pique*, which Arthur Young had allowed to be "one of the most useful implements that can be seen." In some districts his ploughs, harrows, and carts were slowly improving, metal replacing wood and wheeled ploughs the wheelless sorts. (The wheel plough had been in use for ages in the North.) Sometimes seed was drilled. But, generally speaking, little was done except on a few of the larger farms. The smallness of the normal holding was all against experiments with expensive implements; and the peasant had a not unjustified faith in the skill of his own hands. The hoe and the spade had accomplished a great deal in Flanders. From 1820 or 1830 onwards, the simple types of threshing machinery available at that date began to spread in the north, the flail giving way before them. Even small cultivators took to using them in some districts, and latterly they made rapid progress. But the south went its old way with wooden-wheeled ox-carts, the flail, the open-air threshing floor and very often with a plough that was literally classic in its simplicity. After all the Romans were good husbandmen in their day and the land of the south was kindly, if you kept off the high ground.

No doubt the hope of agricultural reformers in the revolutionary and Napoleonic age, that France would shortly make a considerable net addition to her supplies of foodstuffs, was in part realised during the following generation. An agriculture so skilful as that of Flanders, or that of the plain of Nîmes, added to its output merely by carrying forward and perfecting old tried methods, assimilating easily any new crop or new rotation which was appropriate to local conditions. The growth of industrial towns in the north gave the Flemish farmer still more of that manure with which he had always fed his land generously. His root crops fattened his beasts and his beasts fattened his land in profitable rotation. The farmers of the adjacent departments, now at length copying his methods, made even more progress than he, for they started from a far lower level. The steady decline of the fallow, in the north and to a less degree elsewhere, with the improvements in the strains of cattle and sheep, added directly and indirectly to the net supply of foodstuffs. Whatever the drawbacks incidental to the local disappearance and the general curtailment of commons, and such drawbacks it must be remembered were far less than in contemporary England, owing to the non-existence of a landless class in France and the fact that the decline in common land did not create such a class—whatever these drawbacks may have been, many hundreds of thousands of acres were added to the cultivated area of France between 1789 and 1848. And by the latter date the potato alone had made an appreciable addition to the national food supplies.

There is no doubt too that the average yield of the staple crops, like the average weight of the cattle and sheep, had increased as the result of an agriculture which, taking the country as a whole and allowing for backward provinces, was perceptibly more varied and more rational. What that increase was it is not safe to guess. Estimates have been made; but the starting point is much too uncertain, and the point of arrival not nearly certain enough, to warrant their quotation. Even with a full modern statistical apparatus, average yields per acre are awkward things to get at, in a country of reticent peasants whose holdings are much divided and scattered.

Each successive decade in the nineteenth century saw a rather more rapid rate of change in agriculture. This acceleration was due in part to the cumulative results of the removal of legal or customary hindrances to the free exercise of initiative, as a result of the Revolution. In part to the increase of technical knowledge; first among those whom the peasants imitated; then among the peasants themselves, as their opportunities for education improved. In part perhaps to the increased vitality of a people lifted from a state of real misery into one of relative comfort. But in the main, there can be little doubt, to improvements in the means of communication. From 1800 to 1836 the improvement was chiefly in high roads and canals. After the law of 1836, which encouraged the building of by-roads, their influence was added. Then—and far more important—came the railways of the forties. These improvements and their effects will be referred to in later chapters.

CHAPTER II

GERMAN RURAL CONDITIONS BEFORE THE RAILWAY AGE

§ 7. In continental Europe political and economic boundaries rarely coincide, most rarely of all in the no man's land between Latin and Teuton. French Flanders and Belgian Flanders, the French Ardennes and the Belgian Ardennes, Alsace on the Rhine's left bank and Baden on its right, are separated by no economic barrier. Moreover, since 1789, French rule and influence had extended far beyond the French frontier as fixed in 1815. So new economic features characteristic of revolutionary France—changes of land ownership and changes in the legal relations of rural classes, for example—had spread over Belgium and parts of western Germany.

The framework of rural life was the compact village, with its open fields, all the way from the basin of the Seine and the Swiss Alps to the plains of the Slavonic north-east, and over the Danish peninsula to the lowlands of Scandinavia. The flats of western and northern Belgium, of Holland, and of the marshy valley of the Ems in western Germany, were an exception, being in the main covered with hamlets and scattered farmsteads. Very special conditions of life and agriculture existed in the polders, won from the sea. In these North Sea flats there was not found that rigid communal routine of agriculture which had dominated Germany proper—the three-crop rotation; the common pasture; the rights of grazing on the stubble; and the holdings scattered in strips all over the open village fields. Land in the North Sea flats was not necessarily inclosed, in the English sense, though drains often did the work of hedges; but the most important consequence of inclosure, as understood in England, that is the complete control of the individual cultivator over the course of cultivation, had existed there for centuries. His land might be a compact or a scattered holding, but it was free of communal routine and intrusive rights of neighbours. He could crop it as he liked; or keep it laid down in rich wet meadows if he preferred.

A traveller moving into Germany up the Rhine from Holland found what might be called Dutch conditions prevailing in the border provinces of Cleves and Gelders. There were scattered homesteads, few compact villages, and an improved agriculture. He crossed a well-marked agrarian frontier near Düsseldorf, and everything changed at once. The people were all in villages. Great bare open fields lay about the villages, tilled on the three-course rotation[1]. Had the traveller come from north-eastern France he would have crossed no such agrarian frontier. He would have seen only a land of compact villages and open fields, broken by forest and vineyard, with its conditions modified in hilly districts, like the Ardennes and the Eiffel, where settlement and tillage had been adapted to the geographical environment. In the Eiffel he might have found, had he stopped to inquire, districts in which full private property in land was not recognised. Holdings in the arable fields were periodically reassigned by lot far into the nineteenth century. But agriculture in these fields was bound by an even more primitive communal routine than in the rest of Germany.

There was another agrarian frontier to be crossed by the traveller who might penetrate through Germany into the Slavonic north-east; but the second frontier was less precise and less visible than the first. It was the frontier between western and eastern Germany. Very roughly it coincided with the line of the Elbe; but western conditions were found east of the lower Elbe, in parts of Schleswig-Holstein, and eastern conditions west of the middle and upper Elbe, in Saxony and Bohemia. This frontier had a racial basis. Varying racial traditions and the economics of conquest had left marks on agriculture and deep marks on the social relations of the agrarian population. Western Germany was purely Teutonic in civilisation and, as is supposed, almost purely Teutonic in blood. Other elements which may once have existed had been thoroughly assimilated in early historic times. The further the traveller went into eastern Germany, the more clear it became that he was

[1] T. C. Banfield, *Industry of the Rhine* (1846–8), I, 57.

in a land conquered by Germans from others. Within fifty miles of the Elbe he found islands of Wendish speech. In Posen and West Prussia he crossed broad stretches of Polish territory, recently taken over by Prussia, to pass into East Prussia, a country conquered centuries earlier, yet with a rural population largely non-German in blood and partly Slavonic in speech. If he turned south into eastern and southern Silesia he came into a land of Slavonic place-names and Slavonic dialect. Returning south-west, say from Breslau, and crossing Austrian territory through Bohemia, he went over a broad belt of German speech in western Silesia and the Riesengebirge to emerge, well on the Bohemian side of the frontier, among the Czechs of the Prague country, passing into Germans again before he left Bohemia on his way over the Böhmerwald to Nuremberg and true Germany once more.

If the traveller were a trained agriculturist, certain outward signs impressed by history on the land would strike his eye as he moved from west to east and back again. There was no change so sharp as that of the agrarian frontier near Düsseldorf. Although isolated districts were to be found in the heart of Germany where the hamlet or homestead replaced the compact village, and other districts in which an individualistic agriculture had developed, east and west alike were lands of villages and open fields. But villages and fields had peculiarities which a trained eye might appreciate. The average western village would have seemed very familiar to an eighteenth century traveller from England. It reproduced almost exactly an old-fashioned three-field village of his own Midlands. The fields were divided, as in England, into roughly rectangular sections, the English "furlong," "shot" or "wong," the German *Gewann*. The *Gewanne* were subdivided into the familiar strips, from a collection of which, in all the three fields, the cultivator's holding was made up. So late as 1845, this scattering of strips compelled the peasantry of Wiesbaden to bring ploughs and dung carts to and fro across the town daily, to the discomfort of residents and visitors. Wiesbaden, at that time, was ceasing to be a village, and had not yet learnt to be a town. But some years earlier even towns, and important towns, had their three fields, with some of the resulting drawbacks. Berlin itself, to take a striking instance from outside western Germany, had its Pankow Field, its Lichtenberg Field, and its Midfield in 1819. During the next ten years the holdings were rearranged and provision was made for individual agriculture; but in 1819 the scattered holdings and the communal routine were intact.

Though generalisation is difficult, it is safe to say that the West German open-field system, early in the nineteenth century, had changed less than that of northern France since the middle ages. It is true that in the German-Danish provinces of Schleswig-Holstein there had been an inclosure movement, like that of England, in the eighteenth century. In Denmark proper the government carried out a regular policy of consolidation and inclosure between 1770 and 1800. Much the same thing occurred in southern Sweden. In all three countries, just as in England, new farmsteads were built outside the villages and the country-side lost its primitive aspect. The old framework of village life gave way before a deliberate attack from above. If no such attack was made, it was extraordinarily tough and resisting. The most dangerous threat to it came from the growth of towns and the solvent influence of their needs and ways of thought. Now, as compared with France, Germany was almost townless. In 1815 the total population of the twelve towns which in 1914 were the greatest of the German Empire was about 750,000. Paris alone had more than 500,000; and this compact mass of people to be fed had long exercised an influence on the agriculture of the adjacent provinces, comparable with that which eighteenth century London exercised on the agriculture of the home counties. It stimulated progress and broke down old routines. The German towns had a similar influence, but it was on a much smaller scale and as yet it had shown no signs of extending. Owing to the terrible sufferings of the seventeenth century the total German population in 1800 was perhaps no greater than it had been in 1600. The age of the Napoleonic wars was not favourable to town growth. Most towns still fitted easily into their medieval ramparts, and exercised an influence much the same in nature and extent as they had exercised on the day when Martin Luther was born. In the neighbourhood of the greater towns specialised forms of agriculture were practised, as they always had been, and the village routine was broken up. Oil-seeds, root crops, fibre crops, the dye-ware crops—woad, madder, and so on—were necessarily grown in considerable quantities to satisfy urban industrial requirements; whereas in the unvarying village life, which began again almost within sight of the high roofs and steeples even of these greater towns, what industrial crops were needed could be grown on scraps of land here and there, without breaking in on the routine of the three fields.

Connected with this industrial agriculture of the actual town radius, there was to be found in 1815 in many parts of the Rhine valley and in some parts of the valleys of its chief tributaries, the Mosel, Main and Neckar, a free and varied agriculture carried on partly within the framework of the open fields and partly in vineyards, hop gardens, orchards, or ordinary arable fields which lay outside them. The agriculture of Alsace, which Arthur Young had so much admired, was of this type, only by political accident it chanced to be French. Maize, tobacco, potatoes and other crops were grown in free rotation with the ordinary grains. Vineyards, in these south-western German valleys, were often in the hands of large proprietors and were worked as capitalistic enterprises, though the peasant also had his vines. There was too some capitalistic agriculture carried on by landowners outside the vineyards. But the compact village, the scattered peasant holding, and the communal routine of the open fields dominated the rural life of western Germany.

A traveller crossing the rather indistinct boundary line from west to east might well have noticed changes in the villages themselves. The usual western village was a jumble of houses, lanes, and courtyards about the Church—primitive in its dis-order. There were important exceptions however. The chief were villages which had been systematically created during the early middle ages in the marshes of the Weser and Elbe and along the Frisian coast. They were the work of skilled colonists from Holland. The houses lay in a line along the main dyke which kept out the water. The holdings were long strips at right angles to the dyke, so that each house stood on the end of its own holding. Such marsh colonies were also very numerous in eastern Germany, as a result of German colonisation eastward in the late middle ages. All along the coast of Mecklenburg and Pomerania, about Stettin and about Danzig, and over considerable areas away from the sea, particularly in West and East Prussia, marsh conditions had led to the reproduction of these well-planned settlements, with their long straight village streets running along the main dyke.

Much greater areas in the east were covered by another type of planned village, which modern writers have called the forest colony. The pattern of these forest colonies seems to have been worked out in the west, and then to have been applied in the east—again in the late middle ages[1]. In the west they were to be found in the Black Forest, in the Odenwald between the Neckar and the Main, and in a few other districts. But their great extension was in the east, in land colonised from the Slav. Beginning on the eastern borders of the Thuringian forest, they were found thickly spread over a broad belt of country into Saxony, across the mountains into Bohemia, over a large part of Silesia and so away eastward into the Carpathians, to mention only the chief locations. Like the village of the marsh colony that of the forest colony was laid out in a thin line, usually along the road by the stream in a valley bottom, for convenience of access to the water. Again as in the marsh colonies, each homestead stood on the base of its own holding, the holding consisting in a long strip reaching from the bottom to the limit of the village lands on the heights above, where forest, waste mountain side, or in easier and thickly settled country the holdings of some adjacent village formed the boundary line. All this is in very sharp contrast with the complicated field system of the typical western village. No amount of agricultural progress would make the well thought-out and economical groundplan of these marsh and forest colonies obsolete.

The more primitive villages of eastern Germany showed what now seems to be evidence of the imposition of one type of agrarian civilisation on another. Many places with Slavonic names were distinctly smaller than the average western village and showed features which were presumably remains of Slavonic custom.

---

[1] Villages of this type are also found in France. Bloch, *op. cit.* p. 46.

In one type, common between the Elbe and the Oder, the houses stood in a small ring about a green. Beyond the houses came a belt of gardens bounded by a hedge; beyond that the fields, laid out not in the tolerably regular fashion of the west, with its *Gewanne* and strips, still less in the scientific fashion of the marsh and forest colonies, but irregularly, in fragments of no given size or shape. Holdings were usually made up of a series of these fragments, scattered about in the fields and tilled on a three-course rotation; so that the agriculture of such a village did not differ perceptibly from that of the more purely Teutonic type. A similar type was common in Bohemia. Beyond the Oder the village was usually laid out on both sides of a short wide street, forming with its hedged gardens a rough parallelogram; beyond which came the irregularly laid out fields. This was the dominant type far into Poland, where there had been no German colonisation. Often between the Elbe and the Oder, and sometimes east of the Oder, a Slavonic name and some traces of one or other of these methods of laying out the village and its fields were found combined with characteristics which suggest the taking over and partial remodelling of a Slavonic village by German immigrants. The village perhaps had grown, and grown irregularly like those of old Germany, whilst its fields showed some compromise between the unsystematic ground-plan of the untouched Polish or Czech districts and the greater system of the west[1].

But there was a more vital distinction between east and west than these curious evidences of a composite agrarian civilisation. This distinction was also connected with the fact that in the east the Germans were a conquering and colonising race. It was the great extent of land which, in almost every eastern district at the beginning of the nineteenth century, was under the direct personal control of the lord of the manor, the *Rittergutsbesitzer* (holder of a knight's fee), vulgarly the Junker. Originally lord over free and unfree peasants, with a holding of his own by which his household lived, the Junker, since the middle ages, had won direct control over more and more land

---

[1] Meitzen, *Siedelung...der Germanen*, 3 vols., 1895, is the primary authority. His opinions on origins have been much criticised, but his facts stand.

from generation to generation. The wide gulf between lord and peasant in the east, due to the lord's never forgotten position as a descendant of conquerors, had rendered the task of putting down peasants, *Bauernlegen* as it was called, relatively easy. In some cases whole villages had been swept away and their lands added to the lord's domain. Quite apart from such deliberate evictions, the wasting of the people in the Thirty Years' War had thrown land into the lords' hands which they had not again relinquished. Any acquisition of fresh arable ground from moor, marsh or forest, had usually been done at the lord's instigation and for his advantage. Such were the main causes of the special social characteristic of east German agriculture, which differentiated it sharply from that of either France or England. The French seigneur of the old order had never been much of a cultivator. The "spirited landlord" of eighteenth century England had bought out small men and laid field to field. Often he kept some kind of a home farm for purposes of experiment. But most of the land which he inherited or acquired he let out to the rising class of capitalist farmers. In eastern Germany the Junker became his own capitalist cultivator[1]. His land might be mixed up with that of his tenants in the fields or it might lie outside the fields; but in either case it had been his business to arrange it in manageable masses.

Eviction and consolidation of land in the lords' hands during the sixteenth, seventeenth and eighteenth centuries had not been confined to the east, nor was its success there solely due to the stronger position of the lord over against the peasant. There had been a similar movement in the west. But in a number of the more important western states—leading examples are Hanover and Bavaria—the governments, like our Tudors, had early set their faces against what was called in England the "putting down of houses of husbandry." The putting down of peasants (*Bauernlegen*) had been countered by a policy of peasant protection (*Bauernschutz*); while in many of the lesser western states, particularly in the ecclesiastical principalities which down to the Napoleonic age occupied so much of the Rhine

[1] Not generally however until the period 1800–30. In the eighteenth century, and earlier, Junkers usually let out these domains. Sartorius von Waltershausen, *Deutsche Wirthschaftsgeschichte 1815–1914* (1920), p. 121.

valley and the north-west, the strength of the peasants and the comparative weakness of the knightly class had been a real protection to the small cultivator.

Ruling princes in the east had not altogether neglected the peasants' interests; but for one reason and another their work had not achieved much. The Dukes of Mecklenburg, for example, had protected the peasants on their own domains, but either they had not been strong enough, or they had not tried, to check very extensive *Bauernlegen* on those of their subordinate gentry. In parts of Pomerania things had gone so far that the true peasant, who lived by his holding, had almost disappeared. In Brandenburg no action was taken by the Electors in the seventeenth century. As kings of Prussia in the eighteenth they put their hands to the work of peasant protection in 1739, too late to save the situation. Even then they only interfered in some of their provinces. So the Junkers of the east had added to their military and administrative functions those of the agricultural capitalist by 1815. A series of events during the next thirty or forty years strengthened their position as capitalistic cultivators, though they curtailed the Junkers' powers over their people. These were the events connected with the formal emancipation of the German peasants.

§ 8. Emancipation in Germany was long drawn out, not a thing done once for all, with burning of châteaux and wholesale abolition of feudal dues, as in France. On the eve of the French Revolution the legal and, in many districts, the economic position of the German peasantry had been lower than that of the French. There was no comparison between east German legal conditions and those of an average French province, so vastly worse were the former. The west German peasant's position was tolerable and, where he was not too heavily taxed, he could easily bear the legal disabilities of his status. He was comfortable enough in some of the quaint and paternal little states of old Germany. Conditions varied infinitely in detail throughout the scores of Grand Duchies, Duchies, Principalities, Electorates, Free Town Territories and Territories of the independent Knights of the Empire. But it is fairly easy to define the limits within which variation occurred. Putting on

one side the very small group of cultivators who were in a
position comparable with that of an English yeoman on freehold
land, and assuming—as is broadly true—that every peasant had
a lord, there is found at the top of the scale in the west a class
in much the same position as the French *cens* payers. (See *ante*,
§ 4.) They held their lands in return for an anciently fixed quit-
rent, paid in money or in kind, a quit-rent which was not an
economic rent. Besides this they might owe some ceremonial
duties to their lord; and he would generally receive dues, which
again might be fixed by ancient custom, when the land changed
hands from father to son. In essentials the system was not far
from peasant proprietorship.

At the other end of the peasant scale, omitting a few unimportant cases of complete servitude, was a class of peasant who
in the eyes of the law could not transmit his holding to his heir;
for in theory the lord held it in full ownership and only let it
out of his free grace and charity. In practice, son followed father
with great regularity. This form of tenure was marked by the
obligation to render personal services, ploughing, harvesting,
help at the winepress and so forth; but the service owed did
not involve a heavy call on the peasant's time. Besides the
labour dues there were, in French terminology, the *banalités*—
the obligation to grind at the lord's mill, bake in the manorial
oven, put the grapes through the lord's winepress, and pay the
lord's agent for the privilege. There were ceremonial duties too,
and always there was the personal deference, obedience, and
honour owed to the "gracious lord."

Between these limiting types lay almost all the peasantry of
the west. Services more and more occasional and formal,
banalités less and less irksome, a legal theory which did not
so obviously underline the peasant's dependence on his lord,
marked the transitions upwards from the lowest to the highest
grade.

There was no landless class, though there might be landless
individuals. But there was, in most districts, a class which could
not live by its holdings. This class supplied the rural wage
labour as in France. The landlord of western Germany had not
usually great domains like the Junkers beyond the Elbe; but

he might have some arable, woodland or vineyard in hand, which
he must get attended to by peasant services or by wage labour.
As services were light, labourers were generally wanted. Sometimes he let to a farmer, as in England, and then wage labour
was also needed. There was also wage work to be done in certain
districts on the land of the big peasants; for the peasant with
a hundred English acres and more was not unknown. In these
various ways the more pressing needs of the small holding class
were met. But, as will be explained more fully when industrial
conditions in Germany are discussed (see *post*, § 22), the small
holder was often obliged to earn all he could by domestic handicraft.

Across the Elbe also the absolutely landless peasant was rare.
Not so rare as in the west, because in some places *Bauernlegen*
had been so thorough. Yet, generally speaking, the lowest
placed peasant in the eastern villages, the *Häusler* or cotter, had
a scrap of garden and the chance of feeding some geese, or even
a cow, on the stubble and the common. Above him came a type
of peasant, the so-called *Kossäth*[1], who tilled land but had not
a regular holding in the organised village fields. Usually he had
no ploughing cattle. The power to harness his own beasts to
the plough was the test of the true peasant, the man who held
land in the fields. *Spannfähig* he was called, capable of harnessing
his yoke of oxen, as the word might be paraphrased. He alone,
in the lawyer's eyes, was a peasant in the full sense of the word.

All these people in the typical eastern manor were servile.
There were free peasants in the east, especially in the marsh
colonies of the Baltic coast and in the forest colonies on the other
side of the great north German plain; but the average village
was servile. In such a village all were amenable to manorial
jurisdiction, they lived in a state of "heritable subjection."
All were bound to the soil. If their fathers had held of a
Bismarck or an Arnim they held inevitably from Arnim's or
Bismarck's heir. Inevitably from their side; but in the eighteenth
century there was a growing tendency for the lord to hold the

---

[1] These are the terms used in the old provinces of Prussia. The same
classes recur elsewhere but not the same names. In Silesia the *Kossäth* was
called a *Gärtner* (gardener).

contract as not binding on himself, and treat the peasants as tenants-at-will, which perhaps they were in legal theory though at one time they had certainly not so been in economic fact. So they might be evicted, if it became expedient to extend the domain land of the manor. Below these soil-bound yet evictable peasants were to be found in places a certain number of people who could not acquire property and might be sold, like the domestic serf of Russia before 1862. From that risk at least the average peasant was free.

But his servility was clearly reflected in the duties laid upon him. He owed his lord heavy services, services of two sorts, the *Spanndienste*, when he went to serve with his ploughing cattle, and the *Handdienste*, when he went to do whatever work the lord required of him. The man who had no cattle gave hand-services only. Services of both sorts had grown with the growth of the manorial domain which depended on them. The services were supplemented by various dues and payments, hens and eggs presented at this season and that, payments for leave to break the rules of the manor, payments on taking up an inheritance, and the other familiar incidents of serfdom all over Europe. Of course there were also *banalités*, strictly enforced. Then there was a most galling and humiliating obligation in the so-called *Gesindedienst*. This was service exacted from the peasant's family. For many years, and for extremely small reward, they were bound to menial service about the manor house, in the kitchen perhaps, or the stables; or to an equivalent in any agricultural work of which they were capable.

In the east as in the west three-field agriculture and all that went with it implied access to commons, and the isolation of most villages made access to woodland essential. Forest was abundant in most parts of Germany. In the west it was generally recognised that much of the forest belonged to the village as a community. In the east the subjection of the peasants was accentuated by the concentration of all woodland in the lord's hands. The peasant's right of access to it was, in law, revocable. Similarly the lord kept control of the commons, regulating and if he saw fit cutting down common rights. This cutting down had been going on for a long time. In all such matters of manorial economy the lord was judge in his own cause. And so, to quote a German historian, the peasant of the east was "gloomy, discontented, coarse, slavish...a hapless missing link between a beast of burden and a man[1]." Nor is it surprising.

That the Junker and his *Kriegsherr* may not be misjudged, note that in the newly won Polish provinces the position of the peasant was definitely worse than in Brandenburg or East Prussia. The Polish peasant, it may be said, had no rights. His land, his goods, his services were all at the lord's disposal. He had no cause to love his country; and it is probable that he found the Prussian government an improvement on his own, even before Prussia began the emancipation.

§ 9. Before the French peasants began burning châteaux, the abolition of agrarian servitude or its remains had been discussed by almost every government of Western Europe. The lesser princes had done the best work. The Dukes of Savoy got rid of feudal dues and survivals between 1770 and 1780. Denmark began a most important series of reforms in 1784. For over twenty years the abolition of personal service and other feudal obligations went on. The Danish peasant became free; sometimes a freeholder, sometimes a free tenant. Emancipation was accompanied by inclosure and consolidation of holdings; and provision was made to help the peasant in meeting incidental expenses by a national agrarian bank. The whole series of reforms, coinciding as it does with the unsystematic and ill-regulated completion of the inclosure movement in England, shows the enlightened despotism of the late eighteenth century at its best. There were repeated delays in completing these Danish reforms, and when Denmark became a constitutional country in 1848 there was still some clearing up of feudal remains to be done; but the progress made before that date is indicated by the fact that the main task undertaken after 1848 was the turning of rent-paying peasants into freeholders.

Many German princes, great and small, had been feeling their way towards emancipation before 1789. The princes of the south-west had not a great deal to do. There the almost free peasant of the *censier* type predominated. His heavy services

[1] Knapp, *Die Bauern-Befreiung...Preussens*, I, 77

had long since been commuted for money, and he paid with ease the quit-rents fixed in the middle ages when the purchasing power of money was high. He owed a few dues; he was subject to the manorial court. But his general economic position was good although he might be legally servile. Therefore the chief pre-revolutionary reforming prince of the south-west, Karl Friedrich of Baden, had a straightforward task when he took the matter up in 1783. In Bavaria, where conditions were less favourable to the peasant, a beginning was made on crown land in 1779; but not very much had been accomplished before the hurricane season set in after 1789. In the Hapsburg dominions, whose detailed study lies outside the scope of this book, a famous beginning of reform on the grand scale was made by Joseph II in the year 1789 itself. His mother before him had fought *Bauernlegen*, had tried to fix or ease the peasant's services, and to get rid of the legal doctrine of bodily servitude.

But the most conspicuous emancipation movement was that in Prussia; and as Prussia after 1815 was the sole state representative of almost all Germany, with lands stretching from the servile Slavonic east to the free Dutch west, the Prussian movement deserves the closest study. It illustrates every point of importance in German agrarian history during the early nineteenth century.

It begins, where most Prussian stories begin, with Frederick. Before his accession the rulers of Prussia had barely begun to take an interest in stopping *Bauernlegen*. They had even practised it not so long ago. As owner of nearly a third of his kingdom, Frederick had an ample field for experiment. On his own manors he could easily define and lighten peasants' services, secure for them the right of inheritance, and begin an attack on the legal doctrine which placed some of them in a state of bodily servitude. He could also attack the technical side of agrarian reform, divide up commons and rearrange fields, so as to allow of more individual agriculture. His work however was not extensive enough to affect the face of the country greatly. Outside his own manors Frederick tried to press these same reforms, together with a policy of *Bauernschutz*. Strong ruler as he was, he had little success. He came up against the

"stiff and for the most part unsurmountable opposition[1]" of the nobility and gentry. As was said of their successors, their doctrine was   Und der König absolut
          Wenn er uns den Willen thut.
Not otherwise. Yet his edicts, the chief of which are of 1771 and 1777, contain the germs of all later legislation.

There followed for Prussia, after his death (1786), twenty inglorious years, during which the only important development in agrarian history was the continuance of his work on the crown manors. Then Jena. In the interval revolutionary France had overflowed into Belgium and western Germany, overturning the moribund feudalism of those parts. After Jena reforms of all kinds went forward, and among them were the famous emancipation edicts of 1807–8. These edicts dealt with principles and they were two-edged. Inspired less by the old Prussian conception of a disciplinary paternal government than by the new Anglo-French doctrine of economic freedom, they removed shackles, but they also broke down some barriers which had hitherto sheltered the peasant. He became a free man. "Heritable subjection" and the yet lower status of "bodily servitude" disappeared. The meanest peasant could acquire property. But what he could acquire he could sell. His lord began to argue that, if these men were no longer his "subjects," it was no longer his business, as in the past, to see that every "full peasant" had a holding big enough to enable him to fulfil his manorial obligations. Some attempt was made in the edicts to maintain the older peasant holdings. But the lord was given formal leave to do as he liked with holdings created in the last generation or two; and he had opportunities for throwing together some even of the older holdings, if that suited his plans. In short the government was dropping the policy of "peasant protection" which had played so great a part in German agrarian history. Its opposite, *Bauernlegen*, "the putting down of houses of husbandry," fitted in well with the current doctrines of economic freedom. It was acceptable to the squires whose fathers had stood out even against Frederick for their right to evict peasants. Also it facilitated agricultural progress, just as inclosure did in

[1] Article *Agrargeschichte*, in *Handwörterbuch der Staatswissenschaften*, 2nd ed.

England, in spite of the accompanying social drawbacks. To this abandonment of the peasantry there was, however, one exception of extraordinary political interest. The Polish peasantry in Posen were sedulously protected; and their position improved in every way after 1815. These poor folk were not dreaming of their lost kings and might be made into good Prussians. They had no cause to love their landlords, who were less likely to make good Prussians. So the checks which were removed from the landowning Prussian were imposed on the landowning Pole. It is an interesting case of calculated humanity.

The edicts of 1807–8 were only a beginning. They were followed by a whole series of edicts, regulations and laws, of which the chief are those of 1811, 1816 and 1821. Policy fluctuated and only a full narrative could do justice to the finer points of the story. It must be sufficient here to indicate the course of events and the results of the edicts in outline, beginning with the east, where the main problems lay.

The highest class of peasants, other than the aristocracy of freeholders whom the edicts did not touch, were those whose land was already regarded as heritable—who in England would have been called copyholders of inheritance. These were to become full proprietors on ceding to their lord a third of their land as compensation for what he sacrificed. Those whose property had not hitherto been heritable, and they were the great majority in many districts, were to cede one-half. If a man had so small a holding that he could not live on the remnant, he might keep all his land and pay a rent. This was under Hardenberg's edict of 1811. The edict said further that the peasant was in no case to get his land in full ownership until all matters had been settled between him and his lord. The settlement often took many years. Moreover a royal declaration of 1816 limited the application of the principle to men who did *Spanndienste*, the full peasants who had plough oxen and a share in the regular village fields. All below them were excluded, left to the old law, liable to be called upon for services. Now the declaration of 1816 remained in force till 1850 and most of the work of rearrangement was done under it for those peasants whose land was not heritable. The higher grades were more fortunate. They bought off their old obligations by a sacrifice of land, or by an agreement to pay a rent without sacrificing land; and there were no great delays in concluding the transaction.

But the "regulated" peasants, as the tenants of non-heritable holdings came to be called, fared badly in the long run. Their lord could make any arrangement he liked with them before "regulation" began. As it did not begin until they asked for it, he could buy out their interest in the land under the free trade legislation of 1808. The petrifying bureaucracy of 1815–45 was not likely to move fast, so he generally had plenty of time for action. And when, perhaps after many years, regulation was complete, Hans the peasant found that he had sacrificed more than a part of his land to make sure of the rest. While his land, and he with it, were still the lord's property, it was to the lord's interest to repair his house, to see that he had wood enough from the manorial forest for all purposes, and to take some care of him in misfortune. Now he must fend for himself in a cold world. Firewood he is entitled to; but if a free man wants to mend his barn he can buy the timber and do it himself. If he falls into debt he can sell his land and go. There is always likely to be a buyer.

The lowest grades of the rural population, the *Kossäthen* with their scraps of land, the still smaller cottagers and others, were not legally true peasants at all and the laws, which were laws for peasants not for the rural population generally, simply passed over their heads. Together with some of the bought-out peasants and all the other wreckage from the upper grades they became labourers, in the English sense of the word. They held bits of land as tenants-at-will if they were fortunate. Someone was needed to work the lord's growing domain and these people came in opportunely. They could not easily leave their native places because, in fact, freedom of migration was not yet established. When the lords ceased to be responsible for the care of the aged and infirm among their people, a problem arose akin to the problem of "settlement" in the history of the English Poor Law. Clearly no commune—the basis of poor relief was communal—could accept indefinite liability for any poor folk who might chance to wander into it. Towns were few, small, and far. The New Worlds were further still, for as yet there were no railways. The new Prussian law of migration was tolerably liberal; but men whose fathers had lived and died time out of mind in the old village and who, generally speaking, were not wanted anywhere else, seldom thought of moving and would probably have failed to move had they tried, especially as the lords, who still had great administrative powers, wanted to keep them. So they mostly stayed to work on the domain land for what they could get. It was not until after 1848 that German villagers began to migrate in appreciable numbers; and the small folk of the east were the last to learn how to do it.

In the western parts of Prussia, as in western Germany generally, the problems of emancipation were far easier. In the Westphalian and Rhenish provinces which Prussia secured in 1815, a peasantry already almost free and reasonably prosperous had become still freer during the French occupation. Where emancipation was necessary the work was fairly straightforward. A large proportion of the cultivators held land which was regarded as heritable, so they fell into those upper peasant classes whose affairs were rearranged without much difficulty or loss to themselves. And as capitalist farming by the lord was the exception in the west, there was no incentive from his side to buy out peasants or stimulate the supply of mere labourers. Moreover, in many of the non-Prussian states, the interests of the humbler folk received more attention than had been given them in the Prussian laws. It is true that in some districts the work of clearing away the remnants of servitude was long drawn out. Bavaria, for example, postponed the business until after the political storms of 1848. But delay in such a case meant far less than it would have meant east of the Elbe; for there was little effective servitude in Bavaria, only remnants of servile customs and tenures. The net result of emancipation in the west therefore was that the peasants gained far more than they lost. They became, in course of time, owners of by far the greater part of the soil. A new landless class was not created; and to this day the vast majority of agricultural labourers have land of their own, and do wage work only because they have not land enough.

§ 10. Peasant emancipation was regarded by men who took a wide national view as only a part of the greater problem of agricultural reform. Frederick the Great had attacked the tangle of the fields and the problem of the commons. They wished to imitate him. In connection with the changes which took place in the fields, on the commons, and in the actual crops during the first half of the nineteenth century, certain considerations must be emphasised at the outset. Firstly, that where the three-field system had broken down, as in parts of south-western Germany (see *ante*, § 7), the question of reform in cropping was the least urgent: crop rotations were already free. Secondly, that where the peasant was, or was in course of becoming, the owner of the greater part of the soil, as throughout all western Germany, his natural conservatism and the fact that he still cultivated primarily with an eye to the maintenance of his own family, rather than with an eye to the market, made it most unlikely that any agricultural change whatever would happen quickly. Thirdly, that the greatest extent of common pasture and common woodland was in the west, and that, as their common use was congenial to peasant habits and on the whole not uneconomical, there was little effective inducement to make a change in it. Fourthly, that, as a natural consequence, the chief pioneers in change of all kinds were the numerous farming squires of the east, who had both an eye on the market and the power of influencing government.

It is common in Germany to date the agricultural, as distinguished from the legal, reforms of the nineteenth century from the appearance in 1798 of Albrecht Thaer's *Introduction to the knowledge of English Agriculture*. Thaer was a Hanoverian who had at one time been a physician at the Hanoverian court. Called to Prussia, where brains were valued, he founded the first Prussian school of agriculture in 1804, and subsequently he became a professor in the new University of Berlin, from which he issued his greater work the *Principles of rational agriculture* in 1809–12. Before his death in 1828 he had been largely responsible, among other things, for the law of 1821 which took up the question of commons and common rights in connection with that of peasant emancipation. With Arthur

Young he held that common rights were a standing obstacle to rational agriculture. Where holdings lay scattered in the fields and access to one was by right across another, where one cropping routine was enforced on a whole village, and where the right of stubble pasture prevailed, reforms were blocked at the start. Before Thaer's day the eastern squires had been working to get as much land as possible "out of the fields" and under their own control. Frederick's legislation had encouraged them in this. Now all the circumstances of the emancipation urged them to go forward, and the law of 1821 came in to help. A lord who was receiving innumerable scraps of former peasant land, in exchange for the rights over peasants' bodies which he was called upon to abandon, naturally did not wish to have these scraps all tilled for him separately under the old conditions. Therefore as emancipation progressed, slowly it will be recalled, what was called "separation" progressed with it. The lord had his fields, in which he could practise a rational agriculture, and the peasants had theirs, where they could go on in the old ways if they liked—as they very often did. If there was much common, the lord might separate a part proportionate to his enlarged arable holding, and do with it as he pleased, leaving the peasants to share the rest. They might have divided it, but generally did not. As woodland was not generally common property in the east, no difficulty arose here. The lord had merely to guarantee to the land-holding peasantry rights to cut firewood in his forest.

"Land-holding" raises an important point in connection with all these eastern readjustments of common rights. Whatever the rights were—in wood or pasture, meadow or stubble—they were treated strictly as appurtenances to the regular holdings in the fields, a view which was no doubt historically correct. But its application had much the same unhappy effect as had that of the corresponding doctrine in England. The mere cottager, that is to say, who had enjoyed customs of common rather than rights of common, just as in England, might find that the few geese, sheep or pigs, worse still the cow, that once he had been able to keep, were no longer within his reach. One hears of the resultant hardships especially in Pomerania, where the labourer class was most fully developed.

As the separation of squire's land from peasants' land proceeded, opportunities presented themselves for rearrangement of the peasant holdings. These opportunities were taken to a considerable extent. Some holdings were consolidated, and frequently the more substantial peasants moved out of the village and built themselves new houses on the land which was now their own. But there was not a complete rearrangement in the first half of the century. It has been seen that the adjustment of relations between the freed peasants and their lords was a slow business, far from complete in 1848; and until these primary details were settled, questions between peasants had to wait. One sees from the numerous very important Prussian laws dealing with the regulation of common rights, from 1850 onwards, how much remained to do in the second half of the century. But by 1850 the bulk of the large landowners at any rate were in a position to carry out agricultural improvement on the grand scale, not much hampered by ancient rights, customs and routines. Everything might not be in order; but they usually had their own grazing land, on which their sheep or cattle need not mix with the mongrel flocks and herds of the village, besides great stretches of arable upon which the crop rotation was in their own control.

In illustration of the considerations emphasised at the beginning of this section, some facts from the history of west German states may be given. In Bavaria, which was mainly tilled by peasants, nothing important happened before 1850, except a little voluntary rearrangement of fields. Inclosure of commons was started and then stopped. Wurtemberg had much the same history. Its peasants were free and fairly prosperous. They had no special wish to see their fields rearranged, for the routine of the old agriculture was already in part broken down. Their commons were, and always had been, communal property. In Baden the first general law to facilitate the rearrangement of the fields dates from 1856; it was not a success even then. In the Prussian Rhine provinces a good deal had been done under French law to get rid of the compulsory cropping routine, and facilities had been provided for the abolition of stubble grazing by mutual consent. Prussia decided not to apply to these newly acquired lands the law of 1821, for two interesting reasons: first, because there was more compulsion in it than the Rhinelanders were accustomed to; second, because the need for rearrangement of the fields seemed less urgent than in the east, since nearly all the holdings were small.

The north-west has rather a different story. In Schleswig-Holstein there had been a great deal of systematic rearrangement of fields, and even actual inclosure, before 1800. In the adjacent Hanoverian territory King George III, that royal farmer, had been keenly interested in the division of commons. With the nineteenth century there came a whole series of laws in the Hanover and Brunswick states to facilitate division. Hanover was rich in commons, many of which—for example, the great Lüneburg Heath—could be cut up and tilled to the great advantage of the community. She had more cultivating landlords than most western states, so the incentives to division which were so conspicuous in the east came into play. The divisions followed Prussian lines: the landlord took part of the common in absolute ownership and the peasants retained the rest for their joint use. Hanover specialised in this division of commons. The first law aimed directly at the rearrangement of the fields did not come till 1842, and an amending law was needed in 1856; so that the first half of the century had little to show on this side.

The rational agriculture in whose interest all these schemes were devised was certainly making progress between 1815 and 1850. The progress was fastest, as has already been indicated, on the manors of the east. The tradition of leadership, the tradition of serving their families and their country, the cruder incentive afforded by the growth of the corn and wool exports from eastern Germany—in the years when the Danzig wheat price was the regular London quotation and when British merchants posted yearly from Calais to the wool sales in Saxony and Silesia—all these things helped to make the eastern squires spirited cultivators. Like Bismarck in 1839, when he threw up the civil service in disgust, many of them worked furiously at their estates. Thaer had pointed out the right lines of work, though Prussia was so hard hit by the wars that in Thaer's lifetime († 1828) few had capital enough to follow them up.

They were—deep ploughing and improved implements after
the English fashion; stall feeding of cattle after the Flemish
fashion; careful attention, in suitable localities, to the merino
sheep introduced into eastern Germany at the end of the
eighteenth century; extensive growth of the oil seeds, rape,
linseed, hemp; a better rotation of crops with clover or grasses
on the fallow and roots as a field crop; finally, and here the
school of Thaer went ahead of contemporary England, a close
attention to agricultural book-keeping.

Among the roots was the sugar beet, whose possibilities had
first been made clear by a German chemist. Beet growing had
not made much progress during the wars. Germany was too
often fought over by the French. The first boom in beet growing
and sugar factories occurred in Silesia and Saxony in the thirties.
It stimulated the use of better machinery, because the beet
requires deep cultivation and drilling: it cannot well be sown
broadcast. About this time, therefore, Germany began to make
the new types of machinery for herself.

Besides the beet there was the potato, not however a novelty.
It had been making headway long before 1800. Frederick had
realised its merits, as the French reporter said to Napoleon
(see *ante*, § 6), *pour les malheureux*. And not for them only.
Here was a new and easily grown raw material, excellent both
in peace and war for making Prussians who could work and
fight. It would appear that the potato had made much more
rapid progress in Germany than in France before 1815. Pre-
judice against it is said to have died out so early as 1770–1, in
consequence of a period of dearth. By 1815 it was grown everywhere, east and west, by squire and peasant; and within a few
years spirit was being distilled from it extensively. In 1831
there were 23,000 distilleries in Prussia, of which between a half
and two-thirds used potatoes.

Agricultural information was spread among the eastern landowners by methods now familiar—cattle shows, shows of
implements, agricultural societies and agricultural colleges. The
first cattle shows, in the early thirties, were wisely combined
with race meetings. Get the squires together for what the most
stupid of them appreciates and work from the known to the

unknown, was the policy. In 1837 exhibitions of machinery were started, which moved about the country like circuses. By the forties the whole movement was in full swing. The societies and colleges were springing up. From England—still leading— there came knowledge of guano and the earthenware drain-pipe; from the German universities, that modern chemistry of agriculture which is specially connected with the name of Justus von Liebig.

And the peasant? Of him it may be said that he was following at his own pace. What amount of progress had been made on peasant holdings, either east or west, by the forties, is very hard to ascertain. Even for contemporaries generalisation was difficult. One witness, from Pomerania, said that up to 1821 emancipation had done nothing at all for peasant agriculture; holdings were scattered, implements unimproved, ignorance abysmal. More than twenty years later (1845) much the same thing is reported by an Englishman from the other end of Germany. "With the old subdivisions of property, the old agricultural implements have in a great measure been retained." He was careful to point out that the Dutch type of agriculture with its scattered homesteads, in Gelders and Cleves, and the high farming of the upper Rhine valley, were exceptional. He mentions, however, that stubble grazing was nearly extinct in the Rhineland, which suggests that the French legislation against it had borne useful fruit. But the stages by which good farming spread among the small folk, whether from peasant to peasant in the west or from squire to peasant in the east, are exceedingly difficult to trace. It is noted, for instance, that by about 1840 even peasants in the east were beginning to understand the scientific rotation of crops[1]; but how general the knowledge had become is not noted. Broadly speaking, no general and thoroughgoing improvement can be registered in peasant agriculture before the railway age, though there are various hopeful beginnings and a great deal of preparatory work without which improvement might never have come at all.

[1] Meitzen, *Der Boden...des Preussischen Staates* (1868), II, 20. The Englishman is Banfield, *op. cit.* I, 57, 59, 66.

CHAPTER III

INDUSTRIAL CONDITIONS IN FRANCE, 1815-1848

§ 11. In the course of the nineteenth century most French industries were remodelled, but it might be said that France never went through an industrial revolution. There was a gradual transformation, a slow shifting of her economic centre of gravity from the side of agriculture to that of industry, and a slow change in the methods of industrial organisation. The transformation accomplished in a century was in many ways less complete than that which Germany experienced in the forty years after 1871. In the first half of the century the movement, if examined as a whole dispassionately and statistically, is barely perceptible, in spite of the noise and controversy which accompanied it and of the fact that, here and there, a town a district or an industry may be picked out in which something really revolutionary happened.

The best general test of the industrialisation of a nation's life under modern conditions is the rate and character of the growth of its towns. Consider the French figures and facts from 1801 to 1851, bearing in mind what was happening in contemporary England. France started the century with a well-developed urban life. Paris was second in all Europe only to London. She had 548,000 inhabitants in 1801 and no rival. She was and always had been *Paris la grande ville*. Of the other large towns, Marseilles had 111,000, Lyons 109,000, more than any English town except London at that time. Bordeaux, Rouen and Nantes were in the group from 100,000 to 75,000. Lille and Toulouse were just over 50,000. These were all old and famous cities, local capitals, leading seaports, likely to grow steadily for political and commercial reasons independently of industrial changes. In the next fifty years, while the total French population grew about thirty per cent. that of Paris nearly doubled, that of Lyons a little more than doubled. Marseilles grew seventy-five per cent.; Toulouse rather more. Neither Rouen nor Nantes grew so quickly as the general population; Bordeaux and Lille very little quicker. In all France, only a couple of towns grew really fast in the half century as the direct result of industrial developments—St Etienne from 16,000 to 56,000 and Roubaix from 8,000 to 34,000. Contrast England. In the single decade 1821–31, Sheffield, Birmingham, Manchester, Liverpool, Leeds and Bradford all grew more than forty per cent.

Or put the French figures in another way. In 1801 six and three-quarter per cent. of the population, or about one in fifteen, lived in towns of 20,000 inhabitants or more. In 1851 the corresponding figure was just over ten and a half per cent. or rather more than one in ten.

If legislative and administrative action could industrialise a country, France would have moved more quickly. The Revolution had removed all obstacles to free enterprise. Both the revolutionary and the Napoleonic governments held that the state must do its utmost to help industry, without fettering it. Weights and measures had been rationalised and unified. Museums of arts and crafts and industrial exhibitions had been projected during the Reign of Terror, though the first exhibition was delayed until 1798. Schools of civil engineering and of mining were encouraged long before England had anything of the kind. Under the pressure of war needs and the British blockade, the scientific aspects of industry had been explored. The Committee of Public Safety patronised Leblanc's method for making soda. Chemists, encouraged by the state, developed the sugar beet industry. They found fresh sources of saltpetre and new methods of refining it. They applied the best knowledge available to steel making for munitions. They popularised bleaching with chlorine and invented a coffee substitute.

All the governments worked hard to acclimatise the new English mechanical knowledge, in spite of the difficulties imposed by an almost unbroken series of wars with England. Frenchmen had just begun to appreciate the significance of that knowledge before the Revolution. One of Boulton and Watt's steam-engines arrived at Le Creusot in 1782. The spinning jenny must have crossed to France about the same time, as it is said to have been generally adopted in the Department of the

North by the end of the century. Arkwright's spinning frame was known also. England did all she could to keep her profitable inventions to herself, even in time of peace, but she was not very successful, even in time of war. They leaked out in one way and another.

For example—the flying shuttle which, though invented much earlier, was only coming into general use in England towards the end of the eighteenth century, was taken up in France about 1800. Napoleon had a model weaving shed set up at Passy, and arranged for picked weavers to come even from remote southern departments to learn how to handle the new device. About the same time Chaptal, Napoleon's minister for industries, secured a Scotchman named Douglas who understood how to make wool carding and spinning machinery, financed him, found him a workshop on an island in the Seine, and was able to boast that he had sold over 300 machines in two years. The prefects were circularised and instructed to encourage the use of machinery in their departments. And when an important textile invention was made by a Frenchman, Jacquard—the loom for weaving figured fabrics which still bears his name—his success was in part due to the care of government, which had recognised his ability and brought him up from Lyons to Paris to work at the *Conservatoire des Arts et Métiers*. Kay and Crompton, Watt and Arkwright, never received such effective backing.

But Napoleonic France had just gone through a destructive and disorganising revolution, accompanied by civil war and national bankruptcy. She was fighting continuously with all her resources, losing men by the million, and eventually becoming herself the battleground of the nations. Her vitality was amazing and the energy of her governments in every way admirable; but a great part of that energy was necessarily spent in making up lost ground. Again and again the watchful officials had to report that such and such an industry, so far from being ripe for re-organisation, had gone back since 1789; that it was short of capital, short of skilled labour, unable owing to war to get the necessary raw material, or otherwise hampered in its activities. They were well content if they could overcome these difficulties.

§ 12. There were reasons much more permanent and deep-seated than revolution and war to explain why no amount of intelligent official action could make France follow in England's steps at England's pace. "We are," wrote Chaptal in 1828 after more than a decade of peace, "far from having that profusion of machines which one sees in England...it is because labour is cheaper with us and because the cheapness of fuel in England enables them to employ machines everywhere with advantage[1]." The second reason was the chief. The total coal resources of France as now known are inadequate, and a century ago she was neither aware of their full extent nor capable of working large parts of them. All her fields but two are very small; and fully a half of what is now the most important field, that of the North and the Pas de Calais, was not surveyed or tapped to any purpose before 1850. There were no pits at Lens or Béthune in Chaptal's day. At best the whole field is only the tail of the more accessible Belgian coal measures. All the old workings were up against the Belgian frontier, near Valenciennes. The other important coal-bearing strata lie on the upper Loire, just west of Lyons, from St Etienne to Roanne, with outliers east of the Rhone in the Department of the Isère. Judging by the number of collieries, as reported in 1807, this field was then the more important of the two. In the departments of the Loire and the Isère there were nineteen collieries, against six in the department of the North. The North was producing only about a third of the coal raised in France. It did, however, contain the one large old established French mining enterprise, the company of Anzin by Valenciennes. Coal was first worked there about 1720, although not with success until 1734, by the Vicomte Desandrouin. Desandrouin, a mining pioneer on both sides of the frontier, brought the Newcomen steam pump into Belgium in 1725 and to Anzin in 1732. His company was amalgamated with a rival in 1757 to make that Anzin company which still exists. It was always pioneering. In 1825 it dug its own private dock, connected with the Scheldt. In 1835 it built one of the earliest French railways, nineteen kilometres long.

At first sight the figures of French coal output under the first

---

[1] De l'industrie française, II, 28. For coal, see Rouff, Les mines de charbon en France au 18e siècle, 1922.

Empire suggest a very solid foundation for rapid industrial development. The output in 1807 was no less than 5,000,000 (metric) tons, from between 450 and 500 collieries. But nearly all these were in territory which in 1815 became Dutch and in 1830 Belgian. France, after the Congress of Vienna, had an annual output of only 800–900,000 tons. She had raised nearly 700,000 in 1789. Under peace conditions this rose to 1,774,000 in 1828 and to 5,153,000 in 1847. The consumption in 1847 was over 7,500,000 tons, imports accounting for the difference.

Throughout this period Belgium raised more coal than all France, and in the early years very much more. Liège and Southern Hainault were the first homes of coal mining on the continent. Regular working began near Mons in the seventeenth century. The French pits near Valenciennes were only opened up when the political separation of French Hainault, in which Valenciennes lies, from what was then Spanish Hainault threatened a fuel famine on the French side of the boundary. By 1789 there were pits near Mons over 600 feet deep, a great depth for those days[1]. The temporary incorporation of the Belgian provinces into France (1797–1814) gave the Belgian coal industry a fresh stimulus. The Belgians were ahead of the French in experience and technique, and now their coal had the free run of the French market. After 1800 the Belgian industries developed so fast that political vicissitudes could almost be ignored. There was sure to be a demand for all coal that could be raised. By 1830 the new kingdom of Belgium contained some 300 collieries, each employing an average of about 100 men and turning out over 6,000,000 tons a year. The next twenty years saw a rapid increase in output; but Belgian demand grew faster still, so that before 1840 English coal was being imported. Belgium was in fact the one country in Europe which kept pace industrially with England, in the first half of the nineteenth century. She had an ancient urban civilisation and brilliant economic traditions. Once she had been England's schoolmistress in industry. French influence and government had broken down many troublesome medieval relics—town privileges and gild regulations—which had hampered her industries in the seventeenth and eighteenth centuries. France

---

[1] The main pits at Anzin were about the same depth.

also opened the Scheldt to her trade, the Scheldt which the jealousy of Holland and England had closed for nearly a century and a half.

§ 13. In the metallurgical industries the story is much the same as in coal mining. The Belgian provinces, with their industrial traditions, profit greatly by their connection with France and start their separate career in 1815 ahead of her in technique. The valleys of the Meuse and the Sambre in Belgium had been full of metal workers in the Middle Ages. Nails were made in Hainault and cutlery at Namur. Dinant was known all over the west for its pewter pots and pans and other hardware, *dinanderie* it was called; and there were few countries who did not buy from the armourers and sword-smiths of Liège. Weapons changed, but Liège adapted herself to the changes, until finally she became one of the main headquarters of the Napoleonic munitions industry. The first railway lines in Belgium, or on the continent for that matter, were laid in 1804 at Liège in a cannon foundry, and thence their use spread to the coal mines. They were railways without locomotives.

Belgium was specially fortunate in the early possession of a true engineering industry. She owed it to a couple of Englishmen and the skill of her own metal workers. The Liège district, especially the town of Verviers, was both an old woollen manufacturing and a metallurgical centre. At Verviers there arrived in 1798 a wandering Lancashire mechanic who had been employed in Sweden and Germany. English mechanics were wanted everywhere. His name was William Cockerill and he is said to have been illiterate. At Verviers, and later at Liège, he made textile machines. In 1813 he imported from England one of Watt's steam-engines, apparently the first seen in Belgium, and this served as a model. Already his two sons were associated with him; and it was John who founded, in 1817, the great iron and machine works at Seraing near Liège which still bears his name[1]. By 1837 Seraing was a huge place containing "within its walls four coal-pits, two blast-furnaces, rolling mills...forges and shops...for making locomotives, engines and machinery of any description." There were over 2000 men there, and 700

[1] William retired in 1813. John who came from England in 1802 was interested in enterprises in several countries by 1840.

more in an allied works at Liège. An English expert reported that the machines were the best then made on the continent, though "very inferior" to English machines. By that time there was much English capital and English skill employed at various other places in Belgium. The situation was explained by the English expert as follows: "One of the most ungainsayable evidences of the progress of manufacturing industry in a country, is unquestionably that of the number of its machine making establishments. In these, for extent Belgium surpasses, in proportion to her size and population every nation in the world; whilst she can hardly be considered permanently second to England in mechanical perfection, when English engineers are at the head of all her establishments, English patents open to her immediate adoption, and English artisans in nearly all her ateliers[1]." Her immense output was explained by the fact that she was sending machinery all over Holland, Russia, and the whole territory of the young German Zollverein. English comments were sharpened by the reflection that the export of machinery from this country was by no means free, as English law stood in 1837. Even when it became quite free, a few years later, the Belgians were not forced, as the English advocate of freedom had anticipated, to "shut up their establishments." By the mid forties Belgian engineering was too securely established for that.

French metallurgy was only remodelled slowly on English lines after 1815—for lack of the new smelting fuel, coke. Within the limits of France as defined in 1815 were turned out about 100,000 tons of pig iron in the year 1812. The statistics of blast furnaces are unsatisfactory, but there were certainly many hundreds spread over a very wide area. As their size indicates, they were almost without exception of the old fashioned charcoal type, which had to be near the forests. Here and there, notably at Le Creusot, experiments were being made with coal and coke. The Le Creusot works began to sell coke-smelted iron in 1810. No other establishment did so under the Empire.

Between 1812 and 1828 the output of pig iron rather more

---

[1] These quotations are from the *Report of the Assistant Commissioner to the Handloom Weaver's Commission*, First Series, pp. 157, 173. For the earlier history see Mahaim on the Cockerills in *Viertel. für Sozial- und Wirtschafts-geschichte*, 1905.

than doubled. It more than doubled again between 1828 and 1847. The figures are: 1821, 221,000 tons; 1847, 591,000. The United Kingdom, it is believed, produced about 400,000 tons in 1821 and about 2,000,000 tons in 1847. France's progress was in great part due to imitation of England and to the arrival of English experts and English capital. There was, however, much less emigration from England to France than from England to Belgium, a fact which helps to explain the slower French development. But the history of Le Creusot furnishes an important instance. Le Creusot was a company founded by royal charter in 1782, with the dignity of *forges et fonderies du roi*. Under Napoleon it was mainly engaged on munitions. But munitions did not produce dividends, and in 1813 the concern passed into the hands of its chief creditors, Chagot Frères. In 1826 the brothers Chagot, while keeping their capital in the business, sublet the management to the English firm of Manby, Wilson & Co., who already had iron-works at Charenton. They modernised, *i.e.* Anglicised, the plant and ran it for eight years. Failing in their turn, they gave place in 1836 to the Schneiders, the firm under which Le Creusot finally rose to greatness. At that time it employed 1200 men in its mines, forges and foundries.

An instance of ultimately successful imitation of England by Frenchmen comes from the history of the iron-works of Fourchambault near Nevers. In 1815 a certain M. Dufaud, manager of the forge of Grossource, west of Nevers, took advantage of the peace to visit England, nominally to buy iron, really to spy out the land. He returned to start puddling furnaces and rolling mills for turning out wrought iron in the English style. At first he had no great success, but in 1822 his son took the Dufaud knowledge and experience with him into a partnership at Fourchambault. Aided by the tariff—of which more later—Fourchambault got well under weigh by 1830.

Le Creusot, Fourchambault, Denain in the north and Decazeville, far to the south in the Department of the Aveyron, were the leading French iron-works in the thirties. A certain tendency to concentration was showing itself, but right down to the middle of the century the French iron industry retained very primitive traits. True the hoary catalan forges went out of fashion, except in the Pyrenees; but the number of charcoal blast furnaces was still increasing up to 1839, though that of coke furnaces was increasing also. The charcoal furnaces had numbered 379 in 1830. In 1839 they rose to 445, which proved to be the maximum, for in 1846—the last statistics before the revolution of 1848—they had fallen to 364. In the sixteen years since 1830 the number of coke furnaces had risen from 29 to 106. The mere numbers are of course not a complete test, as the charcoal furnace was much less productive than its rival, especially when the latter was equipped with the hot air blast invented in Scotland in 1828. But it has been reckoned that, in 1846, approximately three-fifths of the pig iron made in France still came from the hundreds of little charcoal furnaces, scattered over the country within reach of wood. It was in this position that the railway age, which for France may be said to have begun about 1845, found the French iron industry. In the early railway years the industry could not meet the demand. Rails for the first lines had to come from England, over the terrific tariff of 275 francs a ton. To provide iron for the Paris-Strasbourg line, money had to be advanced to erect blast furnaces along the route. It is not surprising that the capital expenditure on the lines was heavy, in spite of cheap labour and relatively cheap land.

For comparison with Belgium and England, the development of engineering and the extent to which machinery was used are more significant than the condition of the primary iron industry. It must be borne in mind that all the early textile machinery, in England and on the continent, was made of wood with metal fittings. In England, textile machinery entirely of metal was coming into general use only between 1825 and 1840. Progress in the use of such things as the jenny and the flying shuttle loom, though important enough, does not imply the existence of the true modern industrial conditions, in which metal machines ranged in great works make other metal machines. Moreover the first textile machinery, if it used power at all, used water power. The jenny and the flying shuttle loom could be made by an old fashioned craftsman working at home. They were driven by hand. From one point of view they were not modern at all, however ingenious and helpful. And the driving of machinery by water was no novelty. The Italians had driven silk-throwing machinery by water since the fifteenth century at least. Every stream in England had its water mills when the Domesday survey was made. So the increased use of the first series of new mechanisms in the textile industries, to which reference will shortly be made, was hardly so important as is sometimes suggested. It did not require modern mechanical engineering in the background.

In France, iron working and engineering were often associated in the early days, though specialisation soon began. Seraing had its blast furnaces and made both spinning frames and loco-motives. Le Creusot was of the same class, though its output was less varied. At the successive French industrial exhibitions, down to the fifties, the steady arrival of the machine-making machines is registered, and frequently it is from one of the greater iron-works that they come. But the official paeans of the reporters at the exhibitions cannot conceal the really small part which the new engineering still played in the industrial life of the nation. The best evidence of this is furnished by the history of the steam-engine itself, which was at once the cause and the typical product of the new engineering.

According to statistics which are known to be defective, but are the best available, only about fifteen French establishments of all kinds possessed steam-engines in 1815. They were mostly pumping engines for mines. By 1820 the figure had risen to sixty-five in the mines only. By 1830 the total stood at 625, with an estimated horse-power of 10,000. The corresponding figures for 1848 are 5200 and 65,000, which suggest a great multiplication of small machines in these later years; since, if the figures are correct, the average horse-power in 1830 was sixteen and in 1848 only twelve and a half. Perhaps the spread of steam-engines from the coal mines to smaller concerns, such as textile mills, explains the rather surprising decline. Very fortunately industrial statistics completed in 1845, and referring to the years immediately preceding that date, enable us to do what cannot be done at any date for England, that is compare the number of steam-power and water-power installations.

There were at that time 22,500 water installations, whose total horse-power must have very greatly exceeded that of the steam-engines, even if the 1848 figures for steam and the 1843–5 figures for water are taken[1]. Most of these water installations, 17,300 in fact, were ordinary corn mills. No doubt many steam-engines also were used to grind corn. Cotton and silk show the two forms of power in competition, and the continued supremacy of water. There were 462 water installations for cotton spinning and only 243 steam installations. In silk, 435 water mills, mainly used for throwing, quite overshadowed the 143 steam mills. Wool spinning used even fewer steam-engines than silk.

Take a single English comparison, the best which defective statistics will supply. In 1839 the English textile mills alone used considerably more steam power than all France used nine years later. The figure is 74,000 horse-power. In addition they used 25,000 horse-power of water power. The number of steam installations was 3000 and of water installations 2200. The English cotton trade in 1839 had 1641 steam and 674 water installations; the French, a few years later, 243 steam and 462 water installations.

§ 14. It is clear from these facts alone that the French textile industries as a whole had not been transformed by 1850, though there had been important changes. From the eighteenth century France had inherited a textile industrial organisation of the familiar outwork type, in which the main processes are done for a manufacturer by workpeople at home and, of course, by the piece. More primitive conditions survived extensively. Often the weaver was an independent master, or worked directly for his customers. On the other hand there were a certain number of big workshops for such things as calico printing, cloth finishing, tapestry weaving, and other specialities. Water power

---

[1] We do not know the power of the French water installations, but we know that the average French steam-engine in the early forties must have had a horse-power between 12½ and 16. From the English figures given below it appears that the average water wheel in the English textile industries in 1839 was of 13 h.p. Allowing for a large number of very small French water mills, it is most unlikely that the average was below, say, 7 h.p. or about half that of the average steam-engine. On these assumptions, the French water installations of 1843–5 had at least two and a half times the power of the French steam installations of 1848.

was used for silk-throwing, for driving fulling mills in the wool industry, and scutching mills for flax. The linen and wool industries were very widespread and most French country-women spun wool or flax. Silk manufacture was concentrated mainly at Lyons. Cotton was worked in the north-west, from Rouen by Amiens to Lille, and in southern Alsace. Silk had the most elaborate and capitalistic industrial organisation. The chief risks were taken and the main profits enjoyed by the so-called *maître fabricant*, who bought raw material and had it prepared for the looms, furnished the designs, and sold the finished silks. Weaving was in the hands of the *maître ouvrier*, who kept a few looms and employed a handful of journeymen and apprentices. Wool weaving was mainly in the hands of small masters, working independently at home, or employing outworkers on a very modest scale. It was in the linen manufacture that really primitive conditions were most prevalent—the village weaver who worked up his customer's yarn into materials for her own use, or the loom in the peasant's house to make linen either for the family or for the market.

The most striking changes in the first half of the nineteenth century were in the cotton industry. The industry was young, having only come into existence in the course of the eighteenth century. Before the Revolution its most flourishing branch was calico printing, the printing of *indiennes* as they were called, in imitation of the Eastern fabrics. The trade was carried on at Lille, St Denis, and elsewhere. There were also important manufactures of cotton velvet at Evreux, Amiens, Dieppe and other places in the north-west. The Alsatian cotton industry began shortly before 1750 with the printing of *indiennes*, a trade learnt from the south Germans and the Swiss. At the start, both in Alsace and the north-west, the calico or muslin was imported. Spinning in the eighteenth century was almost confined to Normandy and the Lille district, and cotton weaving was still a small trade. By 1800 the jenny was well acclimatised in the department of the North and weaving was also progressing. But rapid progress was quite impossible under war conditions, with English frigates on all the trade routes. The government did not facilitate progress. Heavy duties were laid on imported cotton in 1806 and 1810, as part of Napoleon's continental policy.

Yet a start was made with the new machinery under government patronage. The most interesting story is that of Alsace, because there spinning and weaving were new trades which came in with the new century. Spinning machines, no doubt jennies, are first heard of in 1803. Two years later weaving with the flying shuttle began, and with it the true Alsatian cotton manufacture. Almost from the first these improved hand looms were often found, not in cottages, but in *ateliers communs*— primitive weaving sheds—as might be expected in a young industry which required *entrepreneurs* who were capitalists, if only on a small scale, to supply the new machines. Five years after the flying-shuttle loom, came the first water driven spinning machines; and two years later (1812), the first Alsatian steam-engine was set up in a tiny spinning mill. Meanwhile a few more important establishments had sprung up in the North. There was a cotton spinning mill with 90 workpeople near Lille in 1801, and a mixed establishment at Valenciennes, in which spinning weaving and printing were all carried on by what seemed the huge number of 126 workpeople. By 1810 there were 22 spinning mills at Lille, each employing on the average from 60 to 70 workpeople[1]. There were 13 mills at Roubaix and 8 at Tourcoing. But there was not much power in these mills. A great part of the machinery was hand driven jennies; some of it was driven by horses. The country about Lille, unlike Alsace, is not well suited for water wheels and there were no steam-engines there before 1818.

With the peace Alsace went rapidly ahead. About Mulhouse there really was an industrial revolution between 1815 and 1850. The new spinning industry there counted 500,000 spindles by 1828 and 1,150,000 by 1847—a third of all the spindles in France. The power loom was adopted perhaps more quickly there than anywhere in Europe, not excluding Lancashire. Experiments with it began about 1823. By 1830 there were

---

[1] For comparison it may be noted that the average number of persons employed in a list of 43 Manchester mills in 1816 was approximately 300. *Economic Journal*, Sept. 1915, p. 475.

2000 in use and by 1846 10,000; and in the latter year only some 12,000 hand looms survived in the whole Alsatian cotton area. Water power, so easily accessible along the slopes from the Vosges to the Alsatian plain, was still dominant; but there had grown up in a single generation a true factory system, its roots well nourished by mechanical invention and by a strong engineering industry. It bore its usual bitter social fruit.

The North in those days moved slowly, because steam came in so gradually. There are said to have been 24 steam-engines in Lille and its suburbs by 1832; but they were all small and so late as 1856 the mills of that district had but 932 h.p. of steam between them. Lille, Roubaix, Tourcoing, Armentières, the whole cotton area of the department of the North, had only 550,000 spindles in 1849; and most of the weaving was still done "out," in the cottages. It should be added that much of the yarn went into cotton hosiery and lace; towards the end of the period also into union fabrics, for which it was mixed with linen, worsted, or silk; and that all these industries remained more backward in mechanical and industrial organisation than the cotton manufacture proper.

The department of the North was not the only region in northern France where cotton was spun, woven or printed. But its history is typical of northern conditions. The Norman cotton district, about the valley of the lower Seine, had far more spindles than the Lille district in 1846 (between one and a half and two millions) because it had more water power; but the general conditions were similar. The intermediate district, Picardy with headquarters at Amiens, never became a manufacturing area on the great scale, though it did some spinning and retained a few important establishments for printing, velvet making, and so on.

In the French wool industries the most important developments of the early nineteenth century were neither in machinery nor in organisation, but in the raw material supplies. French wool in the eighteenth century was inferior in quality and was not used at all in the best cloths. Spanish merino took its place. But between 1775 and 1825 the systematic breeding of merino sheep in France itself altered the position; and subsequently the home supplies of merino wool could be augmented, though

with difficulty owing to tariff conditions, from Australia *via*
the London market. Several important branches of the French
wool manufacture owe their modern prosperity entirely to this
new state of affairs. Such are the worsted (combed wool) industries of Reims and of the Le Cateau district, which drew
their fine wool from the new flocks of the Tardenois and the
Picardy downs.

Fine wool was not the only new raw material. At the other
end of the scale France learnt from England, between 1820 and
1840, how to make "unions"—wool goods with a cotton warp—
and shoddy cloth, or as it is called in French, *drap de renaissance*,
twice-born cloth, the wool in which has seen service once before.
These goods for the multitude were woven mainly in Normandy,
where the practice of spinning up ends of yarn and waste wool
had been known in the eighteenth century before the *drap de
renaissance* proper, made from torn up rags, came into fashion.
The chief Norman manufacturing centres were Louviers,
Evreux and Elbeuf. Towards the middle of the nineteenth
century, these cheaper goods were being turned out also at
Sedan, which until about 1840 had been the seat of the finest
cloth manufacture only, and also in the wool manufacturing
towns of the far south, Mazamet, north of Carcassonne, and
Lodève in the Cevennes, towns which had come to the front
as manufacturers of stout and coarse army cloth for the troops
of the Bourbons, and then for the innumerable armies of revolutionary and Napoleonic France.

The towns just mentioned do not nearly complete the list
of French wool manufacturing centres, but they illustrate the
widespread diffusion of the industry. Two more must be
mentioned, even in the most summary account—Roubaix and
Paris itself. The little town, or big village, of Roubaix grew up
most literally under the shadow of Lille, in the old days when
the French law said that without special leave industries must
be confined to the real towns. Lille fought hard for its privileges.
By 1789 Roubaix had about 5000 people and a miscellaneous
weaving trade. For thirty years it grew slowly. In 1824 it was
still only connected with Lille by a country road, impassable in
winter. It had no post, no water power, hardly even water

enough for its ordinary needs. But its population grew to 15,000 by 1830 and to 34,000 by 1850. Its trade was mixed—worsted weaving primarily, and secondarily all the mixed fabrics of worsted with silk, cotton and mohair, for clothing, hangings and furniture. Roubaix demands attention as one of the very few mushroom industrial towns of modern France—Paris, because *la grande ville* always managed, and manages, to have a hand in nearly every French industry. For the wool industry of 1815–50 Paris did a great deal of dyeing and finishing, and a certain amount of combing, spinning and weaving. It was also the home of capitalist *entrepreneurs*, who furnished patterns and materials for weavers working on fancy goods and articles of fashion so far away as Le Cateau.

Round every one of these manufacturing centres were the weavers of the countryside. Wool weaving was untouched by power during the first half of the century. In spinning and the preparatory process of carding, machinery made considerable conquests. Much of this machinery was hand-worked. But water-frames, the Arkwright type of spinning machinery, had come in for the spinning of worsted yarn. The big cylindrical carding engines were also being driven by water; the fulling mills always had been. Here and there, after 1830, especially in the flat industrial district of the north, little steam-engines were set up to drive one or other type of machine. At the very end of the period, effective machinery for combing was being worked out by Heilmann in Alsace and by contemporary inventors in England; but it had not yet come into general use. Reims, the main headquarters of the combed wool trade, was still reputed to have its 10,000 hand combers, working independently for piece wages or grouped in small workshops. Dyeing and finishing were done by hand in rather larger workshops; though machines were appearing in the dye-houses, and shearing machines for cutting the nap of woollen cloth had come into general use, in spite of strong opposition from the old hand shearers. Everywhere the industry was rich in small masters and small concerns. Behind them stood the organising *entrepreneurs* of the towns, like those of Paris; but these were not a new industrial type.

The remaining textile industries were even less affected by
new inventions than that of wool, until the late forties. The
Lyons silk trade had always used some water power for throwing,
i.e. twisting the fibres into yarn strong enough to stand the
strain of the loom. It now added a little steam power. It
adopted Jacquard's loom for figured fabrics, as did the mixed
weaving industries of the North; but power was not yet applied
to the Jacquard loom. The first mention of a power loom, even
for plain silk, is in 1843-4. Flax and hemp spinning by hand were
still carried on in all parts of France in 1840. Hemp was spun
entirely by hand to 1850; and, although a few flax spinning mills
were rising in the North, it was guessed that mill yarn was not
much more than a tenth of the total output of France in 1844.
Five years later, however, there were said to be 250,000 power
driven flax spindles in about 100 mills; and their product was
beginning to beat the hand yarn. The power loom, though very
well suited for plain linen weaving, had only just begun to
compete with the linen hand looms, which were to be found in
every department and in most fair-sized villages.

§ 15. The reports of the industrial exhibitions facilitate the
dating of new industries or new methods. Some illustrations of
importance may be taken from them. Among the outstanding
new industries was that of gas. Gas was first tried at Paris in
1815. A few years later the Palais Royal was illuminated, and
after that movement was rapid, as speed was then reckoned. By
1844 Paris was most proud of her 65,000 gas burners—say one
burner to every fifteen of the population, for both indoor and
outdoor illumination. There was in fact very little of the
former; and even the street lamp brackets, *les lanternes*, only
vanished slowly. Among other new industries with a scientific
foundation which arose in these years, may be noted india-
rubber, the daguerrotype—in 1845 there were thirteen professional photographic artists in Paris—and electroplate. The
chemical industry proper made considerable progress, and new
processes were steadily introduced. The chemistry of fats was
explored, with consequences which were eventually revolutionary for the soap and candle trades. The beet sugar industry,
struck down for a time by the competition of cane sugar when

the blockade lifted, made such satisfactory progress that by
1836 nearly four hundred little factories in the north-west were
turning out 40,000,000 kilograms of sugar yearly.

About 1840 machinery began to affect a number of trades
previously untouched. The invention of riveting machines for
boots prepared the way for factory conditions in an ancient
handicraft, but the factories did not spring up at once. They
waited for the sewing machine, a later invention. Leather
cutting and leather hammering machinery began to affect the
industry on which bootmaking rests. The nailers began to feel
the competition of nail-making machinery: and so on.

But true factory conditions were exceptional in the France
of 1848. It was still possible for a social reformer to argue that
big establishments, where they existed, had an artificial life;
that they were due to a servile imitation of England; that
they were not typical and certainly not desirable, though perhaps
necessary for certain classes of undertakings[1]. This view of the
past or of the future may be questioned, but not the generalisation that the workshop and the small establishment were really
typical of French industrial organisation in 1849. The revolutionary Parisian workmen were not factory hands in the
English sense. All the numberless artistic trades of the capital,
together with the vast majority of French industries, had ample
room for the small master and the working craftsman. No doubt
there was usually a commercial middleman between him and
the consumer, as for instance in the silk manufacture or in the
clothing and cutlery trades, where the actual work of production
was all conducted on the tiniest scale. No doubt too the middleman, even in trades of this sort, tended to develop into the
regular employer of outworkers. But such development was
neither universal nor complete. Nearly three-quarters of a
century earlier Adam Smith, who knew something of France,
had ventured on the conjecture that "in every part of Europe,
twenty workmen serve under a master, for one that is independent[2]." No one in his day had collected figures by which

---

[1] Ch. de Laboulaye, *De la démocratie industrielle. Etudes sur l'organisation
de l'industrie française*, 1849.
[2] *Wealth of Nations*, Bk 1, Ch. 8.

his conjecture could be tested. Nor had anyone in 1848–9 Statistics from other countries before the machine age, and from France herself after it (see *post*, §§ 18 and 66), show that Smith's figure of workpeople was too high, at least for the continent. For France it was probably still too high in 1848, even if the word employer be taken to include every kind of capitalistic middleman, and the word workman every half independent domestic piece worker. If these are excluded, four to one is probably nearer the mark. The number of concerns employing more than a hundred people in 1848 was so small that they could not much affect the average for the whole country. Outside mining and metallurgy they hardly existed; and there were plenty of small mining and metallurgical establishments to bring down the average even in these industries. More than twenty years later, out of 101,000 people in Paris classed as *fabricants*, 62,000 worked alone or with only one assistant, and nearly fifty years later the average staff of industrial establishments was officially returned at 5·5.

§ 16. Charles de Laboulaye thought that the few large establishments of his day had been nursed into life by a misguided policy of high tariffs. In part he was certainly right. It is most doubtful, for instance, whether the cotton trade of the North could have grown had it been exposed to Lancashire competition. Just before the great Revolution, French industry had felt for a short time the full effects of British competition under the very remarkable free trade treaty of 1786. French industry had not liked this, and there had been much unemployment. The unemployment had swelled the dangerous mobs of 1789. Then came twenty years of war, blockade, retaliation, high duties and hothouse conditions for the French manufacturer. Then the peace. The government of the restored Bourbons, yielding to the pressure of its English backers, began in 1814 to break down the prohibitions and reduce some of the monstrously high duties, which had marked Napoleon's anti-English commercial policy. Although the first steps taken affected mainly raw materials, like cotton and colonial produce, the manufacturing interest took fright. "From manufacturer to workman," wrote the Rouen Chamber of Commerce, "all demand, doubtless with reason, the right to provide for the whole consumption of the land they dwell in[1]." A deputy claimed an "eternal prohibition of all foreign yarns and fabrics," and the Chamber did prohibit cotton. A similar outcry from the iron-masters led to the fixing of a 50 per cent. duty on imported iron. Officials trained in the Napoleonic school were entirely sympathetic, so Anglophile tendencies were kept in check. Subject to special modifications, the high tariff of 1806 remained operative until the new government had leisure to go into the matter thoroughly; and then (in the customs legislation of 1816–18) it bowed to business and official opinion. The French peace tariff was therefore based on the principles of high duties or absolute prohibition.

An example or two from the laws themselves and from the comments of interested parties will best illustrate the spirit which inspired them. Article 59 of the law of 18 April, 1816, runs —"As from the publication of this law, cotton yarn, cotton and wool fabrics and hosiery and all other prohibited foreign fabrics shall be sought out and seized throughout the kingdom." The hosiery manufacturers complained later that the law was badly carried out, because the customs officials were content to stop foreign goods at the frontiers, and failed to make domiciliary visits on private individuals. "It is certain," wrote the Chamber of Commerce of St Etienne, "that the progress of French industry is mainly due to the prohibition of a large number of manufactured articles."

Year by year, under the government of the Restoration, the system was strengthened and amplified. Iron had started in 1814 with a 50 per cent. duty while steel had only 45 per cent. In 1820 steel got 60 per cent. The wool-growing interest secured, in spite of the manufacturers, easy terms of export for French wool and a duty on wool imported. There had always been a duty on raw cotton. In 1822 the duty on English iron was raised to 120 per cent. in the interests of the forge-masters and the landowners who supplied them with charcoal. Here was a case, one of many in fact, in which the tariff acted as a premium on old fashioned methods of production. The tariff of 1826

---

[1] Noel, *Histoire du commerce extérieur de la France*, p. 43.

completed the Restoration system. Wool duties were run up
still further. The duties on blankets, cast steel, ropes, and many
other commodities were doubled, trebled, quadrupled.

Meanwhile, as part of the system, France had imitated the
agricultural customs policy of contemporary England. The
Restoration began with a small duty on grain. During the bad
harvest years 1816–17 imports had even been encouraged by
a bounty. But this encouragement had led to the first import
of grain from the young Russian port of Odessa. The thought
of the virgin steppes terrified the landowners of the west, just
as that of the virgin prairies terrified their grandsons sixty years
later. They had the ear of government. The manufacturing
interest could hardly dispute their claim to participate in a
policy which it regarded as essential to its own life. By the law
of July 1819, heavy corn duties came into force. "Perhaps for
the first time," writes a French historian, "tariff restrictions on
the grain trade of France were aimed no longer at export, with
the object of securing the subsistence of the people, but at
import, with the object of checking supplies from abroad[1]."
Subsequent laws completed the system. In 1821 a sliding scale
of corn duties was worked out, followed by taxes on fresh and
salt meat and on cattle fattened for market. Further taxation
of colonial sugar had already saved the beet growers and beet
sugar factories from the depression which had followed the
collapse of the continental system, a depression so severe that
hardly any of the original factories came through.

The government of Louis Philippe from 1830 to 1848 introduced no fundamental change in tariff policy. Ever since 1815
there had been a current of liberal opposition; and from time
to time attempts were made to moderate the excesses of protection and prohibition, which had in effect carried on a system
of war economy into times of peace. But there was never a
true reversal of policy. The tariff law of the thirties cut down
the duties on raw wool and iron, among others; substituted
duties for prohibitions in certain cases; and removed a number
of export prohibitions imposed with a view to giving French

[1] Levasseur, *Hist. des classes ouvrières...et de l'industrie de* 1789 à 1870,
I, 574.

manufacturers the monopoly of such commodities as silk, hides, and building timber. But reaction set in, led by the manufacturing interest now very powerful in politics; and the tariff law of 1841 raised more duties than it lowered. A scheme for a customs union between France and Belgium, propounded immediately after the creation of the Belgian state in 1830, which would have revived the situation that had existed under the Empire, had broken against the opposition not only of the great powers, who feared an increase in the economic strength of France, but also, as might have been expected, against that of the French manufacturers. Belgian industry also, strong as it was, was hardly prepared to open its market to such commodities as French silks and other luxury manufactures, though the Belgian metallurgical industries, and certain branches of the Belgian textile industries, would almost certainly have invaded the French markets, in the absence of a tariff. The French government negotiated a number of commercial treaties between 1830 and 1840, but their terms illustrate rather the strength of the protectionist spirit in France than the growth of any decided belief in the benefits of free international intercourse. Ministers from time to time took halting steps in the direction of freedom; but their general attitude is well summed up in Guizot's declaration, made in 1845, that "he was not one of those who believed that in matters of industry and commerce established interests...ought to be lightly exposed to all the vicissitudes of unlimited foreign competition." The "conservative principle" ought in his opinion to be adopted "by every rational government[1]. '

This declaration of Guizot coincided with the great free trade campaign in England, a campaign which was welcomed and furnished with effective ammunition by French economic thinkers. Frederic Bastiat's *Economic Fallacies*, perhaps the best series of popular free trade arguments ever written, began to appear in 1844 and soon became the text-book for controversialists of his school throughout Europe. Richard Cobden was fêted in Paris, and in 1847 there was held at Brussels an international Congress of Economists, the first thing of its kind in

---

[1] Quoted in Levasseur, II, 83.

modern Europe, at a time when economist and free trader were interchangeable terms. Bastiat had his organisation and his journals in France, where the bare word freedom evoked memories of the great days of 1789 among people sick of the bourgeois liberalism of Louis Philippe's ministers. But when revolution came again, and the bourgeois king was smuggled out of his country by the British consul at Havre, the restrictive system remained almost intact.

It must not be supposed that it was altogether effective at any time. Smuggling was a fine art in every country, and France has a frontier difficult to watch. Nor was it merely the ordinary consumer who was ready to pay for smuggled articles of good quality. There were whole industries whose interests ran counter to the national policy. As weaving and spinning were usually distinct trades, the weavers, or those who supplied them, had no economic incentive to use yarn spun at home if foreign yarn suited their purpose better. In consequence fine cotton and worsted yarns were smuggled extensively. One industry in particular, the muslin manufacture of Tarare in the Department of the Rhone, made constant use of prohibited and smuggled yarn—Swiss and English—down to the middle thirties. "The customs houses," it is said, "shut their eyes and made no use of their right of search[1]"; because muslin must have the best materials. Finally a duty took the place of the prohibition; and, as there was now a legal way of getting fine yarn, the muslin people of Tarare were obliged either to pay the high price or content themselves with the best imitation of the foreign yarns which French mills could produce.

§ 17. The industrial workman was not the representative Frenchman in 1848; he is not to-day. In 1848 he had not as a rule become a factory hand. In many trades he had a fair chance of becoming a master. But as a rule he had the interests and point of view of the wage earner. In the largest trade group of all, the building trades—a group which economic historians are astonishingly apt to neglect—he had worked before the days of mechanical invention, and continued to work after them, under an ordinary wage contract, even though he ranked as a

[1] Reybaud, *Le coton* (1863), p. 133.

master mason or master carpenter. Among such men the wage earners' point of view was likely to prevail. It was certain to prevail among those of them who were not ranked as masters. The nineteenth century was witnessing a slow increase in the average manufacturing establishment properly so called, which increased the gap between wage payer and wage receiver; but it had so far seen no increase in the size of the average house. Earlier centuries could show single building enterprises of a size which it had not learnt to surpass or even equal—a Versailles, a Fontainebleau or a Notre Dame de Paris. This then is no case of a nineteenth century revolution, but of the continuance of an ancient system of relationships involving the wage contract on a large scale. Unskilled labourers also, in building as in all other trades, had inherited the wage earner's standpoint from earlier centuries; for at the bottom of society there had at all times been a mass of unskilled diggers, carriers and haulers, who did a penn'orth of work for a penny, as they said in medieval England.

The Revolution had swept away the ancient gilds (*Corporations de Métiers*) in which the bulk of the skilled men had been organised. On the average an eighteenth century handicraftsman served a four or five years' apprenticeship, followed by three years as journeyman (*compagnon*), before he was legally eligible as a master craftsman. Napoleon, who was attracted by the disciplinary side of gild life, went near to recreating the gilds; and after the Restoration their revival was for some years under discussion. But it never came about. The widespread survival of apprenticeship and regular *compagnonnage* was a matter of custom not of law; just as apprenticeship survived by custom in England after the abolition of the apprenticeship clauses of the Elizabethan labour code, in 1813.

Not content with destroying gilds, the revolutionary legislation in 1791 had declared all associations of either masters or men illegal. Such a law always acts more effectively against men than against masters. This blow at the right of combination had been followed, under the Empire, by definite legal recognition of a privileged position for the employer in wage disputes. Under Article 1781 of the Civil Code, the master's word was to be taken as decisive in courts of law, when questions arose as to the amount of wages due. The standing argument in favour of this clause, which remained in force until 1868, was that as the wage contract was made between master and man, usually without witnesses, you had to take the word of one or the other. So a clause which sprang out of conditions in which collective bargaining was rare or unknown became a permanent obstacle to its introduction. The Civil Code was reinforced by the Penal Code. Under Articles 291–294 associations of more than twenty persons were prohibited; and under Articles 414–416 any concerted striking or picketing became a criminal offence. Evidently the characteristic methods of collective action were understood by workmen, or the clauses would not have been drafted. It is worth recording also that the law of 1791 against combinations was largely the result of employers' complaints about collective action and incipient trade unionism. Masters in the building trade complained of the "tyranny" of a recently formed "Federal Union of working carpenters," which pretended to be a mere benevolent society but was really something more[1]. England can supply many parallels.

Lastly, the government of Napoleon, in 1803, had initiated and subsequently had generalised the *livret*, the workman's book in which were inscribed his various employers' names. No man could be hired unless the record of his last employer was satisfactory; and the whole machinery of the *livret* was under the control of the powerful Napoleonic police. So the hand of the state lay heavy on the working man.

Neither the Restoration nor the government of Louis Philippe made any change in the law, except, from the workman's point of view, for the worse. A law of 1834 forbade associations even of twenty persons if they were parts of some larger whole. This was a direct blow at an illegal association, the *Devoir Mutuel* of the Lyons weavers, which had organised great strikes for better piece rates and other privileges in 1831 and 1834. It had three thousand members and all the methods of a typical and somewhat revolutionary trade union. There were other so-called "societies of resistance," fighting unions, formed

[1] See Levine, *The Labor Movement in France*, New York, 1912, p. 17.

secretly from time to time between 1815 and 1845. The most important was that of the Paris printers, started in 1839, which, in spite of the complete illegality of the whole proceeding, appears to have successfully established a joint committee of masters and men for regulating wages and arbitrating in disputes. It was often possible also to carry out trade union policies under cover of friendly societies—*bureaux de bienfaisance* or *caisses de secours mutuels*—which were not discouraged by government, so long as they kept to their ostensible business. In 1823 there were over 130 such societies in Paris; but the average membership was small—not much over 80 if the available figures are to be trusted. The government made no protest. But if behind such an organisation there lay a "secret syndicate with compulsory contributions," wrote the Minister of the Interior to the Prefect of the Department of the Loire in 1819, "these are things exceedingly blameworthy which one must strive to destroy[1]." And if the trade union activities of an ostensible friendly society led to strikes, then the arm of the law might always be raised, though often it was allowed to hang idle. The statistics of prosecutions for striking, which exist from 1825 onwards, although they are known to be incomplete, suggest either that strikes were very rare or that prosecution was very frequently neglected.

These figures may refer to strikes organised by some society, or to spontaneous strikes with no permanent organisation behind them. Probably the latter type was the more common. From 1825 to 1847 the largest number of prosecutions in any one year, for the whole country, was 130; the number of persons accused that year was 682; the number acquitted was 139; the number sent to prison, 498. In 23 years the average number sent to prison annually was just under 200. But even if the law was laxly administered, it was there. The workmen of France resented it as a direct challenge to liberty, equality and fraternity.

Anything that could be called trade union organisation, even if disguised or ephemeral, was rare in this period. But some of the work done later by unions was done in these years, mainly in

[1] G. and H. Bourgin, *Le régime de l'industrie en France de 1814 à 1830* (1912), p. 202.

the south, by the curious ancient organisations of the *compagnon-nages* among the *élite* of the journeymen, organisations from which many unions ultimately sprang. *Compagnonnages* had always existed in defiance of government, since their history first comes clearly into light in the sixteenth century. They were too old and too strong for the laws of the Constituent Assembly or the police of Napoleon. In the long run the railways did more to kill them than ever the law had done[1].

The *compagnonnage* sprang up and was always strongest in the building trades. Its members were single journeymen, skilled and tested. Marriage or recognition as a master involved retirement; and incompetence was, at least nominally, a bar to entry. Building labour had always been migratory. Outside the building trades too there was an old, but not universal, custom by which the skilled man moved from town to town, to find work and perfect himself in his craft. He made the *Tour de France*, became a *Compagnon du Tour de France*. As he moved about, his *compagnonnage* provided help for him in many ways—the inn or boarding house, kept by a "father" or a "mother," where he lodged; food and shelter until he had found work; assistance to find it through a recognised member of the society called the *rouleur*, who assigned men jobs in rotation, and was well known to employers; help in sickness; help in his quarrels; help to leave a master who offended him or was on the *rouleur's* black list; help to get away from a town where he could not earn enough; help perhaps in a strike; and always good fellowship when the wine was tapped or the funeral bell was tolling.

Compagnons were not organised primarily according to trades, though trade distinctions made themselves felt. The whole body was split into sections called *devoirs*, bearing ancient fantastic names, whose legendary explanation bears witness to the origin of the system among building workmen. The Children of Solomon, or *Devoir de liberté*, reckoned themselves the most ancient group; and among them the masons were the senior division. The other original divisions were joiners and lock-

---

[1] See Martin-Saint Léon, *Le compagnonnage*, and Levasseur, I, 511 *sqq.*

smiths. The coopers were admitted in 1839 and the bootmakers in 1844. Solomon's children made no special religious profession and were largely recruited among southern Protestants. The great rival group, the Children of Master James, an imaginary builder of Solomon's temple, were also originally composed of the same three building crafts, plus the carpenters; but they were strict Catholics. They had admitted many other trades into their company before 1789. The list is long but historically significant. It runs thus—tanners, dyers, ropemakers, basket-makers, hatters, white tawyers, founders, pinners, smiths, cloth shearers, turners, glaziers, saddlers, stove-builders, gilders, cutlers, tinsmiths, harness-makers, wheelwrights, tilers and plasterers. Recently recognised were the canvas-makers and the farriers; and in a more doubtful position came the bootmakers, bakers and makers of sabots. Note the absence of miners, of most kinds of weavers, of all kinds of spinners— spinners were women in the eighteenth century—of all kinds of transport workers, and of the few classes of eighteenth century craftsmen who had any knowledge of machines, clockmakers, instrument-makers, millwrights. Note, in short, how those groups which were to dominate the European labour movement of the later nineteenth century were not yet even counted worth recognition by the *élite* of the skilled journeymen, either because they were so few, like the machine workers, or because they were so lowly, like the miners and the carters

There was an old world flavour about the *compagnons*, with their legends and their rites of initiation, their passwords and elaborate greetings when they met on the high way, their canes and ribbons full of symbolism, the speed with which they fell to brawling for the honour of Solomon or Master James, or for the right to wear ribbons and to wear them in a particular way. They had the apparatus and the quick temper of members of secret societies all the world over; for in their long career they had never been favoured by the governing powers. Repressed for a time during the Revolution, they recovered under the Empire and the Restoration, to the dismay of the powers. "At the funeral of a mason," the police of Bordeaux reported in 1818, "a numerous cortège of masons has been observed

adorned with all the emblems of the ancient *compagnonnage*."
The illegal cortège was dissolved and two men were arrested
"still wearing their hats adorned with ribbons. These individuals, being natives of Bordeaux, were sent home, but the
ribbons were seized and the affair was reported to the public
prosecutor to frighten those who might imitate their example[1]."
The same sort of thing had happened before. It did not discourage the *compagnons*. Theirs was the most permanent and
important working class organisation of the Restoration period;
and it only gradually lost ground after 1830. They had the true
old world intolerance, which led to rebellions among the younger
men, who resented the patronage and bullying of their seniors.
Their queer old rites were becoming ridiculous to the critical
mind of the nineteenth century workman. Industries with
which some of them were connected began to be transformed.
A type of organisation strictly according to trades became more
and more attractive to the average wage earner. A labour movement was taking shape among workmen who had never belonged
to the *compagnonnages*, and were not likely to imitate them.
Last came the railway, to change the life of the migratory workman and destroy the companionships of the open road. But
the building trades in which the *compagnonnages* had begun,
being as yet untouched by machinery, remained a stronghold
for them in 1848; and it was only in the second half of the
century that they finally sank into obscurity.

---

[1] Bourgin, *op. cit.* p. 133.

CHAPTER IV

INDUSTRIAL CONDITIONS IN GERMANY, 1815-1848

§ 18. If, as was suggested in the last chapter, the best test of a country's industrialisation is the size and growth of its towns, the states which were eventually to become Imperial Germany showed an exceedingly low level of industrialisation in 1815, and a level very little higher in 1850. When discussing German agriculture, it was pointed out that, in 1815, what finally became the twelve largest towns of Germany only contained between them about 50 per cent. more people than Paris. In 1850 the twelve towns contained 1,340,000 people and Paris more than 1,000,000. She had actually gained on the twelve in those thirty-five years. Add Lyons alone to her, and you get a population about equal to theirs. Or take another statistical test. In the Prussia of 1816, which from this point of view was thoroughly representative of all Germany, 73·5 per cent. of the population was classed as rural. In 1846 the corresponding figure was 72·0, and in 1852, 71·5. The towns managed to grow just a fraction quicker than the population as a whole. Very many of them were still the quiet little places of the fairy books, with huddled roofs and spires, from which the view over the ploughlands and the orchards was so easy. Germany, quite unlike France, started the century with an urban life that was in many ways medieval, and in many places less vigorous than it had been in the days of Dürer and Hans Sachs. The glory of Augsburg and Nuremberg was in the past. It had been imperfectly replaced by the recent efforts of princes and princelets to develop and beautify their "residence towns."

Down to 1800 Germany, as a whole, had retained a sharp economic and social division between town and country. The townsmen might have an easy view over the fields; but the peasant must not share the industry of the streets. Some eighteenth century princes had encouraged manufactures on the land, particularly rural weaving; but the assumption that the peasant should keep to his plough and that handicraft was the burgesses' business was not easily uprooted. In eighteenth century Brandenburg each village had its officially assigned number of necessary craftsmen—the smith, the wheelwright, the carpenter—a number which might not be exceeded without special royal permission. Yet Brandenburg was not a backward province. When leave was given, in the eighteenth century, to practise unusual industries on the land, they were practised entirely in cottages. A big workshop even was unknown.

The division between town and country was not merely economic. It was also legal. In Prussia, for example, peasant, burgher and gentleman had each his own law. You had a society of estates not of economic classes. This legalised division into estates was swept away by Stein after 1806. Anyone might buy land of any sort. Hitherto a noble could no more buy free peasant land than a peasant could buy urban ground rents. Now anyone could carry on what business he pleased. Bismarck of Schönhausen might go into trade. In all these matters some of the western states started the century ahead of Prussia, quite apart from the levelling and rationalising influence of the conquering French. On the other hand, there were states both in the south and the north—Bavaria, for example, and Mecklenburg—which lagged behind her. Even in Prussia a mere legal permission did not change century old habits. Bismarcks of Schönhausen did not go into trade, though they sold the produce of their manors—but that they had always done. Peasants would not have found ready sellers of urban sites, even if it had occurred to them to buy these things. A generation is a short time for such changes to enter into the daily life of a nation. How slowly peasant emancipation was carried through in Prussia has been already seen. The melting of the old divisions, and the establishment of a freely working industrial society, were not less slow.

There was no summary break up of the old gild system in the towns, except in so far as the French broke it up in the west. Of all European gild systems that of Germany had been the most rigid; though there had been some reform during the eighteenth century. In Prussia, for instance, reform began early, but the principles were retained—apprenticeship; severe tests before admission to the "mastery"; exclusion of all irregularly trained men. Prussia showed her enlightenment by not re-imposing the gild system in Westphalia, where it had vanished under French rule, when that province came into her hands in 1815. But Prussia was not Germany. In Bavaria no serious attempt at reform was made before 1848; and very little had been done in 1862—except in the Rhenish Palatinate, which had been part of Napoleonic France. The most rigid gild rules prevailed, for instance, at Nuremberg. In Wurtemberg reform began in 1828; but it made very slow progress and a man could not really practise what trade he pleased in the fifties or even in the sixties. In Saxony gild organisation existed side by side with more modern developments right through these years and indeed much later. A law of 1840, for instance, which eased the old gild restrictions, solemnly enacted that every village might have one tailor, shoemaker, white bread baker, butcher, smith, saddler, harness-maker, carpenter, glazier, rope-maker and cooper. These were all gild trades. No other gild trade was to be carried on in villages without special permit.

On the whole, some sort of gild system, provided it was reasonably elastic, suited well enough the stage of industrial development at which Germany had arrived, and at which she remained, broadly speaking, in the generation which followed the wars. The exhaustive statistics of the Prussian and other bureaucracies make it easy to illustrate the characteristics of that stage, and to indicate the beginnings of the stage which was to succeed it.

The old restrictions had not done the ordinary gild handi-craftsmen of the towns much good. The masters had kept down the numbers of apprentices, yet their own numbers were often excessive for the stagnant demand of their town. Masters of their craft they might be; but they were masters of little else. In some places 80 to 90 per cent. of them had neither journey-man nor apprentice. Prussian statistics for the early nineteenth century reveal a state of things not so grotesque as this, but still extraordinary. They are available for two very useful dates— 1816, just after the peace, and 1843, just before the effective start of the railway age in Germany. In 1816, for every 100 masters there were only 56 workpeople—journeymen or apprentices. By 1843 the latter figure had risen to 76; nearly a quarter of the masters still worked alone. Take certain instances. Nearly half the tailors and hatters worked alone and the rest averaged one assistant. The average tanner had one assistant. But the dyer was an important fellow; he had two[1].

Under such conditions the routine succession of prentice, journeyman, master could run well enough. The difficulty in many trades would be the keeping up of the number of masters. The prentice had a certain hope of the mastery, a situation which has often been idealised. Its real merits depend on whether or not the mastery is worth having. Most of these German master craftsmen were simply jobbing workmen, and ill paid at that. Like many of the same class in the middle ages, they generally worked direct for the consumer. There were no architects or building contractors, no middlemen tailors or bootmakers or hatters, in the old Germany.

It is true that many of the industries which had a gild organisation in the German towns were of the class which, in all countries, was the last to feel the influence of capitalism in any of its forms. But the tiny scale on which the operations of the dyers and the tanners were carried on is significant. They had not even arrived at the workshop stage. And an examination of the condition of those trades in which capitalism developed earliest in other countries confirms the impression of German backwardness in industrial organisation, which the figures of these old town crafts suggest. Capitalism, it will be seen, was not altogether absent, and it was of course gaining ground during the early years of the nineteenth century; but it still remained weak in the forties. German industry in general could in no sense be called capitalistic; and before 1840 large enterprises of the factory type were extraordinarily rare.

§ 19. A few such enterprises had come into existence during the eighteenth century, often as the result of direct government action. Frederick the Great started a fair sized iron-

---

[1] In Prussia, master tanners, 5639; journeymen and prentices, 5479; master dyers, 4792; journeymen and prentices, 9388. Dieterici, *Der Volkswohlstand im Preussischen Staate*, 1846, p. 353.

foundry at Berlin. The Grand Duke of Baden, so early as 1745, had induced a Swiss manufacturer—the Swiss were ahead in capitalistic development—to start a calico printing establishment which, to the amazement of the South Germans, was planned for two hundred men. It was however long before this figure was reached. There were substantial sugar refineries and other seaport industries in Hamburg and Bremen. More instances of the same class could be cited. But the only type of capitalistic industrial organisation which played a great part in the life of old Germany was the loose association of home workers, mainly in the textile trades, that clustered about a commercial *entrepreneur*, who marketed the goods. These home workers were not true wage earners, as a rule. They owned their looms or other appliances. They usually procured their own materials, unless the material was an exotic like cotton. When wars and vicissitudes in commercial policy broke the *entrepreneurs*, as so often happened in the eighteenth and early nineteenth centuries, the associations dissolved into their component atoms. The unfortunate craftsmen struggled on as best they could, trying to dispose of their goods to peddlers, or falling back on agriculture; for many of them were half peasants.

Most of the help which the princes of the eighteenth century gave to industry went, not to create factories, but to encourage these associations of home workers. If the association was concentrated in a capital city, it was most likely to assume a coherent form. The workers tended to become regular wage earners, especially in luxury trades where access to the raw material was difficult. The more prosperous among them remained independent; they bought materials and sold their goods to the commercial *entrepreneur*. The less prosperous were in the position of the ordinary outworker of England or France: they got their materials from the *entrepreneur*, and worked them up for a piece wage. There were a good many trades of this sort in Berlin, for instance. They had been created by government, and by hothouse methods as German historians admit[1], in order to provide the luxuries appropriate to an ambitious capital, or goods for export to meet the needs of a mercantilist policy,

---

[1] Wiedfeldt, *Entwickelungsgeschichte der Berliner Industrie*, p. 71.

IV] SLOW GROWTH OF MODERN INDUSTRY 87

z

eager for a favourable balance of trade. The collapse and poverty of Prussia after Jena (1806) and Napoleon's continental system ruined most of them. By 1816 the industry of Berlin had slid back into the state from which only an "artificial and expensive governmental policy" had raised it—a state in which the typical figure was the independent master craftsman, with few employees or none. There were 10,000 fewer people in the town in 1810 than there had been in 1801. With the peace, its industries had to start afresh.

What is true of Berlin is to a great extent true of all Germany. She had been fought over again and again. Political boundaries, and with them the lines of customs houses, had been changed every few years. Napoleon's continental system had lain heavy upon her. Blockade conditions, as in France, had called into existence industries which had no natural vitality, especially in face of English competition. Many little spinning mills— of a very primitive type—and many little sugar factories sprang up in war time; only to collapse when England poured her yarn and her stored up colonial sugars into the Hanse towns after Waterloo. The artificial products of eighteenth century mercantilism had vanished with those created by blockade conditions; and everywhere there was lost ground to be recovered.

There was a great deal to learn in the conduct of the new English type of industry. Englishmen were called in, as in France. Cockerill the younger of Seraing paid a visit to Berlin. Some nameless Englishmen started a wool factory there after Waterloo, and made their own machines. Then, in 1821, the Prussian government took an important step. It created the *Gewerbe Institut* (Institute of Trades), somewhat on the lines of the French *Conservatoire des Arts et Métiers*, with the object of spreading the knowledge of new industrial methods and encouraging experiment[1]. In the early days, its products were sold chiefly to officials and institutions, to help government in the task of industrial education. Hand-worked machinery, such as improved looms and spinning jennies, was comparatively easy to introduce; but there were special difficulties to be over-

[1] The first Berliner to make steam-engines was apparently Freund, in 1812; the second, Egells, in 1821. Sombart, *Moderne Kapitalismus*, 3rd ed., I, 868.

come before power could be applied to industry in or about Berlin. Water power is hard to get on the North German plain; and there is no coal within many miles of its Prussian capital. After sixteen years of work by the Institute of Trades, in the year of Queen Victoria's accession, there were only thirty steam-engines averaging 13 h.p. each in the city. Now Berlin at that time had over a quarter of a million inhabitants.

Even in those parts of Germany best fitted for industrial development, such as Saxony and the new Rhenish provinces of Prussia, there was no rapid movement. For fifteen years at least after Waterloo the dislocations due to both war and peace acted as a drag on progress. There was no tradition of individual industrial enterprise or of large scale operations. Capital was scarce. The accumulations of the commercial *entrepreneurs* had been dissipated, and the process of reconstruction was necessarily slow. Industrial freedom was not yet guaranteed. The eighteenth century method of direct government action had gone out of fashion, with the arrival of those new economic doctrines which Germans called *Smithianismus*, the doctrines of Adam Smith. Political questions occupied men's minds. The political divisions and rivalries of the German states limited the possible scale of industrial operations. There were so many different laws and such an endless succession of frontiers.

The Rhine provinces had the great advantage of having been for many years in French occupation, with the results that much antiquated legislation had vanished and—even more important —that good roads had been made. These roads were improved and extended in course of time by the Prussian government. By 1845 an Englishman could report that "not only good, but luxurious roads...traversed those districts in all directions[1]"; and although much of the work on them had been done after 1830, there had been roads enough to be a real assistance to industry and trade ever since 1815. Yet so slowly did things move before 1840, that in 1837, the year in which Berlin reported its 390 h.p. of steam, all the territories of Prussia, including the coal-fields on both sides of the Rhine, that of the Saar, and that

[1] Banfield, *op. cit.* I, 24.

of Upper Silesia, were only employing 7500 h.p. for mining, metallurgy, spinning, milling and every other purpose—mainly mining and metallurgy. By 1846 the h.p. had risen to 22,000, of which over 14,000 was employed in mining and metallurgy.

§ 20. Before the nineteenth century, Germany had made very little use of her extensive coal resources. Her iron and steel industries, though ancient and well developed in certain districts, were carried on entirely along the old lines of charcoal smelting and handicraft work. The mines of the precious and rarer metals, in the Harz mountains and elsewhere, had lost the important position which they held in medieval and early modern times. They were not large enterprises. Thirty or forty men was the ordinary working staff of a copper lead or silver mine in 1837. But at least they had bequeathed to the country a store of technical knowledge and experience. What the old German metallurgical industries were like at their best can be learnt from an account of the iron-working district of the Sieg valley, east of Bonn, and of the famous steel-working district of Solingen, written in 1846, at a time when the new methods which were coming into use elsewhere had not yet affected these ancient industrial centres.

The wooded valleys of Siegerland contained an endless series of little metal working establishments. There were stamping mills for crushing the ore; charcoal smelting furnaces; tilt-hammers for the production of wrought iron and steel; slit-mills which cut sheets of iron into rods for nail-making; wire mills, with rollers for drawing out the metal—"all worked by water power and on the most diminutive scale." The mines from which the ore came rarely employed so many as ten men. "Manufacturing," the English account[1] continued, speaking of the Solingen district further north, "as in the greater part of Germany, is dependent on the land. The furnace owner and forest owner, as well as the miner, club their property together to make iron, living the while on the produce of their little estates." Iron making in fact was a peasant's by-industry. The peasant-miners habitually wore their white "furnace skins" of calf's hide "when haymaking or working in their

[1] Banfield, *passim*.

meadows." Having made the iron, they sold it on credit to the small "hammer master"; who beat and refined it into steel and sold it to the working cutler; who sold to the dealer; who sold to the shipping house. Perhaps, at these last two stages, something which might be called capitalism cropped out.

The Solingen cutler of the forties was an independent crafts-man, working at home or in a small hired workshop, under-taking work "by the dozen." "No large establishments were anywhere to be found," except a single cast steel factory recently established at Burg. This Solingen industrial organisation, it should be added, is not an instance of German economic back-wardness; rather of the conservatism of an old skilled handicraft. As the English traveller did not fail to notice, it had a great resemblance to the Sheffield organisation of his day; or, he might have added, to that of many hardware trades in the English Black Country. The need for charcoal iron in cutlery making, iron which England drew from the forest furnaces of Sweden, helped to keep alive the old methods of iron production in the Rhineland, and so to keep the whole scale of industry small.

The great Ruhr coal-field, the heart of the Rhenish manu-facturing district, only began to be worked effectively after 1815. Much the same is true of the Roer field, by Aachen, which is the German tail of the Belgian coal-field. As for what became, in the later nineteenth century, the third main field of Germany, the field which lies where three empires met, on the former boundaries of Silesia, Galicia and Russian Poland, serious work on it began much later—towards 1840[1]. On the western fields large scale operations were hardly known before 1830; but from that time joint stock businesses of some magnitude took up the work of development. The capital came mainly from the merchants of Cologne. In 1846 all the Ruhr mines are said to have been worked by companies. About Aachen, too, the English observer said, coal mining "was nearly all managed by pits, and it therefore required large and concentrated capitals, as we found to be the case on the Ruhr." And yet, so recent was the development, so comparatively small was the

---

[1] But ironworking, on old-fashioned lines, was well developed in Silesia by 1800. There were 49 blast-furnaces there in 1804, and already great noblemen, *e.g.* the Princes of Pless and Ratibor, were "industrialists." Sartorius von Waltershausen, *op. cit.* p. 44.

scale of operations, that the whole Prussian output from the three
fields just mentioned and from some lesser fields, including
that of the Saar, was only about 3,200,000 English tons a year
in 1846. At that time France was raising 4,500,000 tons, Belgium
a great deal more, and London was consuming more than Prussia
raised[1]. If the comparison were taken a few years earlier, it
would be much more unfavourable to Prussia—which for this
purpose is almost equivalent to Germany—for her development was the most recent of all. In engineering and iron
working it is the same story. There was nothing in Germany
to compare with Cockerill's Seraing works in 1837. In the early
forties, Belgium was turning out more iron than the whole of
the Zollverein. By that time however a few German concerns
had become important. At Berlin the official attempts to found
a machine making industry, by means of the *Gewerbe Institut*,
began to tell. Borsig, a pupil of the Institute, set up as a machine
maker in 1837 with fifty men. Ten years later he was employing
twelve hundred. In the Rhine provinces there were a number
of large scale undertakings. At Ruhrort, for example, the firm
of Haniel, Huyssen and Jacobi had a big engineering works
where "the order, quiet, and businesslike arrangements were
quite English." They built river steamboats among other
things. The same firm controlled large iron-works at Sterkerade
and Oberhausen. At Oberhausen in 1846 they used Nasmyth's
steam hammer; they smelted with a mixture of coal and
charcoal; the blast was heated by gas taken from the top of the
furnace—an early instance of judicious fuel economy; and the
working staff, which it is interesting to learn was composed
mainly of landowning peasants, numbered over a thousand.
Again, "at Essen there is a cast steel works belonging to Messrs
Krupp and Co., who enjoy the reputation of making good steel;
and, it is said, sell a great deal as English." Before our eyes, the
independent peasant ironworkers of the Siegerland type are
turned into landowning wage earners, where capital for big
concerns is forthcoming. In a generation, their children, the
land probably sold, will learn to think of themselves as a wage

[1] Not actually more in 1846, but more on the average 1845–7. Porter,
Progress of the Nation, p. 581.

earning proletariat. But, as yet, these few big establishments stand out, gaunt and lonely, against a background crowded with busy little figures of peasants and handicraftsmen. The background is the real Germany of the forties[1].

§ 21. How truly, a glance at the textile industries shows. All over Germany the peasants grew flax and hemp, and often madder to make dye. The flax was "heckled," that is prepared for spinning, by the village rope-maker, one of the recognised rural craftsmen, and spun at home. Very likely it was woven at home too. If not the village "customer" weaver, as he was called in England, worked it up for a piece wage. Failing a supply of his own dye, the peasant took the stuff into the nearest town and got it dyed in one of the diminutive dyeing workshops, whose average working staff was a master, a journeyman, and a prentice. These were the heavier materials, for blouses and outer clothes. Underclothing could be finished at home. If the wife was not able to make coats or blouses, another jobbing craftsman—the tailor—would come over from the town for a few days' work and equip the family.

This was the course of things in flax, from which the staple clothing of a large part of the peasantry was made. Where the peasant was a sheep master—which was by no means often— his wool would be handled in the same way. If he had no sheep, he would get any woollen goods he might want in the town market. It will not be forgotten how large a proportion of the population, and so of the national consuming power, these peasants formed.

Prussian loom statistics, from the year 1831, bring out the facts admirably. There were no less than 252,000 linen looms in Prussia; but of these only 35,500 belonged to linen weavers whose weaving was their sole livelihood. They were mainly to be found in Silesia, where a linen industry for the market had been fostered by government in the eighteenth century The rest belonged to people who had some other source of maintenance. Either they were worked by peasant families in their spare time, or they were worked by village weavers who cultivated land. The professional linen weavers in Silesia were

---

[1] Krupp only employed 122 men in 1846. S. von Waltershausen, *op. cit.* p. 92.

sometimes townsmen, sometimes countrymen. They were not of course in factories or even workshops. But they were to some extent dependent on the commercial *entrepreneur*—in German the *Verleger*, the furnisher—because, in view of the large scale on which operations were carried on, it might be necessary to get his assistance in procuring sufficient yarn; though generally the master weaver would buy his own yarn from a yarn peddler. In any case, the *Verleger's* success or failure in remote markets meant happiness or misery in Silesia.

The wool industry marks a further step in what might be called professionalism. We are getting out of the society of peasants into that of handicraftsmen; and occasionally we may meet what might be called a manufacturer. Yet in 1831 out of 22,000 woollen looms in Prussia—the figure is low because there were important German woollen centres outside Prussian territory—6500 belonged to people with another source of maintenance, peasants and village weavers. The rest were the property of the old fashioned type of master weaver, usually a townsman with the townsman's tradition; a member of his gild where gilds survived; of course a domestic worker. Like the professional linen weaver, his economic status was indeterminate. He might be entirely independent, buying handspun yarn and selling cloth to the cloth finisher; or he might be in some degree dependent on a *Verleger*. The better his work, the finer the materials required and the wider the market, the greater was the probability of dependence on the commercially minded *Verleger*, who knew where to get fine wool and how to dispose of fine cloth. But there was not a great deal of fine cloth made in Prussia, or in any other part of Germany; and cloth was not extensively exported at this time.

With cotton and silk the peasant had nothing to do, because he did not produce either. The industries were necessarily more professional and more capitalistic than wool or linen. Neither was very large in Prussia. Both were concentrated in the Rhenish provinces—about Krefeld and Elberfeld mainly. The silk industry proper in 1831 employed 9000 looms, the cotton industry 25,500. There were also 32,500 "ribbon" looms for narrow weaving, which might use linen, cotton or silk.

Most of the German silk working was in Rhenish Prussia; but there were growing cotton manufactures in Saxony and the central and southern states. In no case was industrial organisation ahead of that in Krefeld or Elberfeld. There, it was the matured *Verleger* or outwork organisation. Materials had to be procured from abroad. Their preparation and spinning had to be arranged for. Then they could be given out to the weavers. If the calico had to be dyed or printed, it went in all probability to something which might fairly be described as a dye works or print works; for calico printing had been modestly capitalistic from the start.

In all these trades, fifteen years after the loom figures just quoted were compiled, weaving remained almost untouched by machinery. In 1846 less than 4 per cent. of the cotton looms in Prussia were driven by power. The remaining textile industries used the hand loom exclusively. In Saxony, at the same date, there were no power looms at all; yet Saxony came next to the Rhenish provinces as a textile manufacturing district. The persistence of the peasant linen and wool weaving system, just described, is shown by the fact that in 1843, of all the looms in Prussia for weaving of all kinds, nearly three-quarters were still owned by people for whom weaving was only a by-industry.

Machinery had made some progress in spinning and other preparatory processes. The collapse of the little spinning mills, which the blockade had called into existence, was not permanent. After 1830, when the period of recuperation was over, they began to grow fast in many parts of Germany. But most of them were of an exceedingly primitive type; and, as has already been indicated, they made very little use of steam power. Water power statistics like those of France are not available; but there is plenty of evidence as to the size and character of the mills. There were, for instance, four wool spinning establishments in Berlin, in 1846. Each employed between twenty-five and thirty workers. The machinery was no doubt mainly hand-driven jennies. At the other end of Prussia, near the coal-field of Aachen, cloth manufacturing in all its stages was still organised on what were really handicraft lines. "The scale on which machinery is introduced is too small to help the working classes or to enrich the master manufacturers." These were manufacturers of the type of the contemporary domestic clothier in England, small working masters employing a few wage earners. "Of ten cotton mills in the circle of Krefeld," it is reported under the same date, "six are worked by hand, two by horse power, and two by steam." In cotton spinning, as in metallurgy, there had recently sprung up in the west just a few factories of the English type. Messrs Jung's mill at Elberfeld contained 20,000 spindles, and delighted the English visitor, who thought he knew what a cotton mill should be like. But the spinning situation in Prussia, taking the textile industries as a whole, was summarised by a Prussian writer in the same year as follows:—"spinning has remained hitherto essentially hand-spinning, although there exist already some larger enterprises, mainly of recent date[1]." The flax spinners, who were a professional class in districts such as Silesia where linen was made for market, were in a desperate situation. Both in the markets of the world and in the home market, they had now to face the competition of British mill-spun yarn and British linen fabrics. The relative quality of German yarns and linens had deteriorated; with the result that all through the thirties and forties the social problem of the distressed spinner, or of the peasant who had lost a by-employment, occupied the attention of German governments. But it was not from German flax spinning machinery that the destructive competition came.

§ 22. The loss of any by-industry was a serious matter for the peasant. Emancipation, while improving his legal status and relieving him of various burdensome obligations, was usually accompanied in the east by the curtailment of his holding. Population was growing and wholesale emigration had not yet begun. Quite apart from all this, there were many districts in which population had always been too great for the rather thankless soil. Any by-industry had come as a godsend to the cultivators. Flax spinning for market was among the easiest and most widespread of such industries. But there were many others, and new ones were always springing up. The peasants of the Thuringian forest had made wooden toys during

---

[1] Dieterici, *op. cit.* p. 254.

their winter evenings in Martin Luther's day. It is said that
the toy types had not altered, and certainly the trade continued,
in the days of Hegel and Strauss. A better known and higher
grade peasant industry was that connected with the making of
wooden clocks in the Black Forest. The industry came into
existence, obscurely, somewhere between 1670 and 1730. Its
greatest days were in the late eighteenth century[1]. It sprang up
among peasants and was recruited from peasant families; but
its highest branches could hardly remain mere by-industries.
The true clock-maker became a specialist who trained apprentices. But there was a great deal of simple wood work needed.
Any man handy with his knife could make a cuckoo or some
other of the familiar accessories of the Black Forest clock; so
that the industry had ramifications all over the country side.
The wars had interfered with its once extensive export. But
it kept alive, in the early nineteenth century, and retained its
old characteristics until, in its turn and at a later date, it became
a factory trade.

These peasant by-industries are only samples from a long list.
The peasant's eagerness to live just a little better made him
always ready to welcome those who would buy from him anything he could make, or who would furnish him with materials
to work up. We have seen how he took to iron smelting and
iron working as opportunity offered. His wood working skill
could be turned to many uses. He made dolls and tubs and
cheap musical instruments. His women sewed gloves or made
rough lace and embroidery. Their goods were collected by
bagmen and carried to the town market or, more probably, to
one of the great fairs. This method of production was exceedingly economical for the dealer, because the peasant lived poorly
and was not dependent on his industrial earnings alone.

§ 23. The acceleration in German industrial development
which is perceptible from about 1835, and conspicuous from
about 1845, was certainly connected with the creation of the
Zollverein in 1834. How much was due to the Zollverein, how
much to better roads and the first railways, how much to that
spread of knowledge which no tariff can stop, cannot be deter-

---

[1] Gothein, *Wirtschaftsgeschichte des Schwarzwaldes*, p. 833.

mined. Many things which happened might have happened without the Zollverein. The tariffs of the German states before 1834 were impediments, but not insuperable impediments, to trade. Men have often attributed economic results to the Zollverein, of which it was not really the cause, because of its immense political significance. *Post hoc, ergo propter hoc.* Germany began to prosper about 1835; therefore the events of 1834 caused her prosperity. The fallacious argument slides easily. No doubt the events of 1834 were a true cause of prosperity. But they were only one of many, and their strength cannot be measured.

This is not the place to tell the political narrative of the fifteen years which intervened between the creation of the Prussian tariff of 1818, from which the Zollverein tariff grew, and the morning of Jan. 1, 1834, when, throughout three-quarters of Germany, long trains of laden waggons stood waiting to cross the frontier lines, with goods now for the first time toll free. But the economic core of the narrative must be laid bare. That Prussian tariff of 1818, immeasurably the wisest and most scientific tariff then existing among the great powers, sprang from the application of trained reason to the very peculiar fiscal position in which Prussia found herself after 1815. It was essentially an economic measure, but it had a political fringe. It was not framed, as is now generally recognised, in order that it might become the tariff of a united Germany. Maassen, the man who made it, did not foresee its future. Ten or eleven years later Motz, who eventually launched the Zollverein, prophesied that the tariff would lead to German unity under Prussian leadership. But that was after its possibilities had been tested.

The fiscal problem which faced Maassen was this—the Prussian dominions were built up of provinces with very varied histories, and at different stages of economic development. These provinces had been shifted politically like the bits of a puzzle, in the decade preceding the final European settlement at Vienna. Prussian Poland had been all taken away, then partially restored. The scattered Westphalian and Rhenish provinces had been curtailed, increased, all taken away in 1807, all restored and greatly added to in 1815, when Prussia became the warden of the German gate against France. In 1815, too, she had received a large part of Saxony, and a considerable stretch of land in Thuringia. But Prussia in the years 1815–50 was never a continuous territory. Hanoverian and Hessian land separated the Rhenish-Westphalian stretch from the great stretch which now began in Thuringia and extended, lapping all round some non-Prussian islands, nearly to Teschen on the south-east and to Memel on the north-east.

This fortuitous concourse of provinces, each with its own fiscal and tariff history, had to be welded into some sort of economic unity. Also the Prussian statesmen wished to get rid of a very troublesome and elaborate system of taxes on commodities produced at home, which they had inherited from the eighteenth century. This was the *Accise* or excise. Further, they wished to discourage smuggling, which was of course astonishingly easy among the mixed up states of Germany, unless immense sums were spent on the customs services. The new tariff, then, had to be one which all parts of the King's dominions could bear; it had to be arranged to yield a respectable revenue; and it had to be so reasonable as to offer no great temptation to the smugglers. Any extensive use of absolute prohibition was excluded, because prohibition is the greatest of all temptations to the smuggler, unless accompanied by constant domiciliary raids by revenue officials.

The sound view was taken that moderate duties are in practice the most productive. Therefore, as revenue was wanted, duties were kept low. On raw materials they were specially low, and many were admitted free. Manufactures were subjected to specific duties, so much on the pound, the gallon, or the yard. At the values current in 1818 these duties were modest, averaging not much over 10 per cent. when calculated *ad valorem*. Anticipating a leading feature of the British tariff during the free trade era of the later nineteenth century, Maassen reserved his heaviest burdens for "colonial wares," chiefly sugar and coffee. On these he clapped stiff revenue duties of about 20 per cent. The only articles whose import into Prussia was prohibited were salt and playing cards, because both were government monopolies.

A feature which became of great political and economic importance was the taxation of goods in transit across Prussian soil. Prussia, as it happened, now lay athwart most of the main trade routes of Germany, in particular the direct route between the fair-holding towns of Frankfurt-on-Main and Leipzig. Except the bottle-neck between Hanover and Cassel, she controlled all north-south routes. Both banks of the lower Rhine were in her hands; and the great trade highway from Leipzig into Poland and Russia cut straight across Prussian Silesia. Here was an obvious and easy source of revenue. It did not matter to Prussia how heavily goods were taxed which merely went along her roads, to be sold and bought by non-Prussians. If the goods were materials going to competing manufacturing areas, there was a strong protective argument for taxing them. In any case, this was a form of taxation which there was a reasonable prospect that the foreigner might be made to pay. At least he could not shift it on to Prussian shoulders. Apparently these fiscal arguments were what appealed to Maassen and his colleagues; but it soon appeared that, in the transit dues, the new Prussia had got hold of a most formidable economico-political bludgeon. From the first there was a howl against this blackmailing of German trade. The analogy between the King of Prussia and some robber baron of the middle ages could not but occur to the least learned pamphleteer. Saxony, who had no reason to love the King even had there been no transit dues, was loudest of all in her protests. But Prussia cared for none of these things.

During the first ten years of the tariff's history she adopted no definite policy of commending it to her neighbours either by argument or by force. One little Thuringian state joined her in the early days, because it was one of the islands already mentioned. Its name was Schwarzburg-Sondershausen. The decisive event occurred in 1828, when Hesse Darmstadt was induced to join, the first important recruit. The next five years, years interrupted by the rather mild German revolutions of 1830, are filled with the schemings of leagues and counter-leagues and much manoeuvring for position. Bavaria and Wurtemberg formed a league of the south in 1828. There was a short-lived central league whose most important members were Saxony, Hanover, various Thuringian states including the Coburgs, and the Hanse towns. England favoured this league because, on the whole, it believed in free imports. But it collapsed in 1831, under the pressure of Prussian commercial diplomacy.

From 1828 onwards Prussia began to force the pace, for now her policy lay clear before her. She broke the Central League by concluding an opportune treaty with the League of the South. She exploited her diplomatic successes with great ability. Little princes learnt that it was well to be in favour at Berlin. If they were, Berlin would find the money for building valuable roads across their territory. Not for love of them, but because the roads were part of a systematic policy for diverting German trade from the territory of those who were not friends of hers. She won the Thuringian states from the Central League by arranging for a great road over the crest of the Thuringian forest, from Langensalza to Gotha and Meiningen, with branches thence to Würzburg and Bamberg in Bavaria. She agreed with Mecklenburg for a road up the Elbe valley, from Hamburg to Magdeburg, with the deliberate intention of diverting the transit trade from Hamburg to Switzerland, *via* Hanover Cassel and Frankfurt, to the line Magdeburg, Langensalza, Bamberg, Nuremberg. Hanover, still in personal union with England, always stood in Prussia's way. To divert Hanoverian trade was therefore, in Treitschke's words, "a legitimate trick of war against open enemies[1]."

In 1833 the Centre and the South finally came to terms, and the Zollverein was agreed upon. But there was still a strong body of irreconcilables, led by Hanover, or, as nationally-minded Germans said—and with a good deal of truth—by England. The body included, besides Hanover, the Hanse towns, Holstein, Mecklenburg and Oldenburg. As the political map of Germany then stood, this meant that the Zollverein had no direct access to the North Sea. The disadvantage was not, however, so great as might be supposed, because the main economic reason which kept this group of states out of the union was that they were

---

[1] *Deutsche Geschichte*, III, 675.

predominantly commercial and agricultural. They did not fear agricultural competition, and they wanted to buy manufactures where they were best and cheapest, to wit in England. The Hanse towns simply wanted to do all the import and export trade they could. This being the policy of the north-western group, the Zollverein had not to fear any obstacles to the free entry of overseas materials or the free outlet of Zollverein wares; though it did to some extent lose the north-western markets for these wares, so far as they were of the types which England was turning out from her factories.

The Zollverein tariff was substantially the Prussian tariff of 1818. But between 1834 and 1848 the tendency was for the duties on manufactures to become a good deal heavier; partly because they were specific, and as the progress of manufacturing skill brought a yard of cotton or a ton of pig iron cheaper to market a specific tariff became a greater burden *ad valorem*; partly because the pressure of the German manufacturing interest secured increases in the rates several times, especially on English pig iron and cotton yarn. "From the period of its foundation," wrote Banfield with gentle reproach, "the history of the Zollverein is unhappily that of a gradual departure from the sound principles on which it was originally based." These were the days of Friedrich List and the National System of Political Economy. After spending his early manhood as an advocate of German economic and political freedom and union, advocacy which had cost him prison and exile to America, List became United States consul, first at Leipzig (1833) and then in Baden. In 1837 he was in Paris; in 1840 he was back in Germany, where he finally settled at Augsburg. In 1841 appeared the first part of his *National System*, with its powerful historical argument in favour of tariff protection for young national industries. His policy was not adopted officially during his lifetime—he died in 1846—but it supplied arguments in support of the pressure which the manufacturing interest was able, from time to time, to put on the Zollverein authorities.

§ 24. It was the considered opinion of Dr John Bowring, who was sent out from England to report on the Prussian Commercial Union in 1840, that "by directing capital to internal in preference to external trade" it had "already had a great influence in improving the roads, the canals, the means of travelling, the transport of letters—in a word in giving an impulse to inland communications of every sort[1]." He was evidently inclined to think that the Union was also acting as a powerful direct stimulus to German manufacturing industry; though he did not commit himself to an equally definite pronouncement on that head. He noted that, for the reasons already given, the duties on cottons worked out at from 30 to 120 per cent. *ad valorem*, and those on woollens at from 20 to 50 per cent., which amounted to a practical reservation of the home markets, for "all the coarser and commoner manufactures," to the German manufacturer.

The most interesting sections in Bowring's report are those in which he enumerates the industries and industrial arts in which to his mind Germany excelled the United Kingdom. Such excellence could clearly have no connection with a six year old Customs Union. It was the flower of Germany's whole economic civilisation and of her intellectual qualities. There is nothing surprising in his statement that "the arts of design and their application to various fabrics" were better understood than in England; for it is doubtful whether any people in Europe had sunk to the level of design tolerated by the English of 1840. Much more significant is his opinion that, in Germany, "metals were more successfully wrought and worked." He was thinking not of mass production, of pig iron in its millions of tons, but of the craftsman's skill—the fine steel and cutlery of Solingen; the metal wares of Nuremberg; the inherited knowledge of how you may procure and work the "half-precious" metals, as the Germans call them. When to this was added the English technique of mass production and factory organisation, the ways would be prepared for the launch of a very powerful and finished metallurgical industry. This was what happened between 1845 and 1880. It was not an accident; not an artificial fruit ripened by the forcing house of the Zollverein; but a natural growth, assisted in some degree by Zollverein, *Gewerbe Institut*, and other devices of governments.

[1] *Report*, p. 7.

The third aspect of Germany's industrial equipment which Bowring selected for commendation is more significant still. A land of peasants and handicraftsmen, she was also a land with an educated middle class, and this had industrial consequences. "Chemical knowledge, in its various branches, is further advanced than with us[1]." The verdict is given without hesitation. And as the industrial age which was opening was to be founded on the alliance of exact science with industry, an alliance which was to become more important with every fresh discovery, the land of peasants, handicraftsmen, and an educated middle class had certain competitive advantages as against what seemed, in 1840, the irresistible economic might of England.

[1] This opinion was not new. "The Germans are by much the best Chymists in Europe and the best treatises on that subject are either writ in Latin or High German." Campbell, *The London Tradesman*, 3rd ed. (1757), p. 61.

CHAPTER V

COMMUNICATIONS AND COMMERCE IN WESTERN EUROPE BEFORE THE RAILWAY AGE

§ 25. In the two or three generations preceding 1815, England, as everyone knows, went through a revolution from means of communication which were infamously bad to a system which, though limited, was the admiration of all travellers. This was not true of many parts of Western Europe. France and Italy had a complete network of Roman roads, which had not altogether decayed away, like those of England, in the later middle ages and early modern times. They had been kept up or added to, in France, on the same scale of workmanship since the seventeenth century. Arthur Young, fresh from his journeys through the ruts and water holes of his own King's highways, broke out into superlatives over the best of the French roads—"stupendous works," "truly magnificent," "we have not an idea of what such a road is in England," "if the French have not husbandry to show us they have roads." His appended sneer that the traffic "demanded no such exertions" was beside the mark; since the road was there presumably to create traffic. When he came to the Canal de Languedoc, driven through a mountain to connect the Atlantic with the Mediterranean, and saw its basin at Béziers "broad enough for four large vessels to lie abreast"—"here Louis XIV thou art truly great," he exclaimed. He was less appreciative of the Canal of Picardy, on which the great tunnelling works between St Quentin and Cambrai were held up for lack of money. But the fact that it was undertaken under Louis XVI shows how continuous was the French tradition of government engineering enterprise. Young could remember when England had marvelled at Brindley's very modest tunnelling work on the Duke of Bridgewater's canal.

Napoleon was a road and bridge builder of the first rank, who had the benefit of an engineering tradition of nearly a century,

preserved in the *Corps des Ponts et Chaussées*, created early in
the reign of Louis XV. He took up the work of the kings his
predecessors. Under him the Canal of Picardy was completed;
and it is his inscription which stands over the mouth of the
tunnel in front of Bellicourt. This was but one of his canals.
Everywhere his roads preceded his armies and opened the way
for French civilisation and French trade—over the Mont Cenis
and over the Simplon; down the Dalmatian coast and along the
Rhine valley. Bridges; great quays at Paris; improvements in
the navigation of eighteen rivers; more than 200 kilometres of
new canals[1]; over 13,000 leagues of road made or repaired, was
the record of his best years. The main roads had been classified
in 1811–13 into imperial and departmental; the charge of the
latter being thrown on the local authorities. Of the former, under
the direct care of the central government, there were 229.
Towards the end, after Moscow and during his last desperate
campaigns on French soil, many roads went out of repair; but
nevertheless he left a great heritage.

The Bourbons did not neglect it. They found nearly two-
thirds of the main roads in bad condition. These were restored,
as means could be found, and the work of improvement and
extension was never allowed to stop.

But the greatest work of the Restoration was on the canals.
The whole position was systematically examined, as soon as the
evacuation of French territory by the allies was complete (1818),
when it was ascertained that nearly 3000 kilometres of projected
canal were unfinished, and that 10,000 kilometres more were
desirable. A regular programme was drawn up. Special loans
were raised on the security of the canal dues; and the operations
were pushed with such vigour, that over 900 kilometres of
navigable canals were added before 1830 to the 1200 kilometres
previously in existence. The Revolution of 1830 was not of a
kind to interrupt work of this sort, and in fact the government
of Louis Philippe did more than any other for the French canal
network. Another 2000 kilometres of finished waterways were
added before 1848, according to the programme. Between 1835
and 1848, several of the great existing canals linking up river

[1] France had 1000 kilometres of canal before the Revolution.

basins were cut; such as those from the Rhine to the Rhone, from the Marne to the Rhine, and from the Aisne (near Berry-au-Bac) to the Marne above Epernay. From this period date also such important "lateral canals," *i.e.* canals parallel to rivers where their navigation is difficult, as those of the Marne, the Loire, and the Garonne. Some work was done, too, in the basins of the Somme, the Scheldt, the Lys and the Oise.

Neither the government of the Restoration nor that of the July Monarchy undertook much absolutely new construction of first grade roads—royal, imperial, or national roads, as they have been called under the various *régimes*. There were 27,200 kilometres of such roads in 1814. Of these 1200 kilometres were in Alsace-Lorraine. Even at the close of the nineteenth century, there were only 38,000 kilometres in the reduced territory of France. Of the 12,000 kilometres completed since Napoleon's day, much the greater part had been made in the second half of the century. But, though few new roads of the first grade were cut, the Monarchy of July did a great work in improving the average level of upkeep and equipment. On the second grade (departmental) roads much new work was needed, and much was undertaken. But probably the most important development under the July Monarchy was connected with roads of the third and fourth grades.

There had originally been three grades of roads only—national, departmental, and local (vicinal), under the state, the department and the commune. A law of 1836 created an intermediate class between the second and third, the so-called local roads *de grande communication*, that is to say, roads in which both the communal and the departmental authorities were interested. They were to be made by the department and commune jointly, but to be maintained by the department. The true local road was the business of the commune exclusively. The law of 1836 did not merely authorise a fresh grade of road; it determined how roads of this grade were to be controlled, and provided regular sources of income for their construction and upkeep. It must be remembered that a "road" not of the first grade might exist without being practicable for wheeled traffic, a point abundantly illustrated from the history of roads

in England. The work of the first twenty years after 1815 upon
these lower grade roads, was so continuous and effective, that
a competent French writer[1] could assert, in 1838, that there then
existed five or six times as much practicable highway in France
as had existed under the Empire. And so important did the law
of 1836 appear to men looking backward from the early sixties,
that one of them could write of how it "had transformed
France," and how "agriculture owed to it the greater part of
the progress made these five and twenty years[2]." There is
more than a touch of exaggeration in this; but at least it indicates the impression made by the law.

§ 26. French road-making enterprise under the Empire had
affected all adjacent countries, as has been already pointed out.
Modern Alpine road engineering may fairly be called a French
creation, in spite of what antiquity, the middle ages and early
modern times had done to make such passes as the Septimer,
the St Gothard and the Splügen practicable. But in most of
the border lands, which for a time became French, means of
communication already stood at a satisfactory level, before the
great age of French expansion. Holland had her old established
and admirable waterways, and a few roads smoothly paved
with brick for lack of road metal. The Flemish towns could
never have existed had they not been linked up by water or
by artificial highways spanning the Flanders mud[3]. In Italy,
and in the parts of Germany west of the Rhine, Rome had once
ruled; and where Rome had stood even centuries of neglect
could not efface the marks of her feet. The Mosel bridge at
Trèves still rests on Roman piers.

Germany beyond the Rhine had not this foundation; and her
political misfortunes, in the seventeenth and early eighteenth
centuries, had prevented her rulers from undertaking work on
the grand scale in imitation of the Kings of France. Something had been done on waterways, especially by the rulers of
Brandenburg and Prussia; for the North German plains invite
work of that kind. But up to 1800, German roads as a whole

---

[1] Michel Chevalier, *Des intérêts matériels en France* (1838), p. 32.
[2] Lavergne, *L'Économie rurale de la France*, p. 442.
[3] Flemish roads were bad in 1715. Pirenne, *Hist. de la Belgique* (1921),
v, 276.

were very bad indeed. When Prussia took over the great
Bishopric of Münster, in 1803, a high official sent to open a
meeting of magnates at the town of Hamm found it wiser to
walk 4¾ (German) miles to the ceremony than to venture upon
the local road in a wheeled conveyance. An extreme case, no
doubt, but instructive. The building of real made and metalled
roads on Prussian soil had at that date only just begun. The
very first road of the kind in Germany was made by the Bavarian
government, in 1753, from Nördlingen to Oettingen. Before
that date, the so-called "Army and Trade Roads" of Germany
were like the King's highways of medieval England—routes
along which travel was permissible, with here and there a
bridge or a ferry. Prussia only began to imitate Bavaria in 1788.
Old Prussia suffered from the handicap of a short supply of
good road metal, in many of her provinces. Her political
troubles and her drained exchequer, during the Napoleonic age,
were yet more serious obstacles for a poor state, in which road
making must be done by government or not at all.

In 1815 Prussia came into the French road inheritance of
her new Rhenish and Westphalian provinces. How important
that inheritance was the following table shows. The figures are
in Prussian miles, which are nearly five times the length of the
English mile.

Chaussée maintained by the Prussian State.

Prussian miles

	Total	In Rhineland	In Westphalia
1816	419·8	147·2	91·5
1826	668·5	186·0	160·6
1831	902·0	200·4	160·6
1841	1280·1	261·1	207·7

The figures show how little made road there was at the start,
outside the two great western provinces—about 800 English
miles all told. The first ten years of peace show an improvement,
outside these provinces, of some 700 English miles. But this
improvement had not, at that time, affected the north-eastern
provinces. There were no *chaussées* in Posen in 1826, and hardly
any in East and West Prussia. So late as 1841, these sandy and
difficult regions were extraordinarily backward, judged by

western standards. There were at that date from 600 to 700
English miles of good road in the two Prussias, but only about
200 in the great province of Posen—not nearly enough to allow
for one road through the province north and south and another
east and west. Napoleon's "fifth element," the Polish mud, was
as yet unconquered. The Prussian government, wisely no doubt,
had been spending its strength on road developments in the
centre and west, which formed an integral part of its Zollverein
policy. Prussia and Poland might wait, making what use they
could of their great navigable rivers and some considerable
artificial waterways. They waited till about 1845, when the
great age of Prussian road-building began (see *post*, § 86).

As an indication of the remarkable difference between the
road history of Prussia and that of England, with its privately-
built turnpikes, it may be noted that the first road ever
made on Prussian territory by a private company was started in
1843.

§ 27. River transport was not dealt with so successfully by
governments, in any country, as transport by road and canal.
For this political causes were in great part responsible, since
most European streams flow through more than one state. But
even France, many of whose rivers lie entirely within her own
territory, was accused by French critics of neglecting them.
Michel Chevalier complained in 1838 that her excellent canals
then made, or making, lost much of their value because they
linked up rivers imperfectly navigable. The swift Rhone presented special obstacles; but he saw no reason why the Seine
should remain just as it was when first Julius Caesar saw it. He
asserted that this was so.

Improvements on the Rhine were not easily made, seeing
that the great powers took sixteen years (1816–31) to regulate
its international status. Other rivers in Germany were only
slowly being freed from an antiquated fiscal system, as harmful
to trade as any rocks or shallows. In 1800 a cargo paid toll
fourteen times on the Elbe between Hamburg and Magdeburg,
and thirty-three times on the Main between Bamberg and Mainz.
The abolition of many petty states in 1803 improved matters;
but only the Zollverein got rid of river tolls—within its range.

The Elbe, coming from Bohemia and crossing Zollverein territory into the north-west German states, still cut at least two tariff frontiers. The political position of the Rhine, as settled in 1831, remained so difficult that the improvement of its course above Mannheim was neglected right through the nineteenth century, even after the events of 1871 had brought both banks under the control of a single state[1].

The one effective stimulus to river navigation before 1850 owed nothing to the state. It was the steamboat, whose arrival revolutionised river traffic before it had really begun to affect overseas trade. On a river any little steamer can make its way up stream in any weather, taking in fuel as needed. Bunkering was the great difficulty for the early ocean steamers with their extravagant engines. In consequence, even in the United Kingdom in 1850, out of a total overseas tonnage of 3,565,000 tons only 168,000 tons were steam driven. Long before that date all large European rivers had their steam services. No sooner had steam been tried on the Calais packets (1821) than it was taken up everywhere for short sea and river journeys. Before 1825 there were services across the Belt and across the Sound; from Stockholm to Petersburg; on the Rhine; and even on the Swiss lakes. Belgium began to build and run river steamers as soon as she came into political existence. The *Société anversoise des bateaux à vapeur*, for instance, was founded in 1835. Fifteen years later Belgium had only three steamers for overseas trade. France was at first rather slow. Her statisticians lamented her backwardness in the twenties. But after 1830 she moved faster. By 1842 she owned 229 steamers and by 1852, 364. They were small and, even in 1852, still mainly used on the rivers. Those that went to sea were almost all coasters and cross-channel boats. Official attempts to create long distance steam services about this time were unprofitable. Government endowed a postal packet service from Marseilles for Italy and the Levant in 1835. The *Scamander* began the service in 1837. But between that year and 1849 expenses were considerably more than £2,000,000, and receipts considerably less than £1,000,000. And when, in

---

[1] Important work had however been done on the upper Rhine between 1820 and 1840 by the Baden engineer, J. G. Tulla. Schnabel, *Deutsche Geschichte*, III, 265 (1934).

1840, the government of M. Thiers had made generous offers of subsidies to those who would start transatlantic services, the first claimant did not appear until 1847, and he gave up his project a few years later.

About 1850, Prussia, Mecklenburg, the Hanse towns and Hanover, that is to say all the important sea-board states of Germany, had 24 sea-going steamers between them, with an aggregate tonnage of under 5500. Norway and Denmark united had more steamers than all the German states together, though the average size was less. Sweden, odd as it may seem at first sight, was at that time the largest steamship owning country on the continent. She had 61 vessels with an aggregate tonnage of 15,200. The reason was that her Baltic trade was more akin to that river traffic, which engaged by far the greater number of European steamboats, than to the long distance traffic of the greater seas and oceans. Even Sweden's 15,200 tons is a tiny figure when compared with the United Kingdom's 168,000; and it has already been noted how small a part that was of the whole British mercantile marine.

River steamers by 1850 were helping to move goods in bulk; though at first they had devoted themselves mainly to passengers. What may be called cross-channel steamers were doing a trade of steadily increasing importance, very largely in valuable and perishable goods. "The ships employed in the butter and cheese trade," said a somewhat naïve witness before a British Committee in 1847[1], "are of a peculiar description; they are steamers, or vessels propelled by steam...capable of making rapid and safe voyages, which seems to be essential to the carrying on of the butter and cheese trade." However successful this "peculiar description of vessel" may have been in the European short voyage trades, on the high seas the movement even of men, mails, and choice cargoes was not as yet a general success. In French or German hands it was no sort of success.

The rate of growth in the use of steam is therefore no test of the growth of the sea-borne commerce of the western European nations. After the long years of British blockade, that growth was inevitably rapid at first, and it was well maintained.

---

[1] Select Committee on the Navigation Laws, Evidence Q. 2313 *sqq.*

In 1820 the aggregate tonnage entering French ports was 690,000. A short table will best indicate later developments.

Tonnage entering French ports.

1820	690,000	1835	1,200,000
1825	740,000	1840	2,500,000
1830	1,000,000	1845	2,300,000

At no time was half this tonnage French; and with the growth of the import trade, the proportion, and not merely the absolute amount, of foreign tonnage grew also. In 1820, 51 per cent. of the entering tonnage was foreign; in 1830, 66 per cent., and in 1840, 73 per cent. After 1840, the proportion declined somewhat, averaging about 66 per cent., except in 1848 when political events scared away trade and foreign shipping.

Britain and America were the great ocean carriers of those years, America gaining on Britain after 1840. The situation in that year and in 1850 is summarised in the following table. For earlier years satisfactory comparisons cannot be made.

Mercantile tonnage of all kinds on national register.

	1840	1850
United Kingdom	2,768,000	3,565,000
United States (foreign trade)	900,000	1,586,000
France	662,500	688,000
Norway	277,000	298,000
Holland	—	293,000
Hamburg	—	71,000
Bremen	44,000	68,000
Belgium	23,000	35,000

The shipping world still thought in terms of wooden sailing ships. In the masses of evidence put before English parliamentary committees, from 1844 to 1849, when the repeal of the Navigation Laws was under discussion, the comparative shipping power of nations for the future was gauged by the costs of oak, teak, and shipwright's labour. Once or twice a far-seeing witness suggested that the future might lie with the iron steamer. A single witness had formed a high opinion of "the Archimedean screw." But the main discussion was about teak-built East Indiamen, Yankee clippers, "colonial builts" from Nova Scotia, and Scandinavians who crawled across the

North Sea with timber, flax and Danzig corn. No Englishman feared French or German competition. The fast growing trade of Hamburg and Bremen might suggest possibilities from that side; but in 1847 the British tonnage trading with Hamburg was double that of Hamburg itself.

§ 28. The goods which the ships moved out and in at the ports of Western Europe were, as yet, very much what they had been three-quarters of a century before or even earlier. In normal years France kept herself in bread[1], and the German states, in the aggregate, had a surplus of grain for export. The Dutch had always used a great deal of imported grain. "Their ships," Thomas Mun wrote in the seventeenth century, "are as our Ploughs to us, the which except they stir the people starve." So it was still. The standard grain quotation on all Western markets in the thirties and forties was that of Danzig. To Danzig came the surpluses of the whole Vistula basin. From Danzig and adjacent Baltic ports the Dutch had got their corn time out of mind. They fed the Spaniards with it in Queen Elizabeth's days, while fighting them. They still fed them in 1820. Russian Black Sea corn began to appear on the European markets after 1815. So did a certain amount of United States and Canadian corn. But these were subsidiary supplies, less important in the early years than those from Sicily and Barbary. In the English corn law debates, the Danzig quotation took the place occupied by the price in the Chicago wheat-pit towards the end of the nineteenth century. There was nothing new in this prominence of Danzig. "From Danskes in Polland," a merchant reported to Secretary Walsingham about 1580, comes "great store of wheat and rye if it be scant in England[2]."

Baltic raw materials, too, have always been shipped to the west. Timber and pitch from all the gulfs; flax and hemp especially from that of Riga and from the roadstead of Libau on the Courland coast—these were the staples. Germany had little need of them, and France's demand for imported flax and hemp was not yet great. This was the old position. Holland and

---

[1] In the two famine years 1846–7 France imported £12,000,000 worth of cereals. Her ordinary excess of imports was under £1,000,000. This was mainly rice and maize.

[2] Document printed in the *English Historical Review*, July 1914, p. 325.

Belgium were more dependent; and so they had been in the eighteenth century.

Nor had there been any change in the general character of those trades with the tropics, for which the nations had fought through centuries, except that England's abnormal position, from 1793 to 1815, had greatly increased her importance as an *entrepôt* for tropical produce. Much French and Dutch tropical and sub-tropical territory had passed into her hands. The German states, having no tropical dependencies, had always relied to a great extent on some *entrepôt*—usually Amsterdam or London; though the Hanse merchants were in a position to bring a certain amount of produce direct. They now relied rather less on Amsterdam and much more on London. France, retaining a thoroughly old fashioned mercantilist policy in her reduced empire, tried to supply her own needs from colonies who were obliged to sell to her only. She did not succeed, but her duties were so arranged that as little as possible should come openly through London, Amsterdam or Antwerp. The coffee or sugar or spices or tobacco that her colonies could not furnish, she tried to get by direct trade with Arabia, the Turkish Empire, the United States, or far Eastern principalities as yet free from the English and the Dutch.

When the trade of France had settled down, after the years of foreign occupation and indemnities, her total imports averaged £16,000,000 a year (1820–4). Twenty years later the average was £45,500,000 (1840–4), prices having remained fairly steady meanwhile. The increase is conspicuous, but it was chiefly due to expansion of established trades. The most important exception is American cotton. Before the wars, the United States had exported but little cotton. After 1815 their exports grew amazingly. In France they made the fortune of Havre, one of the few French towns which was growing fast. By 1840 France was spending £4,000,000 a year on cotton— mostly American. Other novel trades, which became important after 1825–30, were those in English iron, machinery and hardware. The import of English coal, which was not novel, increased greatly. The French government discouraged all these imports; but France was not able to do without them.

The English coal export trade illustrates admirably the difference between early and late nineteenth century conditions. Before 1828, England had never exported in one year 250,000 tons of coal to foreign countries—all foreign countries. The figure first rose above 500,000 tons in 1835. It was 1,000,000 in 1838 and 2,100,000 in 1845, by which time the railway and steamboat demand was beginning to tell. Contrast this with the 44,000,000 tons of 1900 and the 73,000,000 tons of 1913, exclusive of bunker coal.

Since France was not at this time a creditor country or a great investor or borrower, the growth of her exports about kept pace in value with that of her imports. Her old staple trades came back to her rapidly, as soon as the seas were opened. The wine ships crowded to Bordeaux, as they had when it was the base for the Black Prince's raids. French silks and ribbons, smuggled into England because of their excellence while the prohibitive system was retained, were imported openly in great quantities as soon as prohibition was replaced by a tariff. In the early forties, France's exports of manufactured silk to all countries averaged £5–6,000,000, out of a total export trade of some £45,000,000. Her fine manufactures of wool and of cotton also found ready markets abroad, as and where tariffs permitted. Coarser goods were marketed in her colonies and the Levant. Her miscellaneous artistic manufactures—furniture, clocks, porcelain, "Paris wares"—had not lost their reputation. The most important new branch of her export trade was that in valuable and perishable foodstuffs—butter, poultry, fruits and vegetables—which grew *pari passu* with the relaxation of the English tariff, that is to say mainly in the forties. It was greatly encouraged by the use of steam in the Channel.

Corn was the main export from Germany, with oil seeds, vegetable oils, wine, spirits and some meat and dairy produce. The merino wool grown in the east was sent in considerable quantities to England, and was an important ingredient in English fine cloth for at least a generation. Some German exports of manufactures, well known before the wars, had declined, notably that of linen referred to in an earlier chapter. (See *ante*, § 21.) Trade terminology in England still recalled the old state of things. People called one sort of linen goods Hessians and another Osnaburgs; but they were generally made in Leeds, Belfast or Dundee. The wars and the rigid protectionism of Russia after 1815 had cut off what had once been an important eastern outlet for German woollens. Austrian protectionism, which was of the strictest kind, blocked the south eastern trade routes. Beyond Austria came Switzerland, whose manufactures were at least equal, and in many ways superior, to those of her German neighbours. Then France, with industries, generally speaking, superior, and wielding a stout tariff; Belgium, competent in all industries and in those of the new age very much superior; Holland, also experienced, capable of meeting most of her own needs, and ready to draw on England for the rest; and so to Scandinavia where there was a modest outlet. Of course German manufactures were exported in considerable quantities; but as yet they did not play an important part in the commerce of the world. No country was in any way dependent on them.

§ 29. Of all the goods whose movement the improved roads and waterways were meant to help, only a small proportion came from abroad or were destined for export, even in countries like Holland and Belgium which were essentially lands of transit. The whole foreign trade of France in 1830 amounted to about 30s. per head of the population per annum. Twenty years later, her wine exports were less than 3 per cent. of her average production in volume, though considerably more in value. Trades which worked primarily for export, like the silk trade, were exceptional in France, and still more so in any other part of the continent. The merchant proper, therefore, the wholesale trader with foreign parts, played a relatively unimportant *rôle* in the economic life of the nations. The further east one went, the less important he became, as life became more local and localities more self-sufficient. Even the wholesale dealer whose operations were confined to his own country was not too common. According to Prussian statistics, which on the face of them are rather suspicious, the number of "Great Traders," that is, people without shops who bought and sold on their own account or on commission, was 358 in 1837! The suspicious circumstance is that they are said to have numbered 4185 in 1843, which suggests a clerical error. Yet even the latter figure is small enough.

That is Prussia. But the greatest merchant cities of Germany, Hamburg, Frankfurt and Bremen, were not on Prussian territory.

Even the trader with a shop was not too common in the Germany of the forties. In most places there were no shops except the workshops of the handicraftsmen, tailors, cobblers, carpenters, and the rest. If the consumer wanted what they could not make, he must buy from a peddler or at his local yearly market. Townsman and peasant met weekly at the ordinary market, to buy and sell food; and so the average town lived on local produce. Few were large enough to need supplies from a distance. But for anything unusual both townsman and peasant had to wait. Spices and condiments, materials for clothes, furniture, tools and implements at all out of the common run, toys and little luxuries, were brought by migratory traders— grading upwards from the peddler to what might almost be called the merchant—to the yearly market. It was a great occasion. There were puppet shows and rope-dancers and "English riders." The peasants poured in to make their little purchases; the squires and townsfolk laid in their stores. There would be selling, too, by the local people—cattle, perhaps, if the yearly market was also a cattle market, or flax and other industrial crops, if the district grew a surplus of these things.

Behind the yearly markets stood the great fairs, above all those of Frankfurt on the Oder for the east, Leipzig for the centre, and Frankfurt on the Main for the west. The last was no longer in full vigour; it was influenced by the all-the-year-round trading habits of Western Europe proper. Indeed, all the fairs began to show symptoms of decline before 1840. Frankfurt on the Oder, it is true, the most easterly, the nearest to Nijni-Novgorod and Eastern Europe, was still growing up to 1855; but it was not of first rate importance. After 1834, all the most important fair business of the Zollverein went through Leipzig, a fact which illustrates the strength of Prussia's position in the days when she was engaged in forcing Saxony into the Union. The great fairs were primarily meeting places for dealers, not places where dealer met consumer. The local trader, who collected from independent craftsmen or peasants the coffee mills of Nuremberg, the clocks of the Black Forest, the linens of Silesia, or the toys of the Thüringer Wald, met at the fairs other traders who knew the outlets for his goods, at home or abroad. The large *Verleger*, for whom cottage wage earners worked on commission, might visit the fair himself. Through the fairs the import merchants, usually from the Hanse towns, spread over the country their "colonial wares" or English manufactures.

"Colonial wares" helped in the creation of real shops, since continuous supplies came to be needed locally; but the work of creation was slow. Before the great wars even Berlin, although it had 200,000 inhabitants and a court, had not many shops. There were a couple of "shopping streets," and a few shops thinly scattered in others. The Berliners span and baked and brewed, and sometimes even wove and slaughtered, at home. There had been nothing to bring about a change by 1815; for the town had gone back in industry, population and wealth, and far back in luxury[1].

Not until about the year 1830 was the movement of the late eighteenth century resumed. Specialised shops increased in the few large cities; and in the little country towns, which were the really representative urban centres of Germany, there grew up here and there those general stores, with a range of goods from sugar and coffee through candles to pins and tape, which in all countries have gradually superseded the peddler and the wandering dealer of the markets and fairs. But the peddler, native or foreign, was too well established in Germany to be easily superseded. Sometimes he was a specialist carrying Black Forest clocks, or glassware, Nuremberg metal wares, or foreign textiles. More often, perhaps, his trade was of the mixed kind which literary tradition connects with the peddler's pack. In a land of peasants, with few outside needs, and of small towns served by markets, such dealers will always retain their place, and the shopkeeper can but slowly emerge.

France was in all these matters several generations ahead of

---

[1] "In no great capital is a Briton so struck with the absence of those splendid and seductive shops which fire the eye and undo the purse in London, Paris and Vienna." J. Russell, *A Tour in Germany* (1825), II, 27.

Germany, thanks to her much more complete urbanisation. Over wide areas, of course, the relations of peasants with peddlers, and with the markets of the neighbouring country town, were, in all essentials, those which have just been described. But France had passed out of that stage of economic evolution in which the great fairs play a really important part. A marked decline in the fairs was recorded about the year 1700. In the nineteenth century they had ceased to be the centres of general commerce, and were sinking towards the position which the surviving fairs hold in modern England. The booths and the rope-dancers and the stalls with their miscellaneous wares, in some cases also great droves of horses and cattle, were there; but not the staples of international trade. Further, the size of Paris, Lyons, and the other leading cities had necessitated, for centuries, a large scale organisation of the food trades, especially the grain trade. This had broken up effectively the old system of localised supply of local requirements. In the seventeenth century already, Paris, which derived its main supplies from the cornlands in the belt south of the city, between Chartres and Chalons, was drawing on Brittany; was competing with Rouen for the supplies of the lower Seine basin; and with Lyons for those of the upper basin of the Saône. All this involved large scale commercial operations, and a corresponding merchant class. So also in the wine trade of Bordeaux and Reims, the brandy trade of Cognac, the silk trade of Lyons—to take only outstanding instances—commercial operations in the eighteenth century were essentially modern. Markets were wide, remote, foreign. Commercial methods had been carried to a high level of perfection.

But retail trade, though widespread and maintaining a regular social class of specialised shopkeepers, was, generally speaking, a poor and humble business. There was little capital in it, except in the luxury shops in a few streets in a few cities; and its operations only covered a part of the field which they were to occupy during the later nineteenth century. In many trades, the shopkeeper had not yet got between the craftsman and the consumer. The most conspicuous instances are the clothing trades. The shop that sells new clothing ready made was almost unknown in the eighteenth century. We hear indeed of "Le sieur Dartigalongue, maître et marchand tailleur à Paris," who. some time before 1770, had "établi...un magasin d'habits neufs tout faits, de toutes espèces, de toutes tailles, et des plus à la mode." But apparently such shops remained so rare that, over sixty years later, the opening by an individual named Thernaux of a ready made clothes shop at the sign of the *Bonhomme Richard*, *Place des Victoires*, was so much commented on that historians have been tempted to date from it the birth of this type of business[1]. As a general Parisian type its birth may in fact be dated from the second quarter of the nineteenth century. And in this, as in most matters of urban economics, Paris led the continent.

[1] In the first edition, I adopted, with a reservation, this view from Levasseur, II, 189 n. I had overlooked Franklin, *Les magasins de nouveautés* (1894), quoted in Sombart, *Luxus und Kapitalismus*, as a reviewer in the *American Hist. Review* pointed out.

CHAPTER VI

MONEY BANKING AND INVESTMENT, 1815–1848

§ 30. The monetary and financial system of Western Europe emerged from the age of the great wars in a state which, as compared with that produced by the world war of a century later, might be called one of health and prosperity. Long as the wars had been, precious intervals for rest and recuperation had been allowed to the combatants, of which the wise among them had taken advantage. England, the paymaster of all France's enemies, had strained her resources rather through mismanagement than through necessity. The Bank of England had suspended cash payments and its notes had depreciated as against gold. But the worst was over before 1815 and cash payment was all but resumed next year. It was fully resumed in 1821, by which time she had put her currency into its modern order by Lord Liverpool's Act of 1816. And what currency troubles she had in no way impaired her real financial strength. She was easily able to lend to all the world, and she did so, with great advantage to herself.

France was in a position of astonishing financial comfort and security. Bankruptcy, against which Mirabeau thundered in the early days of the Revolution, had come and gone before ever the nineteenth century opened; and she had seemed little the worse for it. By the Law of 7 Germinal in the Year XI (March 28, 1803) she also had reorganised her currency; and no event of the next twelve years deranged it. About the same time she had built up a national bank upon foundations laid at an earlier date; and the Bank of France remained in excellent working order after Waterloo. Napoleon had made war pay for itself; and though at the finish France had to bear some of the financial burdens of the conquered, they were so small compared to her resources that she bore them with the most perfect ease. Her national debt, when peace came, was far less burdensome to her people than that of victorious England.

As might be supposed, there was most wreckage in countries which had felt the weight of France's hand. Prussia had been bled white after Jena. The national effort during the war of liberation had prevented recovery. But Prussian economics were primitive. Her people had suffered and lived hard. Her King's treasure had been drained away. The old fashioned little State Bank which Frederick had started in 1765—it was more nearly a branch of the exchequer than an independent bank—had been roughly handled. It found itself in 1815 burdened with loans on mortgage to landowners crippled by the wars. It was carried on until 1846 with a hidden deficit, and then reorganised. But its prosperity or misfortune hardly reflected the strength or weakness of the country. The returns of the national bank were not the barometer of national prosperity, as in a commercialised country like England. Happily for Prussia, her simple economic life had rendered overborrowing, or the complete debauching of the currency by inflation, difficult during the wars. There was no one at home or abroad to overborrow from. England, after one unhappy experience in lending to a continental ally—it was the Hapsburg Emperor in 1795—had decided that there was less worry and disappointment in the subsidy than in the loan. She never lent again; she always gave. Prussia had known the evils of excessive paper money during the Napoleonic troubles; but its use had not been sufficiently widespread to produce those dangerous price inflations from which the more highly organised world of the twentieth century suffered after 1918.

The more delicate financial system of Holland, on the other hand, had suffered severely from the earlier French wars and from the blockade. After a life of two centuries, the famous bank of Amsterdam had collapsed in 1791, before Holland became involved in war. It had been doing bad business for some time. Private Dutch bankers, who led the very small *haute finance internationale* of the late eighteenth century, were hard hit by the wars of the nineties. But the country was not again fought over. It recovered in the Napoleonic age. A new state bank—the Bank of the Netherlands—was successfully started in 1814. Immediately after Waterloo, Hopes of Amsterdam were almost the only firm in Europe ready to join with Rothschilds and Barings in the flotation of international loans.

All up the Rhine, before the great wars, there had been a good deal of old fashioned money dealing and banking—in Cologne; still more among the Jews of Frankfurt, the home of Nathan Rothschild down to 1784; and at Basel. The Swiss bankers, Baselers and Genevese, had been world famous. They had given Necker to France, though indeed Necker had not saved French finances. These Rhenish and Swiss financiers had suffered much. Frenchmen fought Russians on the St Gothard and Austrians at Zürich. The Rhine was crossed in every campaign. Latterly, Switzerland had got rest as a republic subservient to France; but she did not recover her importance as a financial centre. Frankfurt revived more completely; for her astutest financiers, the Rothschilds, had served both sides. She played a rather important part in West European finance from about 1830.

Belgium, early absorbed in France and after 1815 attached to Holland, shared the imperial prosperity of the one and the vigour in peace of the other. Economic grievances had much to do with her separation from Holland in 1830; but neither in 1815 nor in 1830 was she suffering from monetary or financial debility.

§ 31. Whereas England finally decided in 1816 for the single gold standard, with silver only as token money, the continent retained the ancient silver standard, in name and to a large extent in fact. The use of silver actually gained ground; for the world's gold output before the Californian and Australian discoveries (1848 *sqq.*) was small, and England, owing to her strong commercial and financial position, was able to draw the bulk of the new supplies to London. In 1792 the United States had adopted a system of bimetallism. Gold and silver were interchangeable for all monetary purposes at the ratio of 15 of silver to 1 of gold. Either metal was to be freely coined for anyone who presented it at the mint; but gold, being under-valued, was not presented. Eleven years later the French law of 7 Germinal,

Year XI, as a matter of history established bimetallism for France. But, in words which no doubt reflected the intention of the legislators, the silver franc was treated as the primary standard of value. Gold was nowhere described as standard money. Only in a late clause of the law was the coining of gold provided for. The ratio of 15½ : 1 was fixed, as such ratios had often been fixed before, in accordance with the then ruling market relationship of the two metals. In his first draft of the law Gaudin, the finance minister responsible for it, had inserted a clause which shows how his thoughts ran—it provided for the recoining of the *gold*, in case the market ratio came to differ too widely from the legal ratio. As France had large stores of both metals, both went to the mints; and the gold Napoleon, successor to the Louis d'Or, came to be a symbol of imperial prosperity. But no one was ever under obligation to pay in gold; the Bank of France usually cashed its notes in silver; and on the Paris exchange it was quite customary, between 1815 and 1848, for gold coins—when wanted in bulk—to command a premium. For ordinary exchanges the two metals circulated side by side; and as no very wide divergence from the ratio of 15½ : 1 occurred in the markets of the world, French currency remained effectively bimetallic, and an alteration in the amount of gold in the Napoleon, the possible need for which had been present to Gaudin's mind, was never in fact necessary. Probably, as bimetallists have always argued, the fact that the French mints were open to both metals, and so tended to absorb whichever was momentarily the more abundant, was in itself one cause of the steadiness of the market ratio. But there were no important discoveries of either metal in those years and no swamping of the market, so the system was not severely tested.

As an illustration of France's monetary comfort after 1815, it may be noted that the coinage of gold was unusually heavy from 1817 to 1819. A marked slackening after 1819 may probably be traced to the English demand which followed the act of that year arranging for the resumption of cash payments. The slackening was accompanied by heavy mintings of silver, which flowed in to fill the gap left by the temporary shortage of gold.

The French franc system, with very slight modifications, was adopted by Belgium in 1832 and subsequently by Switzerland and Sardinia. The amount of gold coined in any of these countries before 1850 was inconsiderable. Holland also had nominally a double standard down to 1847; but almost all the money that she coined was silver. So decidedly did silver prevail in her currency that in 1847 she went over to the silver standard—an unfortunate step in many ways, because within a few years gold again became plentiful.

In the German states silver was everywhere standard money. A certain amount of gold circulated side by side with it, as it always had, but the quantity was less than in some earlier centuries. German currencies reflected German political divisions. Most states used silver thalers equal to three marks; but there were various sorts of thalers; various relations between silver and gold; and an inextricable confusion of small coins and token money. One of the chief businesses of most bankers was the conduct of the bewildering German exchanges. They were mainly what the earliest bankers had been exclusively, guardians and changers of cash. The Zollverein improved the situation by adopting as the union money, in 1838, a two-thaler piece, which was equivalent to seven of the gulden used in some southern states. But nearly twenty years later there was still only approximate unity of currency between north and south; and in the north, the Hanse towns, Mecklenburg and Holstein had systems of their own.

§ 32. French banking history in this period is very nearly a history of the Bank of France. Started in 1800 with a privately owned capital of 30,000,000 francs, which was soon greatly increased; endowed with the exclusive right of note issue; in close and intimate relations with the government; by government saddled with the duty of discounting even the tiniest bills for the good of French trade; it was at once semi-official and popular, the patron of the small Parisian trader and the issuer of paper money for all France. As cheques were unknown in the France of 1815–48, the issue monopoly of the Bank was of special importance. No hampering conditions were attached to the right of issue. There was never any law or order resembling the English Bank Act of 1844, though the maximum possible issue was fixed from time to time. So judicious was the management that freedom was never abused. Even in 1814 the Bank had avoided a suspension of cash payments, though only just. It came through the difficulties of war-indemnity finance (1815–18) with equal success.

From 1817 onwards, independent note-issuing banks were sanctioned by the state in a number of provincial centres; first in Rouen, Nantes, and Bordeaux; between 1835 and 1838 in Lyons, Marseilles, Lille, Havre, Toulouse and Orleans. At first not hostile to this development, the Bank—in the late thirties—reverted to the policy, which it had followed in its early days but subsequently abandoned, of opening branches in provincial centres. This brought it into competition with the provincial banks. When its charter was renewed in 1840, it bargained for a better position in face of its rivals. Henceforward a new provincial issuing bank could only be set up by a special law, whereas a ministerial order sufficed to create a new branch of the Bank of France. In its competition with the provincial banks, the political crisis of 1848 came to its aid. For the first time in its history it was unable to cash its notes. The Provisional Government thereupon declared the notes legal tender. The provincial banks were similarly assisted. But while their notes lost credit, when they became inconvertible, those of the Bank of France held their position. The Bank took advantage of its competitors' distress to offer terms of amalgamation. The terms were accepted and the period closes with the restoration of the Bank's monopoly of issue in May 1848.

The struggle for provincial business in the thirties and forties is an index of French industrial and commercial development in those years. That development is also reflected in the growth of the note issue, which in the absence of a cheque system is a fairly exact test of commercial expansion. In 1820 the Bank of France had a maximum note circulation of 172,000,000 francs. By 1830 it had risen to 239,000,000. That of the three provincial banks was at this time negligible. In 1840 the Bank's maximum circulation was 251,000,000 francs. The provincial banks now had an aggregate circulation of 50–60,000,000. In 1847 the

Bank's maximum was 288,000,000, and the provincial banks, soon to become its branches, issued another 90,000,000 Against this total of 378,000,000 there was a maximum cash reserve in 1847 of 149,000,000 francs. But 1847 was a year of financial crisis, in which the reserves were unusually low. In 1845 the minimum cash reserve had been about 216,000,000 and the maximum about 320,000,000. The consolidated Bank of France in 1848 had a share capital of 92,250,000 francs and the right to issue notes up to 452,000,000 francs. It was in a position to lend to municipalities, to departments, and to the central government, and had never been stronger. Thus ended half a century of sound, successful management and steady expansion, in a political atmosphere which had often been far from healthy.

Centralisation of note issue in the national bank was even more complete in Holland than in France, from the establishment of the Netherlands Bank in 1814 right through the first half of the century—and indeed later. In Belgium there was a more complex, and a most interesting, series of banking developments. In 1822, while the country was still united to Holland, there had been founded a great "general utility" joint stock company, the *Société générale pour favoriser l'industrie nationale*. It had the right of note issue. It was government banker for Belgium and custodian of the funds of savings banks. But it was mainly known as a great lender on mortgage, an exploiter of church lands for their new owners, and a supporter of numerous industrial enterprises. King William of the Netherlands and his family—who had much land in Belgium—held a large part of the share capital. "It appears," writes M. Emile Vandervelde, "that the Société Générale, that mighty capitalist machine, which was ultimately to get all Belgian industry into its grip, was originally just a man of straw—an umbrella for the royal speculations[1]." However that may be, it is significant of Belgium's place in the economic history of Western Europe that this powerful society, anticipating as it did both institutions like the French *Crédit mobilier* of the fifties (see *post*, § 94) and that type of half industrial bank which became characteristic of Imperial Germany, should have grown up so early in Belgium.

Whatever its relations with the unpopular Dutch ruling house may have been, they did not prevent the *Société Générale* from coming safely through the revolution of 1830. But in 1835 a strong rival appeared, the *Banque de Belgique*. Three years later, at a time of financial pressure, the *Société* forced the *Banque* to suspend cash payment, by presenting 2,500,000 francs' worth of notes to be cashed in a few days—an old device of warring banks. The *Banque* survived, however, and the rivals fought for another decade, until both had to suspend payment during the political and economic troubles of 1848. To save the situation the state declared the notes of both legal tender. Two other important joint stock banks existed in Belgium at this time, the *Banque Liègeoise*, founded in 1835, and the Bank of Flanders, in 1841. Belgium was thus equipped with banking and investment facilities proportionate to her industrial and commercial development.

In Germany meanwhile banking development tarried. The Royal Bank in Berlin was a state bank in the strictest sense. Without shareholders, and managed entirely by officials, it carried on a slow and old fashioned business of mortgage, bill discounting and advances against goods, without either note issue or a cheque system. It had issued true bank notes up to 1806; but since that date the only credit documents it handled, other than bills of exchange, had been deposit notes and treasury bills. Its discounting and advancing expanded rapidly, as the railways stirred up trade in Germany. By 1846 the need of an institution better fitted to the new age was recognised, and the Prussian Bank took its place. A main object of government in creating it was to silence the growing demand for privately managed joint stock banks of issue, by creating a compromise institution, with rights of issue but no real independence. The Prussian Bank was a joint stock organisation. Most of its capital was privately held. But its direction was entirely official, though there was an advisory "central committee" of business men. It was to pay a preference dividend to the private stockholders and to share up any further profits between them and the state. It was to have branches similarly organised, and it was to issue notes—to a maximum of 21,000,000 thalers in the early days. The notes were to be convertible into cash, at sight in Berlin, but at the branch banks only if conversion was convenient. On January 1, 1847, the doors were opened and the modern period of Prussian state banking began. Twenty-eight years later this Prussian Bank, only slightly modified, became the Imperial Bank of Germany.

Down to 1846 the Prussian government, remembering its financial trouble after 1806, had been very suspicious of note issue. For a time, from 1824 to 1834, the privately managed "Knights'" Bank of Stettin had issued notes, but the privilege was withdrawn. About the time that this happened, the foundation of banks of issue somewhat of the French type, banks with private capital and management but under government supervision, was under consideration in the German states. Bavaria sanctioned such a bank in 1834, and Saxony approved of the Leipzig Bank in 1838. Both institutions were successful and contributed to the great expansion of German industry which set in during the forties. Nowhere in Germany was the true private bank of issue tolerated; and as has been seen, the average German private banker—before 1840, at any rate—conducted a very primitive business

Those Swiss private bankers, who in the eighteenth century had financed kings, retained a practical monopoly of local business during the first third of the nineteenth century, though they never recovered their international position. Then, between 1830 and 1840, a series of cantonal banks of issue were established—first the Cantonal Bank of Berne, a pure state bank, in 1834; then the banks of St Gallen and Zürich, joint stock banks with official status, in 1836 and 1837. These last were eventually absorbed into the *Schweizerische Kreditanstalt*. In the second half of the nineteenth century the cantonal banks were mostly run with state funds, on the model of that of Berne, and managed by committees appointed by the governments. Side by side with them, however, there existed private and joint stock banks in great variety and some cantonal banks which were also joint stock companies.

§ 33. Banking history illustrates the way in which the joint stock company was coming into general use for large and semi-public undertakings. This was a special feature of the age. In previous centuries only important foreign trade companies, a few banks, and occasionally a public utility concern such as the Paris waterworks, had been organised on the joint stock principle, outside England and Holland. Even in England joint stock enterprise had gone out of fashion between the South Sea Bubble and the canal era. The first joint stock concern in Germany was Frederick the Great's Asiatic Company, started at Emden in 1750 and ruined in the Seven Years' War. Very few of these older companies had a continuous history into the nineteenth century[1].

Nineteenth century company history may be said to begin with the company clauses of the French Commercial Code (1807). They became the basis for the company law of Belgium, Holland, Switzerland, Italy and Spain, and for the earlier company law of Germany. The Code distinguished between the true joint stock company (*société anonyme*), which might or might not have limited liability according to its constitution, and any form of the traditional sleeping partnership (*société en commandite*). Already in the eighteenth century, the device of splitting up the capital supplied by the sleeping partner into regular shares had been hit upon and freely used. Such capital had limited liability, though that of the active partners (*gérants*) had not. Companies of this type were not legally treated as corporations, and were not subject to the official sanction and close official oversight which the Code of Commerce provided for the *société anonyme*.

Neither type was much used before 1820. Only a dozen *sociétés anonymes* were created in the Napoleonic age, and not many more between 1815 and 1820. But for the whole period of the Restoration there were 122, to which must be added a much greater number of the sleeping partnerships with share capital (*sociétés en commandite sur actions*). These latter were used for businesses of many kinds, whereas the true joint stock companies were mainly used for banking, insurance and public utility enterprises—water, gas, railways, and the like. A great

---

[1] The trading company was the type first developed everywhere, *e.g.* the English Muscovy and East India Companies. See Schmoller, *Volkswirthschaftslehre,* I, 441 and literature there quoted.

outburst of company promotion followed the July Revolution. In consequence of a decision of the courts in 1832, the practice of making out the share certificates to bearer, in *sociétés en commandite sur actions*, became legal and very general; though the older practice by which certificates were made out in the holder's name continued side by side with it. Bearer shares were very easily transferable, and their existence in large numbers coincided with a period of company promotions and swindles, in the late thirties and forties, which France has never forgotten. Shareholders with limited liability put up *gérants* who were really men of straw in nominal control of speculative undertakings; and *gérants* of another type carried on businesses of every degree of insecurity, without the participation or sanction of their shareholders. Meanwhile a slow but continuous creation of *sociétés anonymes* went on, still mainly for public utility services, especially railways. From 1840 to 1848, for example, there were floated 177 *sociétés anonymes*, or an average of 22 a year, as compared with over 1400 *sociétés en commandite sur actions* of the two types—an average of 175 a year.

Between 1800 and 1815 Belgium was under French law. Holland also took over the *société anonyme* in principle—as the *naamlooze Vennootschap*. Belgium had known the eighteenth century type of joint stock company well. She was the seat of that Ostend Company, which gave so much trouble to English Foreign Secretaries, and of several important insurance companies. Her first nineteenth century *société anonyme* was also an insurance company—the *Securitas* of 1819 which still exists. Then came the *Société Générale* of 1822, under royal patronage, followed by more than twenty other royally favoured companies, established before the troubles of 1830. Many of them succumbed during those troubles. But the *Société Générale* and its younger rival the *Banque de Belgique* soon began to promote new ones. Between 1834 and 1838 promotion was extraordinarily active. Most of the chief mining and metallurgical companies of Belgium came into existence as *sociétés anonymes* during these years. For five years the average yearly output of *sociétés anonymes* was 25, greater than that of all France in the next decade.

The crisis of 1838, in which the *Société* for the time being smashed the *Banque*, put an end to this quinquennium of company promotion. After a few years of commercial distress and lethargy, promotion was resumed about 1845, this time mainly for private railway enterprises (see *post*, § 37), to be interrupted once more by the dearths, crises, and revolutions of 1845–8. About 120 Belgian *sociétés anonymes* survived these years and were at work in 1850. It will be noted that the figure is less than that of the promotions between 1834 and 1838. There had been heavy casualties among the companies, just as in contemporary England.

Almost to the middle of the century Germany had no proper company law. If joint stock companies were founded at all it was by special charter from the state, as in the eighteenth century. The Hanse towns were an exception, since they had adopted the French Commercial Code. A company which complied with the rules of the Code had a right to exist, whereas elsewhere in Germany the creation of each company was a special act of grace. Until the forties such acts were exceedingly rare. In 1838 came the railway company law of Prussia (see *post*, § 39), which was based on the *Code de Commerce*, as was a more general law for joint stock companies issued in 1843. Down to 1850 no other state had a general company law. Enterprises which required associated capital applied for individual charters in the old way. This was by no means all loss. If promotion was delayed, fraud was averted. The caution of her officials saved Germany from outbursts of unsound speculation.

§ 34. Viewed from the side of the saving public, the joint stock developments of the early nineteenth century mark a stage in the growth of the investment habit. The Mississippi scheme, the South Sea Bubble, and the repeated repudiations even of great states—France was technically bankrupt three times in the eighteenth century—had confirmed the older generations in an inherited fear of putting their savings into anything but land, a strong box, a business which they themselves controlled, or one which they supposed they understood. Only in Holland and England had investment become something of a habit. Even in England, when Adam Smith wrote in 1776, he was a daring man who put money into anything but land, the known business, Bank of England stock, East India stock, or "the funds." However, the canals were at that time beginning to attract what a great modern economist called blind capital, the capital that does not know the business. In war time "the funds" took most of it, and produced that race of investors whom Cobbett used to call tax eaters. After the peace, blind English capital multiplied. It found an attractive outlet in the foreign state loans, which were floated so extensively on the London market by Nathan Meyer Rothschild and Baring Brothers, from 1815 onwards. Nathan Rothschild, who had gained his experience and built up his organisation in handling Britain's war subsidies to her allies, forced the borrowing governments to guarantee interest in sterling, and so quieted the fears of the blind capitalists who did not know about thalers and roubles. They became so trusting that, quite apart from some doubtful European loans, they lost ten millions in South America during the twenties.

On the continent only the Dutch took any share worth mentioning in this international investment, in the early years of the peace. France was a borrower, not a lender. The Rothschilds, Barings, and Hopes of Amsterdam floated loans for her as for the other continental powers. Her own private financial houses were at first not strong enough even to lend a hand. They began to do so on a small scale after 1820; but for the next thirty years they were overshadowed by London firms and by the great international house of Rothschild, which had its members in four capitals[1] and Frankfurt. But owing to her inherent economic strength, and to the excellent management of her currency and finance, France's credit recovered at an astonishing rate. In 1817 she had been forced to float a 5 per cent. loan through Rothschilds and Hopes at 57, at a time when English 3 per cent. Consols stood at 60–70. Before 1830 this loan was regularly quoted well above par, and had been as high as 109–110. At that time English 3 per cents. stood at 80–90. This meant, approximately, that France could raise a loan as easily as England by offering 1 per cent. more than the English gilt-edged rate

[1] London, Paris, Vienna, Naples.

of interest. She was becoming mistress in her own house again; but she was not yet in a position to lend much to her neighbours. Only three types of foreign government securities were quoted in the official list of the Paris stock exchange in 1830, and only six types in 1848. It is true that others were dealt in unofficially; but the official figures indicate the limited interest taken in even the safest foreign investments.

Foreign "commercials" and "industrials" had not attracted interest at all; though there was a certain amount of private investment of French capital in Belgium, and *vice versa*. There were not, of course, many joint stock industrial concerns anywhere before 1850. England again led the way in sending capital to develop the trade and industry of her neighbours. Some of it went with private firms like Manby, Wilson and Co. of Creusot. More went into the continental joint stock companies for gas-works, iron-works, coal-mines, railways and engineering establishments—especially those founded in Belgium in 1834-8 and 1845-7. As is well known, not only English capital and English material, but also English navvies helped the railway development of France. The English navvy of the forties and fifties, in the employ of the first Thomas Brassey, taught many people how to handle pick and shovel, and how a man who would work well must eat largely.

Although, down to 1848-50, France had only taken a small share in international investment, she was preparing by industry and thrift for the days, now very near, in which her share would be far from small. Twenty years later, when her trial came, she had £5-600,000,000 worth of foreign investments. The beginnings of this great holding were made in the late thirties and forties; and the investment habit was acquired by experience with the *sociétés en commandite sur actions* and the *sociétés anonymes* of the reign of Louis Philippe, painful though some of that experience was. When you had learnt to trust your money to a local railway company, waterworks, or sugar refinery, you might proceed to trust it to the government of Spain or Mexico, or to M. de Lesseps for his projected Suez Canal.

The Dutch and the Belgians were, if anything, ahead of the French as international investors. Most of Holland's surplus capital was absorbed in the development of her magnificent colonial empire; and, though she has always been rich for her size, what remained was comparatively inconsiderable. Belgium was fully occupied with internal development down to 1850, and was a borrower for that. But her capitalists, like the French, were beginning to take an interest in international securities, though on a small scale. As yet she had no colonial interests of her own.

§ 35. International investment, in the strict sense, was only one, and perhaps not the most important, cause of an economic interlocking of nations which was becoming closer every year after 1815. In spite of tariffs and other law-made barriers, Western Europe, including the British Isles, was tending to become a single commercial and industrial society, with certain common characteristics, common needs, and common economic diseases. The tendency was not marked until the railway and telegraph era; but it was perceptible while railways were still in the experimental stage, and even earlier. The continent needed England, her goods, and her capital as never before. England needed the continent; though until the tariff reforms of the forties she was reluctant to admit the extent of her need. A main cause of these reforms was the desire of her business men to sell abroad, and the recognition that if you wish to sell you must buy. Both England and the continent needed America. American cotton was the first sub-tropical raw material that was consumed on a large scale by all industrial nations. The nations were becoming so much interlocked that pressure on the economic nerve centres—food or raw material markets; leading industries; banking systems—in London, New York, Paris, Amsterdam, Antwerp or Hamburg, was felt in all the rest, in a way the eighteenth century had never known. This was the beginning of economic vicissitudes and financial crises which were European, or almost world wide.

In 1815-16, the inability of the continent to buy so freely as England had anticipated, helped to produce a commercial and financial collapse there. Merchants were ruined and banks broke. Two years later there were simultaneous financial difficulties in London and Paris, arising from France's heavy borrowings to pay her war liabilities and England's share in the French loans. Both the Bank of England and the Bank of France were in trouble, but not of the most serious kind. There was no panic and no dramatic catastrophe. Seven years later there was panic and catastrophe enough in England during the great crisis of 1825. It followed that notorious period of over trading and crazy speculation, in which, as the story goes[1], skates and warming-pans were exported to Rio, and loans were subscribed on behalf of a fictitious South American republic —one of the classic follies of blind capital. From the European side, its interest lies in the loan of nearly £2,000,000 made by the Bank of France to the Bank of England, when the latter was in the gravest difficulties, an instance of cooperation between "natural enemies," which an earlier generation could hardly have conceived. Incidentally the loan illustrates the strength and excellent management of the Bank of France.

Thirteen years later (1838–9) the interdependence of nations was shown on a wider and more varied field. The United States was in continuous financial and commercial unrest from 1837 to 1839. There had been over issue of paper money, and a politico-economic struggle between President Jackson and the Bank of the United States. There were fluctuating cotton prices and suspensions of cash payment by the Bank of the United States and many lesser banks. Finally came the winding up of the Bank of the United States, and the loss of £6,000,000 of European capital invested in America. The reactions of America's cotton troubles were felt in London, Liverpool, Antwerp, Havre and Hamburg. Leading English firms which traded with America went down in 1837. Deeply involved in the same troubles, and herself just concluding a period of eager and not always sound company promotion, diversified by the conflict between the *Société Générale* and the *Banque de Belgique*, Belgium saw the *Banque* suspend payment in 1838. In 1839 England felt the strain both from Belgium and America, since Belgian financiers turned to the Bank of England for aid. Its reserves ran low, and again it got help from the Bank of France, through the Barings. There was trouble that year also in Hamburg.

[1] The story of the skates is told by McCulloch (*Political Economy*, 2nd ed., p. 329) of 1808.

France had not been spared. The powerful firm of Hottinguer in Paris had been involved in the cotton speculations of Mr Biddle of the United States Bank, and had to suspend payments. But cotton meant less to France than to England; no large part of the European capital lost in America was French; and once more the Bank of France showed judgment and strength.

With the forties came railway building and railway speculation, national and international, followed by bad harvests and by that European failure of the potato crops which, in the British Isles, produced the great Irish famine. The potato failure began in 1845 when corn harvests were short. In 1846 harvests were bad everywhere. In 1847 the English harvest was satisfactory, but that of France was bad and that of Germany very bad. So, when 1848 opened, all Europe was restless and hungry. It was also in financial difficulties. The unprecedented deficit in the harvests required unprecedented imports from long distances—South Russia and America. These had to be paid for, and the payment drained away gold. There were sharp price fluctuations; and, in England particularly, speculative dealings in foodstuffs aggravated the situation on its financial side. The crisis of 1847 began in England with failures among the corn importers. It was made worse because masses of capital locked up in railways had not yet begun to yield a return. Some of it would never yield a return. In France there had been far less railway building, and better regulated. The food situation was less serious than in the United Kingdom, though heavy imports were required in 1846–7. To help finance these, the Bank of France borrowed a million in England, at the beginning of 1847. But France escaped the panic, the wholesale mercantile failures, and the collapse of banks which occurred in England in October 1847. The short suspension of cash payments by the French banks in 1848 (see *ante*, § 32) was due almost entirely to the Revolution of that year, though the outbreak of the Revolution found French finances weakened by the strain of the year before.

These recurring commercial and financial troubles showed with growing clearness how the Western nations were becoming

members one of another. But it was not until the troubles of
1857, after the forces which were knitting them together had
been at work for another decade, that their solidarity was fully
realised.

§ 36. In spite of financial vicissitudes, Europe had not to
undergo, during the early nineteenth century, that most dis-
turbing of all economic revolutions, a marked change in the
purchasing power of money. France had recovered from her
trouble with the *assignats* before 1815. From 1815 to 1850
prices fluctuated violently, but about a fairly steady mean level.
Local price variations were, of course, very much greater than
in the late nineteenth century. No one country even was
approximately a single market for bulky or perishable goods.
These local prices were liable to abrupt changes, when a harvest
failed, for example, or when road, canal or, later, an early railway
linked up a low price area to some great market, and brought its
prices up to metropolitan level. But if metropolitan prices
were taken, or if a curve of ideal national mean prices were
constructed, by combining local and metropolitan prices for
a series of years, the steadiness of the mean level would probably
be remarkable.

Its general trend from 1815 to 1850, judging from the English
facts, would be slightly downward. It was an age of low output
for both precious metals, and of rapid increase in all kinds of
consumable goods. True, the work of the precious metals was
being continuously eased by the growing use of notes, cheques
(in England), and other credit documents. But for this, the
quantity of goods purchasable with a given amount of gold or
silver might have increased greatly, or in other words prices
might have greatly fallen. As things were, the downward movement of mean prices, in the great centres of trade, was not
enough to be perceptible to the business man with attention
concentrated on the short period fluctuations; and therefore was
not enough to exert that dragging influence on business enterprise, which is often found in an age when prices are falling so
sharply and continuously as to make everyone conscious of
the fact.

Again, although there were terrible year to year vicissitudes in the cost of living, there was not a marked and continuous movement in one direction or the other—no movement of the kind so familiar to the sixteenth century or to the years since 1914. It was just as well. There were abundant sources of social distress and bitterness. Short period fluctuations in the cost of living, in the years 1845–8, helped to bring Europe quite near enough to a general social upheaval. Had a more profound and more obscure fluctuation, due to monetary conditions, also been in progress, things must have been worse, worst of all where wage labour was most fully developed, that is in England.

CHAPTER VII

THE MAKING OF THE FIRST RAILWAY AND TELEGRAPH NETWORK, 1830—1869

§ 37. A historian once said that, when Sir Robert Peel was called from Rome to London in December 1834 to preside over an exceedingly short-lived ministry, he travelled no quicker than one of Agricola's couriers might have travelled, when taking back to Rome news of his master's British victories. Peel had an easier journey, because the roads all the way were in his time, as the French say, "coachable." They had just been made so, though probably he had some bad stretches on the Italian side. At that date, in Peel's country, the Stockton and Darlington and the Manchester and Liverpool railways had been open for some years, and progress had been made with the London and Birmingham and other trunk lines. On the continent, two or three short but rather unimportant lines were open, and one short but important line was nearing completion. This line was not on Peel's route. It ran from Brussels to Malines. Opened in May 1835, it carried over half a million passengers in its first year—actually more than were carried on all the English lines in 1835. The fact is significant. In some ways Belgium led Europe in railway building. She was ahead of all the continent in ordered construction, and ahead of England in that she had a railway policy, when England was fumbling for a policy which she never found.

The beginnings of the coal-mine tramway, which preceded the railway proper on the continent as in England, are of no great interest. There was one at Anzin early in the century, and others among the Belgian mines, besides the tramway at the Liège cannon foundry mentioned in a previous chapter. No sooner was Belgium a nation—she became a nation, it will be recalled, in the year the Manchester and Liverpool was opened—than her press began to fill with railway schemes. The first suggestion was a direct line from Antwerp to Cologne, which, in the form then proposed, was never built. Next year the Minister of the Interior began to have plans made. At once the question arose of state *versus* private railways. There were no precedents, so Belgium had to make her own. She was one of the few countries, at that time, in which private capital and private enterprise might not unreasonably have been expected to create a railway system; so that it really was an open issue. But after discussion in Parliament, during the autumn of 1833, it was decided, partly for the glory of the young state, partly because the government was resolute that the whole work must be carried out systematically, that the projected Belgian railways should be a national undertaking. The scheme was voted with acclamation (1st May, 1834), and put in hand without delay. There is no doubt that "this magnificent project," as the first and greatest English scientific writer[1] on railways called it, raised the prestige of Belgium, as the Belgians had hoped it would.

Belgium meant to exploit the advantages of her position as a land of passage. Her railway system should begin with a cross, linking, north and south, Antwerp, Malines, Brussels, Mons and France; east and west, Ostend, Bruges, Ghent, Malines, Louvain, Liège and Germany. Malines was the point of intersection. There were to be branches, on the western arm, from Ghent towards Lille *via* Courtrai, and from Ghent northwards to Antwerp; on the eastern arm, from Tirlemont to St Trond; and on the southern from Braine-le-Comte to Charleroi and eventually to Namur. So Belgium would link up England, France, Germany and Holland, by 347 miles of railway, and draw across her territory the trade of all. Lebeau and Rogier, the two men mainly responsible for the policy, deserved well of their country. It was a simple but brilliant plan.

Part of it was executed quickly. By May 1836, the line was open from Brussels to Antwerp. By January of the next year, the western main line was working from Malines to Termonde. Forty-five more miles of the system were opened in 1837, and seventy-one miles in 1838. By 1844 the original plan was approximately

---

[1] Dionysius Lardner, *Railway Economy: a Treatise on the New Art of Transport*, 1850, p. 416. This chapter owes a great deal to Lardner.

complete. Engineering difficulties, very formidable for those days, had been successfully overcome on the eastern arm, including a tunnel more than half a mile long and the crossing of a watershed five hundred feet high. "The extraordinary expedition with which the Belgian rail roads were completed," wrote Lardner in 1850, "has been mainly caused by the circumstance of their having been executed by the state, and the execution being conducted under the superintendence of a special railway committee, invested with adequate powers. By this expedient innumerable official formalities were avoided." Lardner no doubt had in mind the private bill procedure of the British Parliament, and the vacillations of British railway policy, in the forties.

The Belgian state system proved far more expensive than was originally contemplated. When all the original lines were open to traffic, the state had spent £5,373,000 on them or, say, £16,500 a mile. The expenditure beyond estimate was natural, as the whole standard of railway construction altered while the work was in progress. The light rails, wooden bridges, and 10 h.p. locomotives of the original project, were out of date long before the eastern line had been pushed over the difficult country between Louvain and Liège. Yet some profit could always be shown. If it was not always a commercial profit, not enough to cover the interest on the railway loans, the government could point to the indirect gain to the country resulting from a long-sighted and rapidly applied policy—the 50 per cent. rise in Belgian imports between 1836 and 1845; the 100 per cent. rise in coal production between 1835 and 1845; the more than 800 per cent. rise in the export of cast iron during the same period. Moreover, by 1853, the state lines could show a profit of 5 per cent., enough to cover interest. By that time, however, the railway administration was showing signs of ossification. No fresh state enterprise was undertaken in the twenty years from 1850 to 1870; and by the latter date the government lines measured not much more than a quarter of the Belgian railway system (800–900 kilometres out of 3000).

There had never been official opposition to private enterprise. Concessions were being sought as early as 1832. But, except for a number of short private coal-field lines, none of the early projects came to anything. The first concession to a company for a public line was made in 1842. Then came English capital, English contractors, and English engineers with experience gained at home. The air was full of projects. Yet by January 1847, there were not much more than thirty miles of privately constructed line open for general traffic. The next three years saw more rapid progress, so that by the beginning of 1850 about 160 kilometres were open, and about as much more in hand. Twenty years later, there were some 2100 km. of private line, consolidated, as in England, under strong companies, no longer merely branches and feeders of the central state system, as they had originally been. That system remained almost stationary, and found itself engaged after 1856 in the ordinary courtesies of railway competition in the mid-nineteenth century—rate wars, discriminations, and other devices to attract traffic. But these things are not so much an epilogue to the early history of Belgian railways as a prologue to the later history, which begins with extensive purchases of the competing private lines by the state in 1870.

§ 38. During the period before 1825–30, a large number of horse-worked railway lines were constructed in England, especially on the South Wales coal-field and in other industrial areas. In France there was a similar development before the days of the locomotive, on the coal-field of St Etienne. In February 1823, a royal ordinance authorised the construction of about fifteen miles of line from St Etienne to Andrézieux on the upper Loire. Three years later, the linking of St Etienne to Lyons and the Rhone was authorised. Then in 1832 came the first locomotive, as an outcome of the world-wide excitement at the success of the Manchester and Liverpool. It ran from Lyons to St Etienne and it dragged passengers as well as goods. Parliament took fire; opened a credit of £20,000 for the study of railway questions; and decided that no railway concessions should in the future be given by royal authority only. It reserved them to itself. Having reserved them, it began to consider the matter deliberately.

The widespread scepticism as to the possibilities of railway transport by locomotive, which was only overcome with difficulty in England, extended in France to leading statesmen. When public opinion, and the pertinacity of the promoter, Emile Pereire, extorted from Parliament a concession for the line from Paris to St Germain in 1835, Thiers is credited with a remark which has become classical: "Il faut donner ça à Paris, comme un joujou; mais ça ne transportera jamais un voyageur ni un colis." Next year the line to Versailles was given, on the same principle apparently. Then Parliament settled down to discussions of immense length and great interest on what would now be called the question of nationalisation. Various far reaching projects were quashed, because the Houses were not satisfied with the principles on which they were based. There was, for instance, a scheme put forward officially, in 1835, for a line from Paris to Rouen and Havre. Private companies were to do the work, but the state was to give assistance by taking shares in them. The scheme was rejected. In 1837 came a more ambitious proposal, for lines from Paris to Havre, to the Belgian frontier beyond Valenciennes, and to Tours; and for a line from Lyons to Marseilles. It was over this proposal that the greatest discussions of principle took place. Lamartine, the most eloquent advocate of construction by the state, spoke of the dangers, political, economic and strategic, of placing in private hands control over the unknown powers of the new age. He revived the battle cries of 1789. He denounced the new feudalism and the railway barons who would impudently levy toll on the trade of France. Echoing a speech of Mirabeau, he pictured the deadly *agiotage* (stock-jobbing) that would surely follow the creation of a mass of privately-owned securities. "Que l'État fasse seul, que l'État possède seul...car, un jour, au moins, vous pouvez donner vos lignes au peuple pour qui tout doit être fait[1]." Thus he summed up his position, a few years later. Against him were the professed economists, advocating private enterprise and *laissez faire*, and suspicious of the delays and political dangers of state construction, under a Parliament not too pure. And with them were the promoters and men of affairs.

[1] Quoted in Guillaumot, *L'organisation des chemins de fer en France* (1899), p. 7.

It was generally agreed, however, that, without a considerable measure of state control and some state assistance, France could not hope to create a railway system appropriate to her economic and political requirements. Gradually discussion narrowed itself down to the form and amount of state assistance. No government was prepared to carry the financial responsibility of a complete state system; though some of the schemes assumed state construction of main lines.

No result was reached in 1837, nor yet in 1838, in spite of commissions and fresh projects. Meanwhile a certain number of concessions were given for short lines of obvious local utility, the state assisting in various ways. It made a loan to the company which was to build a line from Alais to Beaucaire in 1837. It guaranteed interest for the Paris-Orleans line in 1840. It helped young companies, when they got into trouble; and itself undertook the construction of the line from the Belgian frontier to Valenciennes, when it became obvious that Valenciennes must be linked to the new Belgian system. As a result of all this, there were from 350 to 360 miles of railway of various sorts open in France in 1841.

At length, by the law of June 1842, an agreement on principle was reached. A national railway programme was drawn up. With Paris as centre, lines were to radiate to the Channel ports and Belgium; to Nancy and Strasbourg; to Lyons and Marseilles; to the Spanish frontier at the east end of the Pyrenees *via* Bourges and Toulouse; to the same frontier at the west end *via* Tours and Bordeaux; to Rouen and Havre; to Nantes and so to Brest. There were also to be lines from Marseilles to Bordeaux and from Dijon to Mulhouse. Government was to find the land, local authorities furnishing two-thirds of the cost, and to construct the road-bed (the *infra-structure*), including bridges and tunnels. Companies were to furnish the *super-structure*, *i.e.* rails and ballast and station equipment, rolling stock and working capital. The local authorities disliked their share of the burden, which was removed in 1845. There remained the state and the companies. For some lines companies were easily found, companies which in several cases were ready to do more than their minimum share of the work. The state, being short of funds, in time acquiesced. For other lines it was hard to find a company at all. On these the state began operations in hope of finding one later.

So the long debated principles of the law of 1842 were never applied as designed. What remained, through these and other changes, was *first*—the general principle of state cooperation, carrying with it a reserved right of ownership by the state; *second*—the principle of state control over the geographical plan of the system; *third*—the full recognition from the first of the state's right to supervise rates, insist on safeguards for travellers, and have its representatives in the counsels of the companies.

The Revolution of 1848 found the position thus. There were from thirty to forty companies in existence, dealing with various sections of the national programme. Many of them were now under obligation to do the whole work themselves, the state retaining merely a right to buy back the lines. The financial troubles which occurred in France, as in England, during 1847 had left several of these companies in grave distress. The Paris-Orleans and Paris-Lyons companies were practically insolvent. Consequently, the new National Assembly proposed to revert to the policy of Lamartine; close on the insolvent companies which could not fulfil their contracts; buy out the rest; and start a complete state system. But government was not strong enough even to make a beginning. The only piece of railway legislation of the years 1848–52 was the concession to a company of the line from Paris to Rennes. The state gave the company what was coming to be recognised as the most useful form of assistance, a guarantee of interest.

By that time over 2000 miles of railway were open; but for lack of willing companies, 360 miles were being worked by the state. The whole position was confused and unsatisfactory. The companies were too numerous for efficiency. The trunk lines projected in 1842 were far from complete. The western line, intended for Brest, was not open much beyond Chartres. South of Tours the south-western line was incomplete; south of Bordeaux it was not begun. The line intended for the east end of the Pyrenees had not yet got into the difficult country of

Auvergne. What is now the P.-L.-M. was in a very complicated situation. It was open from Paris to Dijon and Chalons-sur-Saône, though the original Paris-Lyons company had collapsed. At the other end there was a line from Marseilles to Avignon, of which the state had borne most of the cost. The section Chalons-Lyons was making progress; but little had been done on the section Lyons-Avignon. Further north the Strasbourg line was more forward. The first section to Chalons-sur-Marne, built by the state and leased to a company as originally contemplated, was open before 1848. The Chalons-Nancy section came into operation in 1851-2, and the final Vosges section was at that time well forward. Nothing had been done on the cross country lines from Marseilles to Bordeaux and Dijon to Mulhouse; but in the north, under an efficient company, travel to both Calais and Belgium was possible, and a few important branch lines had been constructed.

The Second Empire saw the completion of the original French railway network. A first step towards completion was the amalgamation of the companies controlling successive sections of one main route. The success of the Northern company, the first developed of the existing great companies, furnished an object lesson. In 1852-3 fusions were going on fast, with the approval and encouragement of the state. It was now anxious to have strong companies, because it wished to bargain for the construction by them of subsidiary lines, in return for the concessions of the trunk routes and any government assistance which might go with those concessions. By 1857 the process of concentration was complete. The state had no longer any lines in hand. All the trunk lines throughout France were controlled by six great companies, each with its recognised area, like that of the North-Eastern which had just come into existence in England. They were the North, East, West, P.-L.-M., Orleans and Southern. Inside the areas there was no competition. Except that of the Southern, they were, roughly, triangles with apex at Paris and base on the frontiers. As part of the bargain between these great new companies and the Imperial Government, the concessions were extended; but a point of time in the future was always con-

templated at which the whole property would fall in to the
state. The stronger companies, like that of the North, needed
no financial help; but some of the others secured a guarantee
of interest. In return for its various favours, the state not only
required the companies to build a subsidiary network of lines
at their own charges, but also overhauled rates and fares in the
interests of the public and of its own traffic.

Unfortunately the world-wide commercial crisis of 1857-8
came just when these agreements had been entered into. The
companies demanded reconsideration. Either they must be
relieved of the burden of new construction, now beyond their
strength, or some further assistance must be given. The state,
unwilling to abandon the hope of national development by
means of subsidiary lines, accepted the second alternative.
It fell back on a general policy of guaranteed interest, plus the
right to a share in profits when profits reached an agreed level.
A series of agreements, called the Franqueville conventions,
after their author, were completed in 1859. Under these all
lines were classed into two groups, the old and the new networks.
The guarantee applied only to lines of the new network, of which
each company had its appropriate share. But if the profits of
the old network got beyond a fixed level, they were to flow over,
as from a full cistern, into the accounts of the new network,
thus reducing the liability of the state on the latter. Then,
when profits on old and new networks had reached other fixed
levels—6 per cent. on the new, 8 per cent. on the old—the
state was to share in them. It was also entitled to repayment
of any sums advanced under the guarantee, with interest on the
advances at 4 per cent.

But the right of the state to share in profits was not to begin
until 1872; and before 1872 things had happened which dislocated all this ingenious financial machinery. Ingenuity was
perhaps more conspicuous than wisdom; for it is easy to imagine
the accounting difficulties which resulted from the system of
the two "networks," each with its budget, difficulties which
were a standing temptation to fraud on the part of the companies, who naturally—to take but one illustration—wished
to increase the content of the "old network" cistern before

allowing anything to flow from it into the cistern of the state.

The two strongest companies, the North and the P.-L.-M., had not to call upon the state to make good its guarantee. The North had always been strong. The P.-L.-M., which stepped into the bankrupt heritage of the old Paris-Lyons, and got its main line through to the Mediterranean open in 1855, had become strong before the date of the Franqueville conventions. The Eastern company was less immediately successful, because, although its main lines were paying, it had subsidiaries in unprofitable country like the Argonne and the Ardennes. But the Southern and the Western were the lines which gave most trouble to the successive governments of France.

The Franqueville conventions of 1859 were supplemented by a series of conventions in the years 1863-9. These dealt with a variety of topics such as:—the re-classification of the "networks," by transferring lines from one to the other; the demarcation of the territorial areas of the different companies as fresh lines were constructed; additions to the new network as extra lines became necessary. Most important of all was a general agreement, by which the companies were to receive the same financial favours as they already enjoyed in connection with expenditure on the "new network," for large additional expenditure on the "old network," in order to make it more efficient for purposes of traffic. As may be supposed, the financial details of all these agreements were excessively complex.

Summarising the railway work of the Second Empire, it may be said that in its early years (1852-60) the 1842 programme of trunk lines was completed, almost as originally planned, together with a considerable number of subsidiary lines; that in its later years the trunk lines were modernised and further additions made to the subsidiaries; so that the French railway map of 1870 contained most of the main features of the map as it was in the twentieth century. A number of minor lines were authorised outside the control of the six great companies. They usually received assistance from the state, but not a guarantee. Of these the most important was the Victor

Emmanuel Company, which made the Mont Cenis tunnel in
the sixties; but this company was taken over by the P.-L.-M.
in 1867. There is no need to insist on its economic significance.
Finally, it may be noted that all this work of concession and
consolidation was not parliamentary, owing to the constitutional
situation under the Empire. When in its last days the Empire
tried to liberalise itself, Parliament claimed the exclusive right
to make concessions for all but the most local and insignificant
lines. The law containing the claim was of July 27, 1870.
France had declared war eight days before.

§ 39. When France got her great trunk lines open under
Napoleon III, Germany, so Treitschke used to boast, had had
her main lines in operation for a decade[1]. "In this peaceful
contest she was far ahead of all continental nations, with the
sole exception of Belgium, ahead both of centralised France and
of wealthy Holland." "It was the railways which first dragged
the nation from its economic stagnation; they ended what the
Zollverein had only begun; with such power did they break in
upon all the old habits of life, that already in the forties the
aspect of Germany was completely changed." There is a dash
of exaggeration in all this; but Germans may be justifiably proud
of an achievement which was the more remarkable because their
country had at that time no central government and no great
reserves of capital.

Some German business men, statesmen, and thinkers, had
occupied themselves with the railway question at an early date.
From 1825 onwards Fritz Harkort, a Westphalian manufacturer,
was pressing railway projects on an incredulous and generally
hostile public. In 1828 Motz, the creator of the Zollverein,
had considered a scheme for a line from the Rhine to the Weser,
in order to avoid the Dutch Rhine tolls. King Ludwig of
Bavaria was passionately interested in railway talk, and sent
engineers to England, France and Belgium in the early thirties
to make inquiry. He brushed aside the assertion of the Bavarian
College of Physicians that railway travel would give horrible head-
aches to both travellers and spectators[2]. He had the satisfaction

---

[1] *Deutsche Geschichte*, IV, 581–2.
[2] The story may be a legend. No memorandum in this sense has been
found in the College archives. Schnabel, *Deutsche Geschichte*, III, 435 (1934).

of knowing, in December 1835, that the first German railway had been opened in his kingdom[1]. It was the five mile suburban line from Nuremberg to Fürth. The distance was covered in fifteen minutes by steam and in twenty-five with horse traction. But it was reserved for Friedrich List, just returned from America, to conceive and advocate with restless energy the idea of a German railway system. It is all laid out in his pamphlet published at Leipzig in 1833—"Of a Saxon railway system as foundation for a general German system." He sketched in nearly all the lines as they were afterwards built. He foresaw, though no Prussian, that the bulk of the lines would radiate from Berlin—six was his number, and six there were twenty years later. Also he attained his immediate object. A company was created to build a line from Leipzig to Dresden. The Saxon government was helpful but took no real part in the enterprise. Within six years (April 1839) the line was at work, and it carried 412,000 people in its first year, including ladies who kept needles between their lips to check familiarity in the single tunnel.

List had been thrown over by the Leipzig business men at an early stage. So he founded a railway journal to spread his views, and went to Magdeburg to interest people there in the extension of the Saxon line, which he saw as a piece of a trunk line from Prague to Hamburg. The Magdeburgers approached the Prussian government. They found the officials suspicious. Having sanctioned a short line near Düsseldorf, and a Berlin-Potsdam suburban connection, they were hesitating over several large schemes recently put forward, including one for a great north-south line strongly backed by Bavaria. Their hesitation is explicable, when it is recalled that Prussia proper was still very badly equipped with roads. One large section of Pomerania (*Vorpommern*) did not contain a single made road. The officials naturally spoke of doing one thing at a time. A report had been put in to prove that there was not trade enough on any of the routes suggested to justify a single railway line. The Minister of Posts was stiff in opposition; he saw all his arrangements upset. So was the leading general of engineers; he said

---

[1] An experimental line had been laid at Elberfeld in 1826.

railways would be of no use in war. The King thought quick
travel should be reserved for gentlemen; but the Crown Prince
(the future Frederick William IV) was a railway enthusiast. He
was always an enthusiast of one kind or another.

In consequence of ministerial coolness, the first Prussian
railway law, compiled before any important line on Prussian
territory had been made, and issued in Nov. 1838, was rather
unsympathetic towards private enterprise and did not con-
template immediate state action. Yet, considering how little
was then known of railways, its provisions were far-sighted and
at least tended to prevent bubble projects and wasteful competing lines.

In spite of official suspicions, however, the Magdeburg
project was allowed to go forward. The necessary funds were
raised with comparative ease; and by August 1840 the Magdeburg-Leipzig line was open to traffic. It paid a dividend that
year. Meanwhile a number of other companies had come into
existence under the terms of the new law—Düsseldorf-Elber-
feld, Berlin-Köthen (Köthen is on the Magdeburg-Leipzig),
Berlin-Stettin. After 1840 the suspicions of government were
allayed, and the work of concession-granting went on rapidly.
The Prussian state even began to give some direct assistance to
railway building. It took shares in or guaranteed interest on the
Berlin-Köthen and the Berlin-Stettin. After 1842 it became
bolder and, finding the exchequer full, planned over a thousand
miles of necessary line, to expedite the construction of which
it was now prepared to offer a guarantee of interest to the constructing companies, whenever the prospects of any given
railway were not good enough to attract capital without
guarantee. Among the lines now planned were the Rhine-Weser,
to link those river basins; the Thuringian line, to do for the
railway systems what the great Thuringian highway had done
for the roads, *i.e.* link Prussia with the south; the Frankfurt-
on-Oder-Breslau, which, together with the Berlin-Frankfurt and
Upper Silesian lines already in hand, would join the capital to
the coal-fields and the delicate strategical area of Upper Silesia;
a Posen line for Prussian Poland; and the great Eastern line
running through the Prussias. The results of this change of

front by the state are clearly shown in the figures of line open for traffic on Prussian territory. They are

$$
\begin{array}{l}
\text{1844 about 500 miles} \\
\text{1848 \quad,, \quad 1500 \quad,,} \\
\text{1860 \quad,, \quad 3500 \quad,,}
\end{array}
$$

The western and southern German states followed the Belgian rather than the Prussian example. The first state railway in Germany was a short stretch of line opened in Brunswick in 1838. In 1842 the Hanoverian state made up its mind to take part in the general development of the German railways, lest trade should be diverted from its territory, which was crossed by the natural routes from Berlin to the lower Rhine and from Hamburg and Bremen to the south. It concerned itself at first only with the east-west route, and had opened about 150 miles of line before 1848. Every line in Hanover was built by the state down to its annexation by Prussia in 1866. Bavaria began with private lines; but as very little progress had been made by 1844, the state stepped in and did all the work itself for the next twelve years, when a period of speculation threw up a number of private companies. Wurtemberg, after long delays, decided for state action in 1845; but its first line was not opened until 1850. Baden also decided on a state system; opened the first stretch of the Rhine-valley line (Heidelberg-Karlsruhe) in 1843, and pushed it southward to the Swiss frontier in the next three years. Of the lesser states it need only be said, that the free commercial city of Frankfurt not only found, through its citizens, much capital for private railway enterprise, but as a state became part owner (with Hesse-Cassel) of the very important Main-Weser railway, which linked the Main to Hanover and the north.

For comparison with the early railway achievement of France, consider the situation in Germany in 1849–50. There were about 3000 miles of line open on what was in 1914 the territory of the German Empire (excluding Alsace-Lorraine), and over 1000 miles more on Austrian territory, compared with 2000 in France (including Alsace-Lorraine) a year or two later. The German through routes were much further advanced than the French. Starting from Munich there was continuous railway communication on to the Saxon system and so to Leipzig. Starting from Bâle there was communication down the Rhine valley to Mainz. The Rhine narrows from Mainz to Bonn were not yet provided with a line. At Leipzig a traveller from the south struck the almost completed trunk lines of northern Germany. From Leipzig he could go to Berlin. From Berlin to Hamburg; or to Magdeburg, Hanover, Düsseldorf and the lower Rhine; or to Halle, Weimar and Cassel; or to Frankfurt on the Oder and so all the way down Silesia to Cracow and Teschen; or to Stettin and the Baltic and thence, a roundabout route, to Posen. The great eastern line from Berlin to Bromberg and the Vistula, and so to Danzig and Königsberg, was not yet in hand.

From Hanover the traveller could not only get to the lower Rhine, to Düsseldorf and Cologne; he could also go direct either to Bremen or to Harburg, on the left bank of the Elbe opposite Hamburg. The now very important southern line from Hanover through Göttingen and Cassel, and so to the Main valley, was not at this time available. Whereas a traveller arriving in France from overseas at Calais, Havre, Brest or Bordeaux, in 1850, could not have got through by rail to any point on the French north-eastern, eastern, or southern frontiers, a traveller arriving at Bremen, Hamburg or Stettin could cross Germany to Cracow or Prague, and could get within easy distance of the western frontier near Cologne, and of the southern frontier near Munich.

It has been seen that there was a considerable amount of railway open on Austrian territory before 1850, linked to the lines of what was to be the German Empire in the north. But the Austrian through routes were not at that time quite complete. Much of the great south line from Vienna to Trieste was finished; but the final difficult bit of mountainous country from Laibach to Trieste had not been tackled. The north main line from Vienna into upper Silesia was built, and so was the line to Prague; which connected with the Saxon system at Dresden. In short, communication was very nearly complete from the North Sea and the Baltic to the Adriatic. As there were no railways of importance on Swiss territory at this time; as the question of an Alpine tunnel was not faced until the sixties; and as the few railways existing in Italy before 1859 were all isolated fragments, linked to nothing, this system of Germanic lines which ended at Laibach was by far the most remarkable piece of continuous railway in Europe.

It is not necessary to follow out in detail the rapidly increasing density of the German railway network between 1850 and 1866. There were no important changes in the principles of railway policy. Prussia exercised a close supervision over all projects, so as to avoid wasteful competition and provide adequately for economic and strategic necessities. Under Moltke, her War Staff thoroughly understood what use the army could make of a properly controlled railway system. Encouragement of essential lines was carried out, as before, by guarantees of interest or other financial devices. But the Prussian government continued to rely mainly on private enterprise to raise the capital and carry on the business management of the railways. Prussia's chief western and southern neighbours relied mainly on the national exchequer as before. Not until Hanover and Hesse-Cassel were annexed in 1866 did the Prussian state own much railway line. Those annexations, followed by that of Alsace-Lorraine in 1871, form the prelude to the railway history of the German Empire; for in no sphere do economics and politics blend more completely than in that of railway policy.

The revolutionary effects of the railway on a country such as Germany was in the early nineteenth century need little emphasis. For eastern Germany at any rate, parallels must be looked for in the railway history of Russia, rather than in that of France or England. Treitschke's saying that the railway changed the whole face of the land was certainly true by the end of the forties. In a country whose road system was still new and very imperfect, and whose towns were almost without exception small and half rural, its revolutionary influence was far more conspicuous than in older developed and more urbanised lands. There was something American about it, just as there was a technical likeness between German and American railway methods. Like America, Germany had got her railways quickly and cheap. Land was cheap in the first place. "The vast expenditure for earth work and costly works of art, such as viaducts, bridges, and tunnels, by which vallies are bestridden and mountains pierced to gain a straight and level line in the English system have not been attempted," Lardner wrote in 1850. "The railways have been carried more nearly along the natural level of the country." They "have been constructed on principles analogous to those which have been found to answer so well in America." The average cost of the lines opened by 1850 was put at less than £11,000 a mile, compared with £16,500 in Belgium, and with an estimated £30–40,000 in England. English estimates were difficult to frame, because many companies were floated only to sink and some lines begun but not finished. There was little of all this in Germany, where state control prevented the haphazard methods of England in the forties.

The German lines did, however, follow the Leipzig-Dresden in adopting Stephenson's narrow English gauge—"for mere love of imitation...and to the damage of travellers' nerves," as Treitschke said[1]. It was in all probability an error. Brunel's broad gauge would have suited German conditions better; but Brunel was never called in to advise, Stephenson was.

§ 40. The electric telegraph first appeared in all countries as an adjunct to the railway. Its predecessor, the cross country line of semaphore poles, with arms like those of the modern railway signal which is descended from it, had come into use in France in 1793–4, when it sent military news from the frontier with unheard-of speed. The inventor, Claude Chappe, died in 1805. The British Admiralty built such lines along the Portsmouth, Plymouth and Harwich roads—predecessors of the existing Admiralty wireless. In Louis Philippe's reign France had 5000 kilometres of the system. Prussia used it extensively. Berlin could get an answer from Coblenz within four hours and, with the help of couriers, from Petersburg in fifty. But the system was expensive. Each pole needed an operator, as readers of the *Adventures of the Count of Monte Cristo* may remember. Signalling in thick weather was impossible. In all countries the system was reserved for

---

[1] *Deutsche Geschichte*, IV, 589.

government. It is said that when the Berliners saw the wooden arms waving all day on the building in the Dorotheenstrasse, then they knew that times were bad.

Meanwhile men of science everywhere had been probing the powers of electricity. In 1833 two German professors—Gauss and Weber—linked the Göttingen observatory with the physical laboratory, by way of the spire of St John's Church and a wire a thousand yards long. Weber offered his invention to the Leipzig-Dresden railway in 1836, but it was declined.

That same year, Morse in America invented the method and apparatus which was, when perfected, to drive all others out of the field. After that the adoption of telegraphy was astonishingly quick. In the forties land lines spread all over Europe, to be followed in the fifties by the submarine cables. "Whilst I am writing these pages," said Lardner with natural awe in 1850, "projects are in progress for electric communication on a scale still more extensive and having objects the importance of which it is difficult to estimate. It is proposed to establish electric wires between London and the Continent." Beyond this "startling project," "it is said that at New York a proposition has been made to establish electric wires between New York and England, by sinking them to the bottom of the Atlantic."

In fact the first underwater line had been laid two years earlier by Werner von Siemens in Kiel harbour[1]. It was in connection with submarine mines. The year after Lardner wrote, the Dover-Calais cable was at work. Similar cables were rapidly laid in all the narrow seas of Europe in the fifties. Then in the sixties, after infinite labour, came cables "sunk to the bottom of the Atlantic," and with them the age in which the world shrank into a single market.

[1] According to P. D. Fischer in Conrad's *Handwörterbuch*, VII, 1153.

CHAPTER VIII

RURAL FRANCE, 1848–1914

§ 41. When Léopold Delisle wrote, in 1852, of how little French agriculture had changed since the thirteenth century, France had several railways but no railway system. In the next ten years the railways grew into a system and the telegraph came. French agriculture did not forthwith cease to be in many ways medieval. It has medieval features to this day. (See *post*, §49.) But forces were set free vastly more powerful than had ever played upon it, forces capable of doing in decades what under all previous conditions might have taken centuries. Within ten years of Delisle's pronouncement, Léonce de Lavergne wrote his *Economie rurale de la France*, a book which was used in an earlier chapter to illustrate the relative immobility of French agriculture down to the fifties[1]. But all through the book the whistle of the locomotive can be heard. Lavergne writes, it may be, of Berri where things have changed hardly at all since Perrette went to market with her milk on her head in *cotillon simple et souliers plats*, and where the *bonshommes* live on in the old way. Yet now, he tells us, since the rail has come, things begin to move and they will move faster soon. So it is of whatever district he writes; and although he praises almost extravagantly what the roads have done, it is clear that he expects far more from the rail. The grain-carrying ocean tramp and the cold-storage steamer he does not foresee.

Fifty years later, a French writer selected the years about 1860 as the turning point in modern French agrarian history. "Already they knew something of foreign competition, of the use of machines, of rising costs of production. But what to-day seems obvious was then at most descried by far-sighted observers. Agriculture was still, in spite of undoubted technical improvements, intensely traditional, marked by the predominance of manual work and by a resigned submission to the...caprice of

[1] First edition, 1860: "to-day" for Lavergne is 1857–9.

nature[1]." The foreign competition, the use of machinery, and the rising costs of production which M. Augé-Laribé picked out as characteristics of the latest age, are all intimately connected with those improvements in the means of transport, which drew land nearer to land, drew the country nearer to the constantly developing engineering and chemical industries of the towns, and called for greater expenditure of capital and effort by the cultivator, who, if he was a hirer of labour, had to bid against the employers of these now easily accessible towns.

During the half century 1860–1910 France, alone among the greater western nations, retained her predominantly rural character. But the rural side of her national life was losing ground. The economic and social forces tending to a more complete urbanisation were so strong, that not even France's inadequate coal supplies, wonderful climate, and landowning peasantry could prevent her following the same road as her neighbours. After 1850 the movement was relatively rapid. It was pointed out, in discussing French industries in an earlier chapter, that between 1801 and 1851 the percentage of the population of France dwelling in towns of more than 20,000 inhabitants only grew from 6·75 to 10·6. By 1891 the figure had risen to 21·1; by 1911 it was 26·0. From about 1875 the population classed as rural began to decline absolutely, the total population growing slowly. In 1846, before the railways had begun to tell, the total population (including Alsace-Lorraine) was 35,400,000; the rural population was 26,750,000 or 75·6 per cent. of the whole. By 1866 the percentage had fallen to 69·5. The course of events under the Third Republic was as follows:

	Total population	Rural population	Percentage
1876	36,900,000	24,900,000	67·6
1886	38,200,000	24,450,000	64·1
1896	38,500,000	23,500,000	60·9
1906	39,250,000	22,700,000	57·9
1911	39,600,000	22,100,000	55·9

The rural population in French statistics is the population living in communes whose *chef lieu* contains less than 2000 inhabitants. The test is necessarily rough. In the south

[1] M. Augé-Laribé, *L'évolution de la France agricole*, 1912; a book to which this chapter is very much indebted.

particularly, where the Mediterranean urban civilisation has persisted from classical times, many big villages or country towns well above the 2000 level are predominantly agricultural. Against this, however, must be set the increase in rural districts of non-agricultural people—traders, lawyers, mechanics and transport workers. So that in whatever way the reckoning was made the result would not be far different. Moreover, if allowance is made for an increase of non-agricultural people in rural districts, it must not be overlooked that many of them, especially the mechanics, are there just because agriculture is, so to speak, less rural than it was. It is coming into the mechanical and business life of the towns. It is being industrialised. This industrialisation of agriculture, very partial as it remained right down to 1914, is a feature of the modern age which will require attention.

§ 42. Nothing has happened since the sixties of the nineteenth century to alter materially the framework of French rural society. The landowning peasantry has not been bought out; very far from it. The slow growth of population, and its actual decline on the land, have prevented any conspicuous increase in the subdivision of the holdings. It could in fact be said with almost absolute truth that population has not grown in order that holdings might not be subdivided; some of the districts where the fairly prosperous peasant owner or the comfortable farmer predominates being those in which the birthrate is lowest. Such are the Garonne valley, Burgundy and Normandy. On the other hand, none of the later political vicissitudes of France have destroyed the class of large landowners as it was reconstituted early in the nineteenth century. Properties have changed hands or have been cut up. The *bourgeoisie* has bought and the old noble and gentle families have sold, in France as everywhere else; but large landowning has not disappeared, though it has lost some of its importance.

Inquiries made in 1908–9 showed that it was generally stationary or declining. In some departments it hardly existed. In a very few it showed a slight increase. Occasionally a new form of large arable estate had resulted from drainage enterprises or recovery of sandy wastes in the south. A recent

transference of large estates to business men from the towns
was registered almost everywhere; also the phenomenon, so
familiar in Britain, of large forests and moors kept under a
single control for sporting reasons. The definitely agricultural
large estate was now comparatively rare, the large agricultural
estate mainly cultivated by or for the owner rarer still. In short,
the position of the large proprietor was economically weaker
than it had been fifty years earlier; but no dramatic change
had occurred. He still held his place in rural society.

One rural class, if it may fairly be called a class, has certainly
declined—that of the *métayers*. The decline set in early in the
nineteenth century. Already in Lavergne's day, *métayage* was
unknown in districts where it had been common before the
Revolution. The ordinary farming lease was taking its place.
Since his day the process has continued. It cannot be traced
statistically, owing to the defects of the French census and other
returns; but it was a matter of common observation that *métayage*,
once common all over France, had become by the end of the
nineteenth century the peculiarity of certain provinces.

Agricultural returns of the years 1882 and 1892—later returns
of the same type are not available—reveal the position to which
métayage had sunk, towards the end of the nineteenth century.
As they do not show a decline in the decade, on the contrary
a tiny increase, it may be assumed that the position was stabilised,
and that in 1892 *métayage* was holding its own as a form of
tenure well suited to certain districts and types of agriculture.
But its place was now very definitely subordinate to that of either
cultivating proprietorship or ordinary farming for a money rent.
The figures are as follows:

	1882	1892
Cultivating proprietor...	2,151,000	2,199,000
Farmer	968,000	1,061,000
Métayer	342,000	344,000

General conclusions cannot be drawn with any confidence
from these isolated statistics; but the reported growth of nearly
10 per cent. in farmers, as compared with the very slight growth
in proprietors, suggests that subdivision of holdings was proceeding on hired land at a perceptible rate. This may, and

probably does, only reflect the growth of market gardening, flower gardening, and so on, which have come to play so large a part in modern French agriculture. Most of the land so used is rented, especially about Paris. As a good living can be got from a very small holding on this system, the whole group of figures must not be taken as in any way suggesting a deterioration in the status or comfort of the average working owner, farmer, or *métayer*.

These same statistics, isolated though they are, help to give a concrete notion of the position and importance of the true labouring class in French agriculture. In reference to the early nineteenth century, it was pointed out that old France did not contain a regular class of landless labourers, and that the Revolution did nothing to produce such a class. Sons of peasants and peasants whose land, whether owned or held by *métayage*, was insufficient for their needs, went out to work; but there was a perpetual movement from class to class. The peasant's son inherited the holding. The day labourer saved and rented a bit of land. The peasant without land enough put in a short day's work for a wage—this was, and is, especially common in the vine lands of the south—and tended his own patch in the evenings. There were of course everywhere some landless individuals, and here and there local conditions resembling those of nineteenth century England. But the real rural labouring class, the proletariat, the "wage slaves" of Marxian economics, did not exist. And the partial industrialising and commercialising of agriculture, in the later nineteenth century, had not produced such a class, in spite of assertions to the contrary. For the average unit of agriculture, the agricultural "business," remains as small as ever it was, and its typical manager is still the working peasant or the very small farmer.

Besides the groups of cultivating proprietors, farmers, and *métayers*, classed as *chefs d'exploitation* in the 1882–92 statistics, there are three groups of "auxiliary and salaried persons." They are *régisseurs*, stewards or bailiffs who manage properties for large owners, day labourers (*journaliers*) and farm servants (*domestiques*). The farm servant is fed and housed by his master and hired by the month, the season, or the year. According to the 1882 returns the total of these "auxiliaries" was slightly less, and according to the 1892 returns considerably less, than that of the *chefs d'exploitation*. Even allowing for some errors, it is perfectly evident that in this decade the proportion of "auxiliaries" to "chiefs" was certainly not rising, and appears to have been falling. At most, in the whole country, there averaged not quite one "auxiliary" to each "chief." And many of these "auxiliaries" had land of their own, or had some chance of becoming "chiefs" in course of time. The figures are as follows:

		1882	1892
Total of *chefs d'exploitation*		3,461,000	3,604,000
Total of *auxiliaires*	...	3,453,000	3,058,000
Composed of:			
Stewards, etc.	...	18,000	16,000
Day labourers	...	1,481,000	1,210,000
Farm servants	...	1,954,000	1,832,000

Of the day labourers, 727,000 in 1882 and 509,000 in 1892, are reported as owning some small scrap of land. The enormous fall under this head suggests statistical error. Indeed the whole series of figures must not be pressed too hard. Nevertheless they give rough arithmetical precision to a situation which changed very little during the nineteenth century, and certainly has not changed appreciably in the twentieth. There can be no question of wage slavery and a proletariat in a society where the number of potential employers is rather greater than that of the actually employed.

Only in a very few districts and in a few forms of agriculture has a labouring class come into existence susceptible to class-consciousness and fit for labour organisation. Such are the great estates of the Bordeaux and other wine districts, the big farms north of Paris, and the forests in many departments. Here alone has it been possible for labour conflicts of the industrial type to arise. The woodcutters and the vineyard workers are those who have most often taken collective action. In these industries a distinct labour class was not a nineteenth century creation. It had long existed in one form or another. The new thing was the organisation, which was worked out in the eighties and nineties.

Nor did the typical peasant's or small farmer's holding change its size or character between 1860 and 1914. It has been pointed out already that France had no general inclosure movement before 1860, apart from inclosure of commons. Holdings were never systematically consolidated, nor fields rearranged. She has had no such movement since 1860. Where open-field husbandry with its scattered holdings anciently prevailed, peasant property is still usually, as the French say, dispersed. French economists, agriculturists and statesmen have lamented this dispersion; but a policy of consolidation has never been pressed on by government, as it has been in many other continental countries. All through the years since the common-field routine lost its ancient binding force, and in France that was long ago, peasants have been exchanging and buying and rounding off their holdings as they had opportunity. But the continued laments over dispersion, its frequency, and its uneconomic character, indicate clearly enough how incomplete the process still is.

The typical farmer, again, is of the smallest. There has been no tendency whatever, so far as the facts are known, towards consolidation of holdings. The big farms are where they have so long been. Occasionally, for some special purpose such as the seedsman's business, a big concern may have grown up here or there. Occasionally, too, but less often than in the early nineteenth century, a large proprietor directs the cultivation of his own estate. For the rest, the typical farmer was and is a small man, not distinguishable from the average peasant cultivator, and often a less prosperous person than many of his peasant neighbours. If all the day labourers and farm servants reported in the statistics of 1892 had worked for the farmers reported in the same statistics, each farmer would have had exactly three "auxiliaries." A large proportion of these labourers did not work for arable farmers at all, but on vineyards and other great estates. Some helped the larger peasant cultivators. When a further considerable deduction has been made, for the solid body of labourers in the districts of really large farms, it becomes clear that the farmer outside those districts would often have no "auxiliaries" at all, and at best would have two or three. The average could hardly be above two, and was probably below.

Statistical discussions about the rise or fall in the size of the average holding are full of pitfalls, even with the best material and in a country where holdings are normally compact, like England. The French statistical material is very defective, and the broken up French peasant holdings invite error. And there is the constantly recurring question, what, after all, is a small, moderate, or large holding? A question as to which, again, French conditions invite error. The economic answer should not be in acres but in net product. The vineyard, the oliveyard, the Parisian market garden, the flower gardens of the Mediterranean coast, cannot be classified with ordinary arable holdings. On a couple of well-watered acres in the country by Avignon a family can live in reasonable comfort. A small holding there, for a peasant who tries to live by it, is an acre and a quarter. In the rather infertile corn lands of *la triste Sologne*, 125 acres is reckoned a small holding. In Burgundy, a man is counted a small holder who has less than about seven acres of vines, or less than 50 acres of corn land. These illustrations are taken from answers sent in to the Ministry of Agriculture in 1908–9 in reply to the question—what do you reckon a small holding for the various regions, and for various agricultural purposes, in your department[1]?

Statistics of holdings were taken in 1862, 1882, and 1892. There are also some estimates put forward by the Minister of Finance in 1909, based on unpublished information and therefore of less value, but still interesting. The figures cover both owned and rented holdings, and are meant to give an idea of the size of the typical agricultural "business" in France. For the purposes of the present chapter the 1882 returns may be omitted. They only differ by very small percentages from those of 1892.

Number of Holdings in France.

	1862	1892	1908
Very small (under 2½ acres) ...	not reported	2,235,000	2,088,000
Small (2½–25 acres) ...	2,435,000	2,618,000	2,524,000
Middling (25–100 acres) ...	636,000	711,000	746,000
Large (100–250 acres) ⎱ ...	154,000	{ 105,000	118,000
Very large (over 250 acres) ⎰		{ 33,000	29,000

[1] The hectare is here, and throughout, taken at 2½ acres. It is actually 2·471.

The table brings out most clearly the stability of the situation since the early sixties. It helps to justify the assertion that the framework of French rural society has not been materially altered. There have been, and no doubt will be, acute controversies as to whether or not it is really true that the "very large" holdings declined by about 12 per cent. between 1892 and 1908, and about what this means if it is true. But in view of the recognised weakness of the figures, in which a 10 per cent. margin of error would not be at all surprising, such controversy is unfruitful. The fruitful conclusions from the table are, *first*, that the statisticians of 1862 and of 1908 only differed by between 3 and 4 per cent. in their estimates of the number of "small" holdings; *second*, that the 1908 estimate of the number of holdings above 100 acres is only 8–9 per cent. less than the 1862 estimate; *third*, that even allowing for a considerable margin of error, there seems to have been a modest growth in the number of middling holdings, mainly at the expense—if the 1908 figures are to be trusted—of the very small and small holdings. It looks as if the fairly comfortable peasants had been quietly buying scraps from their smaller neighbours, an assumption which fits in with what is known of the facts from other sources than statistics.

English readers will note the very different standards of size for a holding applied in the two countries. That 100 acres should be classed as a large holding and 250 acres as a very large holding, and that there should be two and a half million holdings under 25 acres, sounds odd in a country where a 50 acre holding is reckoned small, and where the average holding, including a great many not really agricultural, is 66 acres.

To complete this sketch of the things which have remained relatively stable in the agricultural life of modern France, something must be said of communal property. In 1815 the communes had owned about a tenth of the whole area of France, chiefly woodland and mountain pasture. There had been no great change by 1860. At that time they owned about 12,000,000 acres, the total area of France being then about 140,000,000 acres. Of the 12,000,000 acres, nearly 4,500,000 were forest and wood including the great stretches of communal forest in the Alps, the Pyrenees, the Vosges and the Jura. About 6,700,000 acres were pasture, heath, and true waste—the stony wilderness of the Camargue, or the still unreclaimed *landes* of the Biscay coast. Here again mountain commons predominated. The rest—about 750,000 acres—was arable, meadow, vineyard, or garden. By 1877 the total area of communal property was said to have fallen from about 12,000,000 to about 10,750,000 acres. The decline represents mainly actual recovery of land from communal waste for individual agriculture. Of the 10,750,000 acres not less than 1,500,000 were completely unproductive; largely rock and glacier, of which a single department contained nearly 750,000 acres of grim Dauphiné peaks, which hardly suggest acreage. While the total of communal property had fallen, the amount of woodland had risen to about 5,000,000 acres as a result of afforestation.

Apart from the mountain pastures, which account for by far the greater part of the unwooded commons of France, it is the communal woodland alone which affects the daily life of the cultivator; and there are important districts, especially in the north-west, where even communal woodland is unknown. While waste has shrunk a little since 1877, woodland and mountain pasture remain much as they were; for the forest code forbids partition of woodland, and the habits of the mountaineers require undivided pasture. Between a quarter and a fifth of all the forests of France belongs to the communes, the total afforested area being about 23,000,000 acres. As a very large part of the remainder belongs to the state, and is administered by it direct, the importance of communal forest ownership is clear. The 5,000,000 acres of communal woodlands formed an appreciable part of the approximately 130,000,000 acres of the French Republic between 1871 and 1918. The communes regulate their use, and are entitled to levy a small charge for their care and maintenance. So the French village can do without much coal, and the villager gets timber for the needs of his holding.

§ 43. If the figures of the French agricultural population quoted above are to be trusted, the number of "auxiliaries," day labourers and farm servants, fell by 400,000, or nearly 12 per cent., in the single decade 1882–92, whereas the number of *chefs d'exploitation*, agricultural *entrepreneurs* large and small, actually grew. It is most unfortunate that similar figures are not available for every decade. But non-statistical information confirms the impression which these figures give—namely that when the rural population began to decline absolutely, about the year 1875, the decline took the form of a migration from the day labouring and farm servant class into the towns. The class, it will be remembered, has always been recruited, first, from the small sections of absolutely landless people in the country districts; second, from the holders of scraps of land by which they cannot live; third, from peasants' sons who see no immediate prospect of coming into property. These groups are composed of men, all of whom, since the introduction of universal military service by the Third Republic, have learnt what town life is like—at least as seen from the barracks. The modest prospects for them on the land fail to satisfy. Moreover, in spite of the natural outcry of employers against the rural exodus, and the fatal charm of the city, it is of course true that with modern mechanical developments in agriculture less labour is required to the acre, for arable farming, than was required in the years before agricultural machinery began to tell. And the economy of machinery is not confined to arable farming. But either the exodus went beyond the point of maximum economy in the substitution of machinery for human labour, or employers, finding that an alternative and cheaper labour supply was available, did not trouble to push the use of machinery to the point of maximum economy; for towards the end of the nineteenth century, before the fall had gone far, these absconding Frenchmen began to be replaced on a large scale by immigrant aliens.

Belgian labourers had for a long time been in the habit of tramping into the north French departments, particularly for gang work in the fields of sugar beet. Their numbers grew. Spaniards tramped round the Pyrenees for the vintage of the south. Italians helped to get in the harvests of the south-east, or were hired as cowmen and cheesemakers by the well-to-do French peasantry of Savoy. A few Swiss and Germans also came, and latterly, in the present century, there began to arrive

in the north-east, and even in the neighbourhood of Paris, some
of those Polish harvesters on whose assistance Germany had
relied for many years. This last is an extraordinary development. The "child-rich" Slav, as the Germans call him, reaches
right across Germany to spill his surplus children in Malthusian
France. As with the Belgian, the Italian and the Spaniard,
earnings and conditions of work, which had made the more
prosperous Frenchman rebel and go to town, were an attraction
drawing him from afar.

These agricultural immigrants were mostly birds of passage.
They came for harvest, vintage, or beet lifting, made their money,
and returned. Some of the Italians, however, and a considerable
number of Spaniards, came with intention to stay, and applied
for naturalisation. No estimate of their numbers, as distinguished from the total number of aliens engaged on work
of all kinds in France, has been put forward; but it must have
been many scores of thousands.

It is quite impossible to determine whether or not the
agriculture of France, from 1875 onwards, did or did not "need"
so many human hands as it had once employed. As has been
already pointed out, the rural population fell in the thirty
years from 1876 to 1906 by 2,200,000 or 9 per cent. But some
of this fall was in the lower age groups—fewer children. And
some of the fall in adults was made good by aliens. The decline
in the working force was therefore small. If France had all
been rearranged into methodical and economical holdings, many
fewer hands would certainly have been required. The small
holding system, and especially the system of small "dispersed"
holdings, is obviously in a sense wasteful of labour. But, assuming that the small holding system is worth preserving for
social reasons, and that dispersed holdings, as things are, cannot
be abolished, it is impossible to determine whether in fact
employers, including some peasants, might have used more
machinery but preferred to hire cheap aliens, or whether—
and this is the critical point—the development of forms of
agriculture which require more human labour very nearly
balanced the economy of labour due to machinery. Leaving the
question unsettled, the two lines of agricultural evolution,

economy of labour by the use of machinery, and demand for labour by the growth of intensive and specialised forms of cultivation, may be followed.

§ 44. Up to the sixties, the only form of agricultural machinery which had come into at all general use in France, was the old-fashioned type of threshing machine, usually worked by a horse or mule. Its use was almost confined to the north, and was not universal there. But by curtailing the business of hand threshing in winter, it had already made an important inroad on the century-old routine of agricultural work, and reduced the need for day labourers on the larger holdings. The agricultural statistics of 1862 reported 101,000 threshing machines. (Note that France then contained 790,000 holdings of more than 25 acres and 3,200,000 ploughs.) They also showed that experiments were being made on the really large holdings with other machines, some of recently invented types, some of types known in England since the eighteenth century. There were said to be 26,000 horse hoes; 11,000 drilling machines; of mowers for hay and reapers for corn, 9000 each; of horse rakes and haymaking machines, together 6000. By comparing these figures with the 154,000 holdings of more than 100 acres in France, a precise notion can be gained of the tiny part then played by machinery. Not quite 7 per cent. of these big holdings owned drilling machines. Less than 4 per cent. of them had any kind of hay making machine. And these are classes of machines known in England quite early in the century.

Thirty years later the picture is different, but the difference is less than might perhaps have been expected. By the early nineties agricultural machinery had won the day in all countries where large farming was the rule. Constantly being improved, especially in America and England, it was undertaking new tasks and doing the old ones faster and on a greater scale. The big power-driven threshing machine had driven out the smaller types. The American reaping machine had become a reaper and binder in the seventies. And so on. The French agricultural statistics of 1892, while not telling nearly all that could be desired, yet throw valuable light on the progress of machinery in a land where the typical holding was small and "dispersed."

Putting on one side the very small holdings (under 2½ acres), as quite unsuited to machinery of any kind, there were 3,467,000 holdings in France in 1892. There were said to be 3,669,000 ploughs of all sorts. No doubt many of the smaller holdings at the bottom of the scale would have no plough of their own, while all fair sized arable holdings required several. Apart from ploughs, harrows, and so on, machinery could hardly be expected on the holdings below 25 acres. Take then, in connection with the other types of machinery, the holdings above that line. There were, as shown in the table in § 42, 746,000 between 25 and 100 acres, and 147,000 over 100 acres. And there was only a little more than one drilling machine and one hay-making machine for every three holdings of 100 acres or more. (Drilling machines, 52,000; haymaking machines, 51,000.) That is to say, hand sowing and hand haymaking dominated even on the larger holdings. There were 29,000 holdings over 250 acres and only 23,000 reaping machines; so that the largest type of holdings did not average one reaper each. There were 252,000 horse hoes, a class of machine which was evidently coming into use on some holdings under 100 acres, and there were 234,000 threshing machines. The last figure is vague; for we do not know how many of these were the big migratory machines, which do nearly all the work in England, and how many small fixed machines of the earlier types. But there cannot be much doubt that the latter predominated. In judging the other implements and machines too, it must be remembered that a name tells little. How often was the plough just the ancient *araire*, the bough of a tree shod with metal, which was still to be seen in corners of France in 1913? No doubt very often. Were the reapers, reapers and binders, or some earlier type? Probably almost without exception the latter.

The conclusion from these figures is clear. Those machines, which are the typical products of the application of nineteenth century metallurgy and engineering to agriculture, had not even conquered the larger French holdings in 1892, if the statistics are at all trustworthy. And they must be trustworthy enough to bear the weight of this simple conclusion. There can hardly be a 50 per cent. error in the enumeration of reapers.

It must not be forgotten that in the eighties and nineties
French agriculture was for the first time struggling against what
seemed overwhelming foreign competition. Prices were falling.
Appeal was being made to the state, and the cultivator was short
of capital. This side of the story will be told later. It is relevant
here, because small, conservative and generally poor cultivators
do not easily learn to save themselves by expenditure of capital
on machines, when their pockets are empty.

For the critical period of modern French agrarian history,
the twenty years following 1892, no comprehensive statistics of
machinery are available. But these are certainly the years in
which it first made general progress. France became a heavy
importer. It was asserted, but by interested parties, that the
imports were to the home production as three to one between
1910 and 1913. Observers were agreed that the most rapid development occurred in the twentieth century, and especially after
the year 1905. By 1911 it was reported that threshing machinery
was now so universal that the flail had vanished almost everywhere. Mowing machinery for hay had become so general,
that in many departments there was arising a generation of
labourers who would not, or even could not, handle a scythe.
An estimate of certain classes of machinery for a single department may serve as an indication of the trend of events; though
it cannot be taken as strictly representative. The department is
that of Haute-Garonne (the Toulouse country), not a country
of specially large holdings, nor specially accessible to new in-
fluences. The estimates are those of a departmental professor
of agriculture[1].

	1892	1900	1908
Mowing machines ...	450	7000	15,000
Reapers (various types) ...	180	1500	25,000
Reapers and binders ...	60	800	1,200

What had been happening in this department since 1892 is
evident. Machinery had been rapidly replacing hand labour for
the times of pressure, hay and corn harvest. And in this at least
the department may be taken as representative of the whole
country. It will be noted that the professor of Haute-Garonne

---

[1] Before an agricultural machinery congress in 1911. Quoted in Augé-Laribé,
op. cit. p. 58.

believed that his department contained considerably more
reapers of various kinds, in 1908, than the official statisticians
had claimed for all France sixteen years earlier. Allowing both
for official omissions and professorial local pride, this fully bears
out the view that these were the critical years for mechanical
agriculture in France.

§ 45. Highly specialised agriculture was difficult before the
modern transport age, except in narrow areas or for very
peculiar classes of produce. There had always been belts of
garden ground about the great cities. Agricultural products
which would keep and stand transport might be produced in
specialised areas, remote from the place of consumption; provided those areas could be fed from elsewhere. Thus, even in
the Middle Ages, there was a highly specialised vineyard
industry about Bordeaux; because the sea and the Gironde
enabled wine to go and corn to come. But such situations were
rare. It was only after good roads and railways had become
general, and had been supplemented by the telegraph for
market news, that any district could easily afford to specialise
on some class of produce for which there were good markets
at a distance. The process began in France early in the nineteenth century, when the quick cross-channel steam packets
began to carry butter and eggs and fruit and poultry to the
London market. The reform of the English tariff in the forties
opened the door wide. But it was only late in the century, in
the period now under review, that a steadily growing demand
for French agricultural produce *de luxe* affected the agriculture
of the whole country. The effects are not always traceable in
statistics, and the total area of highly specialised cultivation
cannot be given. But its products were known in all luxurious
markets. The devices of French market gardening, the bell
glasses and the weather screens, the mushroom and the as-
paragus caves, are familiar. Brittany sent early vegetables all
over Western Europe. The prunes and crystallised fruits of the
south-west, the flowers and strawberries of the Alpes Maritimes,
the fruit of Burgundy which was turned into the *confitures* of
Bar-le-Duc—the list of good things, and of the places where
they are grown, is long and might easily be lengthened.

Still more widespread was the dairying industry in all its forms—the milk, the butter, and the cheeses whose names strung together would make music for the enumerative poet. Here statistics help a little. The official figures of grass land show an apparently enormous increase between 1892 and 1909; but there are pitfalls in the figures which forbid quotation. International comparisons of cattle are safer and more useful. In 1911 France had 7,600,000 cows as against 4,400,000 in the United Kingdom in 1912, and 8,100,000 in the considerably larger and more populous Austro-Hungarian Empire in 1910–11. She had more cattle per head of the population than Germany and very nearly as many per head as pastoral Switzerland. She had always been rich in cattle. The absolute number had not grown very rapidly. There were 11,760,000 in 1840; 12,810,000 in 1862; 13,000,000 on the reduced area in 1882 and 14,440,000 in 1911. But the quality, and the proportion of milch kine to the total, had greatly improved. A disproportionate number of the whole in 1840 and 1862 were draught oxen.

The growing importance of this group of dairying and gardening industries enabled the peasant to compete effectively in the world's markets. Hand labour, patience, a touch of artistry were needed; and all these he could give. It is in such occupations that every few acres can carry their family; and so the depopulating tendency of agricultural machinery was checked, though to what extent it is impossible to say. It can only be repeated that the two sets of forces have worked against one another and, as the rural population and employment figures suggest, not altogether unequally.

§ 46. Even if the rural working population did decline somewhat after 1875, this did not carry with it a decline in the productivity of French agriculture. The dairying and gardening industries were expanding, as has been seen. Wheat is the test cereal crop. It is the master crop of France, and France has always been the leading wheat growing country of Europe, Russia only excepted. In the years immediately preceding the war she had more than three times Germany's wheat area, more than eight times the wheat area of the United Kingdom, and even 20 per cent. more than Austria-Hungary with its rich

Danubian plain. The French wheat area declined steadily between 1862 and 1910 from over 18,000,000 to about 16,000,000 acres, but the crop harvested from the declining area as steadily grew. It was a little larger on the average of the ten years 1876–85 than it had been in 1856–65, in spite of the lost territory. The figure for 1896–1905 was over 13 per cent. and that for 1906–9 over 19 per cent. higher than that of 1876–85. This of course means a constantly increasing yield per acre. There had been a similar increase for oats and barley, specially marked in oats. Meanwhile the grains on which poor and backward peoples live, such as rye and buckwheat, had been losing ground, though so far as they were still cultivated they shared in the increased yield per acre of all the cereal crops.

The potato, starting from humble beginnings early in the nineteenth century, had become a staple crop everywhere by 1850. Once the peasant had overcome his prejudices, he relied on it more and more, and the larger holders grew it for urban markets. By 1882 there were over 3,000,000 acres of potatoes in France, and by 1911 over 3,750,000 acres. (Great Britain at that time had about 600,000 acres.) Between the same two years the French total crop had increased 66 per cent.; but this is not a decisive test owing to the great fluctuation in the yield of the potato from year to year. The crop of 1892 was over 50 per cent. but that of 1900 not much more than 20 per cent. beyond the level of 1882. Yet allowing for these variations, the general movement was decisively in the right direction.

One method by which the output of agricultural produce had been increased was by the reduction of fallow. It has been seen (see *ante*, § 2) that down to the middle of the century the old two-course and three-course rotations, involving a high percentage of fallow each year, were still very common. Gradually, but by a process of which few records have been kept, the extension of roots and fodder crops on the fallow got rid of this old fashioned and wasteful husbandry. Lavergne's estimate was that fallow had declined by two-thirds before 1860; but this is probably sanguine. The process continued after his day. France is unfortunately one of the few countries whose modern agricultural statistics do not contain an estimate of the amount

of fallow from year to year. Figures exist for Spain, even
for Rumania and Bulgaria, but not for France. However, the
steady increase in roots and fodder crops indicates what was
happening. By the end of the century, fallow had been reduced
to something near the necessary minimum. It cannot be altogether abolished; for in certain soils or certain seasons,
fallowing may be advisable to clean the fields, or unavoidable
owing to weather conditions.

As a result, animals of all kinds increased in weight and value,
and most kinds increased also in numbers. Sheep are the
exception. From 32,150,000 in 1840 they fell to 29,500,000 in
1862, to 21,100,000 in 1892 and to 16,400,000 in 1911. This
fall in the head of sheep is conspicuous in the agrarian history
of all Western Europe since about 1860. It has been much more
conspicuous in Germany than in France (see *post*, § 56). Continental cultivators have never succeeded in fitting the sheep
into the system of mixed arable farming as practised in England.
There is no district on the continent which, like Lincolnshire
for instance, excels both in corn and sheep. The reasons are
many and can only be suggested here. Chief among them are
the smallness of the holdings, their dispersion, and the lack of
inclosures. As commons and open grazing land have declined
sheep have declined with them. But sheep stand alone. Between
1862 and 1909 horses in France increased from 2,914,000 to
3,236,000, and swine from 6,000,000 to 7,300,000, in spite of
the decrease of territory in the interval. The growth in cattle
has already been noted.

To this story of improvement and growth some qualifications
must be appended. The disaster which overtook the vineyards
in the seventies will be dealt with later. In consequence of this
disaster, the work of the closing years of the nineteenth century
was one not of progress, but of recovery and reconstruction.
The work was well done, yet the area under vines early in the
twentieth century was much less than it had been in 1873.
Owing to the extreme variations in the quality, yield and value
of vineyards, area is not in itself a satisfactory test. Taking
quality, value, output and employment into account, it may
be said that vine growing was reconstituted by 1900–5. Also

the wine industry was re-established on a new and more scientific basis.

Sugar beet growing has been the sport of tariff makers and international agreements. Its history is exceptional and highly technical. The test of success is neither acreage nor weight, but the sugar-yield of the roots. France always protected her sugar industry. Partly as a result of protection, acreage grew steadily up to 1901, when it was over 800,000. The French sugar output rose from about 50,000 metric tons in 1852–3, to over 500,000 tons in 1892–3 and over 1,100,000 tons in 1900–2. In the nineties France was both protecting the industry and, in effect, giving a bounty on export (see *post*, § 47). Under the international Brussels sugar convention of 1902, bounties ceased in 1903. The effect was felt at once. Acreage fell off, and the sugar output, after a few years' fluctuations, fell to an annual level varying between 736,000 and 803,000 tons for the years 1907–11. But in spite of these vicissitudes, a comparison of 1907–11 with 1852–3, or even with 1892–3, shows progress enough.

The most important reservation to be appended to the story of rural progress is that, in view of the possibilities of modern scientific agriculture, this progress was not so great as it might have been. Take, as test cases, wheat and potatoes, two standard and essential crops. The figures on which the comparisons are based were collected in 1911 or 1912. They represent therefore the final position of French national agriculture in the century 1815–1914. It appears that in those years Belgium and Holland got nearly twice the weight of wheat from a given area that France got; Germany rather more than half as much again; Great Britain rather less than half as much again. For potatoes Holland's yield per acre was considerably more than twice that of France. Belgium was only a little behind Holland. Germany had not quite twice France's yield. Great Britain's was to France's as $1\frac{5}{8}$ to 1. There are palliatives of these unfavourable comparisons. France grows so much wheat that she cannot afford to reserve only her picked areas for it, as for instance Germany does. Southern France is not by nature a good potato country. Figures might have been selected rather more favourable to France. But when all has been said, and however the figures are handled, it remains true that, largely, no doubt, owing to the extent and character of her peasant agriculture, she is behind her neighbours in arable farming. And it might be added that, excellent as her dairy farming is, it is inferior to that of Denmark.

§ 47. So far the agrarian history of France in the railway age has been treated as a whole. It remains to break the history up into its sections, to follow the short period vicissitudes of agriculture, and to see how difficulties were accentuated or overcome.

In the years from about 1855 to 1875, an immense stimulus was given to the production of the two great staples, wheat and wine. English free trade and the railways levelled up wheat prices to the English price all over Western Europe during the sixties. Population was growing everywhere, and the taste for wheaten bread was growing faster than population. The Black Sea lands had not yet been effectively opened, and American grain did not begin to flood the European markets until, *firstly*, the railway network of the prairies had been created (1865–75), and, *secondly*, the ocean tramp had appeared as a successful grain carrier (about 1875). There was therefore a great extension of wheat growing everywhere. Between 1850 and 1869, the amount of land under wheat in France increased about 33 per cent., wheat being raised from land hitherto considered only fit for inferior crops, or for no crop at all. Between 1860 and 1870, the land under the vine also increased and the output of wine increased greatly. The main cause was the growing domestic consumption which followed the building of the railways. A subsidiary cause was the series of commercial treaties, beginning with the Cobden treaty of 1860, which opened the markets, first of England, and then of other countries to French wines.

The French wine output mounted steadily, with an interruption in the early fifties due to the ravages of the *oidium* fungus, until it touched its maximum figures—nearly 70,000,000 hectolitres in 1869 and 1874, and 78,000,000 in 1875. (The drop to 36,000,000 in 1873, in these years of maximum output, well illustrates the great variability of vintages as compared with harvests.) But already the vines had begun to feel the attacks of the phylloxera, a plant louse akin to the aphis, and during the

next decade the French wine industry was struggling for existence. At first it seemed as if the attacks were local and incidental,
like those of any other insect pest. But they returned and spread
year by year, until whole districts were devastated and in some
cases whole departments lost their vines. Every suggested
remedy and preventive was tried with no great success, until
at last a large number of vineyards were replanted with imported
vinestocks which were found to resist the phylloxera. But the
wine industry took twenty years to recover. The area under
vines fell almost continuously from 1873 to the end of the
century, the total fall being 33 per cent. After the maximum
yield of 1875 (78,000,000 hectolitres) came ten years (1876–85)
in which the maximum was 55,000,000 and the minimum
26,500,000, then ten (1886–95) in which the maximum was
51,000,000 and the minimum 23,000,000. Then at length the
turn came; for although the vineyard area was still falling, better
management and better wine making had greatly increased the
yield. The concluding figures are as follows:

	Maximum yield	Minimum yield
1896–1905	67,400,000 (in 1900)	32,300,000 (in 1898)
1906–1913	66,100,000 (in 1907)	28,500,000 (in 1910)

In the lean years after 1880 the French wine trade had been
put on a new basis. Before 1877 there had been no imports
worth mentioning, apart from small quantities of the finer
table wines. Now, ordinary wine began to be imported in
bulk, in part for direct consumption, in part for *coupage*—
mixture with French wine before sale. The import of ordinary
wine rushed up from 600,000 hectolitres in 1877, a figure only
equalled once before, to 7,000,000 in 1880 and 12,000,000 in
1887. This wine was mostly Italian. In 1888 began a Franco-
Italian tariff war which first checked the trade and later diverted
a large part of it from Italy to Spain. By the end of the century
the recovery of the French vineyards began to tell. After 1896
imports of ordinary wine seldom got above 8,000,000 hectolitres. In 1901, after the great vintage of 1900, they were down
to 3,350,000, and the average for the ten years 1904–13 was well
below 7,000,000.

Whilst France had been a great wine exporting country, her

vine growers had been with her wine merchants in the small
free trade camp. They had supported the treaties with England
of 1786 and 1860 against the manufacturers, because those
treaties widened the wine market. After 1880, when France
had become on the balance a regular wine importer, they learnt
to sympathise with the manufacturers. They began—it is the
recognised opening to the game of protection—with agitation
against the fraudulent and unwholesome wines, raisin juice
and potato spirit, which certainly were coming in. Raisins
themselves were suspect, as fraudulent wines were made also
at home. For a good many years, however, after 1881 France,
being bound by commercial treaties, could not alter her
moderate import duties. A little was done, "on hygienic
grounds," to check the fraudulent wine trade, native and
foreign; but for the time wine growers were left to join in
the chorus which was now going up in favour of protection
from every agricultural interest.

With the late seventies had begun that world-wide fall in
prices which continued, broadly speaking, until the end of the
nineteenth century. Many causes were at work (see *post*, § 93),
but the main causes, in the agricultural sphere, were the railway,
the marine engine and the telegraph, working internationally.
And the article most affected in the early days was wheat.
Before 1860 France had been on the average self-sufficing in
wheat. Between 1861 and 1880 she had an exportable surplus
in five years, and had to import more or less in the remaining
fifteen.

The bad harvests of 1878–9 which she shared with England
had necessitated heavy imports, or what seemed heavy to
Frenchmen, unaccustomed to get their bread from abroad.
The figures were 18,000,000 hectolitres in 1878, 29,000,000
in 1879, and 27,000,000 in 1880. For comparison it may be
noted that the average annual production of wheat in France
for the decade 1876–85, was 102,000,000 hectolitres. The
French producer found that instead of getting high prices, the
compensation ordinarily expected for a poor harvest, his prices
in 1878–80 were actually lower than they had been in 1877.
The result was a regular tariff campaign conducted by the

Société des Agriculteurs de France, who denounced most of all the American invasion. Their first campaign may be said to have failed. In the general tariff of May 1881, foodstuffs were left free or subject only to small duties, except such things as coffee and cocoa which paid stiff revenue duties.

Various commercial treaties were arranged on the basis of this tariff, which prevented serious alterations in it for a decade. But the government never bound itself to give another country any special terms affecting either cereals or meat, so that policy with regard to them was left open. As the years passed and the price fall continued, complaints came in about one agricultural commodity after another. German and Austrian sugar helped by an export bounty, Japanese silk, Scandinavian timber, were added to American wheat and cattle and "hog products," and Italian or Spanish wine. Meat imports, like those of adulterated wine, could be checked on grounds of health. Already in 1881 government showed its complaisance by forbidding American pork. Three years later, the grievance of the beet sugar growers and makers was met by a complicated rearrangement of the sugar taxes, and an increased surtax on foreign sugar. The rearrangement did not include an export bounty in so many words. But the tax was levied, in imitation of Germany, on the weight of the beets when delivered for manufacture. Provided the sugar yield of the roots was increased, by better farming and better handling, this left a certain amount of the sugar practically untaxed. Thus a stock of duty free sugar could be created which might be shipped to foreign markets.

In 1885 and again in 1887 the low duties on cattle were pushed up. Rye, barley and oats began to be taxed in 1885, for the first time since 1861. The flour duty was raised both in 1885 and in 1887. Wheat was dealt with in 1885. Under the 1881 tariff it paid only 60 centimes per 100 kilos (1s. 1d. per quarter). This was raised to 3 francs in 1885 and to 5 francs in 1887.

The figures below illustrate the wheat position at this time.

	Average home production in hectolitres	Highest year's net import	Price in the year of highest import
1876–85	102,000,000	29,000,000 (1879)	22·1 francs
1886–92	104,000,000	19,600,000 (1891)	20·5

The average import in 1886–92 was only 14,000,000 hectolitres, less than a seventh of the home production, which was
not falling; but the average price was only 18·3 francs, and it was
this which kept the *Société des Agriculteurs de France* active.
The duties seem to have prevented French prices from falling
as English prices fell, but the resulting price level was still not
what the French producer had hoped for.

The Italian tariff war of 1888, due to a quarrel about tariffs
in general, gave further openings for agricultural protection
against a near and dangerous competitor. Wine duties, as has
been seen, were pushed up enough to divert the trade to Spain.
Eggs, butter, dried fruit, flax, silk, hemp, all were subjected
to extra taxation until January 1892. After that the two countries
traded with one another under their general tariffs, until a fresh
treaty was concluded in 1899. Trade under the general tariff
meant that neither gave the other favours accorded to nations
with whom a treaty existed, so that for eleven years continuously
there were special obstacles to Franco-Italian trade.

While this war was in progress France had consolidated her
tariff system. It was in 1890 that the wine growers were cheered
by a tax on raisin wine. The same year duties on rice, maize,
and meal were raised. Finally came the so-called Méline
tariff of 1892. It was aimed partly at the system of tariff bargaining by commercial treaty which, in the eyes of its makers,
had injured France. There were to be two scales of duties, one
for the world at large and one for countries who gave France
favourable commercial treatment. That is to say, the most that
bargaining could extract from France, to wit the minimum
tariff, was known precisely before bargaining began. The
Méline tariff did not alter the grain duties. That on wheat,
for example, remained at 5 francs per 100 kilos, or 9s. a quarter.
Most other agricultural duties were raised about 25 per cent.

But even the Méline tariff was not the last word. In 1897
the wheat duty was pushed up from 5 to 7 francs. Next year
the butter duty went up again. The wine duties were revised
and raised in 1899. In 1903 the rates on cattle and meat were
advanced. The details need not be followed further. Up to
1914 there was no change in principle; although, as has been

already seen, the beet industry lost its export bounty and suffered accordingly.

French agriculture in the last age must be thought of as working behind a stout tariff wall. If one object of this was to make France self-sufficing in bread, success can be claimed; though it may be argued that she might have had more children and better nourished had her bread been cheaper. For not only the townsman but most of the smaller peasants were buyers of bread. However, the increased home yield of wheat and the stagnant population kept down the need for imports. Whereas in 1886–92 the average net import of wheat was nearly one-seventh of the home production, in 1896–1902 it was less than one-seventeenth, and in 1906–12 about one-thirteenth.

So it was all along the line. France remained almost self-supporting—at a price. The price was paid in many ways. Part of it in rather stagnant exports; for the nation that will not buy neither shall it sell. Part in the failure to develop home industries connected with the handling of imported food, and food export industries which require cheap materials. France suffered in 1914–18 from a shortage of refrigerating plant directly due to her refusal to buy frozen meat in time of peace. She had nothing to compare with the export trade of, say, Huntley and Palmer, though it seems absurd to suppose that a Frenchman could not devise better biscuits than an Englishman. Whether she bought approximate self-sufficiency too dear may be doubted by one writing after 1914. But that problem is not a problem in economic history.

§ 48. Tariffs on agricultural produce may be better or worse, but there can be no question about the merits of the two other cures for agricultural distress to which France turned in the eighties—cooperation and education.

It has been pointed out that the French peasant, in spite of his intense individualism, had certain inherited cooperative instincts. The old agriculture of the common fields was in a sense cooperative. Drainage and irrigation can never be purely individual enterprises in a community of small cultivators; and it appears that societies for sharing the cost and responsibility of such works were in old days called syndicates. The peasantry

7

of Savoy and the Jura, as a natural outcome of common mountain pasture, have practised cooperative cheese-making time out of mind. You draw cheese in the autumn, in proportion to the milking record of your cows, from the stock made in summer on the alp. But these are curiosities, whose connection with the modern agricultural syndicate is at best remote. A more real connection exists between the syndicates and the provincial societies of agriculture started in the eighteenth century. The index to the 1794 edition of Arthur Young's travels contains an entry: "Societies of agriculture, their absurd conduct." The first of the four passages to which this concise heading refers runs: "This society does like other societies—they meet, converse, offer premiums, and publish nonsense." The fourth passage runs: "similar are the employments of societies everywhere! In England busied about rhubarb, silk, and drill ploughs:—at Paris, about fleas and butterflies;—and at Milan about buttons and scissors." This is needlessly severe. In spite of some inanities, the societies did all that was done for a long time to spread agricultural knowledge. They tried to popularise English methods before the Revolution. They lived on through all the political changes of the nineteenth century, and they are living still. Purely absurd institutions would have broken down earlier.

Next come the so-called agricultural *comices*, organised during the Restoration. These were humbler and more local than the agricultural societies, but hardly popular. They started shows of fat beasts. They gave prizes to aged and faithful farm servants. Under Napoleon III, they were used to keep the country folk quiet and imperially minded. They also aided in the spread of agricultural knowledge; but on the whole, their utility was not great.

In the seventies, the war against phylloxera involved a good deal of concerted action. In 1879 government created what were called vine defence syndicates to carry on the struggle. This is the first modern application of the term syndicate to an agricultural organisation. While the phylloxera war was still undecided, foreign competition and falling prices stirred the rather lethargic agricultural societies and *comices* into action, all over the country. They supplied recruits for the *Société des Agriculteurs de France* and furnished local evidence of the dangers of the American invasion.

But the best among their members turned towards positive measures, and considered the further improvement of French agriculture. Agricultural cooperation was making headway in Denmark and Germany during the seventies, and its successes were reported in France. Local professors of agriculture pointed out the value of joint action, especially for the purchase of chemical manure, the full value of which was just beginning to be appreciated. An association for the purpose was founded in 1881 by the *comice* of Villeneuve-sur-Lot. Next year the *comice* of Rouen followed. And in 1883, M. Tanivray formed what became the model syndicate of the *agriculteurs du Loir-et-Cher*.

Next year the French Parliament was occupied in legalising trade unions (*syndicats*). When the bill was in the Senate, a clause was being discussed which authorised associations for the defence of "the industrial and commercial interests" of their members. "And agricultural," said M. Oudet, Senator of Doubs. The addition was accepted, as no one meant to exclude agricultural labourers. And thus syndicates of quite a different sort were legalised by accident, so much by accident that when the syndicates were about to celebrate the twenty-fifth anniversary of their foundation, the Court of Appeal had just decided that many of their activities were in fact illegal. But they were not interfered with and the law has since been adjusted to their needs.

Growth was extraordinarily rapid. The figures are difficult and uncertain, but the general movement is clear. The syndicates were not alone in the field. The old agricultural societies and *comices* kept up the work of discussion and exchange of ideas. Some of the *comices*, besides helping to found syndicates, developed active policies. That of Carpentras worked to get the local strawberries on to the London market. There were also the *associations syndicales*, mostly older than the syndicates and not to be confused with them. These were associations of the type already referred to, for regulating irrigation, drainage, dyke-

building and so on. The syndicates proper grew as follows.
Round numbers, and not the exact official numbers, are given
because the latter are both defective and contain duplications.

Date	Syndicates	Membership
1885	39	?
1895	1900	400,000
1905	3000	660,000
1910	5000	750,000

So far no definition of an agricultural syndicate has been
given. It is hard indeed to define. At law it is a union of
persons exercising the same profession, for the promotion and
defence of their common interests. That is wide enough, and
the syndicates from time to time did nearly everything which
might be brought within the definition. At first they were
associations of agriculturists of all grades, often led by a man of
title and ancient family. Their first function was the purchase
of manures, seeds, and other requisites collectively. Then they
began to develop special activities, or throw off daughter
societies—cooperative banking, mutual insurance work against
loss of cattle, losses by frost and hail and other farmers' risks;
cooperative dairies, egg societies, and so on. The normal type
of syndicate had wide general objects. Its area might be a commune, a canton (rural district), or a department. In course of
time, departmental federations of local syndicates were formed;
then wider federations, such as the *Union de Bourgogne et
Franche-Comté*, which groups together syndicates of fruit and
vegetable growers over the wide area indicated; then federations
for whole sections of France, like the powerful *Union du Sud-Est*.

The picture is so various as to be indistinct; and naturally
there was a good deal of overlapping and some confusion.
However the forms of organisation are of less historical importance than the methods of work and the results attained. After
the first fifteen or sixteen years, *i.e.* with the twentieth century,
it was noticed that the large syndicates were dropping somewhat
into the background as federations developed. This was
natural, since a departmental association, for example, can hardly
be a real economic unit. Life was tending to be concentrated
in the communal syndicate, with its various specialised activities

or daughter societies, and in the federations which could carry
on propaganda and deal with the government or with associated
traders. Whether a particular function was carried on, legally
speaking, by the syndicate of so and so or by a society created
by the syndicate of so and so is, for present purposes, immaterial.
In the twentieth century the functions of syndicate and cooperative society were generally kept distinct, as this was legally
convenient and correct. But at one time or another, all the
functions already mentioned and others still to be mentioned
have been carried on by a syndicate.

Buying was the primary function. Manures, seeds, cattle,
cake, insecticides, compressed fodder, American vinestocks,
sometimes pots and pans, clothes, and soap were among the
articles handled. Some syndicates in fact acted as rural cooperative retail stores. At times they bought agricultural
machinery and hired it out to their members. This was perhaps
the most fundamentally important of all their activities. Then
they began to organise cooperative selling, which carried with
it collecting, grading, and handling produce of various kinds.
Where a syndicate's basis was a branch of production in some
locality—fruit, vegetables, wine—rather than the locality itself,
the work went forward easily and naturally. Vine growing and
dairy farming lent themselves specially well to cooperative
handling and collective sale. In the west centre cooperative
dairying made rapid progress from about 1890. In the east
some of the old mountain *fruitières* (cheese-making associations)
were federated and adapted to the new conditions. And there
were many other French rural industries to which the method
could be applied—sugar beet, olive oil, the distillation of scent
from flowers, of brandy from wine, of commercial alcohol from
potatoes. The syndicate's position was, of course, particularly
strong and its task correspondingly easy in the districts of
highly specialised agriculture in which France abounds. Here
the local bond and the trade interest coincided, and the cultivators could unite to face such natural enemies as the railway
companies.

Two specially interesting though late developments from the
syndicate movement were the cooperative credit societies and

the insurance societies. Neither was easy to start in France. Long after village credit societies were an old story in Germany, assistance from the state was necessary to make the French societies a success. Many of the best cooperators in all countries would look with suspicion on a system in which local societies were, in effect, begged to make use of credit put at their disposal by the state. This was what happened in France after 1894. When the charter of the Bank of France came up for renewal in 1897, it was forced to help in financing them. By laws of 1906 and 1910 the credit societies were authorised, one might almost say ordered, to make long term loans, fifteen and twenty-five years, to individuals and agricultural cooperative societies, for such development purposes as the acquisition of a holding or the equipment of a dairy.

Cooperative insurance also has been a nurseling of the state. The commercial insurance society in all countries is prepared to deal with many of the risks which face the peasants' property —fire, murrain, lightning. The state wished to encourage the cooperatives to compete with it. Therefore a law of 1900 relieved them from various fiscal and legal burdens, and in 1912 they were given financial assistance. Again the self-help and self-reliance, which to many advocates of cooperation are of more importance than the direct economic results, have been sacrificed in order to hasten the ripening of the movement. No judgment can yet be passed on the wisdom of this policy.

Rapid as was the growth of the agricultural syndicate and its affiliated organisations, they cannot be said to have conquered France by 1910–14. Not all the syndicates were vigorous. Their 750,000 reported adherents in 1910 were not all active members; and there must have been by that date between $3\frac{3}{4}$ and 4 million peasants, farmers, landowners and so on who might have joined. To say that one independent cultivator or landowner in every eight was an active cooperator, in the years just before the war, would be a generous estimate; possibly one in ten would be nearer the mark. Many promising fields for cooperative action had hardly been scratched. The co-operative sugar and wine and alcohol and oil enterprises were interesting rather than important; and there were rich dairying districts in which the cooperative dairy was unknown or in-significant. The credit associations, fostered and fed by the state, were making slow headway. Active official propaganda in their favour was tried; but the peasants' suspicions and stubborn individualism were not easily overcome. "Why, then, are these gentlemen so anxious to lend us money and make us reveal to one another our affairs?" Loans to societies were more readily taken up than loans to individuals. The movement was gaining ground, but it was young and its future uncertain.

The belief that the syndicates would further "social solidarity," that catchword of late nineteenth century France, was prominent in the minds of many of their promoters. All country folk should learn that they were members one of another. From landlord to labourer they should unite in defence of their interests and in the sober study of their great calling. Agri-cultural practice and agricultural science were to come into fruitful alliance. They certainly did. That the syndicate move-ment had a powerful educational influence, and opened channels through which new knowledge could flow out over the land, is beyond dispute. It also no doubt increased "solidarity" within economic groups. But whether it drew closer economic groups naturally inclined to be hostile is another matter. The labourer either left the syndicate to work in the higher sphere of buying and marketing, where he did not expect or hope to penetrate, or—when conditions were favourable—he inter-preted the word syndicate in its urban and industrial sense, and set about making trade unions of his own.

§ 49. Agrarian conditions in France are such that a trade union movement was bound to set in late and could hardly become general. The scattered farm servants, who form con-siderably more than half of the small wage earning class (see *ante*, § 42), had little opportunity and usually not much spirit for combination. Socialists tried to stir up within them a noble discontent, in the alcoholic atmosphere of country town hiring days, but generally retired in disgust. The servant had his drink, made his bargain and went to live in his master's house, where he usually slept on straw in the stable; and the socialist went away to tell his comrades at a congress, not without truth, that a detestable social system had reduced these men to the level of the beasts[1].

Here and there, however, a class conscious group of rural wage earners fell into line with the labour movement of the towns. There were serious strikes among the woodmen in the great forests of the departments of Cher and Nièvre in 1891 and 1892, and the strikers formed unions. These were followed by a few unions among the vineyard workers of the south; and there were mutterings among the farm labourers north of Paris, who were wage earners of the type assumed in socialist doctrine, and were near the centre of the French labour movement. But these new developments went almost unnoticed during the nineteenth century. With the twentieth century came, among other things, a world-wide rise in prices which automatically reopened the wage question in all countries (see *post*, § 93). Add to this systematic propaganda from the towns by political parties ranging from extreme socialism, through radical socialism, to radicalism, each with an economic programme more or less well defined. And do not omit most substantial grievances. The first woodmen's strikes were strikes of men, many of whom were making less than a franc a day. When the vineyard workers struck in 1904, they had just come through a long spell of unemployment and low wages, due to frost having stopped work in the vineyards. Their demand was for a daily wage of 2 francs 50 centimes and a six hour day. The six hour day is explained by the fact that most of them had land of their own and wanted to work it.

This vineyard strike of 1904 was the first big thing of its kind in France. It was in Languedoc and did not affect the Bordeaux vineyards; but it included a wide area from the Pyrenees to Nîmes. After that, wherever true agricultural labourers existed, syndicates and strikes became the order of the day. There were great harvest time strikes on the farms of Seine-et-Marne in 1906 and 1907, and similar, though less important, strikes in subsequent years in the large farming district of the north. Then all sorts of people went on strike— labourers in the flower gardens of the Côte d'Or, Parisian mush-

---

[1] From a Congress speech quoted by Augé-Laribé, *op. cit.* p. 243.

room labourers, labourers on big horticultural farms about
Lyons, labourers who tapped the pines for resin on the sand
hills of the Biscay *landes*, and always, again and again, the
woodmen of the central provinces. In 1912 came the troubles
of which the outside world talked most because a familiar name
was involved—the workmen on the vineyards of Champagne
struck, and struck with sabotage, for higher wages.

A large number of these strikes succeeded in their immediate
object—wages. The farm servants of the Paris area actually
secured better accommodation. Syndicates were as often the
result as the cause of a strike. So it has been in all countries.
People were still discussing in 1912–14 how effective these
syndicates were likely to prove, and how durable. It was recognised that as fighting organisations they had shown their
value. It was known that they had no funds to speak of, and it
was said that they had not much control over their members.
So some anticipated their dissolution. But there has always been
a stage in the history of every trade union movement of weak
associations, which rise when a crisis has to be faced and sink
again in quieter times. Provided the conditions favour collective
action, even dissolution is not likely to be permanent.

Perhaps the most interesting rural syndicates of the trade
union type are those of a group which came into existence in
the Bourbonnais (department of the Allier) in 1904. They did
not achieve much at that time. The interest lies in their com-
position; for they were recruited among small peasants, small
farmers, *métayers* and labourers. They were specially strong
in *métayers*, and one of the main items of their programme was
the abolition of certain old customs, which linked the *métayage*
of the twentieth century with that of earlier times. The share-
tenancy often carried with it payments in kind and in labour,
which came straight from the Middle Ages, and were described
by the modern peasant, in terms borrowed from the old order,
as *corvées* and *redevances*. Payments in kind are an essential
part of *métayage*. It was their troublesome and trivial character
of which men complained—the scattered deliveries of eggs,
and butter, and hens which formed part of the contract. The
métayer complained also that he was called off from his own

work to lend a hand to his lord, arbitrarily and at inconvenient times. His complaints read like those of a fourteenth century villein grumbling at his "boon work."

Another grievance of the *métayers* of the Bourbonnais recalls not the fourteenth but the eighteenth century. There had grown up between them and their landlords a group of middle-men known locally as "farmers general." These men rented estates and sublet, in holdings of from 50 to 150 acres, to *métayers*. Here was precisely the capitalistic parasite of whom politicians talked. The *métayers* needed no modern terminology. They just said that, when you had to keep three pots boiling instead of two, your own was apt to be *bien maigre*; and they put the abolition of "farmers general" on the programme of their syndicates. They were not abolished, nor were the *redevances* and *corvées*, down to 1914; but it is said that *métayers* in another district, the Biscay *landes*, have got rid of similar old abuses by an appeal to violence since 1918[1].

§ 50. This intrusion of the capitalist middleman might be taken as symbolic of a process which, as is alleged, was going on everywhere in the later nineteenth century. Agriculture, the contention is, was being steadily commercialised and industrial-ised by its intercourse with the capitalism of the towns. If it was actually untrue to say of countries like France, where peasant ownership predominated, that land was falling into fewer and fewer hands, untrue also to say that a rural proletariat was growing visibly—and such statements would have been untrue; was it not true after all that the peasant, while retaining his nominal independence, had become subject to capital in other ways? Was not his dependence on the chances of the market, and so on the middleman who understands markets, an evidence of subjection? Worse still; was he not often directly subject to some agricultural manufacturing concern, which took his produce and dictated prices?

To the partial truth of these contentions the cooperative movement bears witness. By the late nineteenth century the times were long past when the normal peasant family lived on the produce of its holding, sent only surpluses and by-products

[1] See the *Times*, April 7, 1920, and the *Rapport...sur la situation du mé-tayage en France*, of 1913.

to market, and bought nothing but a few clothes, tools, utensils and luxuries. That was the complete and uneconomic independence of the early middle ages. Strong remnants of it were to be found all over France; but agricultural specialisation, and the peasant's growing need for all kinds of implements, fertilisers, and clothes which he could not produce, were curtailing it more and more every decade. Specialised produce had to be sold, and household needs met by purchase. The peasant, who had learnt his helplessness in face of the impersonal forces of the market and the trained skill of the dealer, turned to cooperative marketing of his produce and to cooperative buying of his fertilisers, his implements, perhaps also his clothes. Whether in the long run he gained directly by cooperation has been questioned. At first he often did. But the dealer soon learns, in self-preservation, to offer terms not less attractive than those of the cooperative society; which is not difficult, as he generally has more capital. Yet though cooperation's direct advantages may be questioned, its existence was a potential check on the exploitation of the peasant's ignorance and isolation, a guarantee against abuses in a commercialised agriculture. The field for such abuses in twentieth century France was the field over which cooperation had not yet spread—a large field.

But the risk that the peasant may be exploited by the dealer can only be called subjection to capitalism by a figure of speech. His isolation and ignorance, in the absence of cooperation, may lead him to pay too much for inferior phosphates or sell his butter cheaper than he might. Yet specialisation and the close linking up of town and country insure a sale for his goods and guarantee his existence. The world needs him, or the capitalist would take no interest in him, and would not trouble to fleece him. The world will give him some credit, though at a price. His personal independence in such a situation is far less interfered with, he is far less "subject" to any one, than he was when in the old days he fell into the hands of the village usurer. He is more independent than he was in days older still, when he starved if his crops failed, because there was no commercial link between himself and the world.

Subjection of the peasant to some agricultural manufacturing concern is a more real instance of loss of economic independence. It is, historically, a development very like that by which craftsmen in the towns, who once worked direct for the consumer, came to work—at a price, which soon became a wage—for a shopkeeping or industrial *entrepreneur*. There has been much of it in modern France; though it is easy to exaggerate the completeness of the subjection. Comparatively few peasant holdings are so absolutely specialised that they can be regarded as working solely for the industrial *entrepreneur*. Take the standard case of sugar beet. Here, up to a point, there was complete dependence. Factories, naturally anxious for a maximum yield of sugar, were in the habit of giving out seed and making contracts in advance for the crop. The peasant thus became a sort of outworker, very like the old hand loom weaver. But the land came to his aid, because no land will grow beet every year. Dependent in respect of one crop in his rotation, he might be independent in respect of the rest. He could live on them or sell them freely in open market. Much the same is true of some other agricultural factories which are pointed at as having imposed rules and prices on the peasant producer, and so brought him into subjection. Breweries have done it, but no peasant can grow continuous and exclusive barley; distilleries of industrial alcohol, but it is unlikely that a peasant will raise nothing except potatoes. A private dairy enterprise, a great wine business, or a jam factory on the other hand may completely dominate its peasant *clientèle*, binding them by elaborate contracts and controlling the whole course of their activities. For a holding can be given up completely and continuously to milking cattle, vines, or fruit. Its owner may become tied to the factory even more securely than an ordinary industrial wage earner; because the land is there and it is his. Cooperation had made little progress by 1914 towards control over industrial enterprises of this type; so there was a real, though limited, domination of the peasant by capitalist rural industries. In spite of the success of some cooperative dairies, cooperative dairying was far from general. As for the other agricultural industries, cooperation had hardly touched their fringe.

CHAPTER IX

RURAL GERMANY, 1848-1914

§ 51. The revolutionary movements of 1848 mark a definite stage in German agrarian history which has no parallel in that of France. Politically most of the revolutions might perhaps be regarded as failures. But they set the air in motion round the "green tables," as the Germans say. The officials who sat at the tables felt the draught and began to move more vigorously. As was noted in an earlier chapter, there were German states in which no real attempt had been made to revise the inherited relations between the peasants, the lords, and the land until after 1848. Bavaria is the chief case in point. There was nothing that could properly be called serfdom in Bavaria, it is true; but until the old relations had been overhauled, the peasant was not free economically, though he might be free legally. In effect he was bound to the soil and bound by tradition in his use of it.

In Prussia the economic consequences of emancipation had been very slowly worked out—everywhere except in Posen where there were political reasons for speed (see *ante*, § 8). The officials lost interest in the business during the thirties and forties. It may be recalled that the ordinance of 1816, dealing with the lower grades of peasants, and the law of 1821, which completed the emancipation of the higher grades, only came into operation at the request of those concerned. You had to ask that your parish should be regulated. Such methods made for delay. Even when the requests had gone up the officials handled them slowly. It may be recalled also that the term peasant had been given a strict legal interpretation. In eastern Germany numbers of little people in the villages found themselves excluded from the peasant class. The law ignored them. They might be bought out, evicted, turned into tenants-at-will, or deprived of that use of the commons to which only the full peasant was legally entitled. The emancipation laws were the offspring of the eighteenth century; and, as has been said, in the eighteenth century the state had "long had a peasant problem on its hands, but there was no recognised labour problem[1]." A few people in the days of the early reform legislation saw that it would tend to increase the class of landless labourers; but most had not yet discovered that the labourer was a person requiring the care of governments. So the creation of the labourer class went on. Only a few of these lesser folk survived, with their economic position unimpaired, to take advantage of the more sympathetic legislation and administration which followed 1848. And often even the legally recognised peasants had not yet got free of the old order. What in England would have been called villein services were still quite common, and semi-servile tenures had not all been wiped out.

The Prussian law of 1850 was the product of the new spirit. It came from that Manteuffel government which Bismarck so despised. Its main feature was an attempt to rectify the injustice done to certain cultivators below the legal peasant line. The line had been drawn at the ownership of plough oxen and occupation of a regular holding in the arable fields. If you were not *spannfähig*, that is, if you could not harness a team to the plough, you were no peasant. Under Manteuffel's law those below the line could appeal to have their status regulated provided they held land by some sort of peasant right, and were not mere tenants-at-will. Even 1848 had not brought the labourer to light. For "regulation" an appeal was still needed. There was no automatic action. And since 1815 many had lost the right to be heard; for they had lost their land or had been turned into tenants-at-will (see *ante*, § 8).

What with carrying on emancipation under the old laws and applying it under the new, Prussian administration had plenty of work during the years of Prussia's rise to the leadership of Germany, from 1850 to 1871. By 1870 the legal side of the work was nearing completion. The bulk of those who could hope to have their peasant status turned into that of proprietor had been dealt with. Remains of the old order survived for a long

[1] Knapp, *Die Bauern-Befreiung...Preussens*, 1, 287.

time, and the Junkers always fought successfully against the
abolition of the manor as an administrative area. They defeated
a proposal to abolish manorial autonomy made by Manteuffel's
government in 1850; and even after a reform law of 1892 most
of the manors continued to be independent administrative units.
The free peasant, and *a fortiori* the labourer, remained under
his old master's eye and rule. Right down to the end of the
century he could still be legally called upon to render service
with hand and team—*Handdienste* and *Spanndienste*—for
carrying out communal works. The call had to come from the
communal council, it is true. But even after 1892 things were
so arranged that the communal council was not likely to go
against the squire.

In western and south-western Germany also there was a
great deal of work to be got through after 1850, before the
average peasant was turned into a full proprietor of the French
type. Two states may be taken as illustrating the extremes.
Wurtemberg had been democratic in temper for a long time and
its peasantry substantially free; but there were still old feudal
burdens on the cultivator to be got rid of after 1848. The
arrangement was that he should make payments over a period
of years and then enjoy full ownership. The work took over
twenty years, but in 1873 the financial business connected with
it was wound up. The peasant had paid his last instalment.
His land was all his own henceforward. In Bavaria, on the other
hand, the work was only begun in 1848 and there were more
and deeper traces of servility to be got rid of than in Wurtemberg. First manorial jurisdiction had to be abolished. The
lords were compensated and the state took over all the work.
Certain more humiliating obligations, including the remnants
of personal service and the lord's right to take the "best beast"
when the holding changed hands, were abolished without compensation. All uncertain payments surviving from the old days
of servility were to be fixed, that is, turned into definite
yearly quit-rents. It was open to the peasant to redeem these
various burdens on his land by paying eighteen years' purchase.
There were also arrangements for dealing with tithe.

This Bavarian law of 1848 did not work very efficiently and

had to be supplemented by a law of 1872 intended to facilitate and hasten redemption. Even then the process dragged. Bavaria was still legislating about it in 1906. The quit-rents had survived into a generation which had forgotten that they replaced much more unpleasant obligations. Their unpopularity increased with the fall in prices towards the end of the nine-teenth century, and a strong movement for their immediate abolition began in the nineties. As a result, the rates at which the rents could be redeemed were cut down and the state sub-sidised the redemption fund. But right down to 1914 Bavaria was occupied with this financial aftermath of peasant emanci-pation.

§ 52. In spite of exceptions and rough edges here and there, it may be said that the German Empire of 1871 was founded in a country of free landowning peasants and powerful cultivating squires. Throughout its history there was no important change in the balance of the various classes of landowners or in their distribution; though at the end of the nineteenth century there was a slight tendency noticeable towards decline in the largest and smallest types of holding. For example, between 1895 and 1907 holdings over 250 acres declined from 24·1 per cent. to 22·2 per cent. of the agricultural area of the Empire[1], and those under 5 acres declined from 5·6 to 5·4 per cent. of the area. About three-quarters of this agricultural area was peasant property, if we include among the peasants small holders who made their living in part by day labour. The contrast between the land of squires in the north and east and the land of peasants in the south and west is brought out with admirable clearness in the imperial statistics. Whereas in the Mecklenburgs, where in the old days *Bauernlegen* had been most thoroughly carried out, 60 per cent. of the land was in holdings of 250 acres and upwards, in Wurtemberg and Bavaria such holdings only occupied 2 per cent., and in Baden 3 per cent. of the area. Half of Bavaria was covered by holdings of between 12½ and 50 acres; rather less than a third by holdings between 50 and 250 acres. An analysis of the Prussian figures reveals a similar, though less

---

[1] This excludes woodland and forest, mountain and other natural pasture, waste land, and all building land, roads, etc.

marked, difference between the eastern and the western
provinces.

In a broad survey of modern German agriculture tenant
farming might almost be omitted. It is true there has always
been a good deal of rented land, amounting altogether to
16 or 18 per cent. of the agricultural area, the higher figure being
the latest (1907). But a third of this rented land consists of the
smallest type of holding, under 5 acres, and is partly garden
ground, partly ground held by people who are not primarily
agriculturists, and partly labourers' holdings. Another large
slice of the rented land is in the hands of men who also cultivate
land of their own. The only real analogy to English tenant
farming is found where large estates are let out to substantial
farmers. A very small percentage of the agricultural area of
Germany, perhaps 5 or 6 per cent., was in this position. By
an interesting coincidence, which is perhaps not altogether
accidental, it was commonest in Hanover and Brunswick, the
districts formerly in closest touch with England. There was a
fair amount of it also in Westphalia. On the estates of the
Junkers beyond the Elbe it was always exceedingly rare.

Far less important than farming, and worth mention only as
a curiosity, was the German equivalent of *métayage*, *Theilbau*
(share farming). It had once been common in the wine-growing
districts, but had almost died out before the nineteenth century.
It survived here and there in those districts and in the tobacco-
growing districts of Baden. An analogous system in which
a labourer, as distinguished from a regular tenant, took a share
of the produce of the land that he worked was rather less rare
and more widespread. Statistics of these survivals were collected
in 1895, when it appeared that, all told, over 30,000 holdings,
mostly very small, were held wholly or in part on produce
sharing terms. The average size was about 4 acres. At the next
occupation census (1907) it was not thought necessary to collect
any figures.

The peasant with a fairly substantial holding has always been
a common type in German society. The "big peasant," for
statistical purposes, is the man who holds from 50 to 250 acres.
Such own nearly a third of Bavaria. They are common also

in the far north, for instance in Mecklenburg, where, as descendants of the old free German colonists, they maintained themselves side by side with those squires who had managed to get rid of the semi-servile land-holding population of Slavonic ancestry. No part of the German Empire was without a fair number of these big peasants, though the biggest among them—the men of 150 to 250 acres—were confined to a few districts. In 1895 "big peasant" holdings, including however some that were rented, covered a larger area than any other class. There were about 280,000 such holdings. By 1907 those held by the typical German peasants, the million or so "middle peasants" with their 12½ to 50 acres, had overtaken them, and covered very nearly a third of the agricultural area of the Empire.

Below them came the "little peasants" with holdings of from 12½ to 5 acres. Of these also there was latterly about a million, but their land covered only 10 per cent. of the cultivated area. Last of all came the people who in the old classifications were not peasants at all, and who, like many of the "little peasants" could not live by their land, the "scrap holders" of less than 5 acres, whose three and a quarter million holdings averaged little more than an acre each, and occupied a bare 5 per cent. of the cultivated area.

The big landlords, when emancipation and its accompanying changes were completed, held about a quarter of agricultural Germany. West of the Elbe an appreciable part of the rather rare big estates was let to farmers. East of the Elbe, where big estates were common, they were nearly all in hand. The typical eastern Junker lived on and directed the management of an estate with perhaps 2000 acres of cultivated land including the meadows, to which was normally attached some forest and perhaps some waste, part of the ancient commons which it had been worth no one's while to bring under cultivation.

§ 53. Before dealing with the modern history of the commons and the fields, something more may be said of the forests. Forest covered a quarter of the new Empire, and the area of forest land remained fairly constant throughout the second half of the nineteenth century. The total was not much less than 35,000,000 acres, considerably more than half the area of

Great Britain. Of these immense forests private persons owned nearly one-half, mainly in the east; the communes owned about one-sixth, mainly in the west; the crowned heads in their private capacity and the state in its public capacity together nearly a third. The privately owned forest area was more than three-quarters the size of Ireland. It may be recalled that east of the Elbe the legal view had long been that forest was the lord's, even when the peasant had customary rights in it. The western view was the reverse of this, though there were private and state forests in the west also.

This great area of forest, of which about two-thirds was coniferous timber and one-third deciduous—mainly beech and oak—gave direct employment in the twentieth century to more people than the German chemical industry. They were not all fully employed in the woods, as forestry is an admirable by-industry for small holders. About 126,000 (of whom 103,000 were wage earners) had forestry as their main occupation in 1907, and about half as many used it as a by-industry. The comparative smallness of the figures when compared with the vast area illustrates clearly what a small addition to a nation's opportunities for employment even a very great forest industry furnishes. On the German scale, Great Britain, if entirely covered with forests, would not carry 300,000 workers of all classes.

It was pointed out in Chapter II, that, as a result of the legislation of the eighteenth and early nineteenth centuries, a considerable part of the commons of Germany had been divided up before 1850. Division in the earlier years had generally taken the form of a separation between the lord's share of the common, over which he secured complete control, and the peasants' share which they continued to use collectively. But as emancipation went forward and the peasant acquired a more individualistic outlook, division of the common among the peasants also made headway. There was even a certain amount of division of forest in those districts where communal forest ownership persisted. Division of the common grazing ground and waste was closely associated, as in the English inclosure movement, with the rearrangement of the common arable fields.

Generally speaking, where the one went forward so did the other, and *vice versa*.

In the west, as has been seen (see *ante*, § 10), there was no great interest in rearrangement of the fields, before the decade 1840–50, save in a few exceptional districts like Schleswig-Holstein. Hanover, having encouraged the division of many of her extensive heaths at an earlier date, first took up the field question in 1842 and pushed ahead with it in 1856. Baden did not touch it until 1856. Bavaria, in spite of a movement in favour of rearrangement, preferred not to associate this policy with the emancipation law of 1848. A small beginning was made in 1861; but as the consent of a very large majority of the interested parties was required before rearrangement could be started, the law was almost a dead letter, since in such matters large majorities are hard to get. Really effective legislation is found only towards the end of the century, in 1886 and 1899. Nor did the earlier laws of Prussia treat rearrangement as an end in itself. They struck at uneconomic aspects of common field agriculture—rights of pasture on a neighbour's stubble and rights of way over his land. The mere fact that holdings were scattered did not bring them under the law, unless they were subject to some such "servitudes." But, incidentally, reform of these matters had encouraged rearrangement. A certain number of holdings were consolidated, and some peasants moved out of the central villages, where with a three-field system and scattered holdings everyone was bound to live, and built themselves houses on their new land. Not until 1872 was rearrangement as such definitely promoted by Prussian law. Henceforward the whole or some part of any common field system could be overhauled and rearranged, provided a bare majority of the owners demanded it, and the assembly of the Circle (one might say the County) approved.

So then it appears that systematic rearrangement only became a general policy in Germany during the third quarter of the nineteenth century, and that even in the fourth quarter the policy was not everywhere pursued with vigour. Consequently the country remained full of scattered holdings in the twentieth century, though long before 1900, in most cases before 1875, the old binding routine of the open fields was dead. Writing in 1909, a German scholar said that Brunswick was "the single German state in which the reform of the old field system could be reckoned as essentially complete[1]." Elsewhere it was in all stages of completion, most incomplete of all in Bavaria and the south-west.

Still there was a policy, as compared with France where there was none. The Germans noticed when they came into possession of Alsace-Lorraine how little had been done to improve the division of the fields. There was a lack of field roads, which involved the old troubles arising out of rights of way over your neighbour's land. This they tried to remedy by a law of 1884. A second law of 1890 introduced compulsory exchange of parcels of land, when the making of field roads, or irrigation and drainage operations, rendered this necessary. But no attempt was made to overhaul the whole system, probably because the adjacent parts of Germany proper were those in which re-arrangement was least popular and had made least progress (see *ante*, § 10). Throughout the upper Rhine valley, open-field routine had long been dead and the peasants had long tilled their scattered acres with conspicuous success. They were therewith content. So the fields of Alsace went back to France much as they were in 1870.

Meanwhile there had been a perceptible change in the official attitude towards common property, as distinguished from common rights. The early nineteenth century, under the influence of eighteenth century thought, was all for its abolition; although in France the shortsightedness of the cutting up of communal forest had been recognised and the movement stopped (see *ante*, § 3). In Germany the process continued later, but by the middle of the century its inexpedience was beginning to be recognised. And as, with the growing complexity and cost of local government in the later nineteenth century, the provision of communal funds became an urgent political question, the policy of individualising communal property went out of fashion. German thinkers had come to emphasise the historical significance and the reputed German origin of *Genossenschafts-*

[1] F. Grossmann, *Handwörterbuch der Staatswissenschaften*, iv, 639.

wesen, the principle of association. So the remaining commons and communal properties were retained, to be used as a source of revenue and a means of education in *Genossenschaftswesen*. Division of forests was generally prohibited. If it was desired to make better use of waste land, the communes were encouraged to let it to competent cultivators, rather than divide it among their members. Common use of the remaining communal property declined steadily, except in the case of forests and mountain pastures; but communal ownership was retained.

What has been said of the persistence of scattered holdings in modern Germany applies only to peasant land and to districts and states where such land predominates. It does not apply even to all peasant land. Quite apart from nineteenth century consolidation of holdings, there were old established types of holding which needed no consolidation. They were in the marsh colonies and forest colonies formed by German settlers in the north and east during the later middle ages. As was pointed out in describing these colonial villages (see *ante*, § 7), their field system was so well devised and so economical that it did not become obsolete. Each homestead stood at one end of a long drawn out strip of land which was, and always had been, the holding of its occupant.

§ 54. By the time the German Empire was founded, the eastern squires had their estates consolidated almost without exception. The process of emancipation had increased the supply of labour available to work them (see *ante*, § 9); but by about 1875 the rural districts were just beginning to feel the effects of that rapid drift of population to the towns and to foreign countries, which was to complicate all German economic problems for the next forty years. A generation earlier freedom had not meant movement. The peasant or labourer was in practice though not in law bound to his native place. Then came the railways; the revolutionary storms of 1848 which weakened customary social ties; a period of increasingly liberal legislation; and finally the effective freedom of movement which resulted from German union. Before 1866, it was not too easy for a Prussian to move into Saxony or Hanover, foreign countries and potential enemies. After 1871, the right to leave his native parish was almost the only bit of true freedom that the eastern labourer enjoyed.

From the first days of peasant emancipation, the squires of the east had been anxious not to lose control over their people. So they had secured, in spite of Stein's opposition, the ordinance of 1810 (*Gesinde-Ordnung*) regulating the relations of master and servant. Every agricultural labourer who could in any way be regarded as living with his employer came within its scope; and it remained the basis of the Prussian law of master and servant throughout the nineteenth century. Under this law, a contract once entered into could not be terminated prematurely from the workman's side; striking was a crime punishable with imprisonment; obedience was due to the point of absolute servility. Now the typical labour system of the east made these conditions applicable to most labourers, because the majority could be regarded as servants in the eye of the law. The leading hands on an eastern manor were the so-called *Instleute*, men hired by the year and housed by their employer. In the early nineteenth century the *Instmann* was sometimes paid with a scrap of land; but latterly his wage was given partly in money, partly in kind, perhaps with the addition of some potato ground. The wage contract very generally included the labour of wife and children, so that during its currency the *Instmann* was not much better off than the old unfree peasant whose family owed *Gesindedienst* (see *ante*, § 8). Frequently, in recent times, the *Instmann* had labourers under him, whom he engaged, lodged and boarded, who therefore also came within the scope of the law of master and servant. Very little of the social legislation of modern Germany (see *post*, § 81) applied to these people, when first enacted, and it was extended to them only partially and grudgingly. Twenty years after the passing of the industrial insurance code, in the eighties most of the agricultural labourers enjoyed no sickness insurance. As wages were always low, though they had grown steadily since 1850, it is not surprising that the Prussian labourer went to town; that recruits seldom came back to their village; and that from 1875–80 landowners raised a long-drawn wail about rural depopulation, and imported all the cheap foreign labour they could get.

Modern agricultural technique made things worse. The estates of the eastern plains were perfectly suited for its adoption; and there were few better farmers in Europe than the best of the Junkers in the later nineteenth century. After the decade 1840–50 Germany had little to learn from any country in agriculture and forestry. In agricultural chemistry she was unquestionably the leader. The network of railways, becoming denser each year, eased the transport of produce, machinery and fertilisers. As a result the best farmed eastern manors became models of their kind, especially after the hard work of their owners during the agricultural depression of the eighties. But a model estate under modern conditions, especially in the climate of eastern Germany, requires a great deal of seasonal labour. Certain forms of agriculture, such as beet and potato growing, are particularly dependent on such labour. For both seasonal and permanent labour foreigners were drawn upon increasingly from about 1880.

It had long been customary for Polish peasants from the Eastern provinces to migrate for harvest into the German districts; but it was not until the date named that foreigners began to do the same. Once started, the foreign immigration grew rapidly. The great majority were always seasonal labourers, but some took longer jobs. By the twentieth century their numbers had become very large. In 1907, 257,000 foreigners engaged in agriculture were reported; and for 1912–13 the figure was reckoned at more than 500,000[1]. They were found in many parts of the Empire, but were most numerous in provinces where large estates predominated, such as Mecklenburg. Both the permanent and the migratory labourers were in the main Poles, Russian and Austrian subjects at that time, and other Slavs from the Hapsburg Empire. There were regular hiring agencies on the Russian and Austrian frontiers; and latterly (in 1907–8) the Prussian government set up a system of licensing the migrants, who might only enter the country after securing their licenses at certain specified places of entry.

[1] S. von Waltershausen, *op. cit.* p. 451.

On large estates the foreign workpeople, who were of all ages and both sexes though men naturally predominated, were housed in rough barracks and kept under strict discipline, so far as possible, by withholding part of the wage and not paying it if the contract was broken, or if the labourer was irregular in his conduct. On smaller estates the foreigners were housed more roughly still. "There is little sentimentality about the treatment of these foreign labourers," wrote an English observer in 1908. "They are heartily disliked, but they are regarded as a necessary evil[1]." They were necessary not only on the very large estates. Many a substantial German peasant, owning 150 or 250 acres on a Prussian or Pomeranian marsh-colony, employed his handful of Poles or Galicians.

Western Germany, and those districts in the east where peasant property was the rule, had a labour problem closely resembling that of France. In the late nineteenth and twentieth centuries there was a certain amount of immigrant labour, Swiss in the south, Dutch in the west, with everywhere a sprinkling of the Slavs. But the bulk of the labour always, and practically the whole of it in the years from 1850 to 1880, was supplied from the families of the "scrap holders," and from a very small landless group at the bottom of the social scale. The frequency of fairly large peasant holdings made the peasant employer a common type. In the north-west, especially in Hanover, Westphalia and along the Dutch frontier, tenant farming required its labouring class. But, taking Germany as a whole and even including the great estates of the east, the proportion of native agricultural wage earners to cultivating proprietors was always low, and latterly it was declining. When the creation of peasant property was finished, there were in the whole Empire about 2,300,000 holdings of 5 acres and upwards. The smallest of these were not always living holdings, in the sense in which one speaks of a living wage; but the owner at least had his stake in the country. Moreover in fertile and favoured districts, for instance the winelands of the Mosel, some of the very numerous holdings of less than 5 acres were living holdings. To set against these, say, from 2,000,000 to 2,500,000

---

[1] W. H. Dawson, *The Evolution of Modern Germany*, p. 291.

living holdings, there were in 1895 only 3,600,000, and in 1907 only 3,300,000, agricultural wage earners, excluding forestry but including market gardening and cattle breeding. It is true that the wives and children of these wage earners often worked also, but so did the wives and children of the peasants. The fact does not alter the balance between families agriculturally independent and those dependent, altogether or mainly, upon wage work. In a typical peasant land like Bavaria the independent families, in this sense, exceeded the dependent.

In such lands the line between dependence and independence was constantly being crossed, just as in France. The industrious "scrap holder" after working for a wage could add to his holding by purchasing, or more probably by renting, further scraps, of which there was generally a supply available.

The decline in agricultural labourers between 1895 and 1907 is only one aspect of the general decline in the agricultural population of modern Germany. An exceedingly rapid urbanisation set in during the sixties of the nineteenth century. From the fifties to the nineties there was also a heavy emigration to foreign countries, especially to the United States, and mainly from the rural districts. Down to 1844 there had never been more than 33,000 emigrants in any one year. For the five years 1845-9 the annual average was nearly 90,000. For 1854 it has been estimated at 250,000[1]. There was a marked slackening in the sixties, because the War of Secession shut America for a time; and the movement was still slack in the first years of imperial prosperity. In the early eighties, a figure of over 200,000 was again reached but not maintained. For 1886-90 the average was just under 100,000. After 1894 the figure became negligible, and never again touched 40,000. In 1912 it was under 20,000. Germany had no longer men to spare. Urbanisation will be discussed more fully in connection with German industrial history. Here only the rural consequences of migration and emigration need be registered. From 1871 to 1890 the official rural population, *i.e.* the population living in communes of under 2000 inhabitants, remained almost stationary while that of the whole Empire grew remarkably fast. In the

---

[1] These early figures are uncertain.

decade 1871–80 rural population rose a trifle. In 1881–90 it fell to just below the starting point, which was 26,200,000. This official figure is not quite satisfactory. Fortunately after 1890 more exact and more illuminating facts can be got from the German occupation censuses. In 1895 the whole mass of people directly connected with agriculture and forestry, from the squire to the *Instmann*, with their dependents numbered 18,500,000 or 35·8 per cent. of the whole population. Twelve years later the corresponding figures were 17,700,000 and 28·6 per cent. This was the period in which Germany became dependent on Slavonic labour from the south-east and east. The reason is clear.

§ 55. The technical progress in German agriculture between 1850 and 1914, and particularly since the decade 1871–80, has already been referred to. This progress was both stimulated and threatened by the two outstanding events in the agrarian history of modern Germany—within a single decade she ceased to be a food exporting country and began to feel the whole pressure of foreign competition of the modern sort in her foodstuff markets. When England ceased to be self-sufficing, towards the end of the eighteenth century, the flooding of her markets with imported food was a physical impossibility, quite apart from any corn law. "An inconsiderable state...," G. R. Porter wrote so late as 1851, "may exist under circumstances which oblige it to be habitually dependent on the soil of other countries for the food of its inhabitants; but...a very simple calculation would suffice to convince us that this can never be the case with a numerous people[1]." His calculation was that to supply the United Kingdom with wheat alone would take more than twice the amount of shipping which then entered her ports yearly. The amount was just over 7,000,000 tons. Twenty years later it was 18,000,000 tons and forty years later it was over 37,000,000 tons. Porter's simple calculation was in danger in 1870, and was becoming a little ridiculous by 1890. It was still true that no great nation could become completely dependent on her neighbours for food; but a measure of dependence was now possible of which, only a generation earlier, no one had even dreamed.

[1] *Progress of the Nation*, p. 138.

Those twenty years from 1870 to 1890 were the deciding years for Germany. The seas were open and the rail had linked her to the Polish and Hungarian plains, the Russian black earth zone, and the cornlands of Rumania. In all these countries the network of feeding railways, subsidiary yet essential to the main routes, was getting denser. From most of them also water carriage by sea and river was possible as an alternative.

Lack of statistics for Germany as a whole, before 1871, makes it difficult to deal with her transition from a food exporting to a food importing country in precise terms. The transition too was gradual. It was marked by harvest fluctuations and delayed by agricultural improvements. So it always is in such cases. So late as the thirties of the nineteenth century, a run of good harvests and some technical improvements made clear sighted observers wonder whether England might not be made self-sufficing in essentials after all. In Germany there was certainly a heavy export balance of grain in the fifties. Danzig prices were still the European standard (see *ante*, § 28). By the eighties there was an import balance. The scales had tipped over slowly between 1865 and 1875. By a coincidence, the modest grain duties which had always formed part of the Zollverein tariff had been dropped in 1865. So the problem of agrarian protection, which had hardly existed for the Zollverein and had attracted no attention during the years of the North German Confederation (1866–71), soon forced itself on the statesmen of the Empire. Their master was himself an eastern squire, quite untouched by that somewhat cosmopolitan liberalism of the sixties, which had made trade between European nations freer in the early seventies than at any other time either before or since. He was the more susceptible because the foreign agricultural competition which Germany felt first and most severely was that of Russia. Grain was coming to the towns through those eastern provinces of his which so recently had been exporters. In 1877 Germany imported nearly two million tons of Russian rye, oats and barley, as compared with less than a million tons, already a high figure, in 1875. The problem was at that time much less of a wheat problem than in contemporary

France or England; for the German of the seventies was not a great eater of wheaten bread.

Before the seventies were over Bismarck had taken action. His motives were primarily fiscal and political. The Empire, as distinguished from its component states, lived on indirect taxes and needed money for a number of social, political and military objects. But there can be little doubt that, among all the cries of the interests suffering from falling prices, trade depression and foreign competition in the late seventies, that from the interest to which he himself belonged seemed to him the most reasonable. The demand for protection of manufactures he utilised for political ends. The demand for protection of agriculture, of the squire and the peasant, touched deeper prejudices and convictions. Very soon he was arguing that low corn prices were economically harmful to a nation.

The new tariff became law in July 1879, and became operative in 1880. At the last the agrarian party, which was strong in the Reichstag, had forced government to raise the duties originally suggested by a considerable amount. Still, they were moderate. Wheat, rye and oats paid 10 marks per metric ton (about 2s. 2d. per quarter); barley, maize and other grains 5 marks. Duties were also laid on live stock, timber, and other produce of the land. The duties did not keep up prices. Twice again, in the eighties, appeal was made to government and each time government listened. By 1890 the duty on wheat and rye stood at 50 marks the ton (10s. $10\frac{1}{2}d$. per quarter), that on oats at 40 marks, on barley at 22·5, and on maize at 20. Timber and cattle duties were also raised.

After the fall of Bismarck in 1890, a cut was made in the corn duties by his successor Caprivi, as part of a general policy of conciliation towards the masses of the towns. By that time the raised duties were beginning to tell, and German prices were being held well above the world-level. The following table, which is carried into the twentieth century, illustrates the development. It may be noted that Caprivi's wheat and rye duties were 35 marks the ton (7s. $7\frac{1}{2}d$. per quarter); oats 28 and barley 20; that is to say far above Bismarck's original tariff.

Average price of the metric ton of wheat in marks.

	1879–83	1886–90	1896–1900	1901–4
Danzig, customs free	198·85	139·63	128·84	127·41
London	200·00	142·73	134·30	129·05
Berlin	205·08	174·21	154·41	165·56

The slight differences between the London average and the customs free average at Danzig are due either to unimportant differences in the cost of handling or to small variations in average quality at the two places. The general coincidence of the two sets of figures is close and unmistakable. The average Berlin price does not exceed the London price by the exact amount of the duty. This was not to be expected; the less so as duties changed rather rapidly in the eighties. But as time goes on the Berlin price tends more and more to coincide with the free world price, whether that is taken at London or Danzig, plus the tariff and something for carriage. In the years 1901–4 the tariff duty was 35 marks per ton. Prices in the Westphalian industrial area ran higher than in Berlin, which lies nearer to the main corn growing districts of Germany.

It is not possible to follow out here the agrarian tariff policy in all its complex detail during the later years of the Empire. The great contests were over the treaties concluded with corn growing nations under Caprivi, and over the revision of these treaties early in the present century, a revision for which the way was prepared by a further overhauling of the tariff in 1902. Whatever the details, stiff corn duties were maintained; and their effect was more conspicuous than that of higher duties in France, because Germany's dependence on the outer world for essential food was greater and more constant. It was calculated, for instance, that during the five years 1895–1900 German agriculture was able to supply 92·6 per cent. of the nation's needs in rye, but only 73·7 per cent. of its needs in wheat. By this time the country had increased its consumption of wheat per head appreciably since the seventies. In the twentieth century, the balance inclined still further against Germany, in the early years, but improved again somewhat in the years just before the war. The figures of the estimated average weights of the chief crops, as compared with the imports

of the corresponding grains, for selected groups of years, illustrate the measure of Germany's dependence.

Millions of metric tons.

	Wheat		Rye		Barley		Oats	
	Crop	Import	Crop	Import	Crop	Import	Crop	Import
1900–1904	3·90	2·03	9·66	·83	3·12	1·17	6·95	·51
1905–1908	3·72	2·32	9·94	·55	3·15	1·96	7·95	·62
1911–1912	4·21	2·08	11·23	– ·32	3·32	3·30	8·11	3·0
				(export surplus)				

Perhaps the most striking facts about this table are *first*,
the way in which Germany had been artificially turned towards
the production of the more highly taxed grains, wheat and rye,
and the import of the less highly taxed, oats and barley; and
second, the successful effort that was being made to retain the
country's impaired self-sufficiency. The total yield of each of
the four main crops was rising, although in wheat the rise is
barely perceptible. This point must be taken up again in
connection with the technical progress of agriculture. In the
present connection the conclusion is that German agriculture
did not go to sleep behind its tariff wall.

The tariff of the early twentieth century was intricate but
interesting. It showed a sustained effort to make agrarian
protection as little burdensome as possible to the consumer, but
yet to protect every recognised home interest. Besides corn it
dealt with oil seeds, except cotton seed; with nearly every kind
of fruit and vegetables; with nearly every kind of meat; with
horses and cattle, but not donkeys; and with most classes of
timber. Potatoes were a special care. They were taxed in
summer, but free in winter. The cheapest human food at any
rate should come in free at the season of greatest need, if the
home supplies ran short—an unlikely contingency, it may be
added, since Germany produced on an average upwards of
40,000,000 tons of potatoes a year against the United Kingdom's
6–7,000,000 tons.

Undoubtedly the policy initiated in 1879 did in the long run
produce many of the results intended. It was in part a war
insurance policy and as such it was reasonably effective. If

tariff changes and the hope of tariff changes led to unwholesome and speculative fluctuations in land values, as they certainly did, the tariff nevertheless saved Germany from reversion to "extensive" methods of arable farming. Towards these England was driven, during the last two decades of the nineteenth century, in her attempt to compete with the produce of virgin soil lightly farmed. Whether the balance was held exactly between the various rural classes is more doubtful. Large peasants no doubt gained; but small ones, "scrap holders" and labourers had to go to market for a good deal of their bread corn. Compensation through taxes on fruit, vegetables, meat and miscellaneous agricultural produce may have redressed the balance for some of them; but the gain of the poorest is the most disputable.

That the policy, taken by itself, was hurtful to the industrial wage earner was never denied. Many of its advocates maintained that he secured some compensation through its twin-policy of industrial protection. That issue is too complex for discussion here. But some of the ablest advocates of agrarian protection supported the policy with the deliberate object of checking the industrialisation of Germany, and were too sincere not to be aware that checks hurt. On grounds of national health and power; from fear lest Germany should become, like England, an "industry state" with agriculture entirely subordinate; from a still longer sighted fear of the social and moral disasters which might conceivably overtake Western Europe, if its population continued to multiply, crowding into the towns, and living on food drawn precariously from without; for these and kindred reasons they took their stand deliberately with those who were thinking of little but the interests of a district or the rent roll of a class.

§ 56. In investigating some more technical aspects of late nineteenth century agrarian history, the absence of national unity and so of national surveys in the years from 1850 to 1870 is specially unfortunate. For in many ways these were the most critical years in the history of German agriculture. Down to 1850 considerable progress had been made on the large estates, very little on the peasant holdings (see *ante*, § 10). By 1870 the arrears of peasant emancipation had been mostly cleared off and, far more important, the railways had been at work for twenty years. A land with many locally self-sufficing areas and many local price-levels had become an economic unit. Endowed at last with complete control over his holding, better educated, brought by the railway into touch with distant markets, the peasant was waking from his long sleep. But only the most elaborate series of local inquiries, so elaborate that even German patience has never carried them all out, could tell the full story of his waking. In the east no doubt the moment of emancipation, or rather of that "regulation" by which the division of land between the peasantry and their lord was completed, would usually be the moment for the breakdown of the old agrarian routine. Regulation was going on with varying speed for fifty years (1820–70). Where it was accompanied by rearrangement of the fields and the creation of more or less compact holdings, the routine was automatically broken; but rearrangement was far from universal. For a complete picture, regulation and rearrangement would have to be traced village by village.

In the west, where old burdens were more often bought off by a series of annual payments than by a cession of land, and where thorough-going rearrangement was not at this time attempted, there was no stimulus to change at any particular moment. What happened there is still more untraceable by the historian. Silently and often without official record, districts and villages, which had remained bound by tradition, learnt from neighbouring districts, where perhaps agriculture had been individual before the nineteenth century, or from some progressive local landlord. Gradually the village fields ceased to present the uniformity of the old three-course rotation—the rye field, the barley field, the fallow field—and became that patch-work of various crops which can be seen from the railway train, or very much better from the air, by the traveller in central Europe to-day. In the early forties the great uniform fields were characteristic of German peasant agriculture; in the seventies the patch-work of various crops.

Scattered thinly among the patch-work fields of the west, and covering a large part of the land beyond the Elbe, were the broad fields of the *Rittergut*, for the most part not hedged, but otherwise resembling those of an English farm in a district of nineteenth century inclosure, like south Cambridgeshire or the Lincoln Wolds. These were the fields on which the fight for scientific agriculture was won.

Justus von Liebig (see *ante*, § 10) lived long enough (1803–73) to see his teaching put into practice on many of those fields, and to foresee its spread to the whole country. The chief books in which he expounded the chemistry of agriculture as now understood appeared in 1840 and 1842. They laid the foundation for the chemical study of soils, and for the use of "artificials"—chemical manures—to rectify soils, or replace the constituents abstracted from them by various crops. The country had need to be educated up to that use. At Liebig's instigation, the scattered and independent agricultural colleges were transferred to the Universities and equipped with experimental stations. Below the University departments came the full time Agricultural Schools, of which the first was founded at Hildesheim in 1858. By the twentieth century the Empire contained twenty-eight. A still more interesting movement began in the years just before the Empire was created. This was the foundation of winter schools, to which agricultural students and agriculturists could go in the dead season when northern and eastern Germany lie under unbroken snow. A dozen such schools existed in 1870; over 240 in 1906. The last link in the educational chain was the agricultural continuation school, to which the sons of small peasants and labourers from the primary schools could go in winter evenings. This development came a little later than that of the winter schools proper. There were over two thousand continuation schools in the decade 1900–10. So, between 1870 and 1900, the channels were provided through which agricultural knowledge could flow even to the lowest ranks of the independent cultivators.

It is generally agreed that the sugar beet industry did more than anything else to make German agriculturists welcome this knowledge. The industry was well established, after various vicissitudes, by about 1845. Its headquarters were in the country on both sides of the Elbe, south of Magdeburg and into

Saxony; though it was found in many other districts. On the experience of this centrally placed area both east and west could easily draw. Beet growing requires deep ploughing and the seed must be drilled if the crop is to be successful. Therefore it called for the best and most powerful implements. Beet is an exhausting crop; therefore its place in a rotation and the problem of maintaining the fertility of the soil on which it was grown required careful attention. The production of a type of beet with a maximum sugar yield, and the chemical problems raised by its treatment in the factories, invited scientific research. The beet-pulp furnished an excellent cattle food. So on every side the industry touched fundamental questions in agriculture. A table will best illustrate its growth since the sixties:

Years	Average number of tons of beet handled annually	Average annual yield of raw sugar
1866–1870	2,500,000	211,000
1886–1890	8,722,000	1,110,000
1906–1910	13,423,000	2,116,000

The remarkable increase in the yield of sugar per ton of beet will be noted; from about 1 : 12 the proportion of sugar rose to nearly 1 : 6 in the forty years. In the twentieth century there were rather over a million acres under beet, on the average. There were approximately 350 sugar factories employing about 100,000 workpeople. The average factory had increased greatly in size and, since 1895, the number of factories had diminished, as the following figures show:

Date	No. of factories	No. employed
1882	390	67,000
1895	455	95,000
1905	376	about 100,000
1912	342	,, ,,

The potato also helped agricultural development. It was extensively grown, and was used for the distillation of alcohol, early in the nineteenth century. The gigantic crops raised in the later nineteenth and twentieth centuries were in large part also distilled. By that time the gross weight of the potato crop was nearly twice that of all the main corn crops put together. Distillation of potatoes for industrial alcohol was a leading German industry. There were about 5000 distilleries. Potato growing had led to improved crop rotations. Potatoes were used extensively as cattle food, and helped to maintain the head of cattle, especially in the east. What the crop meant, directly and indirectly, for the national food supply was shown to the outside world in 1914–18.

So much of the north German plain is sand, heath or marsh-land, that the problem of increasing the average fertility of the north was not easy. Surface and subsoil drainage were under-taken on a large scale. Nitrates and phosphates were freely applied and special attention was given to "green manuring" —the ploughing in of crops such as the clovers. In various ways the area of cultivation was appreciably increased between 1860 and 1900. The acreage under the main crops between 1880 and 1910 is shown in the following table. It covers a critical period in agrarian history, that of the great fall in prices and the recovery from it. Incidentally, it illustrates again the effect of the tariff in maintaining the cultivation of the principal food grains:

Area under main crops in millions of hectares.

Year	Rye	Wheat	Barley	Oats	Potatoes	Meadow hay	Total
1880	5·9	1·8	1·6	3·7	2·8	5·9	21·7
1891	5·5	1·9	1·8	4·1	2·9	5·9	22·1
1900	5·9	2·0	1·7	4·0	3·2	5·9	22·7
1906	6·1	1·9	1·6	4·2	3·3	5·9	23·0
1912	6·3	1·9	1·6	4·4	3·3	5·9	23·4

This means that 1,700,000 hectares, or over 4,000,000 acres, were added to the area under the main food crops during a bare generation. There was also an increase in some secondary crops, such as beet. There are a few entries on the other side, but they are of no great importance, as the areas affected were not large. The crops concerned are the industrial crops—flax, hemp, and so on—which declined. It must be noted that only part of the added crop area was land newly brought under the plough. A great portion of it was land now used for crops which was formerly left fallow, owing to the survival of the old wasteful crop routines, especially on peasant holdings. It took a good deal more than a generation for the peasantry, so many of whom in the early forties had known only the inherited routine,

to learn how a crop of some kind could be got off their land
nearly every year.

The peasant was also slow to learn how he could get the
maximum yield per acre out of what land he did cultivate. On
the great estates this vital figure was improving steadily in the
fifty years from 1860 to 1910, so steadily that the total agricultural output of the country was enormously increased in that
period. It was improving also on peasant land, but more slowly.
Perhaps the simplest available illustration of the point, at the
close of the period, when peasant education had done its best, is
that given by a comparison of the yields per acre in a German
state where almost all the land is peasant farmed with those in
a state where large holdings predominate. The comparison is
not exact. Differences of fertility may affect it; and there is
no province entirely given up to large holdings. But the one
selected (Mecklenburg-Schwerin) has 60 per cent. of its area
in holdings of over 250 acres, and another 26 per cent. in
holdings of over 50 acres. It is the typical land of the big squire
and the big peasant and it is not naturally very fertile. The
peasant land chosen, Bavaria, of which nearly 70 per cent. is in
holdings under 50 acres, is partly high and infertile but also
contains some very favoured districts.

Average yield in 100 kilogrammes per hectare for the decade
1902–11.

	Rye	Wheat	Barley	Oats	Potatoes	Meadow hay
Mecklenburg	17·9	23·7	22·4	21·2	141·6	41·2
Bavaria	15·8	16·0	17·1	15·6	116·9	48·6

The figures, if not exact, are telling. Where agricultural
knowledge is least needed, in the hay field, Bavaria leads.
Everywhere else it is hopelessly outdistanced, worst of all in
the best crop—wheat. It may be added that Wurtemberg was
rather worse than Bavaria, Baden and Alsace-Lorraine only a
trifle better, in spite of their rich Rhine valley bottom. Even in
potatoes the peasant fails badly. Perhaps he did not keep abreast
of the production of new and fertile varieties. The figures do
not prove that a peasant land cannot be well tilled. A comparison
between Mecklenburg and Denmark might show a different

result. But they are pretty conclusive for the areas, crops, and date selected.

The increase in Germany's crops was more than equalled by the increase in her head of most classes of live stock during the imperial age. These are the figures, in millions:

	Horses	Cattle	Sheep	Pigs	Goats
1873	3·3	15·8	25·0	7·1	2·3
1883	3·5	15·8	19·2	9·2	2·6
1892	3·8	17·5	13·6	12·2	3·1
1900	4·2	18·9	9·7	16·8	3·3
1912	4·5	20·2	5·8	21·9	3·4

The decline in sheep is amazing. The Empire may be said to have dropped sheep farming altogether. In discussing French agriculture, it was pointed out that a decline in sheep was a general feature of the agriculture of Western Europe in the later nineteenth century. The French flocks fell by one-half between 1840 and 1911. In Germany the fall began later but was far more headlong. For this there are general and special reasons. The general reasons are the same as in France (see *ante*, §46)—the difficulty of handling sheep in a land where holdings are mostly small and uninclosed; the decline of rough grazing land before the plough; and the failure, even on large compact holdings, to combine sheep rearing and arable farming as in England. Special reasons were the German distaste for mutton, and the absence of a duty on wool. All grains, nearly all animals, all meats, most timbers were taxed, with a view to keeping German prices above world prices. But the manufacturing interest would not stand a wool duty. Naturally, when a landowner was working out the future of his stock and his crops, wool, the sole product in selling which he would have to face world competition unprotected, would fall into the background of his plans; especially if its joint product, mutton, was not in great demand.

Apart from sheep, the record is one of continuous and brilliant progress, progress most rapid since the price fall and depression of the eighties. It will be noted that the growth in cattle did not coincide, as in England, with a decline in cereals, and that the increase in the number of pigs alone, since 1883, added immensely to the country's resisting capacity in the event of

war, an event which every German agrarian writer and every
great landowner had constantly in view. No discussion of
German agriculture ever omitted the military aspect.

Yet with all her labour and travail Germany was not self-
sufficient at the end in animals and animal products. Take a
few illustrations from the year 1912. She imported 200,000
cattle of all kinds; over £2,000,000 worth of beef; £1,000,000
of bacon; £1,000,000 of milk and cream; over £16,000,000 of
butter, lard, suet, margarine and animal fats of all kinds; but
only 133,000 pigs—excluding sucking pigs. She also bought
horses, sheep, and goats, but the figures here are relatively
unimportant. Dependence on foreign trade for fats was the
critical point. But, for a war of reasonable length, most difficulties could be surmounted by a little extra slaughtering of pigs,
and this was the 1914–15 policy.

§ 57. It has been seen how in France one of the results, and
much the most fortunate result, of the price fall and agrarian
troubles of the eighties was the development of rural cooperation. Of Germany too it was said in 1908 that the cooperative
societies had "done more for the small farmers than all the
agrarian and protective laws together[1]." But in Germany these
societies were not simply products of depression. They were
products of a principle well tried in earlier years and applied
in turn to the various problems of the small—and sometimes of
the large—holder, as those problems became acute.

Germany was the pioneer in cooperative peasant banking—
in cooperative banking generally for that matter; but here only
cooperation on the land is in question. Her peasant banks will
always be connected with the name of Friedrich Wilhelm
Raiffeisen (1818–88), an ex-soldier and burgomaster of a
group of villages in Prussian Rhineland. Raiffeisen's work was
a direct outcome of the famine years 1846–7, years of distress
throughout Europe. To meet the distress he started, among
other experiments, a village cooperative bakery. He followed
this up with various more or less charitable societies which had
not the hall mark of true cooperation. Later (1862) he adopted,
like the other great German cooperative fore-runner Schulze-

---

[1] Dawson, *op. cit.* p. 297.

Delitzsch, whose first activities had been in the towns, the idea
of a small society with unlimited liability, whose members
should lend to one another and go surety for one another. From
1873 onwards this type of organisation became universal for
the Raiffeisen rural banks, their founder and his followers
erecting into a kind of dogma the rule that there should be no
regular subscribed capital, but only a loan fund into which the
peasants put their savings and from which advances were made
to individuals on personal security, with the security of their
little holdings and farming capital in the background[1]. The
true security was the depositing peasants' close personal knowledge of one another, to guarantee which the rule "one bank one
village" also became a dogma in the Raiffeisen school. Liability
was unlimited, partly because in the early days nothing else was
possible, partly because it promoted the maximum of care from
all members when an advance to one of their number was
decided on.

In 1876 Raiffeisen founded a Central Bank at Neuwied to
stand behind the village societies. Its shares were mostly held
by them and all were expected to be affiliated to it. In 1877
a general union of the Raiffeisen banks was started for all
Germany. Its strength was in the west. In 1905 it formed a
loose alliance with a younger and previously independent
association, the Imperial Union of Agricultural Cooperative
Societies.

The Delitzsch banks, whose *clientèle* in time included a fair
proportion of cultivators, were more complex and more commercial. When limited liability was permitted for cooperative
banks, in 1889, they turned towards it; and early in the twentieth
century about a third of them were "limiteds."

The controversies between upholders of the two classes of
banks are as unprofitable, as the history of their relations with
the state, the law, and the churches is intricate. Suffice to
say that in 1895 Prussia, and subsequently several other states,
set up state Central Cooperative Banks to make advances to
associations of cooperators; also that the prominence of Christian

---

[1] To meet subsequent legal requirements the Raiffeisen banks have, since
1889, had small nominal shares for each member.

profession in Raiffeisen circles, together with the leading part taken by the clergy, both Roman Catholic and Protestant, in the promotion of the movement, have provoked hostility among German anticlericals and socialists.

One of the original objects of rural cooperative banks in all countries has been the elimination of the village usurer—the "fist" of Russia, the "gombeenman" of Ireland, and in Germany as a rule the Jew. Raiffeisen in his early apostolic days used to stand in the village market place outbargaining the Jew on behalf of the peasant. This first object had, on the whole, been well attained before the end of the nineteenth century. Most peasants had a good chance of finding a creditor more ready to lend, and much better endowed with bowels of compassion, than the village Jew. As advanced agricultural knowledge spread to the peasantry between 1870 and 1890, the Raiffeisen banks invariably came to act as collective purchasers of fertilisers and cattle feeding stuffs, so reducing or eliminating those chances of fraudulent dealing between experienced trader and simple peasant which before had been unusually high. It was in fact the Raiffeisen teaching that the bank, directly or indirectly, should be the economic centre of village life. The central authorities of the Union at Neuwied set up in course of time organisations from which the village societies could buy tested agricultural requisites at reasonable prices. By the end of the century there was a central factory for artificial manures, a machinery depot at Frankfurt, and in Cologne a wholesale warehouse from which the village societies could buy their more essential requirements, so dispensing with the mercantile middleman. It is the regular sequence of cooperative evolution, as has since been shown in many peasant countries, from Ireland to India.

So, just as in France rural syndicates formed for collective purchase developed all sorts of other activities, in Germany the bank often became the village trading organ. The fact renders interpretation of statistics difficult. It was also a subject of warm controversy in German official and economic circles, for Raiffeisen developments never went unchallenged. This manysided activity was specially characteristic of the Raiffeisen group, and was less developed among other groups of banks, of which there were several besides those already mentioned.

It was in the eighties and nineties of the nineteenth century, the difficult times for all European agriculture, that the cooperative movement, working outwards from the banks, laid strong hold on German peasant society and did for the peasants "more than all the agrarian and protective laws together." By the twentieth century, the fields of activity were pretty well mapped out, and it was a question of steadily occupying them. The sketch of the system in its final form, now to be given, relates to the years 1907–8. Between 1907 and 1911 the whole cooperative movement increased about 30 per cent. in membership. In 1907 the total was 4,000,000; by 1914 it must have been over 6,000,000. And, as will be seen, a very large part of this membership at both dates was rural. There was however no important change in system between 1908 and 1914.

At the centre stood the agrarian credit banks (*Spar- und Darlehnskassen*) of the Imperial Union, which since 1905 included—for statistical purposes at any rate—the Raiffeisen banks. The number was 11–12,000, the membership over 1,000,000. Round, approximate figures are given, because this class of statistics is never exact. Some lesser local agrarian unions, not associated with the Imperial, reported some 200,000 members. To these rural cooperators must be added about a third of the members of the Union of the Schulze-Delitzsch banks, which, though mainly urban, reported approximately that proportion of "independent agriculturists" among their members. The total of the three groups was about 1,400,000 in 1908. Of these a large but uncertain number were also associated for procuring agricultural materials, being members of Raiffeisen organisations.

Outside the Raiffeisen group, the so-called agricultural "procuring societies" were distinct from the banks. It was of course likely that most of those who joined such societies would also be connected with one or other of the different classes of credit societies. This applies also to all the various societies whose object was not the supply of credit, to which reference must now be made. So to some extent the total

figures of cooperators were a paper army. But as it is impossible
to say how far this was so, and as the total figures are much less
important than the figures for the various specialised forms of
cooperation, the point needs no more than this passing reference.
The "procuring societies" proper numbered nearly 2000, with
a membership of over 200,000. Their activities were much the
same as the "procuring" activities of the Raiffeisen banks—
purchase of fertilisers, cattle food, machinery, plough oxen and
other beasts, and so forth. The purchase of plough oxen, with
funds advanced by the societies, had in some cases proved to
be a very valuable form of cooperative enterprise, especially for
small holders who, in the old agrarian terminology, had not
been *spannfähig* (see *ante*, § 8) and so had been forced to hire
at ploughing time, often at ruinous rates. Cooperation was
helping to make these people *spannfähig*; they now had teams
to harness.

Next in importance came the various groups of cooperative
dairies (*Molkereigenossenschaften*). This was a type of society
which had come rapidly to the front since the early nineties of
the nineteenth century. There were in 1908 nearly 3000 cooperative dairies with a membership not much under 250,000.
The high average membership implies efficient local organisation; but inter-local organisation, which would have enabled the
dairy farmers to speak with one voice to the urban consumers,
was somewhat defective—a drawback from the peasants' point
of view but not perhaps altogether a misfortune for the public.
These societies were strongest in the north, in the Prussias,
Brandenburg, Mecklenburg, Holstein and Oldenburg; but there
was also an important group in Saxony and another in Hesse
within reach of the Rhenish industrial region; and a smaller
group down in Wurtemberg. The north had in many parts an
old tradition of cattle tending and an agriculture appropriate
to it. These had developed naturally, just as in Holland, in the
inclosed districts of Schleswig-Holstein and in the "marsh
colonies" of the North Sea and Baltic coasts (see *ante*, § 7).
Holdings in these colonies had always been of fair size, compact,
and often separated by ditches which facilitated the care of
cattle. Climate and soil were favourable to pasture farming. To

these favouring circumstances were added, in recent years, the demand of such cities as Hamburg and Berlin, and the example of the neighbouring Dutch and Danish dairy industries. Pasture farming spread from its original homes, and the substantial peasants and farmers who carried it on began experiments in cooperation, at a comparatively early date. The Oldenburg central society, which dates from 1875, and the Schleswig society (1886) were organisations for selling butter made, not in a cooperative dairy, but by the individual peasant proprietor or farmer. The cooperative dairies proper, to which milk is brought to be made into butter, started in 1888 in Hesse. They were organised in the Baltic provinces and elsewhere during the nineties.

Among the vineyards cooperation had done little. There were about two hundred small vine growers' societies with a membership of 11,000; but they handled a very small part of the grapes grown on the 300,000 acres of German vineyard. Cooperative distillation made no better showing. There were also about two hundred societies, a good deal richer than the vine growers' societies, but with a much smaller total membership—under 4000. Among fruit growers, vegetable growers, and cattle breeders there were a fair number of cooperative societies; among fishermen, forest workers, and slaughterers a few were scattered here and there.

Statistics will not measure exactly the growth of the retail stores (*Konsumvereine*) in the rural districts. The total membership of *Konsumvereine* in 1908 was 1,100,000, appreciably less than the total of the credit societies, and less than half the membership of retail cooperative stores at that time in the much smaller population of the United Kingdom And of these retail cooperators the vast majority in all countries were townsmen. So it cannot be said that the store movement had made a deep mark on German rural life, though, owing to the peasant's familiarity with cooperative methods, it had probably made more progress in rural Germany than in the rural districts of any other country.

Great and beneficial as the progress of rural cooperation had been, its size and its benefits must not be overrated. It has been seen that in the year 1908 there were about 1,400,000 rural members of credit societies. There were nearly 2,500,000 peasant holdings above five acres and about 3,250,000 holdings below five acres in Germany. That is to say something like a quarter of the peasant holders were enrolled in credit societies of one kind or another—on the assumption that every member of a credit society was a peasant holder. This justifies what was said above; that when the twentieth century began, few peasants were in danger of being forced into the hands of usurers for lack of credit facilities. It was a great achievement both for the pioneers and for the rank and file of the cooperative movement. But it would be a mistake to use vague ambitious phrases about the peasant living in an atmosphere of cooperation, or about cooperation having revolutionised the conditions of peasant life. The peasant was a good cooperator crossed on a natural individualist: at times his individualism emerged. In Germany, as in other countries, capitalist commerce and industry hastened to offer him terms and wares nearly, if not quite, so good as those which cooperation could secure. This was from one point of view a cooperative triumph; from another an indefinite postponement of a cooperative victory. The proportions of the total trade in agricultural credit, agricultural produce, and agricultural necessaries which were handled cooperatively were, after all, not very great; even the proportion of the peasant trade so handled was small, credit apart. But, given the shortness of the period during which cooperation had been a powerful force, it would have been no mistake to use ambitious phrases about the prospects of the movement in 1914. The world has yet some time to wait before it can tell how succeeding dark and changeful years have modified the reasonable expectation of 1914[1].

§ 58. The problem of the rural labourer in the east was a matter of earnest official consideration during the last five-and-twenty years of the Hohenzollern Empire. He was discontented and the towns were drawing him away. The restoration to him of his lost interest in the land (see *ante*, § 9) was an obvious solution. But it was a solution which did not get much support from the average manorial lord of the east. Nevertheless Prussian laws of 1890 and 1891 provided for state acquisition of land to be cut up into small holdings. The holdings were to

[1] In 1931 there were about 2,000,000 members of rural credit societies, compared with about 1,400,000 in 1908.

be let out for a rent charge, part of which was to be permanent, in order that the state might keep its hand on the new holders. This was necessary because it was intended that these holdings should never be subdivided or mortgaged. This policy of "nationalisation"—which is almost identical with a policy recommended but not adopted in connection with the Wyndham land purchase scheme in Ireland—was in essentials modelled on the old policy of *Bauernschutz* (see *ante*, §7), and is an interesting illustration of the universal reaction in the late nineteenth century against the individualism of the century's earlier years. The Prussian state was proposing to do laboriously what might have been done much more easily at the time of emancipation and "regulation."

The laws were applied with most vigour where they were most needed—in Pomerania and the Prussias. By 1905 over 300,000 acres had been turned into small holdings, and the state had more than as much again in hand to be dealt with in subsequent years. The great majority of the newly created holdings were of the size usually classed as "middle peasant" holdings, that is $12\frac{1}{2}$ acres and upwards. Only a few hundreds were under $6\frac{1}{4}$ acres. They were conceived of as living holdings, and so did not greatly affect the problem of the labourer proper, except in so far as the prospect of inheriting or procuring such a holding might tend to keep men on the land in provinces, such as Pomerania, where hitherto that prospect had been remote.

With the experience bought in the course of this experiment, the Prussian government eventually set itself to provide real labourer's holdings on the same system. An order of Jan. 1907 authorised the provision of plots so small as one-third of an acre. The avowed object was to guard against the failure of those foreign supplies of labour upon which the east had come to depend. Characteristically, it was enacted that in "nationally threatened districts," *i.e.* where Danes or Poles abounded, such holdings were to be kept in true German hands. There is not much evidence to suggest that in the next seven years the policy did what was hoped of it; but this is a matter on which the historian must speak with reserve.

Side by side with these official attempts to better the economic position of the labourer, there was a growing recognition that the problem was not entirely, perhaps not primarily, one of property. Conditions of work and service had to be humanised, homes made tolerable, village life given some measure of variety and interest, before the situation could be expected to improve. Various individuals and organisations were working in this direction latterly; but since the imperial government had never taken in hand the reform of the law of contract and the law of association (see *ante*, § 54), laws which were in essence relics of serfdom, it was not to be expected that a little well meant philanthropy would heal the labourer's spirit, or make him conscious of "solidarity" with a master who still felt and often spoke as his feudal overlord.

§ 59. The clause of the small holdings law, which contemplated the retention of the newly made holdings in safe German hands, links it to a parallel series of laws by which an attempt had been made to Germanise the province of Posen and those parts of Prussia where Poles predominated. German colonisation eastwards was an ancient story. Its continuance appeared to the imperial government a political necessity, to the academic systematisers of German policy what they called an historical necessity. Early in the nineteenth century, when the Polish ex-serf had no consciousness of nationality, he had been given preferential treatment that he might become a good Prussian. But by the time the Hohenzollern Empire was established, educated by his German masters and infected by the Polish national movement of the sixties, he had become conscious that he was not and did not wish to be a Prussian. The nineteenth century had created what the eighteenth had hardly known, an educated Polish middle class. The education for which Prussia, to her great credit, had made universal provision was turned against her. The new middle class became the guardian of Polish national feeling, and from it the peasantry learnt. As this middle class grew in strength, towards the end of the nineteenth century, "Polonism" spread from the country into the towns of the east, many of which had been predominantly or almost exclusively German in the days when Poland was essentially a land of gentlemen and peasants.

This is not the place to examine the various anti-Polish policies of the Prussian government—the prohibition of Polish speech in all official relations; the floggings of Polish school children who would not say their Lord's Prayer in German; and other less grotesque manifestations of the will to rule. The agrarian policy is in itself sufficiently representative.

Bismarck set on foot the first systematic attempt to colonise the German Polish provinces in 1886. After considering the possibility of simply expropriating the Polish landowners, much as Oliver Cromwell expropriated Irish Papists, he fell back on the modern method of buying them out. Over £17,000,000 were spent on this in the next twenty years. Many Poles made excellent bargains. Some used the purchase money to buy other estates which they sublet in small holdings to Poles, as a counter-weight to their old estates now cut up for Germans. The Poles also set up a cooperative land bank to help small men, Polish men of course, to buy land. They found that German pro-prietors were not unwilling to sell to them, to the disgust of the government. Ten years after Bismarck's law, as many new Polish proprietors had been created as the German proprietors whom the government was establishing at such heavy cost. The Polish land bank often outbid the official Land Commission. So in 1907 the imperial government harked back to something like Bismarck's original idea. If Poles would not sell voluntarily they were to be forced to sell, not at their own price but at the Land Commission's price. This was the last phase.

That the colonisation policy had failed of its main object by 1907 was beyond doubt. About 12,000 families of colonists had been settled, chiefly in West Prussia and Posen. Many of them had done excellently as cultivators. Crops were heavier, live stock far more abundant, waste land much less seldom met with on the colonised land than in the old days. Over three hundred new villages had been created. Economically these people set an excellent example to the Poles, by which the Poles in time profited. But the political aim, the creation of a dam against Polonism, had simply been missed. The Poles continued to multiply and possess the earth. If they were kept from it here and there, they went to the towns and Polonised them, or to Upper Silesia, which was not part of the spoil of the old Polish kingdom, and Polonised its growing industries. The whole policy heightened their national self-consciousness and stimulated their powers of economic organisation. They profited by the money and prosperity which the Prussian government was bringing among them, and gave the Prussian government no thanks. They went on buying land. Between 1896 and 1906, in the two provinces of Posen and West Prussia, the area in German occupation actually declined. Facts such as this explain the last phase in Prussia's Polish agrarian policy. It is most unlikely, in view of what had gone before, that the more ruthless policy, if persisted in, would have achieved what the earlier policy had failed to accomplish, even had it been pursued like its predecessor for twenty years. It lasted a bare seven before the kingdoms were moved[1].

"The tearing away of the Polish speaking provinces of Prussia would only be possible if Prussia were worsted in war," Bismarck said. To reduce this risk he tried to Germanise them while Prussia was at her strongest. He failed, and those very districts to which the colonisation policy had been applied were torn away in 1919. By the irony of history the new Poland took as her inheritance a standard of agriculture and of economic life generally, which she owed in great measure to German diligence and German knowledge. Her recovered provinces would have been less efficient than they now are, had not the determination to beat Bismarck and his Germans acted as an economic spur.

---

[1] It was not vigorously pushed, 1907–14. Sartorius von Waltershausen, *op. cit.* p. 456, complains of Bethmann-Hollweg's inertia. Max Sering, *Manchester Guardian—Reconstruction in Europe*, VI, 370 (1922), says expropriation was only applied in three unimportant cases. Hans Delbrück *Regierung und Volkswille* (2nd ed., 1920), p. 12, who thinks the whole system of German colonisation in the Polish districts was "bankrupt" in 1914, argues that Bismarck did not believe in it and adopted it purely on tactical grounds—hardly a compliment to Bismarck's statesmanship.

CHAPTER X

INDUSTRY INDUSTRIAL POLICY AND LABOUR IN FRANCE, 1848–1914

§ 60. Before the war French statisticians were prophesying that half the population would be urban by 1920 (see *ante*, § 41). In 1851 just a quarter had been urban. This slow movement is a further confirmation of what has been said in earlier chapters about the absence of a thoroughgoing industrial revolution and the maintenance of the rural side of national life in modern France. But the townward movement, if never very rapid, was extraordinarily uniform from year to year. Each decade down to 1911 saw roughly 3 per cent. of the population transferred from the rural to the urban group. Urbanisation and industrial-isation are not interchangeable terms; but, following the practice adopted in previous chapters, the one may be taken as a fair test of the other.

It need not be supposed that this leisurely movement towards industrialism implies any lack of inventiveness, endurance, or organising capacity in the French nation. Under all industrial conditions Frenchmen have shown themselves unusually inventive. France's contributions to the development of the car and the airplane show the same intellectual qualities as Jacquard's loom or Heilmann's combing machine. The endurance of her peasants did not fail their children when turned into factory workers. And it is hard to believe that the nation, which created the ordered routine and flexibility of the modern army, has any fundamental incapacity for that brigading and handling of men and materials in industry, without which the huge standardised production of a modern cotton or steel or chemical manufacture cannot be perfected. It is probably true that often the act of artistic creation in industry—as in many other spheres of life—has come from France, and that more docile and commonplace peoples have standardised and multiplied some product of the French conception with greater success than the French themselves. Perhaps there is something in national character which causes the Frenchman to flag when set to work of standardised monotony. But real proof of such a thesis is not to hand.

That opportunities for industrialism on the largest scale were limited by the course of political events in France, during the later nineteenth century, there can be little doubt. And as little that geographical causes, affecting her supplies of fuel and power, have remained not much less important than they were in the days when Chaptal ascribed England's early leadership to cheap coal and dear labour (see *ante*, § 12). Political forces delayed the creation of a railway network. When that network was fairly complete (1855–60) an age of vigorous industrial expansion began. But the war of 1870, even more the Parisian turmoil of 1871 and the long years of national gloom and self-distrust which followed, chilled the confident ardour without which no nation ever did great work—even in factory building. France was doubting the value of her government and her Republican institutions, and doubting of her own destiny, for the best part of a generation after 1870. Contrast the self-confident, not to say self-satisfied, frame of mind in the England of 1860, in the Germany of 1875, in the United States always.

Until the railway network was complete the fuel position was a constant handicap. Even with the network completed that position was not good. Fresh sources of fuel were discovered at home, but they were hard and expensive to work, and very rarely yielded coal of first rate quality. The discoveries were made in the north, where the coal measures of the Valenciennes field were traced under the cretaceous and tertiary deposits of the western parts of the departments of the North and of the Pas de Calais. Late in the reign of Louis Philippe, coal was found at a depth of from 1000 to 1500 feet south of Lille. The first pit to be worked was at l'Escarpelle, where coal was struck in 1847 and working begun in 1850. Thence the pits were opened up westward—at Courrières and Lens and Loos, and so away towards Béthune and St Omer, during the next thirty or forty years. The joint basin of the North and the Pas de Calais passed from the second to the first place among French coal-fields between 1852 and 1869. In the former year, out of a total French coal output of 5,000,000 metric tons, the Loire basin produced 1,640,000, the North basin 1,000,000, the basins of Le Creusot and Blanzy 400,000, the smaller basins the rest. By 1869 the national output had risen to over 13,000,000 tons. The North and Pas de Calais combined raised 4,300,000; the Loire 3,100,000. Alais in the far south (Department of Gard) came third with 1,300,000 tons, having outdistanced Le Creusot where the coal reserves are small. But, productive as they were, the newly opened deposits about Lens and Loos—still more some of those opened up later towards St Omer—were hard to work. The seams are thin and they dip sharply to the south. There were often difficulties with the overlying strata. Pit-head prices were relatively high; and the coal is inferior to the better English and German coals. As an illustration of cost, it may be noted that in 1912 the average pit-head price in France was put at 15·63 francs. The corresponding German price was 13·25 and the British 11·25.

France's coal output increased steadily in the later nineteenth century, but never became impressive. It was 16,000,000 metric tons in 1872; 21,000,000 in 1882; 33,000,000 in 1900; and 41,000,000 in 1913. The final figure, which contains a little lignite, may be compared with Great Britain's 292,000,000 tons, Germany's 279,000,000 (of which however 87,500,000 were the inferior lignite), and Belgium's 23,000,000 tons. French production never nearly met the home demand. France imported steadily about half as much as she raised—8,000,000 tons in 1872; 21,000,000 in 1912. Partial dependence on imported coal was not in itself a handicap to industrial development. Germany was a great buyer of British coal down to 1914 (see *post*, § 71). But Germany had large rich coal deposits of her own, placed conveniently for other industrial developments, and she used imported coal chiefly in places easily accessible by natural or artificial waterways; whereas very many important parts of France neither had French coal within easy reach nor were easily accessible by water. In spite of the care given to her canals, France only had really heavy traffic on those of the north-west. It is possible that more public enterprise and efficiency in canal development might have produced heavy traffic, and so greater industrial facilities, elsewhere. If so, we have once more an instance of a cause mainly political.

The war showed that France had neglected one natural aid to industry, the water power of her mountain regions. Compared with Switzerland or Germany her record in hydro-electric work was not good. The vast power latent in such streams as the Rhone or the Isère ran to waste, and that in districts remote from the sea and from the better French coals. It is believed that there were 8,000,000 h.p. easily available. In 1913 only 750,000 h.p. had been harnessed. Again the political factor comes into play; for the utilisation of water power on a large scale is necessarily a matter in which governments have the deciding voice. Any governmental hesitation, incompetence, or indifference will make itself felt. It must be remembered however that efficient and economical hydro-electric developments only became possible, in any country, towards the end of the period with which this chapter deals. The French power problem until the very end of the nineteenth century was a problem in coal. And even the most complete utilisation of her water resources will leave a huge demand for power which only coal or oil can meet.

§ 61. With coal, under modern conditions, go the primary iron and steel trades. Down to the middle of the century France was still smelting more than half her iron ore in little charcoal furnaces, which could not be highly concentrated. They had to be within easy reach of the woods. The transition of all, or nearly all, furnaces to the modern fuel took place under the Second Empire. Political troubles from 1848 to 1852, accompanied by relative stagnation in railway building and industrial development, gave the industry a setback. The output of pig iron had touched a maximum, of nearly 600,000 tons a year, in 1846–7. It did not pass 600,000 tons till 1853. By 1869 it was at 1,400,000 tons. Once more political disasters led to a setback; and it was not until 1874 that the 1869 figure was improved upon. And then the French iron industry, which had been unable to take full advantage of the great iron and steel "boom" of the early seventies, because it had been thrown out of gear by war, was hit by the depression of the late seventies.

The output of the worst year of depression (1879) was hardly any better than that of 1869. Not until the nineties did the output definitely establish itself at over 2,000,000 tons, though twice in the eighties it touched that figure. Meanwhile the decisive inventions of the modern age of steel had been made in England and adopted in France. Down to the sixties France had produced inconsiderable quantities of steel, almost exclusively for cutlery and weapons. The total output in 1851 was only 14,000 tons. Nor had she attained a very large output of wrought iron, the material which, before the steel inventions, was used for railway metal and many other purposes for which steel has since supplanted it. Her output of wrought iron had risen to over 450,000 tons in 1847. After five years of decline, comparable with that in the cast iron figures, the output rose to about 550,000 tons, a point at which it remained almost stationary from 1855 to 1860. In the latter year 30,000 tons of steel were made.

During these years of stationary output, Bessemer in England was working at the process for making cast steel rapidly and in bulk which bears his name. The London Exhibition of 1862 made it known to the world. Between 1863 and 1867 Bessemer converters, paying royalty to the inventor, were adopted in six great French iron works, among which may be noted Le Creusot and Hayange near Thionville. With the Bessemer converter, there came the Siemens furnace, by which higher temperatures for iron and steel working could be attained than hitherto. Steel rails, which cost 600 francs a ton in the early sixties, were to be had for 315 francs in 1867. By 1869, 110,000 tons of Bessemer steel were being turned out yearly; and the total French output of steel and wrought iron combined had for the first time reached 1,000,000 tons, more than that of any country except the United Kingdom, and more than that of all the states which two years later were to form the German Empire. Frenchmen claimed that they had raised Bessemer's invention from its merely empirical stage, and that they were ahead of other nations in scientific metallurgy. Only a metallurgical historian could test the claims. The figures at least suggest that they were not without foundation.

The leading steel producers of France in 1869 were Petin Gaudet of Rive de Gier near St Etienne, the Terre Noire Company in the same district, Schneiders of Le Creusot, the Wendel Company of Hayange, Moyeuvre and Stieringen-Wendel, all in Lorraine, and Dietrich of Niederbronn in Alsace. Other great iron firms were at Commentry and Fourchambault in the centre, at Fraisans (Franche Comté) in the east, Longwy in the extreme north-east, Anzin and Denain in the north. Le Creusot had nearly 10,000 men; Petin Gaudet had 6000; the Wendel Company 5000. All were doing standardised work on the greatest scale—though not, as will appear (see *post*, §67), without some help from tariffs to balance geographical disadvantages.

Two years later all the works of the Wendel Company and those of Dietrich were on German territory[1]. There were German armies of occupation at Longwy and Fraisans. Le Creusot they had never reached nor yet—in that war— Anzin and Denain. Neither had there been much damage in any of the great metallurgical centres. But the cession of Alsace-Lorraine not merely transferred important going concerns; it cut off from France part of a great system of iron deposits whose full value was not known at the time. These are the deposits of the Moselle basin, north and east of Pont-à-Mousson, Metz and Thionville. They were on both sides of the new frontier, for Conflans, Briey and Longwy—all iron towns—remained French. Their ore, the *minette*, is easily worked but not very rich in iron and not well suited to Bessemer steel making, owing to its high proportion of phosphorus. Its full value therefore only came to be realised after the invention of the basic method of making steel, in which phosphorus is removed during the process, by Thomas and Gilchrist in 1878.

For twenty years after 1869, the France that remained improved very little on the 1,000,000 tons of wrought iron and steel turned out in that year. The average output for the five years 1886-90, for example, was only 1,300,000 tons. But with the nineties a rapid change began in both cast iron and steel.

---

[1] Wendel's various establishments were still worked with French capital in 1914. *Rapport sur la situation des principales industries avant la guerre*, 1919, II, 960.

The cast iron output which had struggled slowly up to 2,000,000 tons in the early nineties, was at 3,000,000 tons by 1905 and over 5,000,000 tons in 1913; the output of wrought iron and steel touched 2,000,000 tons in 1899, and rose rapidly from 2,400,000 in 1908 to a maximum of 3,775,000 in 1912. By this time over 3,000,000 tons of it was steel—nearly all basic, made either by Thomas' process or by the open hearth basic process, in a type of furnace invented by the Frenchman Martin. These are the figures for "worked" iron and steel—billets, rails, girders, plates and so forth—given here because they can be compared in a continuous series with those of earlier years. The figure on which recent international comparisons are generally based, the gross figure of steel cast, is a good deal higher. Together with the comparatively insignificant quantities of wrought iron and cutlery steel, it stood at a round 5,000,000 tons in 1912–13. France had increased her steel output in the twentieth century at a greater rate than any other country, though not to a greater extent. In 1913 her 5,000,000 tons compared not too ill with Great Britain's 7,500,000, if not too well with Germany's 17,000,000.

One grave geographical handicap to French metallurgy has not yet been noted. France is short of coal. She is still shorter of coal that makes good coke; and the foreign coal which lies nearest to her eastern metallurgical districts—that of the Saar basin—is not a good coking coal either. Whereas she always imported some 33 per cent. of the coal she used, just before the war she was importing 45 per cent. of her needs in coke. The imported coke was nearly all Westphalian, its price controlled from Germany. On the average a French steel works paid from 50 to 60 per cent. more for its coke than a British or German works. One element in the price, it may be noted, was an import duty which in recent years stood at 1·20 francs the ton.

Although France had lost so much iron ore in 1871, so much remained that an immense development in iron mining was possible in the twentieth century. But the development was more the result of German than of French industrial activity; and German firms became largely interested in the French iron mines. Whether coke moves to ore or ore to coke, in any iron industry, is a matter of relative costs. In the conditions existing as between north-eastern France and Germany it was easiest for ore to go to coke. It went in immense quantities after 1904. In that year France raised 7,000,000 tons of ore. In 1913 she raised 22,000,000 tons, of which 20,000,000 came from the one department of Meurthe et Moselle, mainly from the north-east corner—Briey to Longwy. Of this great output, much greater than that of the United Kingdom, she exported no less than 10,000,000 tons. She had become the greatest exporter in the world. One understands why the German industrial expansionists in 1915 wanted to retain that north-east corner. They would have crippled the French iron industry, in all probability for ever, and guaranteed their own supplies of raw material.

For local reasons, a certain amount of the *minette* moved from Germany and Luxemburg into France. France also drew some Bessemer—non-phosphoric—ores from Bilbao. But as she was unable to consume much more than a half of her own ore output, and as her southern departments had special difficulties in procuring fuel, she made very little use of the rich ores of Algeria. The bulk of these went by sea to Middlesbrough, to be smelted with the excellent Durham coke that was produced only a few miles away.

Fuel costs being high and the tariff on iron and steel also high, it is not surprising that the French iron masters habitually made far better prices than those of England or Germany—nor that they were in a poor position to compete in outside markets; although, after 1890, they were organised into powerful associations, central and local, such as the *Comité des Forges de France* and the *Comptoir Métallurgique de Longwy*.

In an earlier chapter the development of French industrialism was measured in terms of steam-engines and, judged by this standard, it was found to have been almost ludicrously slow down to the forties. From what has just been said of French mining and metallurgy in the second half of the nineteenth century and the opening years of the twentieth, the progress in the use of power may be inferred. Only a few figures need be given in further illustration. They are those of steam power used in industry, including the generation of electricity, but excluding locomotives, tramways, and marine engines:

1840	34,000 h.p.	1890	863,000 h.p.
1850	67,000 „	1900	1,791,000 „
1860	178,000 „	1910	2,913,000 „
1870	336,000 „	1913	3,539,000 „
1880	544,000 „		

When to the later figures are added the 750,000 h.p. generated by hydro-electric installations, nearly if not quite all created since 1900, it might easily be argued that an "industrial revolution" began in France somewhere about the year 1895. All the power used in French industry in 1890 would only have driven a few squadrons of the capital ships of 1920.

In all countries, the most conservative branch of the metallurgical trades has been that of cutlery. In France, its history furnishes a specially striking instance of the late and partial adoption of power and of modern methods of organisation. Early in the nineteenth century the trade was still carried on as a pure handicraft by master cutlers of the medieval type. It had long been concentrated at Thiers, in the hill country of Auvergne, with minor concentrations on the head waters of the Marne—Langres and Nogent—at Châtellerault in Poitou, and, like almost every other French industry, in Paris. By 1839 it was supposed to employ 16,000 workers, of whom 12,000 were in Auvergne. At Thiers the blades were made in the workers' homes, and the master cutlers simply mounted and finished them. Water power had long been used for grinding. About 1840 the first factory is heard of; and by 1862 Thiers seems to have been ahead of other European cutlery centres in the use of water driven machinery for stamping, boring, and so on. It had built up a considerable export trade. It had also adopted a most elaborate division of labour, though most of the workers were still half cutlers half peasants, and individual businesses were very small.

And so things remained there right into the twentieth century —cutler's shops scattered about the adjacent villages; grinders renting their own work rooms by the water side and regulating their own hours of labour; small power driven factories doing by machinery such processes as might be so done with advantage, and giving out other processes to the appropriate specialised workers.

At Nogent a strong body of hand workers continued to turn out the very finest cutlery all through the period with which this chapter deals, though water and steam driven factories grew up there in the late nineteenth century. About Châtellerault on the other hand, the factory system, which was introduced in the third quarter of the century, had almost completely ousted the domestic workshop when the century closed. But the factories were small. At Paris about a thousand highly skilled cutlers continued to make or finish for market the finest hand made goods, especially surgical instruments. In 1906 there were in all France 3400 cutlery businesses. They employed 18,500 workpeople, or an average of 5·4 per firm. Of the 3400 firms only 130 employed 10 or more workpeople. Even if it be assumed that the smallest concerns had not more than one or two, the figures leave no room for any considerable number of large establishments, and reveal a very primitive organisation in the trade as a whole.

As compared with other metal using industries, Parisian cutlery was a small affair, merely one of the innumerable artistic or skilled crafts which have always had their home in the capital. Most of them were still conducted without the characteristic organisation of modern industrialism in the third, and even in the fourth, quarter of the nineteenth century. Paris of the siege was essentially a town of workshops rather than of factories, just as it had been in 1848. Not much of the 336,000 h.p. employed in industry in 1870–1 was to be found there. But under the Third Republic it continued to exert its old attractive power, and, as time went on, became the chief centre for many of the finer and even for some of the less fine branches of engineering, besides dominating all the artistic metal industries. No doubt its position, midway between the coal of the north-west and the iron of the north-east, fitted it to become a home of the secondary metallurgical trades. The heavier branches were represented there, during the last quarter of the century, by the iron works of Eiffel at Levallois-Perret, by rolling mills at St Denis, and by boiler works at Belleville and elsewhere.

Among lighter trades were the manufacture of specialised machinery and machine tools, mainly in relatively small shops. The average machine-tool shop, for example, in 1913 employed only 150–175 men. Latterly Paris also became the home of those firms which did so much to develop the characteristic transport mechanism of the current century—Panhard, Daracq, Renault and the rest.

A secondary metallurgical industry which had already developed on modern lines in France before 1870 was the manufacture of textile machinery. Machine making had started in Paris (see *ante*, § 11) in the days when most machines were made of wood with metal fittings. In the period which saw the transition from wood to metal (1825–50) England went ahead once more. Not until the sixties did even leading French textile mills adopt the self-acting metal mule in place of the wooden jenny. By that time textile machine making was best developed in Alsace. Schlumbergers of Mulhouse were the first firm in France and one of the first in Europe. When Alsace was lost some businesses migrated across the Vosges; but much of the industry was lost with Alsace. Certain types of textile machinery were made in fair quantities; but in no important type did France ever again become even approximately self-sufficing. For cotton machinery she relied mainly on England; while most of her wool-combing and wool-spinning machinery continued to come from Alsace. Her linen machinery in 1913 was four-fifths English or Irish. A single French manufacturer produced the rest at Lille.

Dependence on imports in the twentieth century is shown also in two metallurgical industries of fundamental importance—locomotives and steel ships. After importing many locomotives in the early railway days, France settled down to make her own. Her engineers had contributed to the invention. The first steam-carriage seen in Europe was the rather kettle-like contrivance with which Cugnot astonished Paris in 1762, and Marc Séguin claimed the tubular boiler. Locomotive building was eventually developed mainly in the north-western industrial area. It was done in part by the railway companies, but chiefly by private firms. After 1870 it was concentrated, as in most countries, into few hands—eventually only six firms apart from the railways. Four of these were in the north-west. So were the chief railway company's works, those of the Nord near Lille, which turned out some of the finest late nineteenth century locomotives. Yet in the twentieth France imported heavily, though imports varied with demand. In years of slack demand France supplied her own need; but in boom years the French shops showed themselves either not equipped to meet a maximum demand or unable to compete with some foreign shops, in spite of a stiff tariff. They met all the calls made upon them in the early years of the century; but with a period of active construction from 1906 to 1912 the deficiency became apparent. The average annual delivery of locomotives for the six years was 535. Of these the companies built on an average 48 a year; French firms 317; and foreign firms 140. The foreign firms were almost all Belgian or German.

§ 62. The story of steel shipbuilding is of far wider significance than that of locomotive building. In the eighteenth century the French were excellent seamen and navigators, and as shipbuilders certainly not inferior to the English. The great wars hindered the development of their mercantile marine and almost abolished their fighting navy. With peace the mercantile marine revived; but it was never able to make up the ground lost to England. In 1848–50 its tonnage was nearly 700,000, as compared with the United Kingdom's 3,565,000 tons, and the ships were all built of wood. Steamers were negligible. In 1860 and in 1870 total tonnage stood at about 1,000,000, being in 1870 just over one-sixth of that of the United Kingdom. Steam tonnage in 1870 had grown to 154,000. The subsequent history was as follows[1]:

		1880	1890	1900	1910
Total tonnage:	France	919,000	944,000	1,038,000	1,452,000
	U.K.	6,600,000	8,000,000	9,300,000	11,500,000
Steam tonnage:	France	278,000	500,000	527,000	816,000
	U.K.	2,700,000	5,000,000	7,200,000	10,400,000

It is interesting to note that the French sailing fleet was larger

[1] These figures are from the British return, Cd. 6180 of 1912. There are various statistical difficulties connected with them which cannot be discussed here. French figures show, what this table does not, that the sailing tonnage reached a maximum in 1906 and declined later.

in 1910 than in 1900. The fact that the French figures are for all boats of two tons and upwards, and so include the fishing fleet, is only a partial explanation. It is evident that circumstances in France were favourable to the survival of the sailer and unfavourable to the early creation of a steamer fleet. One circumstance was artificial. The government in 1892 gave a specially generous bounty to builders of sailing ships. Another was natural. The character of the Mediterranean coasting trade helped to keep sailing ships at sea. But far more important are the circumstances which hindered the construction of steamers.

As a competitor for the steamer traffic of the high seas under modern conditions, France was hampered by the date at which the transition to those conditions occurred; by the geographical situation of her metallurgical and shipbuilding industries; by the nature of her seaborne trade; and by her commercial policy. The transition fell in the twenty years 1870–90. In the former the United Kingdom had a steam fleet of 1,100,000 tons, still largely wooden; in the latter a fleet of 5,000,000 tons, mainly of steel. During these years France was recovering from the war and just realising the full mineral resources of her remaining eastern provinces. But those resources were particularly ill-placed for shipbuilding. The long and expensive haul of coke to ore was repeated in the haul of plates to shipyards. The northern coal-field was near tide-water but was not a first rate producer of metallurgical coke and was short of iron. Although its facilities for procuring seaborne ore supplies were fairly good they were not comparable with those of Middlesbrough or the Clyde. The Channel ports are not naturally convenient for shipbuilding. Havre, which did more than any, is an artificial creation. The Atlantic, Biscay and Mediterranean ports are all far from French coal or iron.

France lacked also bulky cargoes for export. An English steamer could always go out in coal. Apart from casks of the cheaper wines and timber from the southern Biscay coast, nearly all French exports were of great value in proportion to their bulk. From the commercial side there were good opportunities for the development of quick liner traffic, but not for that of the slow tramp traffic which employed so much British tonnage.

It is hard, if not impossible, to determine whether commercial policy in its details hampered or encouraged mercantile shipbuilding between 1870 and 1910. The policy included bounties, and so, from one side, was encouraging. But the import duties on coke, steel, machinery and nearly all ship building requisites were accompanied by high home prices for these things; and it is doubtful whether the adjustment of bounty to prices was so accurate as to produce a net balance of encouragement. However the details may have worked, France's general commercial policy certainly hampered maritime enterprise, and so shipbuilding. A nation which aims at self-sufficiency, as she did, broadly speaking, must not expect to be a great ocean carrier. History seems to show that people who carry much for others have always first been obliged to carry much for themselves. Medieval Venice, Holland in early modern times, and nineteenth century England are cases in point.

However the forces may have combined, the result was that France's steam fleet, including steamers bought abroad, only increased about 3½-fold between 1870 and 1900, against the United Kingdom's 6-fold. Between 1900 and 1910 the French rate of increase was faster than the British; but by this time France was so far behind that her greater proportional growth was only a fraction of Great Britain's actual growth. And she only secured this growth by buying British built ships. Figures of French construction and purchase, even for the present century, are far from satisfactory; but apparently in the last years before the war France was buying from 50 to 60 per cent. of the amount of tonnage that she built. It was estimated that her total productive capacity for merchant ships in 1914 was not more than 140,000 tons gross per annum, as compared with the United Kingdom's two to three millions.

§ 63. Industrial progress outside the metallurgical industries was most rapid, under the Second Empire, in the cotton industry. It has been seen that this industry had undergone revolutionary changes in Alsace before 1850 (see *ante*, § 14). The changes continued. By 1870 Mulhouse could compete with Lancashire at some points. Its textile machinery was first rate. It span the finest yarn in France. It did as good calico printing as any place in Europe. It had almost got rid of the hand loom. Of 47,000 looms reported from the whole Alsatian and Vosges area in 1867, only 9000 were hand worked, and these were mostly in out of the way places. For France as a whole the figures are very different—200,000 hand and 80,000 power looms.

They show clearly the continued predominance of hand weaving in the other great manufacturing districts, those of Rouen and Lille. Rouen did more spinning than any other district. In the fifties it was surrounded with fair-sized mills, many driven by water. There were 225 mills, with an average of 6000 spindles, in the department of Seine-Inférieure in 1859. By 1867 the number had fallen to 198, but the spindle average had risen to 7500. The eight intervening years had seen the American civil war and the European cotton famine, and an accentuated competition from England in consequence of the Cobden Treaty of 1860. In 1867 the Norman district contained more than half the spindles of France; the Lille district just over one-sixth; the Alsatian district rather more than a third, but it did the finest work. The estimated total was 6,800,000. Both Normandy and Lille had a fair number of power looms, though proportionally to the hand looms far less than Alsace. A fourth district should be noted, if only because it still used nothing but hand looms. This was the muslin weaving area of Tarare and Roanne, north-west of Lyons. It was not a spinning region. When transport and tariffs permitted it used English yarns; failing them, Alsatian.

Once more the Treaty of Frankfurt dislocated a great French industry. Many Alsatian manufacturers refused to accept German nationality and made a fresh start on the French side of the Vosges, in the districts of St Dié and Epinal, districts to which the cotton industry had already spread from Alsace. But this took time and it was impossible to improvise a manu- facturing equipment comparable with that of Mulhouse. How- ever, by 1874 the French consumption of raw cotton had risen above its previous maximum (124,000,000 kilograms, in 1869) thanks to the energy of Rouen and Lille. The universal trade activity of the mid-seventies carried the figure rapidly up to 158,000,000 kilos in 1876—a figure that was not reached again for fifteen years. The following table gives the years of maximum and minimum consumption, and the year's consumption in kilos, for each decade:

1870–9 { Max. 158,000,000 in 1876
        { Min. 87,000,000 in 1873

1890–9 { Max. 216,000,000 in 1897
        { Min. 147,000,000 in 1890

1910–9 { Max. 346,000,000 in 1912
        { Min. 106,000,000 in 1914

1880–9 { Max. 155,000,000 in 1887
        { Min. 122,000,000 in 1888

1900–9 { Max. 319,000,000 in 1909
        { Min. 193,000,000 in 1900

The net result is easily summarised—stagnation from 1876 to 1890 and steady growth for the next twenty-four years.

The French cotton interest, and the spinning branch in particular, has always credited this stagnation to the commercial arrangements made with England and Belgium in 1873, which maintained the system of 1860, and to the commercial treaties based on the tariff of 1881 which provided for "most favoured nations," a group including both Belgium and England, duties which were on the whole rather easier than those of the previous decade. There was never anything approaching to absolute free trade; but the tariff barrier was one which the better English goods could generally cross. In 1892 begins the most modern era of French commercial policy with the high duties of the so-called Méline tariff. There can be little doubt that the marked increase of cotton consumption in the nineties, coinciding as it did with a great development in metallurgy and the use of power, was closely connected with the new policy, though not entirely attributable to it. France was deliberately forcing industrialism, for reasons which she judged adequate.

The forcing process completed the technical transformation of the cotton industry. For example, during the twenty-five years from 1867 to 1892, the hand loom had been steadily losing ground in Normandy and the north; but in the latter year there were still a few thousand hand loom weavers in the Norman area. By the end of the century they had gone. There remained however right down to 1914 one important centre of hand loom weaving and some scattered hand looms in many places. The centre was Tarare. There were hand looms in the town itself;

9

and in the surrounding district lived many of the old fashioned peasant weavers, who tilled their fields and wove in their spare time. Tarare was hit in a curious fashion during the early years of the twentieth century, the suppression of religious orders and the decline in the ceremonial taking of the *première communion* having greatly reduced the demand for fine lawn and muslin; but the trade as a whole remained fairly active.

Perhaps the most striking features in the history of the industry between 1880 and 1914 were the growing importance of the eastern area, whose development was so closely connected with the events of 1871, and the relative decline of Normandy. The east had the advantages of complete modern equipment and cheap labour; though against these had to be set the heavy transport charges on cotton from Havre and Antwerp and on coal from wherever it came. The water power of the district had not been effectively harnessed. Nevertheless in 1912, out of 7,600,000 spindles in all France the east claimed nearly 3,000,000. Lille with Roubaix and Tourcoing had 2,500,000 and Normandy 1,500,000. The rest were at St Quentin and a few other places. Of 110,300 power looms, 60,700 were in the east, 18,600 in Normandy, 16,000 in the north and 15,000 in the Tarare district, which also contained the greater part of France's 25–30,000 cotton hand looms[1].

As an indication of the size of the French industry in 1912, its 7,600,000 spindles and 140,000 looms may be compared with Germany's 10,500,000 spindles and 230,000 looms, or with Great Britain's 57,000,000 spindles and 725,000 looms. The comparison with Germany, whose population was more than 50 per cent. greater, is not unfavourable. Moreover, in spite of the high costs both of machinery and of fuel, France had succeeded in increasing her cotton exports considerably between 1909 and 1914. In 1913 they were valued at over £15,000,000 as against £2,000,000 of imports. But more than half the exports went to her own colonial markets where she had made for herself an artificial monopoly; so this branch of her trade can hardly be taken as a test of manufacturing efficiency. The balance, some £7,000,000, can be so taken; for it was chiefly

[1] See Forrester, *The French Cotton Industry* (1921), p. 34.

composed of specialities which she was able to force into neighbouring markets, headed by that of England, through their
sheer quality.

§ 64. It has been pointed out (see *ante*, § 14) that, in the first
half of the nineteenth century, France's great achievement in
connection with the wool manufacture was the creation of a home
supply of fine wool, which provided material for the combed
wool (worsted) industries of Reims, Fourmies and Le Cateau.
Imports of Australian and other wool did not become important
until about 1835; and it is probable that in 1850 the home clip
was nearly three times the total imports. From that date imports
increased very rapidly. These were the days of the new combing
machinery—Heilmann's from Alsace, Holden's and others from
England—and of the creation of combing firms by Englishmen
at Reims and at Roubaix. This machinery handled the fine
but rather short Australian wools with special success. By
the early sixties more wool was imported than was grown at
home; and the French merino had lost its quality. Twenty
years later imports were four times the weight of the home clip;
twenty years later again (1901–2–3) six times; and on the eve
of the war nearly eight times the home clip. The home clip,
whose mere weight had been maintained fairly well down to
1891, had fallen continuously from that time, until at last it
was not much above half what it had been in 1890 or in 1860.

In the sixties the French worsted industry was equipping
itself rapidly with modern spinning machinery, built mainly
in Alsace. Roubaix was now the dominant spinning centre,
with nearly half the spindles of France   Then came Reims and
Le Cateau Cambrésis; in a minor group Amiens, St Quentin,
Guise and some others. The power loom made headway,
especially after the treaty of 1860 had scared French manufacturers with the prospect of Bradford competition. But
towards the end of the Second Empire, there were still twice as
many hand looms in the country about Reims as there were
power looms in the town. At Le Cateau and at St Quentin the
hand loom was almost unchallenged. There were economic
reasons for this, reasons which kept the hand loom alive down
to 1914. The industry specialised on light women's fabrics and

always had an export trade in expensive "novelties." Such
fabrics require delicate manipulation and are made in small
quantities of any one pattern, conditions which favour the hand
loom. In the twentieth century the small towns and villages
of the Cambrésis—Solesmes, St Python, Viesly, Neuvilly—
still had a population of weavers on whose old oak looms, worth
about £4 each, "novelties" were made for the great houses of
Reims, Roubaix, Fourmies and St Quentin. There were
weavers also in the St Quentin villages—Estrées, Epéhy,
Hargicourt. They all lived by the trade *de luxe* and were in
some danger of dying with it. They worked 13–14 hours a day
and when work was slack they went on the land[1].

Meanwhile the town industries had gone over to machinery
for all processes; and Roubaix had profited by its nearness to
the coal, and to the ports where the overseas wool was landed, to
strengthen its mechanical equipment and its industrial predominance. Yet, even at Roubaix, a twentieth century factory
wool comber would find work on the land in slack seasons.
By 1910 there were some 2,000,000 worsted spindles in France;
England had about 4,000,000. Nearly 800,000 were in the
joint towns Roubaix-Tourcoing. Just over 900,000 were
divided among Fourmies, Avesnes and various places in the
Cambrésis. Half the remainder were at Reims. Nearly all the
wool combing of France was done at Roubaix though Reims
still shared in the work; and Roubaix contained in 1900 over
a hundred worsted power weaving businesses, which controlled
a large, but not definitely known, proportion of all the looms
of France.

Moreover Roubaix, or to be exact Tourcoing, had by this
time pushed into the woollen industry proper, the industry for
which the wool is carded, not combed, and whose fabrics are
relatively heavy—the broadcloths, blankets, flannels, overcoat
cloths and tweeds; the industry also which makes *drap de
renaissance*, Anglicé shoddy cloth, from the short fibres of
torn up rags. The woollen industry had at one time been spread
over almost the whole of France; but under the old conditions
it had not been strong about Roubaix. By 1910 Tourcoing had

---

[1] *Enquête sur l'état de l'industrie textile*, 1906, II, 485, IV, 426.

more woollen spindles than any other centre. Next came the
Norman cloth district of the lower Seine (Louviers, Evreux,
Elbeuf) and Mazamet in the far south, where an ancient
industry had adapted itself more successfully to modern conditions. Sedan, once famous, had sunk to the fourth place.
The events of 1870–1 had not helped it. These were the four
important centres. After them came Reims, Vienne, and a
crowd of minor places.

As in all countries, the woollen industry had been slower
than the worsted industry to adopt concentrated production
and full mechanical methods. Before 1850 very little progress
had been made, and even late in the nineteenth century movement
was slow. At Elbeuf there were still some 250 small manufacturers of the old type in 1880; by 1904 there were only 35,
but the individual businesses were much larger. The power
loom had not come in effectively until the eighties, and the whole
district had lost ground to the more adaptable manufacturers of
Roubaix; partly because worsted yarn, the Roubaix speciality,
came to be used more and more in fabrics which formerly were
made entirely on "woollen" lines, and partly because certain
old types of fine woollen fabric, such as broadcloth, went out
of fashion. On the coarser side Elbeuf and Sedan lost ground
to the towns of the south, which took up vigorously the manufacture of *drap de renaissance*.

Except for a few specialities, French woollens, which are
chiefly men's wear, never held a position on the international
markets comparable with that held by French worsteds, which
supply the women's demand. And the worsteds always had
to face those tariffs which, in all countries except England, fell
with special severity on articles *de luxe*. Nevertheless the export
of French fabrics, mainly worsteds, was seldom below £8,000,000
a year under the Third Republic and was often much higher.
With the general rise in the world's tariffs, towards the end of
the nineteenth century, France became increasingly dependent
on the open English market, which took between one-half and
two-thirds of all her exports. She lost trade especially in the
United States owing to the high tariffs of the nineties. Her
dependence on England led to a certain instability in her whole

wool industry; because any change in English taste or in English competitive capacity was felt throughout it. The demand in her protected colonial markets was a poor compensation for possible losses in England; since the colonies wanted neither warm cloth for men nor fine dress goods for women in any great quantity.

The classical textile industry of France, silk, had also become extraordinarily dependent on the English market during the two generations which preceded the great war. In 1913 the United Kingdom took 65 per cent. of all the exports; the United States 15 per cent.; the rest of the world the balance. Throughout the entire nineteenth century, any relaxation of the prohibitive mercantilist policy of the eighteenth had brought a rush of French silks into England. The complete freedom established here in 1860, and maintained subsequently, in contrast with the growing protectionism of other countries after the late seventies, had produced the situation of 1913. Meanwhile the French industry had undergone a twofold, though incomplete, transformation. From a pure silk industry *de luxe* it was turning into a more popular industry, which made much use of other materials. And, whereas in the decade 1845–55 it had barely become acquainted with specifically nineteenth century technical methods (see *ante*, § 14), by 1904–14 these methods had conquered a great part of the industrial field. Further, the late nineteenth century saw a marked change in the main sources of raw material.

France had never been completely self-sufficing as a silk producer; but down to 1850 the silk-worm industry of the Rhone valley had supplied the greater part of her needs. Her imports, of cocoons, raw silk or thrown silk, came mainly from Italy and the Levant. It was reckoned that she produced some 25,000,000 kilograms of cocoons in the forties. Then came a disease among the worms, as fatal as the phylloxera in the vineyards, and an average annual output for the decade 1856–66 of not much over 7,000,000 kilograms. There was some recovery in the later sixties; but in 1870 the figure was only 10,000,000. After 1880 even this low figure was only reached once (in 1894); the normal figure down to 1910 being about 8,000,000. After

1910 there was again a sharp drop; and there was no reason to anticipate a recovery.

From the very earliest times silks had come into Europe from the Far East; but it was only after the opening of the Suez Canal (1869) that Far Eastern raw silk began to compete seriously in the Mediterranean markets. With every year after 1870 that competition became stronger. At first the silk was chiefly Chinese, but with the twentieth century there set in an exceedingly rapid growth in the exportable surplus of Japan. Italy's export surplus dwindled as her industries developed, so France drew the greater part of her silk from Asia. Her home production was now not a twentieth of her needs; and of her total consumption (1912) only 15 per cent. came from Europe or the Levant, and over 80 per cent. from the Far East, including Indo-China. *En revanche*, Lyons had become the headquarters of the world's trade in raw silk.

Power looms are first heard of in the Lyons trade before 1850 (see *ante*, § 14); but they made slow progress under the Second Empire. Mechanical "throwing" however made great progress and its technique was much improved. Throwing machinery was not a novelty but its use had hitherto been far from universal. The story of power looms in Lyons and the Lyons area down to the twentieth century is summed up in the following table[1]:

	Power looms	Hand looms town and country	Hand looms Lyons alone
1873	6,000	110,000	35,000
1888	19,000	75,000	12,000
1903	38,000	50,000	4,000

The power looms in 1903 were managed by women; the hand looms were, and always had been, family concerns, at which man, wife and children might all lend a hand. For certain fabrics two women could manage three power looms; but one loom one weaver was the ordinary rule in both branches. By the twentieth century the old fashioned hand loom weavers were refusing to take apprentices, for reasons easily surmised;

---

[1] These are local estimates given before the *Enquête sur l'état de l'industrie textile* in 1904, III, 46. There is a wide margin of possible error. Pariset, *Hist. de la fabrique lyonnaise* (1901), says there were 18,000 power looms in 1879 and 30,000 in 1898, p. 385.

and the fear that Lyons would in consequence be no longer able to produce the finest and richest fabrics was freely expressed. There were still some thousands of these little *maîtres ouvriers* in the town in 1909, a few of whom had a hired assistant; and some of the power loom businesses were on a very small scale. Moreover in the year 1894 electricity began to be applied to the looms where they stood. This was first done in the silk ribbon industry of the St Etienne district. After ten years trial there were 11,000 looms in the district driven through the wires of the *Compagnie électrique de la Loire*, and another 1000 owned by manufacturers who produced their own current. Electricity helped to keep alive the small weaving shops and the cottage looms; but it also tended to drive men from the trade and let in women and girls.

With the steam driven power loom ordinary factory conditions had entered the industry. The *maître fabricant*, the *entrepreneur* of the old order (see *ante*, § 14), tended to become a mill-owner; though even after 1900 he often carried on business in the old way. Joint stock enterprise was rare. There were only two *sociétés anonymes* at Lyons in 1904. But private firms were almost equally effective in curtailing the sphere of the working masters. In spite of electricity such curtailment continued in the decade 1904–14; though at the latter date the transition to factory conditions was not completed; and, owing to the small size of many businesses, promotion from the ranks was still possible.

The competition in home and foreign markets of cheap silk goods, or of goods made from a mixture of silk and other materials by the Germans and the Swiss, had stimulated the transition from domestic to factory conditions. Already in the sixties the wonderful figured silks for which Lyons was once famous were giving way before plainer and more popular fabrics. The use of cotton, of silk spun from waste and broken ends, and later of artificial silk and of mercerised cotton, all encouraged factory methods and fabrics with a popular appeal. Artificial silk was first made in France about 1890; but in 1913 both England and Germany were larger producers. In all three countries the industry was growing rapidly.

The popularisation of "silk" goods had, as one consequence, a slight diffusion of the industry from its old headquarters in the Rhone valley. Silk can go to cotton as readily as cotton to silk; and there is no need to make artificial silk in a mulberry country. But the Rhone valley easily kept its pre-eminence. Heavy tariffs retained for it the home market; its own skill and taste combined with England's free trade policy gave it its great share in ours. And no market could quite forego its finest goods, whatever the price. In the aggregate exports were some 66 per cent. of the total production, or, say, £16,000,000 out of £24,000,000. England alone often took more French silks than France retained.

Against this prosperous if somewhat dangerously situated industry may be put that of linen, which was in a state of absolute decline in the later nineteenth century. It had this in common with silk—that it retained, and in a far greater measure, something of the old technique. In 1913 there were about 42,000 looms for weaving linen or hempen goods in France, and of these 20,000 were hand looms—to be found mainly in the Cambrésis, Maine and Anjou. The total of both classes is small. Figures are lacking for the early nineteenth century; but it is hard to believe that looms were not much more numerous, if in some cases much less efficient, seeing that until after 1860 the power loom was never employed. It is known that the number of factory spindles fell from 907,000 in 1866 to 450,000 in 1904. And the French flax crop fell from 370,000 to 114,000 metric tons in the thirty years from 1883 to 1913. The period since the seventies was one in which the European linen industry as a whole was contracting, losing ground to cotton, and in which the English—though not the British—industry almost died out; but the contraction was much more pronounced in France than in Europe as a whole. It must be traced to a backward technique, which made earnings in linen less than those for corresponding work in cotton; to the absence of special climatic advantages, such as those which have favoured Ireland; and to the competition of a neighbouring population with a lower standard of life, a less exacting factory code, and a greater acquired capacity for certain processes of the industry—the

Belgians. Neither flax-growing nor flax-spinning, as at present carried on, is congenial to a prosperous and assertive industrial democracy. Both declined in France for much the same reasons as in England. The flax and hemp industries in France were only partially replaced by a small jute industry, about Dunkirk and in the Somme valley, an industry whose 130,000 spindles fed 8000 looms in 1913.

§ 65. Among the industries which rose to power in the later nineteenth century, and prepared the way for the twentieth, there were two groups in which France hardly took that rank among the nations which might perhaps have been expected. These were the chemical and the electrical groups. She had in her day led Europe in the application of the young science of chemistry to manufactures, and her succession of distinguished chemists had never failed. Before all others, her government had sought to bring science and industry together. But, until late in the century, it had failed so to organise education as to provide a constant stream of trained working technologists and a body of workpeople responsive to their lead. Here France was far behind Germany. And she lacked the geographical endow-ments which facilitated the growth of a powerful chemical industry in England, with or without adequate educational backing. She had no parallel to the Lancashire and Cheshire chemical district, with its coal, salt, and tide-water; to the south Welsh district where the coal slides down hill to meet the rare ores or the sulphur or the pyrites at sea level; or to the Tees estuary where coal and salt again lie so handy for the sea. France, to take but one illustration, had rock-salt in the east and in the south-west, and she had always made quantities of "bay" salt on the Biscay coast; but there was no coal near any of these regions. Nor had she special deposits of peculiar chemical value, such as Germany had at Stassfurt (see *post*, § 76). Lastly— the point recurs in the discussion of almost every French industry—she had neither cheap coal nor, consequently, a cheap and abundant supply of coal-tar products.

For the finer chemical industries such obstacles are easily overcome, since cost of carriage is no great burden. It is well known, for example, that Germany, before the war, drew chemical by-products of the coking process from England, for the use of her dyeware and other industries. But in the so-called heavy trades—soda, chlorine, the commercial acids, the bulky chemical fertilisers and so on—the obstacles were a grave handicap; though it must not be supposed that the trades were insignificant. They were, however, definitely inferior to those of Germany and England; so that France in spite of her tariffs was a great and growing buyer of foreign chemicals, in the five and twenty years before the war, while French chemicals were not prominent in the world's markets. Only an elaborate technical and statistical analysis could even suggest the extent to which this inferiority was, so to speak, culpable and to what extent it was inevitable.

Facts do suggest a certain lack of perception and initiative in the electrical industries. Here many of the materials are drawn from outside Europe; the workmanship is fine; science and practical subtlety have their full reward; the value of the products is usually high in proportion to their bulk. For such trades France would appear to have certain definite advantages. On the other hand, until she began to harness her water power, the generation of electricity was expensive, a fact which checked consumption and so handicapped the trades; and in these as in other trades not only fuel but also machinery, whether imported or home made, was relatively dear. Yet, on the balance, it is hard to see why the French electrical industries should not have been at least as efficient as those of, say, Switzerland; and it is very doubtful if they were, at any rate up to 1900. With the twentieth century there began a more vigorous development, accompanied by the effective utilisation of water power. But even in 1913, the capital invested in the French electrical industries was not much more than a third of that invested in the corresponding German industries, and, in spite of the high tariff, the imports of electrical generating plant amounted to about a seventh of the estimated total home production; though for some other classes of electrical equipment, for instance lamps, France was nearly self-sufficing.

§ 66. Throughout the series of sketches which have just been given of certain features in the recent history of leading

French industries, the late and incomplete development of industrial concentration has been repeatedly illustrated. It is only necessary to recall the extensive survivals of small scale production in cutlery, silk, and engineering, or the very recent transition from small to fairly large scale production in the Norman woollen industry. For statistical reasons, it is not often possible to trace the process of concentration with precision. For the sugar industry however this can be done and the results are worth quotation, the more so as this industry is an important link between French manufactures and French agriculture. In the season 1883-4, 483 active sugar factories produced 406,000 tons of refined sugar, or an average of 840 tons each. In 1900-1, the year of France's maximum sugar output, 334 factories averaged just over 3000 tons each. In 1912-13 213 factories averaged just over 4000 tons each. The recent concentration is not less conspicuous than is the small output of the average factory in the eighties of the last century.

But in considering concentration in French industry as a whole, the innumerable minor and local trades, to which it has not been possible to give individual attention, must be taken into account. In any country, consideration of those groups will modify the general impression of an overwhelming tendency towards concentration, which examination of the greater industries of the late nineteenth century always produces. In 1898 the 8500 power using "factories" of all sorts, in London, employed on the average only 41 wage earners; and if the 750 greatest concerns are set on one side the average was only 20. And France remained to the end a home of artistic trades, of *ateliers*, of small workshops, many of which made no use of power. In 1896 a census of industries and professions showed that the 575,000 "industrial establishments" in the country averaged 5·5 workpeople each. Only 151 establishments had 1000 or more workpeople. More than 400,000 of the establishments had only one or two workpeople, and another 80,000 had only three or four. Of the 575,000 establishments, 534,500 had less than ten. There is no regular series of such censuses[1],

---

[1] One was taken in 1861; but it is not comparable with that of 1896, as it obviously omitted all the smallest establishments. Instead of 5·5 it gives an average working staff of over 13. Cf. Levasseur, *op. cit.* IV, 576, and Meredith, *Protection in France*, p. 114, where the figures of 1896 are quoted.

and even if there were, the inclusion of all such things as
cabinet makers' and blacksmiths' and wheelwrights' shops is
from some points of view misleading. Fortunately the course
of concentration in power using industries can be conveniently
tested by the statistics of steam power which the French government has collected for very many years. They give the number
of industrial establishments containing one or more steam-
engines and the total horse-power of steam available in France.
Use has already been made of the total figures to illustrate the
aggregate utilisation of power since 1840 (see *ante*, § 61). The
following table gives the facts now required:

Date	No. of establishments	Total h.p.	h.p. per establishment
1852	6,500	76,000	11·7
1862	15,000	205,000	13·6
1872	23,500	338,000	14·4
1882	37,500	612,000	16·3
1892	47,700	966,000	20·2
1902	58,700	2,000,000	34·0
1912	63,000	3,235,000	51·3

These figures confirm strikingly what was said before about
the revolution in the use of power in industry which began
between 1890 and 1900. Down to 1890, the average amount of
power available per establishment is almost incredibly small,
especially when it is remembered that the figures contain the
really great mining and metallurgical concerns. Obviously the
rest were using little 5 and 10 h.p. engines, just as they did in
the fifties and sixties. And even for 1902, though perhaps not
for 1912, the increase in the average utilisation of power is
no doubt to be explained mainly by the expansion of the great
concerns. The relatively small increase in the number of power
using establishments during the final decade will be noted;
though it must not be forgotten that it was precisely in this
decade, and the closing years of the decade 1892–1902, that
the application of electric driving was prolonging the lives
of some small establishments. The ribbon-weaving shops of
St Etienne are not included in these figures. Nor are gas-
engines included; and they played a great part in small establishments everywhere.

In short, it may be said that only in the twentieth century

was the life of the small concern even seriously threatened in France; and that, in this very century, the electric motor and the gas-engine were tending at worst to delay execution, at best to give permanent vitality.

§ 67. It has been seen that, in the nineties, the government of France finally reverted to extreme forcing tactics for the maintenance and development both of her industries and of agriculture. This is therefore the point at which to take up again the history of commercial policy and to discuss its relation to the industrial activity of the period 1892–1912.

When Louis Philippe fell, the system of restrictive industrial tariffs, which the government of the Restoration had built up on Napoleonic foundations, remained almost intact. High duties or absolute prohibitions characterised it. Even the socialists of the short lived Second Republic made no sustained attack on the system, which Louis Napoleon inherited substantially unaltered, although there was a fairly strong free trade minority in the Assembly. He lost very little time in altering it, for he admired Sir Robert Peel and had a measure of real faith in free trade. Between 1853 and 1855 duties on coal, iron, steel and various raw materials and foodstuffs were reduced by imperial decree. If he fought in the open, Napoleon had to face, and sometimes yield ground to, a powerful protectionist majority; and it was for this reason that the famous Cobden Treaty of 1860 was a product of the most secret diplomacy. Napoleon's motives in negotiating it were by no means entirely economic; but its political aspects must be passed over here. The treaty was for ten years. It abolished prohibitions and paved the way for a substantial reduction of duties. On the side of England, it provided for complete abolition of the remaining duties on manufactures and for a great reduction of those on wines and spirits. More—it set an example which all Europe followed during the decade which ended with Sedan. This series of commercial treaties almost all contained the "most favoured nation" clause, by which the contracting parties were pledged to treat one another in the matter of tariffs as favourably as they treated the "most favoured nation"; with the result that any bargain for reduction of a tariff between any two nations applied to all other nations with whom the bargainers had treaties of this type. Of this series of treaties the one which was to become most notorious was that signed between France and the German Zollverein on Aug. 2, 1862. Under this treaty system there grew up in France a so-called "conventional" tariff, applicable to all the countries with which she had treaties —and they were many—and a "general" tariff for the rest of the world. The general tariff itself was revised in a free trade sense.

Closely associated with the policy of 1860 was the reform of the French Navigation Law in 1866. Under the old law, the coasting and colonial trades were reserved almost completely for French ships. Goods imported under the flags of countries which did not produce them were subject to surtaxes. So were non-European goods imported through non-French markets— cotton from Liverpool or coffee from Hamburg. This was the so-called *surtaxe d'entrepôt*. Lastly, foreign-built ships could not be imported at all. This prohibition had been replaced by a duty of 25 per cent. in 1860. Under the law of 1866, most surtaxes, except the *surtaxe d'entrepôt*, disappeared. The colonial trade was partly opened, but the coasting monopoly was retained.

The Chambers never liked Napoleon's policy; and after 1871 the direction of French economic affairs fell into the hands of two of his strongest parliamentary critics—Thiers, as President, and Pouyer-Quertier, a Norman cotton-spinner, the first minister of finance. But they did not attempt a complete reversal of policy. Certain duties were raised for revenue purposes. In matters of navigation, the *surtaxe d'entrepôt* was extended and the *surtaxe de pavillon*, on goods imported under the flags of countries which did not produce them, was revived. Perhaps most important of all, it was decided that duties should be laid on a number of raw materials which had been admitted free since 1860, and that the duties on the corresponding manufactures should be raised. But this brought up the question of the treaties, by which these latter duties were fixed, or at least frequently affected. To free his hands, Thiers denounced the treaties with England and Belgium; but he was still bound by many others, notably by the Treaty of Frankfurt, by which the 1862 treaty with the Zollverein had been transferred to the new German Empire and most favoured nation treatment guaranteed by France to her conqueror. After much negotiation and after the fall of Thiers the whole scheme was abandoned; treaties of July 1873 with England and Belgium revived the system of 1860; and the *surtaxe de pavillon* once more disappeared, after a very brief revival.

Under this "Napoleonic" *régime*, France was left to face the depression and falling prices of the late seventies. Her customs laws were singularly complex; for while her conventional tariff retained the stamp of 1860, her general tariff, though revised to some extent, retained the stamp of a much earlier date. Parts of it went back to 1791 and it still included a large number of absolute prohibitions. Various schemes for a revised general tariff were defeated in the late seventies. There emerged eventually the new general tariff of May 1881, still almost free trade on its agricultural side (see *ante*, § 47) and not excessively protectionist on its industrial side. Raw materials, like foodstuffs, generally remained untaxed. The duties on manufactures were in most cases 24 per cent. higher than the existing conventional rates; but as this was only a basis for bargaining, it was quite likely that, so long as the old type of commercial treaty continued, something like the old conventional rates would continue also. And countries with whom no treaty existed certainly found trade freer than it had been under the former general tariff.

Ten year treaties were concluded with most European states during 1881–3, and in 1882 England was given most favoured nation treatment without a formal treaty. So the system of 1860 was perpetuated in principle and in some cases aggravated, from the point of view of the French protectionist manufacturer and his political sympathisers. The new tariff law was accompanied by a new shipping law (Jan. 1881). Free entry of most raw materials had not given that stimulus to shipping which had been anticipated. France therefore reverted to the ancient policy of bounties—tonnage bounties on shipbuilding, and distance bounties on long voyages.

Speaking generally, prices of all kinds continued to fall throughout the eighties and the French manufacturers' complaints
came in recurring chorus. The agriculturists, as has been seen
(see *ante*, § 47), were able to secure further protection, because
the chief agricultural products were excluded from the commercial treaties; but the manufacturing interest had to await
the expiry of the treaties and a general revision of tariffs. Italy,
for reasons of her own, denounced her treaty in 1888, but tried
to secure most favoured nation treatment by special agreement.
She failed, and France applied the general tariff to all Italian
goods, followed by a special fighting tariff, when the difference
had brought on commercial war. But as France was not a
heavy importer of Italian manufactures, the war is less important
in French industrial than in French agrarian history. It did
interfere with the export of French silks and woollens, and so
tended to annoy the manufacturing interest, which had no
adequate corresponding gains.

The general features of the great "Méline" tariff of 1892,
which was the final outcome of the complaints of the eighties,
have been already mentioned in the discussion of French agricultural policy (see *ante*, § 47). It was intended to tie the hands
of government in tariff bargaining, by means of its fixed minimum rates for commercial friends and its maxima for other
people. As friends were only to be guaranteed the minima, not
a particular level of duties, it was hoped that the hands of
Parliament would remain free to adjust these minima if required.
The schedules were excessively elaborate, and exact comparisons
between the new tariff and its predecessors are therefore difficult.
But its character can easily be illustrated. Though most raw
materials were still allowed free entry—such were wool, silk,
flax, hides and oil seeds—others were now subject to duty.
Of these the most important were timber, coal, and such
iron compounds as ferro-manganese and spiegeleisen. Many
commodities very near to the raw material class were taxed,
for the first time since the sixties—bricks, cement, paving stones
for example. The duties on rough steel manufactures were
reduced, but only because steel had fallen so very much in
value since 1860. Finer steel goods—tool steel, steel wire,

machinery—were subjected to heavy increases, as were most other metal wares. In the textile group, thrown silk, formerly admitted free, was now taxed. All yarn duties were raised, except those on worsted and on some classes of woollen yarn. Duties on linen and cotton fabrics were raised considerably; on jute fabrics slightly; on wool fabrics hardly at all. There were also important increases on rubber goods, paper, and furniture; less general and marked increases on china, earthenware, glass, leather and leather goods.

A feature of the new tariff was the extensive use of bounties. Bounties were given to silk hemp and flax growers, to reconcile them to the free entry of imported silk hemp and flax. Manufacturers using taxed yarns were in certain cases given what amounted to an export bounty by way of compensation. The existing bounty system for sugar and for ships was maintained.

The shipping legislation was in form distinct from the tariff, but was closely associated with it. The *surtaxe d'entrepôt* remained; but the French legislators found they could not afford to apply it to colonial wool imported *via* London. The London market was too strong for them. They used it however to divert imports from Rotterdam and Antwerp to Dunkirk and Havre. Bounties were so oddly arranged that they gave a great stimulus to the construction of sailing tonnage, at a time when everywhere else the sailer was going out of use (see *ante*, § 62).

As a whole the tariff was one of the stiffest in the world, though not so stiff as those of Russia and the United States. On British goods exported to France the duties were reckoned, early in the present century, to average 34 per cent. *ad valorem*, being of course very much higher than that in many leading cases. This then was the wall behind which French industry worked during the period in which it probably expanded faster than at any previous time, and during which the characteristics of modern industrialism began to show themselves conspicuously in French society[1]. Although the system failed of its object in certain cases—it must, for instance, be considered a failure as applied to shipbuilding—it can hardly be doubted that

[1] There was a tariff revision in 1910; but there was no change of principle, and the revised tariff had hardly time to exert much influence before 1914.

French industry, or at any rate certain French industries, which had not at any time been open to the full blast of competition, might have suffered severely had the tariff movement been in the opposite direction. On the other hand, it is impossible to estimate how far the undoubted dearness of many half manufactured goods and of machinery in France, since the nineties, prevented industrial developments which might otherwise have occurred; or to what extent French manufacturers may have been encouraged to maintain antiquated methods by the comfortable shelter of their tariff. The way in which their predecessors were stirred to activity by the free trade treaties with England of 1786 and 1860 suggests that such comfort has its dangers.

To link the industrial activity of 1895–1910 crudely with the tariff, as effect and cause, would be a blunder. No credit can be given to the tariff for some of France's most brilliant industrial achievements in those years—achievements in automobilism or in aviation for example. Yet on the whole it seems reasonable to think that the tariff was, what on previous pages it is assumed to have been, an industrial stimulant. Whether such a stimulant, in association with an agrarian tariff, is, either in the short or in the long run, also a stimulant to the wholesome development of national life is a problem which cannot be entered upon here. There is certainly no evidence that it did anything to promote social harmony; although its advocates constantly appealed to the interests of the wage earning masses who, as it was argued, would have suffered most from the unrestricted competition of foreign manufactures. No doubt this was true; but intensified industrialism merely widened the field of industrial strife, increased the armies of industrial combatants, and awakened among them memories of 1871, of 1848 and of 1789.

§ 68. The story of urban Labour in modern France begins unhappily, with the collapse of the Second Republic and the exilings of Republicans and Socialists after the *coup d'état* of 1851. It has been seen (see *ante*, § 17) that, although the French town workman of the forties was seldom a factory hand, he had nevertheless the wage earners', the so-called proletarian, point of view. He was still very often illiterate; and it is hard to picture the shape in which the social thought of the early nineteenth century had come through to his mind. No doubt he attached an economic meaning to the equality in whose name his father had fought after 1789. No doubt he was conscious of the inequality of the law, and of the complete absence, under every subsequent *régime*, of the political liberty which that father had enjoyed, in name at least, under the First Republic. How soon he fell in love with the word "socialism," coined about the year 1830, and just what meaning he attached to it it is impossible to determine. Some few among the picked minds of his class were attracted by what they read or heard of the fantastic institutional communism of the *bourgeois* Fourier († 1837), who believed that, when once the way had been shown by a few examples, human society would crystallise easily into a series of college-like communities, in which all things would be in common; where spells of work and play, industry and agriculture, education and the arts, would dovetail into one another without friction. The aristocrat St Simon († 1825) they hardly needed to read. He had made fun of the pomp and futility of the Bourbon court; had belittled politics and exalted economics; and had criticised the right of property and the right of inheritance. These views, in their cruder forms, come without teaching to the disinherited, who have been taught to reverence an imperfectly comprehended equality. St Simon's more philosophic speculations were outside their range.

After 1840 social thought began to take more popular forms. In that year appeared Proudhon's notorious question and answer: *Qu'est-ce que la propriété? La propriété c'est le vol.* This was easily remembered, and perhaps its qualifications, in which Proudhon explained that only property enjoyed without labour was theft, were not always read. Still more attractive was Louis Blanc's *Organisation of Labour* (1841), with its attack on the abuses of competition, its assertion of the right to work, and its half finished scheme for cooperative production. But there were still a multitude of very straightforward legal and political reforms needed, before even the least ambitious schemes of social reconstruction could be undertaken with any

hope of success. The failure of the Revolution of 1848 postponed
many of these reforms for another generation.

What the mass of Parisian workmen were probably thinking
most about in 1848, and what the working class leaders and their
bourgeois sympathisers were dreaming of, are best illustrated,
the former by the schemes of the provisional government for
pacifying the capital, and the latter by the debates at the Workers'
Commission, which met subsequently in the Luxembourg,
under the presidency of Louis Blanc. It will be remembered
that there had been bad harvests and trade depression in 1846-8,
and that trade depression always produced an abnormal amount
of unemployment in the luxury trades of Paris and of the other
great urban democratic centre, Lyons. The first offers of the
provisional government were the return of all articles worth
less than ten francs pledged at the pawn shops, and the dedica-
tion of the Tuileries as a place of retirement for the veterans of
labour. The second offers were a guarantee of "existence for
the workman by his work"; a guarantee of "work for all
citizens"; a formal recognition of the workman's right of association; and a present "to the workmen to whom it belongs" of
the balance of Louis Philippe's civil list.

The Luxembourg discussions cannot be so easily summarised.
It is necessary to make selection. They began with an insistent
demand for the organisation of a shorter working day—eleven
hours was the rule in Paris—and for the abolition of sweating
by middlemen, the characteristic abuse of the small workshop
and garret industries of 1848. Government at once decreed a
shorter day and the abolition of "exploitation of workers by
middlemen," both easy things to decree. Later, Louis Blanc
brought forward for discussion what would to-day be called a
town-planning scheme, which recalls Fourier's communities—
groups of buildings each for a hundred families with baths,
schoolroom, reading room and communal kitchen. But the
great debates were those on the organisation of labour, or in
modern terms cooperative production. Honour and not gain,
said Blanc, was to be the motive for work. Wages were to tend
towards equality, until the day came when every man would
give to society the best of his work, and demand from it only

the satisfaction of his needs. As a beginning, the state should establish or acquire factories and workshops, and let them to cooperative associations. The levelling of wages, it must be noted, was not attractive to the rank and file, who were sending up almost daily petitions against levelling competition. The workers of Montmartre even protested against an influx of "Parisians." To secure an outlet for all wares under the new order, governmental "bazaars" were to be established, where the producer could deposit his goods receiving in exchange a negotiable warrant—a proposal which seems to show the influence of Robert Owen's Labour Exchanges of 1832.

The phrases of the Luxembourg passed into the street, and petitioners before the national assembly demanded such things as "the establishment of a democratic republic," "the abolition of the exploitation of man by man," and "the organisation of labour by way of association" (cooperation). Meanwhile extremists like Louis Auguste Blanqui were preaching stronger doctrine and working for that type of revolution which Karl Marx outlined this very year in his Communist Manifesto, with its appeal to the proletarians of all lands to unite. But these were a small minority.

The Luxembourg Commission was not a mere debating society. It did good work in arranging for arbitration between employers and the half organised trade unions, which sprang into life as soon as the pressure of government was relaxed. It also prepared the ground for the establishment, with government assistance, of a few cooperative associations of producers. It was not responsible for the "national workshops"—they were really huge ill-managed relief works—with which the government tried to palliate unemployment. The failure, as some hold the calculated failure, of these works was the immediate cause of the collapse of the provisional government. The dreams of the Luxembourg dissolved. The Constituent Assembly, chosen by universal suffrage, listened to Proudhon expounding his modified doctrine of property and voted him down; listened to Considérant expounding with a half-religious fervour the economic gospel according to Fourier, and laughed. Only a small minority voted even for the bald principle of the right to work; though the majority was ready to endow co-operative associations and discuss with sincerity measures of social reform. Louis Napoleon became President, then Emperor. Blanqui, and many less extreme men, went to prison or exile. There remained a few struggling cooperative associations, a little legislation about savings banks and friendly societies, and many bitter memories.

An attempt had been made to revise the law of 1791 against combinations (see *ante*, § 17). But combinations of all kinds remained illegal under the law of Nov. 1849. Article 1781 of the Civil Code, by which in a wages dispute the master's word was taken as final, and the articles in the Penal Code which made concerted striking or picketing penal offences remained in force. The Empire stood for order, though it was Napoleon's wish to show benevolence so far as benevolence was safe. Had he not himself once written a pamphlet on the extinction of pauperism? But during the fifties he did not feel safe. So none of the legislation of these years was really progressive, from the standpoint of the wage earner; though the tension of official control over economic life was at certain points relaxed.

Between 1860 and 1870, the government moved decidedly towards a system of greater industrial freedom, and took definite action for the betterment of the material life of the towns. Urban sanitation and the housing problem were handled seriously and with some sympathy. Friendly societies were encouraged. In 1864, the clause of the Penal Code which made concerted industrial action a crime was abolished. Four years later the hated article 1781 of the Civil Code disappeared. Trade unions, if not legalised, were tolerated, and prosecutions, which had been numerous in the fifties, slackened. The formation of cooperative societies was encouraged. A deputation of working men was sent to the London international exhibition of 1862, and there agreed to the suggestion that an international working men's association should be called into existence—but that was not part of the imperial plan. And in connection with the Paris exhibition of 1867 an official congress of workmen was again patronised.

One result of the official tolerance of the sixties was that *compagnonnage* (see *ante*, § 17) showed itself still alive, if moribund It had been declining ever since 1830, but so ancient an institution died hard. It was still fairly vigorous among carpenters, wheelwrights and farriers, trades whose organisation had not been affected by nineteenth century developments. The old formalities and turbulent rivalries were not dead; but the system had become an industrial curiosity with no future.

Of infinite significance for the future was the early history of "the International." Three French delegates went to London in Sept. 1864. The delegates met at St Martin's Hall. Mazzini addressed them and so did Marx. The French deputies at this and succeeding conferences were as a rule not extremists. They were advocates of cooperation and of the nationalisation of banking and large estates. But every type of extreme opinion found expression through this "First" International—Marxian communism; the doctrine of revolution for revolution's sake associated with Blanqui; and the more reasoned anarchism of the Russian Bakunin. In all its gatherings and activities there were trials of strength between opportunist and uncompromising revolutionary. The revolutionary element was growing stronger in the seventy trade unions of Paris, during the last years of the Empire.

§ 69. It was common in 1871, when the Empire had fallen and the war had been lost, to put the terrors of the Commune in Paris to the credit of the International. History has rejected this explanation. There were prominent "internationalists" in the government of the Commune. All socialists in matters of economics, in politics they favoured local autonomy—"communalism" as distinct from communism—and so fell into line with those who hated the whole spirit of France's over-centralised government, as the first Napoleon had left it and all succeeding *régimes* had preserved it. But these men, so far as the history of 1871 is known, were not terrorists, not fanatical disciples of Robespierre and St Just like the communal leader Delescluze. They protested against suppression of journals, arbitrary arrests and the other beginnings of terrorism. The bloody episodes of the Commune have no place in any orderly economic evolution, either of opinion or of fact, and cannot be credited to any one group. They were the offspring of hunger, defeat and armed idleness, begotten on the class divisions, class hatreds and suspicions of Paris. "At bottom," wrote one who lived through it, "it is a war of the proletariat against property and the wage system; nearly every wage earner is on the side of the Commune[1]." He was; but not entirely for economic reasons. His national pride was humiliated. If others had fought as we have, might things not have been different, he was saying. We would have died, but these surrendered to the Prussian. What else would you expect of the *bourgeois*? The capitalist is a born capitulator. He would save his dirty wealth.

To this day, in socialist histories of 1871, the confused and savage emotions packed into that jingle of words—*capitaliste* and *capitulard*—are stirred again, to the detriment of clear thinking and of the peace of France[2].

The men whose army had crushed the Commune, and shot the communards in heaps against the walls of Père la Chaise, did not think clearly either. Survivors were transported wholesale and the International, their reputed instigator, was proscribed by law in March 1872. Amnesty to the political offenders of 1871 was not offered for eight years; and the Third Republic had been thirteen years in existence before, by the law of 1884, complete freedom of association was granted to the wage earners of France.

French industry had not been up to that time a good soil for the growth of large working class organisations, quite apart from the legal difficulties. But trade unions were tolerated after 1871, provided they kept reasonably quiet. So they grew almost as quickly as industrial conditions warranted. In Paris, the task of reorganising them after the tragedies of 1871 was undertaken by Barberet, a Republican journalist whose activities were specially favoured by government because he held that strikes are acts of treason against democracy. His policy was much the same as that of the Liberal trade unionists of contemporary England. In Paris the unions grew rapidly. There were between 130 and 140 in existence by 1875. Next year they organised

---

[1] Dauban, *Le fond de la société sous la Commune*, p. 77.
[2] See, for instance, the huge *Histoire socialiste*, edited by Jaurès.

the first French Labour Congress, a Congress which clung to cooperative ideals and repudiated Socialism as "a *bourgeois* Utopia." But already by 1879 the "nationalisation of the means of production" became one of the avowed ideals of the Congress; though it is exceedingly hard to say how much active socialist conviction such a resolution implies at any time or place. The change to avowed socialism came about with the return of exiles and the conclusion of terms of imprisonment, as in the case of Jules Guesde, a southern journalist who had fled to Switzerland to avoid a sentence of five years imprisonment, inflicted on him for expressing sympathy with the Commune. He came back a Marxian, to fight and beat the "moderates" and the "co-operators."

With the eighties, begins the stormy and difficult history of the socialists as a political party or group of parties—a group from which sprang many of the great political names of modern France. This is not the place to record party struggles, dissensions, programmes and hopes; but rather spontaneous economic development and the economic achievements of the state. Now in the France of 1914 there was probably less "practical socialism," less socialist achievement in the broadest sense, than in any other country of Western Europe. The state owned a few more railways than it had owned in 1871. There was a certain limited amount of what used to be called municipal socialism; but private ownership of the land and the means of production, wage labour, inheritance and the other hall marks of "the capitalist age" were untouched. So it was everywhere; but France was not even leading in "socialistic" developments. Factory acts and state care for the aged and helpless were developed further in the United Kingdom; the subordination of individual interests to the collective life of the municipality, further in Germany; urban cooperation much further in England, and rural cooperation much further in Denmark. The British death duties and income tax of the twentieth century were more "socialistic" than any French taxes. With her endless array of small holdings, her little workshops, and her thrifty peasantry and *bourgeoisie*, France was a difficult field for the pure socialist to till. So she became a home of compromise parties—radical socialists, liberal socialists and the like, who accommodated their doctrine to facts, and generally managed to find room in it for various kinds of property which they were not prepared, with Proudhon, to call theft.

The syndicates, both before and after the law of 1884, were a battleground for the socialist parties and for those parties who went beyond or aside from socialism proper—anarchists and, latterly, syndicalists in the specialised twentieth century sense of the word. To the end the typical French syndicates were weak, poor, and ill organised, compared with the great British trade unions. In the eighties and early nineties of the last century their total membership was insignificant. Statistics of syndicates legally constituted, which are probably not exhaustive but are the only figures available, show a total of only 140,000 in 1890 but of 420,000 in 1895. These figures exclude the agricultural syndicates and are comparable with British trade union statistics. The British figure remained fairly steady at about 1,400,000 in the early nineties. In France the growth was continuous after 1900, following a period of stagnation from 1895 to 1899. There were 589,000 unionists in 1901, 836,000 in 1906, and 1,029,000 in 1911. Even allowing for France's much smaller industrial population, this 1,000,000 compares badly with the United Kingdom's 3,018,903 for the same year; although it reflects a great deal of successful organising work in a relatively short period. There were many British Unions with a continuous history of fifty years and more, whereas the French syndicates were almost all young.

The typical French syndicate remained small throughout. The average membership was 140 in 1890 and only 200 in 1911. This helps to explain the great importance of federation in the later history of the French labour movement. With her small towns and coal-fields and her generally scattered industries, France did not easily produce such powerful single organisations as the Lancashire cotton spinners or the Durham miners; so that if her syndicates were to become a real force, federation of some kind was essential. In fact the French labour world was torn by successive and often conflicting schemes of federation, propounded in the interests of the varying sects and parties.

Already in 1886 a National Federation of Syndicates was projected. It soon became a political organisation for the Guesdist —or Marxian—socialists. In opposition to it was the better planned Federation of Labour Exchanges (*Bourses du Travail*). As originally conceived, far back in the nineteenth century, a *Bourse du Travail* was to be a meeting place for employer and employed, and a centre from which labour prices might be circulated, just as stock and produce prices are circulated from their exchanges. Under the law of 1884, the *Bourses* became centres for the activities of the various local syndicates. Municipal authorities were to encourage their creation and subsidise the necessary building operations. The nearest English parallel to the *Bourse*, as it developed in the nineties, is the local Trades Council.

The Federation of Labour Exchanges, which was not officially started until 1892, was followed within three years by yet another federal organisation, the General Confederation of Labour of 1895, soon to be notorious far outside France as the C.G.T. Its headquarters became the focus of all that was most revolutionary in the French world of labour. The moving spirits of the C.G.T. repudiated all political associations, put the general strike into their programme, and worked out the doctrine and practice of "direct" as opposed to parliamentary action. It was from them and their teaching that "syndicalism" acquired its modern meaning—a doctrine revolutionary rather than evolutionary; despising parliaments and the old democratic machinery; holding that organised groups of wage earners are destined to dominate the state; and looking forward to a condition of society, very indistinctly pictured, in which control of the means of production by such groups will have superseded capitalism, and excluded nationalisation under a central government, as advocated by parliamentary socialists.

When the nineteenth century closed, the C.G.T. and the Federation of Labour Exchanges were rivals for the allegiance of the workmen and their syndicates, partly for personal reasons. But in 1902 the Federation was merged in the Confederation; and the latter became the official mouthpiece of organised labour during the stormy decade which followed.

Since 1893 the Socialists had been a powerful body in parliament; and round about 1900 professed socialists began for the first time to find places in its ministry. Their entry into office coincided with a fresh activity in social legislation—a ten-hours factory act in 1900; more thoroughgoing factory inspection; and the organisation of joint consultative councils of labour, from among employers and employed, to advise the government and mediate in labour disputes. There is no need to explain that such measures were apt to be treated as bribes and insults by the stalwarts of the C.G.T., who saw hope only in revolution organised by "self-conscious minorities," not in the slow conversion and parliamentary procedure of majorities. And the collaboration of classes, which parliamentary socialists like Millerand and Briand were now preaching, was rank treason, not to say blasphemy, to those for whom class warfare was an article of faith. In which connection it must not be forgotten that, in their memories of 1871, Frenchmen of all parties had a picture of actual class warfare at its worst.

The French temperament, the determination of governments to govern, and the teaching of the C.G.T. combined to make the numerous strikes of the twentieth century critical and sometimes bloody. A general strike was proclaimed more than once but never attained. Even in 1906, the year of maximum unrest, when May 1 was spoken of as the day of the coming revolution, the total number of men on strike at one time or another was returned at less than 450,000. Both sides claimed success; society because it had endured; the "self-conscious minority" because it had drawn the attention of working men everywhere to its method and its cause—its cause, the "integral emancipation which can be realised only by the expropriation of the capitalist class"; its method, the general strike.

In all these half revolutionary movements, the lead was constantly taken by members of a trade group which had been surprisingly little affected by the characteristic industrial developments of the previous century—the building trades federation, reputed the most revolutionary syndical organisation in France. Perhaps it is only an accident that these trades had been for many generations the stronghold of *compagnonnage* (see *ante*, § 17), with its secret organisation and its traditions of hostility to a series of repressive governments; but even if accidental, the coincidence is interesting. What picture the French mason or carpenter made for himself of the building industry after "the abolition of capitalism" one does not know: nor probably did he. He knew vaguely that for centuries laws had been made by payers of wages for earners of wages, and that the state enforced them. He would probably have said that this was still the position. People had never talked favourably of the state in his circle. "Syndicalism" came easy to him. There was a fighting tradition in his race and his trade. So he took ground in the forefront of the fight. He knew what he disliked and trusted for the rest.

Organised wage earners remained a minority in France in 1914. The C.G.T. was a minority of this minority. And the active revolutionary forces in the Confederation were probably a minority of itself. In 1910–14 there were about 5,000,000 potential members of industrial syndicates in France. There were about 1,000,000 enrolled members. The membership of syndicates affiliated to the C.G.T. was approximately 400,000. Affiliation was often a fragile link. Most syndicates were very poor. Even the smallest subscriptions for any remote object were paid with difficulty and constantly allowed to fall into arrears. The C.G.T. therefore never had a useful fighting fund. This was one reason for the methods which it adopted, methods whose dramatic appeal served as propaganda, even when they could hardly hope for any prompt success. A second, and more powerful reason, lay in the revolutionary memories of France. Again and again resolute minorities had overthrown governments. Why should not a resolute minority bring down a whole social system, by one well directed blow, instead of laboriously accumulating fighting funds, or bargaining and compromising with politicians? The thing seemed at least worth trying. It was open to the socialistic workman to use both methods and he very often did. As a politician he would support the United Socialists, or some other socialist group. As a member of his little syndicate he could vote for affiliation to the C.G.T. and perhaps take part in a strike with a wider, vaguer, more soul-satisfying aim than that of the local strike for the local grievance. His parliamentary representative and his ultimate leader in the governing councils of the C.G.T. were always warning him against the dangers of that concentration of industrial power into fewer hands, which had been making steady progress since about 1895. If the progress was slight in relation to the whole economic life of France, it was still definite enough to give support to Marxian dogma and to strengthen his instinctive dislike of a system which, as his leaders told him and he was disposed to believe, imperilled liberty, made nonsense of equality, and bred hatred in place of fraternity.

CHAPTER XI

INDUSTRY INDUSTRIAL POLICY AND LABOUR
IN GERMANY, 1848–1914

§ 70. The swift industrialisation of Imperial Germany is one of the commonplaces of contemporary history. The ground was prepared before the Empire came into being. The decade from 1852 to 1861 showed the familiar symptom, a particularly rapid drift to the towns, as a result of the railway enterprise of the forties. But pre-imperial industrial and commercial enterprise did not leave a very deep mark on the recorded and measured life of the country. In a previous chapter it was pointed out that, in 1816, 73·5 per cent. of the Prussian population was classed as rural, and that in 1852 the corresponding figure was 71·5. Despite the townward rush of the fifties, the figure stood at 69·3 in 1861 and had only fallen to 67·5 by 1871. The change since 1816 is astonishingly small. Some states of less area, such as Saxony, being more dominated by industry than Prussia have a different story; so that the whole Empire in 1871 was slightly more urban in character than the kingdom of Prussia. But only slightly. An exact comparison cannot be made, because the Prussian definition of a town in the early nineteenth century was legal, not statistical—a place with such and such rights, not a place with a given population. But taking for the Empire the usual statistical division, by which the population in communities of 2000 and upwards is classed as urban, it appears that 63·9 per cent. of the population was still rural in 1871. What happened in the next forty years the table shows:

	Total population	Rural percentage	Urban percentage
1871	41,059,000	63·9	36·1
1880	45,234,000	58·6	41·4
1890	49,428,000	57·5	42·5
1900	56,367,000	45·6	54 4
1910	64,926,000	40 0	60·0

The figures suggest a whole nation rushing to town. The rush was greatest into the greatest towns. In 1890 there lived in cities of 100,000 inhabitants and upwards 11·4 per cent. of the German population. In 1910 the corresponding figure was 21·3 per cent. (13,823,000 souls). The rural population remained almost stationary throughout; and the enormous increase in the total population was absorbed by the towns. The maintenance of so large a rural population, under modern agricultural conditions, is a considerable achievement, especially when it is considered how small an area of Germany is naturally suited to intensive agriculture; but note that the attraction of industry and the towns was so strong, or the drag of the land so weak, that these 26,000,000 cultivators needed latterly a great body of migratory helpers from outside. There were not Germans enough on the land to gather the land's produce.

The huge absorbing capacity of German industry and commerce is further shown, when it is borne in mind that the period after 1890 was one of dwindling emigration, and that after 1900 emigration was negligible. Or again; compare the population of 1849, in the area which was to become the Empire, with that of 1910. The total in 1849 was 35,128,000, in 1910, 64,926,000. The rural population in 1849 was at least 25,000,000, probably more; in 1910 it was nearly 26,000,000. In sixty years an urban population of 10,000,000, at most, was replaced by one of nearly 40,000,000; and far more people were living in towns of over 100,000 inhabitants in 1910 than in "towns" of every sort, down to the tiny country market town of 2000 inhabitants, in 1849.

All the forces tending towards industrialism and urbanisation had struck Germany at once. She began the century with no highly developed urban life, like that of Napoleonic France (see *ante*, § 18). Down to the forties she went through no industrial revolution, like that which in England was filling the towns before the railway age. Then, crowding fast on one another in two generations, came the railways; the abolition of the last remains of medieval economic restriction after 1848; the expansion of the Zollverein (see *post*, § 78); the creation of a modern financial and banking system (see *post*, § 96); the great

steel inventions; the swift, cheap, glorious and exhilarating
achievement of national union; and the period of electricity,
overseas expansion and world policy. All the time population
was growing at a rate which would have terrified Malthus, and
might, if continued, have brought his teaching again to memory
early in the present century. However, about the year 1904,
the German birth rate began to fall swiftly; so that continuous
growth at the late nineteenth century rate had ceased to be
anticipated long before the present possibility of actual decline
had become thinkable.

§ 71. The railways, as Treitschke said, first dragged the
German nation from its economic stagnation—and with astonishing abruptness. In spite of Germany's huge wealth of
coal, to take the industry most obviously and vitally associated
with transport developments, she was not raising so much as
either France or Belgium in the early forties. What the position
was at that time has already been pointed out (see *ante*, § 20).
On the Ruhr, Roer, Saar and Saxon coal-fields effective development had started. The great Silesian field was still almost
untouched; its really effective working did not begin until the
seventies. The early and successful creation of a railway network
took Germany rapidly ahead of France and Belgium as a coal
producer between 1845 and 1860. She developed not only her
deposits of coal proper, but also the very extensive deposits of
lignite (brown coal) found along the middle courses of the Oder,
Elbe, Weser and Rhine. Lignite has a low heating power, but
it is easily won, in shallow pits and open workings; for geologically it is far younger than the coal.

By 1860 what was to become Imperial Germany (including
Luxemburg) had attained an output of 12,300,000 (metric) tons
of coal plus 4,400,000 tons of lignite. Belgium in that year
produced 9,600,000 and France 8,300,000 tons—in both cases
practically all coal, since Germany is the only West European
country with important resources in lignite. But if the Germany
of 1860 was ahead, though not so far ahead, of little Belgium and
of France with her scanty and inaccessible coal measures, she
was still an immense distance behind Great Britain, whose
output in 1860 was 81,300,000 (metric) tons, all good coal. The

year the Empire was founded, the German output was 29,000,000 tons of coal and 8,500,000 of lignite. France and Belgium in that year had each an output of from 13,000,000 to 14,000,000 tons; Great Britain an output of over 118,000,000. France and Belgium were not yet hopelessly outdistanced; Great Britain, in her isolated strength, had hardly become conscious of Germany as a coal producer. A dangerous rival she never became down to 1914; but how the relative positions of the four powers changed after 1871 the annexed table shows. The trifling output of French lignite is included with the coal.

Output in Metric Tons.

| | Great Britain | Germany | | France | Belgium |
		Coal	Lignite		
1871	118,000,000	29,400,000	8,500,000	13,300,000	13,700,000
1880	149,000,000	47,000,000	12,100,000	19,400,000	16,900,000
1890	184,500,000	70,200,000	19,100,000	26,100,000	20,400,000
1900	228,800,000	109,300,000	40,500,000	33,400,000	23,500,000
1910	268,700,000	152,800,000	69,500,000	38,350,000	23,900,000
1913	292,000,000	191,500,000	87,500,000	40,800,000	22,800,000

Even if lignite be excluded, as it often though improperly is, in comparing the fuel resources and fuel output of Germany with those of other countries, the table illustrates in a way which needs no comment the stupendous industrial momentum of the imperial age, and also, as in the case of the town statistics, the relatively small achievement of pre-imperial enterprise, striking as that achievement was in its day. Disunited Germany had been helped by her railways and her far superior resources to get ahead of France and Belgium. United Germany was almost ready at the last to challenge England on England's chosen ground.

To win this position she had had to augment and house her coal mining population at an amazing rate. In 1861-5, just before Sadowa, there were about 120,000 coal and lignite miners in Germany with Luxemburg; in 1887 there were 247,000; in 1906 there were 570,000, of whom 511,000 were coal miners. The number of lignite workers had increased almost threefold in the forty years, that of coal miners considerably more than fivefold. The coal miners were a highly concentrated population;

the lignite workers were scattered over wide stretches of country. Owing to the geological differences in the deposits, coal and lignite produced totally different types of mining. The late development of the coal-fields allowed the workings to be laid out, from the first, on that large scale which yields the maximum economies. In 1895, for instance, the average coal mining concern employed over 800 men, a remarkably high average figure for any industry and any country. The lignite pits, on the other hand, averaged only 66.

In the twentieth century the great Westphalian (Ruhr) coal-field was still by far the most important producer, averaging something like a half of the total German output. The Saar basin in 1913 produced 13,000,000 tons. The Saxon basin (Zwickau), which fed the textile manufacturing district of Chemnitz, was only of local importance and had no great reserves untapped. But, at the very extremity of the Empire, in a land where "it seems to the traveller as if a curtain fell and shut off the rich life of west Germany," where "close by the busy anthills of workers lie wide expanses of woodland... divided into the preserves of great landlords[1]," Silesia had reserves so immense that they were said to exceed all those of the United Kingdom. The Silesian output in 1913 was 43,000,000 tons, rather more than that of all France, and it was capable of indefinite increase.

In spite of these great resources, it was only towards the end of the nineteenth century that Germany became, on the balance, a regular coal exporting country; but her net export, whether in the form of coal, coke or briquettes, soon became large, judged even by British standards. Early in the present century it was 10–12,000,000 tons and it had risen by 1912–13 to about 20,000,000. She sold to France and Belgium and Holland and Switzerland and Austria, to name only her chief customers; but she was always a heavy buyer of coal from Great Britain and of lignite from Austria. Her coal-fields all lie far from tide-water, and she has no steam coal to equal that of South Wales. Hamburg and Bremen were therefore specially good customers of Cardiff and the north-east coast; and so excellent were the

---

[1] Partsch, *Central Europe*, pp. 272, 274.

facilities for water transport on the north German plain, a
region geologically too young to contain any coal of its own,
that twenty per cent. of the coal burnt in Berlin in the year 1906
was also British. In 1912 Germany paid Great Britain between
£8,000,000 and £9,000,000 for coal and Austria over £3,000,000
for lignite. Her own exports of coal, coke, and briquettes in
that year were valued at just over £30,000,000.

§ 72. Before the introduction of modern technique, Germany
like all other countries had possessed a dispersed iron industry.
But the excellent ores found in the eastern tributary valleys of
the lower Rhine, from that of the Ruhr to that of the Sieg, had
long since supplied localised industries, far stronger than those
in any other district. Their primitive industrial organisation
was described in an earlier chapter (see *ante*, § 20). There was
abundance of metallurgical knowledge in the old Germany,
and a high level of skill among her craftsmen. Fortunately for
the Rhenish industry the Ruhr coal-field provided a first rate
coke for smelting. The creation of an iron industry on the new
English lines had therefore been only a question of capital and
organisation. By 1845 a start had been made (see *ante*, § 20).
Then the railways came both as carriers and consumers; but
down to 1860 progress was relatively slow. In 1850 the territory
of the future German Empire (with Luxemburg) produced only
838,000 tons of iron ore, against France's 1,821,000 tons, and
the United Kingdom's 5–6,000,000. In 1860, France was still
producing more than twice as much ore as Germany, and the
United Kingdom nearly six times as much. In terms of pig
iron, a better test than ore because the iron content of ore is
so variable, the relative positions of the leading countries in
1860 were:

	tons		tons
United Kingdom...	3,888,000	Belgium ...	320.000
France	898,000	Austria ...	313 000
Germany	529,000	Sweden ...	185,000

It will be seen that Belgium, who in the early forties had
produced more iron than all Germany, was still not so far
behind her.

In the sixties and early seventies the German iron industry
took a leap forward, a leap which does something to confirm the

saying that "the German Empire was built more truly on coal and iron than on blood and iron[1]." France was passed before she was beaten in the field. In the first flush of victory, and after the acquisition of the ores and iron-works of Lorraine, the creation of fresh metallurgical businesses proceeded with reckless speed. It is said that more businesses for iron-smelting, iron working, and engineering were started in Prussia between 1871 and 1874 than in all the previous years of the century. In 1875, when the *post-bellum* boom was already beginning to slacken, the new Germany was turning out 2,000,000 tons of pig iron against France's 1,448,000 tons.

Then came a check, almost a collapse. The overtrading of the victory years coincided with the removal of the iron duties, which the Empire had inherited from the Zollverein tariff (see *post*, § 78). Great Britain, who was producing 6–7,000,000 tons yearly in the seventies, poured in her iron and her Bessemer steel; for prices were falling and fresh markets were welcome. Between 1873 and 1874 the number of men employed in iron smelting fell 40 per cent. In 1876, of 435 blast furnaces in Germany, 210 were "blown out," standing idle.

By 1880 the tariff had been revived and, more important by far, the basic process of steel making had been worked out in England by Thomas and Gilchrist. Germany was poor in Bessemer (non-phosphoric) ores and, owing to the situation of her iron industries, she had not Middlesbrough's facilities for importing them in "black Bilbao tramps." But in Lorraine and Luxemburg were almost inexhaustible reserves of basic ore, now available as foundations for the age of steel. The Germans have always acknowledged their debt to the English inventor. To this day they call the phosphoric by-product of the process, known in England as basic slag, "Thomas' dust."

In the eighties, when all over the earth prices were falling and laments about industrial depression were going up from the world of business to governments, the German iron industry, having recovered from the disasters of the previous decade, was the only iron industry in any important European country which made satisfactory progress. In that decade Great Britain hardly

---

[1] J. M. Keynes, *The Economic Consequences of the Peace*, p. 75.

increased her pig iron production at all, though her output of
steel increased by some 40 per cent. In France both iron and
steel outputs were almost stationary, and in Belgium the rise
was inconsiderable. But the German Empire doubled her output of steel and nearly doubled that of iron. Comparisons
between her and the United Kingdom, which hitherto no one
had thought of making, began to have an international significance. Below are the figures for 1880 and subsequent years.
It must be noted that they are probably too favourable to the
United Kingdom, whose output is given gross (with certain
omissions), while those of the other countries are "worked"
steel—not however always defined in quite the same way. But
for a rough indication the table will serve.

Output in metric tons.

		1880	1890	1900	1910
United Kingdom	Pig iron	7,873,000	8,031,000	9,103,000	10,172,000
	Steel	3,730,000	5,301,000	5,981,000	7,613,000
Germany	Pig iron	2,729,000	4,658,500	8,521,000	14,794,000
(with Luxemburg)	Steel	1,548,000	3,164,000	7,372,000	13,149,000
France	Pig iron	1,725,000	1,962,000	2,714,000	4,038,000
	Steel	1,354,000	1,407,000	1,935,000	2,850,000
Belgium	Pig iron	608,000	788,000	1,019,000	1,852,000
	Steel	596,000	716,000	927,000	1,857,000

The period 1890–1910 is shown to have been that in which
Germany took the lead in Europe, with a speed and decision
which confirmed the most confident faith of her people in
their industrial and political future. Only the United States—
half a rich continent—was ahead of her as an iron and steel producer. At the end of the period her exports of iron, steel, iron
and steel goods and machinery were approaching £100,000,000
in value (£86,000,000 in 1912 and over £100,000,000 in 1913).
Given but another half generation of peace anything seemed
possible.

As the export figures suggest, there had been built up, on
the basis of the huge output of crude iron and steel, a system
of metallurgical industries of infinite variety. There was no
category of iron or steel goods, or of goods composed mainly
of iron or steel, of which Germany's export in the twentieth
century did not vastly exceed her import; with a single exception

—tin plate from South Wales. There were naturally special classes of machinery the imports of which exceeded the exports; but even these were few. Fine cotton spinning machinery from Lancashire and reaping machinery from the United States were the only really important classes.

Perhaps the most remarkable achievement had been the creation of a modern shipbuilding and marine engine industry, mainly at Hamburg, Bremen and Stettin. In 1870–1, when it first became possible to speak of a German mercantile marine, there were about a million tons of shipping owned in German ports. The steam tonnage was insignificant, less than 100,000. In 1880 it had risen only to 216,000, against nearly 3,000,000 tons on the register of the British Empire. Spain had more steam tonnage than Germany in 1880, and France considerably more. A good deal of what Germany had was not German built, and not built of iron or steel. Six years later, the Secretary of the Boiler Makers' Trade Union, giving evidence before a British Commission on trade depression, could speak easily of England's practical monopoly of iron and steel shipbuilding. But, by purchase and skilled imitation, Germany was, at that very time, acquiring a steam mercantile marine. By 1890 her steam tonnage was 724,000; by 1900, when it was practically all steel-built, 1,348,000; by 1910, 2,397,000. Between 1910 and 1914 she was capable of turning out nearly 400,000 tons of mercantile shipping in a year, besides the ships of a swiftly growing navy. The United Kingdom's maximum output of merchant ships was about 2,000,000 tons, and the British Empire's steam tonnage in 1910 was 11,369,000.

In the twentieth century, although the Rhenish-Westphalian district still held its leading position, the primary iron and steel industries were strong elsewhere. Westphalian coke was sent to the blast furnaces of Lorraine and Luxemburg; there were important works on the Saar basin; and away in Silesia, though local iron ore was not abundant, coal was so good and so cheap that it was profitable to move in ore from other places by water and rail. But Silesia and the Saar between them only produced about 15 per cent. of the German pig iron, against some 30 per cent. in Lorraine and Luxemburg, and from 45 to 50 per cent.

in the Rhenish area. Secondary iron and steel trades—the making of structural materials and engines and machinery of all sorts—were exceedingly widespread, almost in exact proportion to the urban population[1]. Where there were no geographical conditions which literally compelled concentration in certain areas, the fact that Germany was a federation of states, each of which had once possessed a separately organised economic life, had tended to industrial dispersion. The Zollverein, the chief force working in the opposite direction, had only been approximately completed in 1852 (see *post*, § 78). The Hanse towns did not come into it until 1888. And since German industry developed so largely in that latest industrial age, during which the perfection of transport facilities had rendered the manufacturing congestion of the earlier nineteenth century less necessary, it was open to business organisers to select sites for their enterprises with considerable freedom, and to build upon whatever industrial foundations remained in each state from the days of its economic independence.

It has been seen already how the late development of German industry facilitated large scale operations in coal mining. The same is true of all the metallurgical industries. Take machine making. The excellent German industrial statistics allow the development to be studied with a precision impossible for France, England, or any other country. German statisticians group businesses under three heads—small, which employ five persons or less; middling, with from six to fifty workpeople; large, with fifty-one or more. In 1882, when the Empire was young, there were more men employed in small and middling than in large businesses, in the industrial group labelled "machinery, instruments and apparatus." The figures are—small and middling, 189,500; large, 166,500. The average business in that group employed only four pairs of hands, and the average large business, 186. Under any conditions the group includes many small businesses—machine repairers, small instrument makers, and so on. Twenty-five years later (1907) there were 231,500 people employed in small and middling businesses and

---

[1] Map 3, *Gewerbe und Handel im Deutschen Reich* (results of the 1895 census).

788,800 in large businesses. The average number of employees per business had risen from 4 to 12, and the average number per large business from 186 to 231. Without any overwhelming change in average figures, there had been a complete change in the industrial life of the group. In 1882 a few large businesses stood out here and there among a thick undergrowth of small ones. In 1907 the ground was well covered with large businesses and the undergrowth was completely overshadowed, though not killed.

In Germany, as in France, the oldest and most specialised of the iron and steel industries, cutlery, is interesting because of its marked concentration and its partial maintenance in the twentieth century of conditions which recall an earlier age. The Solingen district in the Rhineland has for centuries made nearly all the German cutlery. It is a far older centre for fine work than Sheffield, but early in the nineteenth century its workmanship and reputation had fallen off. The old independent master cutlers had become outworkers for mercantile *entrepreneurs* (*Verleger*), just as the master craftsmen had in a number of other German industries. The master cutlers employed on an average one man each in 1809, when their old gild, which had already lost its character as an association of really independent craftsmen, was abolished. Down to 1850 the outwork system remained unchanged. It developed all its worst abuses—sweated piece rates and payments in "truck"—and the quality of the cutlery deteriorated *pari passu*. In the succeeding half century quality improved and industrial organisation was profoundly modified. The first factory appeared in 1851. By 1895 there were 55 large establishments with an average working staff of 119 in the whole German cutlery industry; but these figures include some branches of the trade—such as saws and tools—not found at Solingen, which is a cutlery town in the strictest sense. In the twentieth century the largest factory there contained about 800 men. These Solingen factories were pioneers in a process which Sheffield was very slow to adopt, the forging of cutlery by mechanical methods instead of by hand.

But the factory, although in time it took over other processes than forging, never killed off the independent outworker. He

retained many of the customs of gild life, and gradually recovered his independence and skill, under the joint influence
of vigorous trade union organisations, which took charge of the
piece rates, sympathetic government inspection, and sanitary
legislation. In 1895, for example, although there were 6552
men in the factories—which were commoner in the tool and saw
industries than in cutlery proper—there were 22,200 workers in
8480 small and middling businesses. Such figures indicate a
large body of men working alone or with a single assistant.
These men were specialists, carrying on the processes subsequent
to forging, such as tempering, hafting, polishing and finishing.
The business of grinding was still more exclusively in the hands
of small people in 1895; for even including a handful of large
and middling establishments, the average grinding business employed less than two men.

After 1895 there was no tendency towards the destruction of
this state of things. Rather the reverse. Electrical transmission
helped the small men conspicuously, giving them good light
and power for lathes, grindstones, and polishing wheels. As
a result outwork actually increased. About 1910 electrically
equipped workshops, mainly for grinders, were being set up
at the rate of 200 a year; and the large Solingen factory, already
referred to, employed twice as many outworking specialists as
it did factory hands. These outworkers were all divided into
the traditional gild groups—legally-bound apprentice (*Lehrling*),
serving for four or, if a razor grinder, for five years; journeymen
(*Gesell*); and fully qualified master. Technical knowledge was
no longer conveyed only from master to apprentice, but was
spread through a highly efficient cutlery trade school. The
cutlery industry thus supplied some, if rather doubtful, support
for the ideals of those German social legislators who, in face
of the growing industrialisation of their country, were anxious
to take counsel with the past (see *post*, § 81).

§ 73. In discussing the textile industries of modern Germany
it will be best to work from the bottom upwards, taking first
those which were last and least modified after the railway age.
At the bottom comes linen. It has been seen (see *ante*, § 21) that
in 1831 out of 252,000 linen looms in Prussia only 35,500

belonged to weavers who lived entirely by weaving. The rest were worked as a by-employment by peasants for their own use, or belonged to men who were primarily weavers, but who also cultivated land. Spinning was all done by hand. In the thirties Germany was still exporting hand-spun linen yarn; but the trade was fast being crushed by the mill yarns of England. In the east there were whole villages of spinners, and the number of those who tried to get a livelihood by spinning had actually increased. Bad times and bad harvests had forced peasants to spin or starve. Conditions among the spinners were terrible. The export of German linens, like that of German yarns, was falling off; cotton was invading fields hitherto occupied solely by linen; and the rural spinner was not an adaptable labourer who could turn easily to another trade. So in the years of bad harvests and bad trade which preceded the revolutions of 1848 thousands of spinners died of hunger typhus.

Very slowly, between 1845 and 1870, power driven mills took over the work of spinning; but in 1870 there was still plenty of hand spinning, and a great German economist, writing in that year, anticipated that it would not easily die[1]. He was right. When the first imperial census of production was taken, twelve years later, there were found to be over 7000 businesses for heckling and spinning flax and hemp. They employed 25,000 workpeople. Of the 7000, only 108 made use of water or steam power; but these 108 mills employed 17,700 out of the 25,000 workpeople. They were real mills, with a fairly high employment average. What the remaining 6300 businesses, with their 7300 workpeople, were like may be inferred. Probably they did more heckling, *i.e.* preparing the flax, than actual spinning.

The twenty-five years between the first and the third census of production (1882–1907) saw the death of domestic flax and hemp heckling and spinning. The 7000 businesses had shrunk to 242. Of these 137 were returned as the businesses of solitary spinners—survivals, perhaps only nominal survivals, from an age that was dead. The remaining 105 employed 18,450 workpeople. The normal flax mill had not grown much

---

[1] Schmoller, *Zur Geschichte der deutschen Kleingewerbe* (1870), p. 467.

since 1882; for the trade was not expanding, and was not one for which modern Germany had shown any marked aptitude. By its side there had grown up a small jute spinning industry with larger businesses—32 mills averaging 400 workpeople each.

The spinning of flax by hand was just alive in 1882, but no more. Linen weaving by hand at that time showed hardly any signs of decay. It is true that the old peasant household weaving had decayed greatly. So late as 1861, there were still more than a quarter of a million linen looms worked as a by-employment in Prussia. In 1882 the number had fallen to less than 30,000 for the whole Empire; but as they were mainly in East and West Prussia, Posen and Pomerania, the two figures are roughly comparable. The professional hand-loom weavers had by no means been crushed by 1882. There were 104,000 linen weavers in the Empire, mostly men. Of these only 8300 were employed in mills where power was used. Of the remaining 95,700 more than half worked alone, the rest having one or two helpers. They were in part outworkers for capitalist *Verleger*, or for the owners of the spinning mills; in part "customer weavers" of the old sort, who worked up the hand spun yarn of the peasant women.

Only a few thousands of this ancient race were still struggling on in 1907; for a true revolution had occurred in the interval. The 72,400 separate businesses of 1882 had fallen to 14,700. The whole industry had contracted numerically to half its former size, and half the workpeople were now women. There is no reason to infer that the productivity of the industry had contracted with its numbers; because the great majority were now mill-hands, though 9000 of the old solitary hand-loom weavers and a few thousands more who hired a helper or two still survived. No doubt some might have been found in 1914.

The linen industry may be classed as one of Imperial Germany's failures. In the hand-work age of the eighteenth and early nineteenth centuries the German industry held a strong international position. Adopting mechanical methods late, it never recovered that position. Whether this was to be regretted is another matter; for it is probable that, lacking the special climatic conditions of Belfast, Germany could only have maintained the industry in power by maintaining a low standard of life—a condition of success not altogether absent from Ulster. The decline of linen manufacture in England and France (see *ante*, § 64) bears out this view. Germany's position in the twentieth century was that she imported a great deal of linen yarn from Belgium, Ireland and Austria, and a fair amount of fine Irish linen. Her exports of yarn and linen were inconsiderable in quantity and in value less than half her imports.

The development of the wool industry must be examined in connection with the collapse of Germany as a wool producer. In the forties the fine Saxon wool, which had been so much prized in England, was deteriorating; and Germany, instead of exporting fine wool, had to begin to think of importing it. The Zollverein, which included the chief German wool-producing districts—Saxony, Silesia, and other parts of Prussia—ceased to be an exporter, on the balance, about 1840; but for ten years the excess of imports over exports was inconsiderable. It was composed of fine Australian and Cape wools. After 1850 the excess grew steadily, although the home clip was growing too. Germany was at her highest point as a wool producer, in quantity though not in quality, between 1864 and 1870. In the latter year the home clip, by weight, was about three-fifths of the total German consumption, a very creditable proportion in the then conditions of international trade.

The imperial age saw the collapse of the home production, accompanied by a rapidly growing demand from a larger and more prosperous population. The old-time German peasant had worn but little wool, and worn it long. By 1880 the home clip was only a third of the total consumption; in 1890 it was less than a sixth; by 1900 it was a tenth; and by 1910 a still smaller fraction. No great nation was so dependent on the outside world for the raw material of its warm clothing. This complete revolution in sixty years helps to explain the contemporary revolution in industrial conditions. The case is parallel to that of flax; but in wool the revolution, both in raw material supplies and in industrial conditions, was more thorough, and the whole process was on a much larger scale.

Early in the nineteenth century, while Germany still supplied almost all her own wool, conditions were favourable to the maintenance of the old types of producers—peasants who made cloth at home; customer weavers who made cloth for them; small independent domestic masters; outworkers weaving at piece rates for a *Verleger*. The two former types were necessarily much scattered; and the two latter, though concentrated in certain districts which made a speciality of the industry, were also found more or less in all parts of the country. Even when imported materials ousted German wool, no economic force came into play which compelled rigid localisation. Consequently there have always been a great number of wool manufacturing centres—Saxony, the Thuringian states of Reuss-Gera and Reuss-Greiz, Lausitz, Silesia, the Elberfeld district, Aachen and München-Gladbach by the Belgian frontier, Hanover, Berlin, Alsace, and others.

The transition to factory conditions was at first slow. It had only just begun in 1850. Such machinery as had been introduced was often worked by hand or by horse, and was within the reach of a small master. Most of the spinning mills of the forties and fifties could hardly be called factories. In 1850 there were only 1200 power looms in the wool industries of all Germany; though there was some concentration of hand looms into weaving sheds by rising employers. Such employers were recruited, either among the *Verleger*, or among the more prosperous domestic manufacturers. A sharp fall in wool prices during the sixties discouraged the German sheepmaster, but gave openings for the rising and as yet not rich manufacturers. They could operate with less capital. Between 1860 and 1869, Cape wool, which was coming into favour in Germany, fell from 1s. 7d. to 1s. a lb. on the London market. The modern technique of wool manufacture had now been fully worked out in England and France. It had only to be taken over. This was done very rapidly in the prosperous years of the North German Confederation, between 1866 and 1870.

But in 1870, and later, there were strong remnants of the old order. There was still enough home grown wool to feed a number of domestic spinners, village weavers, and domestic manufacturers. And capitalist manufacturers, who were using more and more imported wool, an article generally out of the small man's reach, still gave out much of this yarn to the hand-loom weavers. The inquiry of 1882 showed that there were over 2000 solitary people in Germany to whom spinning was a "business," besides 2–3000 little spinneries with not more than five people in each. These types were still to be found in 1895. Even in 1907 there were said to be 554 domestic wool spinners in Germany. Can any have lived on till 1914? Or was there some error in the returns? It is immaterial. For four-fifths of the spinners, even in 1895, were in large establishments with an average of over 200 workpeople, a high figure for wool spinning in any country. The rest were nearly all in real factories, if not such large ones.

Weaving had not become entirely a factory industry. Of 153,000 weavers reported in 1895, 28,000 were home workers. Curiously enough the number of these domestic weavers was greater than had been reported in 1882. This surprising result was due in part to statistical omissions and technicalities; but mainly to a true cause—that hand-loom woollen weaving, in the nineties, happened not to be suffering so much as linen and cotton weaving from the inroads of power; so weavers driven from the two latter trades took refuge in the former. This of course could not endure. Power resumed its inroads, and by 1907 the domestic weavers numbered only 13,800. No doubt there were still a few thousands in 1914; though it is unlikely that they were so valuable a group as in France (see *ante*, § 64).

An important feature of the German wool industries after 1870 is the rapid development of the worsted (combed wool) branch. The old German cloths had nearly all been woollens in the technical sense, *i.e.* the wool was not combed. Consequently factory wool combing, and the processes associated with it, made their appearance late. When they did appear, they were often carried on in the spinning mills. But the rapidly increasing dependence of Germany on imported wool, and the great distance of some of her manufacturing centres from the ports, made it desirable to have the wool washed and combed *en route*. This tended both to make twentieth century Germany a considerable buyer of combed wool (technically "tops") from England, Belgium and France, and to encourage the erection of combing plants in Western Germany, at München-Gladbach for instance and near Bremen. It tended also to strengthen the very intimate commercial bonds between the German and the Belgian wool industries. In Germany itself, it accounts for the remarkable increase in the personnel of wool combing mills from 5800 in 1882 to 21,600 in 1907, whereas wool workers generally only increased from 182,000 to 238,000 in the same period. With this increased staff of combers, Germany was able, while buying combed wool with one hand from the West, to sell nearly as much with the other hand in Austria, which was still further from the great wool ports of Europe.

Rapidly as the worsted branch had grown, it had not become in every way self-sufficing. It bought not only combed wool but huge quantities of worsted yarn of certain types out of Yorkshire. Just as in the case of the combed wool, however, it sold an approximately equal quantity of other types to its eastern and south-eastern neighbours. But for the German tariff very great quantities of English manufactures would have followed the English yarn; and even with the tariff the quantities that went were not small. But on the balance Germany, in the twentieth century, had become a very large exporter of wool —raw, half-manufactured, or fully manufactured. It was fourth in the great groups of her exports in 1913; just below coal and coke; rather further below machinery; far below iron and steel goods other than machinery; but above cotton goods, and far above any other single group. A mighty industry, not one-fourteenth part of whose raw material came from Germany or from any German colony or protectorate.

§ 74. The cotton industry, started with an exotic raw material in the days when Germany had no colonies or protectorates, was necessarily in the same position. This fact had always influenced its industrial organisation. It had no natural ties with peasant life. Few Germans wore cotton before 1850. It was not a large industry. It was localised and more or less capitalistic in the early days of the Zollverein. In 1846–50 the German cotton consumption was only 15–16,000 tons a year as against France's 55,000 and Great Britain's 230–240,000 tons. There was quick development in the fifties and sixties, especially

in Saxony (Chemnitz) and about Elberfeld. There were minor
centres also, whose existence again illustrates the influence of
the separate economic life of its component states on that of
Germany as a whole. The chief were Bayreuth and Hof in
Bavaria, Stuttgart in Wurtemberg, and Breslau in Silesia. In
1871 the great Alsatian industry was captured, rather to the
discomfort of the trade in other parts of the Empire; and cotton
consumption rose at once, from an average of 68,000 tons in
1866–70 to an average of 116,000 in 1871–5. Comparisons with
Great Britain now ceased to be ridiculous, as her consumption
was still under 600,000 tons.

As the machine age progressed, there was no widespread
domestic industry to be killed off except that of weaving. And
the normal cotton weaver had never been a really independent
master. He was an outworker who wove an employer's yarn
to the employer's pattern. Cotton spinning on the handwheel
had been the speciality of a few districts. Its decline was
gradual. Hand-driven jennies superseded the wheels, and little
water-power plants superseded the jennies, without creating
a grave social problem like that of the flax spinners. The
industry grew with machinery, instead of being revolutionised
by it. What industrial tragedies had occurred had been connected with English competition. From the twenties and
thirties come tales of how an ambitious peasant or miller would
build a cotton spinnery, only to go under when next England
dumped cotton yarn. Hence the Zollverein tariff, which the
North German Confederation and the Empire retained.

Some of these little spinneries, and even a few isolated persons
called spinners, though perhaps improperly, survived into the
imperial age. As many as 5000 of the latter were reported in
1882; and in 1895 there were nearly 4000 people in spinneries
which did not average twenty workpeople apiece. But these
are the curiosities of economic history; for even in 1882 there
were over 61,000 cotton spinners in Germany. There was a very
rapid process of industrial concentration going on among the
larger businesses, which had long dominated the trade. Between
1882 and 1895 the number of large spinning businesses declined
by one-half, and their average number of employees more

than doubled. The figures for 1895 were—large businesses, 304; persons employed in them, 69,441; that is, 92·8 per cent. of all spinners whatsoever. Here is a fully developed factory industry. It was consuming in 1895 more than 250,000 tons of cotton a year. With the growing use of cotton for all domestic purposes in Germany, and also with a growing export, consumption drew nearer to that of the United Kingdom, until finally (1910–14) the latter was only about twice the former, reckoned in bales. But if the trade is measured not by weight but by quality, the gap is far wider. Germany spun much more coarse yarn than the United Kingdom. She was a heavy consumer of the inferior East Indian cottons, which Lancashire rather despised. Consequently the number of her spindles was only one-fifth of the United Kingdom figure—10·9 as against 55·6 millions in 1913. And in spite of Alsace, she was not at the last far ahead of France's 7·4 million spindles.

Cotton weaving was still predominantly a hand industry in 1871. The power loom had made steady progress since 1850, and was now well on the road to victory; but the crisis of the contest was only just beginning. In 1875 nearly two-thirds of the cotton weavers of the Empire were domestic outworkers, weaving by ones and twos and threes in cottage garret or cellar. Seven years later the proportion had fallen to a half. Then came the final rout. Out of 224,000 weavers of cotton, or mixed materials partly cotton, in 1895, 50,000 were still struggling on outside the factories. In some cases their work was of a fancy kind, which for a good many years longer resisted the competition of machinery, just as in the case of the fancy weavers of Northern France; but nearly half of them were crushed out during the next intercensal period (1895–1907). They had no real significance for the story of the German cotton industry in the twentieth century, during which the consumption of cotton increased faster than in any other country, as population grew and outside markets were exploited.

But, as has been seen, cotton did not become Germany's chief textile export. Of raw cotton she naturally exported little, beyond what passed through from Bremen into Austria. As in the case of wool, neither technical developments nor tariffs

freed her, even at the height of her strength, from dependence
on England for the finest yarns. For the five years 1908–12, for
example, the average import of yarn and "twist" (doubled or
trebled yarn) was worth very nearly £5,000,000. For the same
period, cotton goods imported averaged just over £2,000,000.
They also mostly came from England. *Per contra*, there was
an export of coarser yarns and twists, which rose in the five
years from just over £1,500,000 to £3,000,000, and an export
of manufactures which rose from £17,500,000 to £21,000,000.
Of these manufactures, the United Kingdom, with its open
markets, was much the largest single purchaser, followed at a
long distance by Turkey and Brazil. The young German
colonies and dependencies were almost negligible as markets
for manufactures, British oversea territories being a far more
profitable field. Herein Germany differed markedly from
France, whose protected colonial markets were of the greatest
value to her home industries.

Silk had been an industry specially favoured by the German
princes of the seventeenth and eighteenth centuries. It was
regarded as a proper accompaniment of their princely dignity,
and an ornament of their "residence towns." But, before 1845,
it had died out in many places where acclimatisation had been
tried, surviving with any vigour only at Krefeld,—where it had
not received much princely patronage—Elberfeld and Freiburg.
In 1871 a silk industry was acquired in upper Alsace; but
Krefeld was always to Germany what Lyons was to France,
though it was never Lyons' equal, except in mechanical ingenuity in the latest times. For the special feature of the most
modern German industry, as compared with the French, was the
thorough and rapid acceptance of machinery. Like all the other
German textile trades, silk weaving was in the hand-loom stage
before 1870. It may be said to have remained in that stage
until nearly 1890. In that year Krefeld, the most progressive
seat of the trade, had only 5400 power looms as against 22,500
hand looms. Then came the now familiar revolution, the more
remarkable because of the special character of the silk industry.
But, as was seen in the case of France, silk goods were
being "democratised" at this time; and there Germany saw her

advantage. She turned her back on the princely traditions of the trade, and concentrated on the production of silk and part-silk goods in bulk. The transformation of the Krefeld weaving industry was carried through with amazing speed, as the following table shows. The figures are those of silk and velvet looms.

Looms at work in Krefeld.

	Power looms	Hand looms
1890	5,400	22,500
1900	9,700	7,200
1905	9,400	3,700
1909	9,900	2,700

Domestic weaving held its own better in some other centres; but the census returns of 1907 show that the Krefeld weaving transformation is broadly representative of the whole industry.

Although there were some (electrically driven) power looms in the domestic workshops, just as there were near Lyons, the whole body of domestic workers—nearly all weavers—was only 14,000 out of a total working staff of 84,000 for the whole industry. All processes other than weaving, including dyeing and printing, employed only 17,000 people. Both dyeing and the spinning of silk waste, the only two branches of the industry besides weaving which employed any considerable numbers of workpeople, were true factory industries. They had in fact been tending towards factory organisation at an earlier date than weaving; for the spun silk trade in particular depends for its success on the application of elaborate mechanical methods.

It was a matter of pride to Germany that her silk exports, in the machine age, became comparable with those of the more ancient and famous French industry. In some years, the value of the German exports was as much as four-fifths of that of the French; but generally the lead of France was greater. Between 1900 and 1913, French exports of silk manufactures varied between £10,000,000 and £16,000,000; those of Germany between £7,000,000 and £10,000,000. The third European exporting country, Switzerland, was somewhat behind Germany; the United Kingdom was far behind any of the three.

§ 75. There were few trades in nineteenth century Germany which had not been recently linked with the land. Peasant iron workers, peasant cutlers, peasant weavers, peasant spinners, peasants who went to sea in the summer, and peasants who made wooden toys in the winter—the list could be drawn out almost indefinitely. The export trades of Germany had in many cases been founded on these peasant industries. They might be either by-industries proper, or might occupy most of the time of the women and children and some of the men, in districts where the rural population was unable to live by the land (see *ante*, § 22). To the end of the nineteenth century, rural industries remained an appreciable part of the total industrial effort of Germany; but they were subject to an increasing competition from factories, which were founded either in the old rural seats of the industry, like the modern watch factories of the Black Forest, or in towns which entered into competition with the trade of these old seats. Originally, much of the output of the cottages had been marketed by peddlers. But at a later date, say in the second quarter of the nineteenth century, a commercial *Verleger* had as a rule organised output and sale and, if necessary, had supplied material to the cottagers.

Among the trades which remained down to the present century in part localised in their old rural seats, was the wooden toy trade of the Saxon Erzgebirge and the Meiningen Oberland, where 20,000 people still got a living—though a scanty living—from this work in 1900. The best "lines" had been absorbed by factories, mainly in Nuremberg and Berlin, during the eighties and nineties; and so only the ruder work was still done on the land. Thuringia maintained also numerous other branches of the toy trade, of more modern creation—toys in glass and clay and papier-mâché, building blocks, Christmas tree decorations, dolls' limbs. The number of the little toy making businesses was growing down to 1907, when the census reported—for the whole Empire—1500 more businesses and 3200 more people in the trade since 1895, figures which suggest plainly of what kind most of the businesses were, especially when it is borne in mind that a number of real toy factories had grown up in the interval.

There was a similar increase in other trades which had once been entirely rural, and still were rural in part. Among these were lace making, another of the trades of the Saxon Erzgebirge, glove making, again a Saxon industry both in town and country, and straw hat making, which as a rural industry was carried on in the Black Forest, in Alsace-Lorraine and Saxony.

Thirty years earlier these trades and others of the same class —knitting, embroidery, the making of trimmings, clock making, and wood working of many kinds—had been both rural and domestic. But even in the rural districts, they were tending to gather about the smaller towns, while remaining domestic. In very few cases were the workers really independent craftsmen. They worked for a *Verleger*, and were usually exploited by him. With the rapid growth of great towns in the imperial age, the exploitable population, the families who were anxious to add to the family income by any possible means, began to be found in greater and greater numbers in the towns, without ceasing to exist in the country. New needs and new ways of supplying old ones were developing fast; and the situation was met by an immense extension of urban domestic outwork (*Verlagssystem*). It arose as a natural successor to the rural domestic outwork which had been so widely practised in the old Germany.

Further; the outwork system laid hold of many industries which, unlike most of the older rural outwork industries, had really been in the hands of independent craftsmen, in direct touch with the consumer. Some trades even passed in a single generation through the three stages—independent handicraft, outwork, and the factory system—an evolution which, as has been said, had taken several centuries in earlier ages. Similar developments have occurred in all countries, but never so rapidly or under such careful observation as in Germany. The most important trades thus transformed and transformed again were those connected with clothing.

Take, for example, bootmaking. Before 1870 the typical bootmaker was an independent craftsman, buying material and selling to the consumer. In one or two districts there had existed, since early in the century, a localised outwork bootmaking industry, run by commercial *Verleger*. Pirmasens in the

Rhenish Palatinate had an industry of this type. Moreover, experiments in mechanical bootmaking had been made before 1870, but again only in one or two places. They are heard of in Saxony in the fifties. But boot factories can only have occupied a very few thousand people in 1870; for in 1882, out of nearly 400,000 bootmakers in Germany, less than 7000 were in businesses employing more than fifty persons. At the same date 18,000 men returned themselves as working at home for *Verleger*; and no doubt many more were in fact so doing. By 1895 the number working for *Verleger* had grown considerably; but it had fallen back again by 1907. Meanwhile the number returned as working in big businesses (over 50 employees) grew fast, from decade to decade. For a moment, in 1895, the outwork system seemed to be gaining ground; but the factory system overhauled it and in the twentieth century was ruling the industry. If the number of boot and shoe makers outside the factories remained large, it must be remembered that their character had changed. Except for a minority, they were no longer independent craftsmen, but sellers and cobblers of factory made boots.

In most other clothing trades, of which needlework and tailoring may be taken as representative, the number of domestic outworkers grew down to 1907, in spite of the rather late creation of clothing factories. For tailoring, figures are available from 1882 onwards. The tailor, like the bootmaker, had normally worked direct for the consumer in 1870. By 1882 only 39,000 tailors out of over 300,000 admitted that a *Verleger* came between them and the public; and there were no clothing factories of any importance. In 1895 the number of self-styled outworkers had nearly doubled, and a small group of fair-sized factories appeared, the 46 largest averaging 88 workpeople. Both outworkers and factory workers increased again by 1907; and thereafter, though figures are not available, the factory went ahead fast. No doubt, at the later dates, there were far more real outworkers than the statistics show; for in all countries, under modern conditions, the working tailor may do some jobs direct for consumers, although during the greater part of his time he is sewing at piece rates for a shopkeeper or wholesale clothier. Such a man is more likely to assert his independence than his dependence.

The innumerable branches of needlework and their industrial development cannot be separately examined. They have been in all countries the great field for outwork and sweating in the modern town; and everywhere the system of urban outwork production on a large scale has been associated with the great urban retail establishments which market the goods. The capitalistic *Grand magasin*, or *Magasin de confection*, was a French invention, unknown to pre-imperial Germany (see *post*, § 91). Indeed the Germans of the sixties and seventies were heavy purchasers in Paris. As their historians explain, the home industry benefited much by the siege and the Commune which cut off Parisian supplies. French and English fashions, the first for women, the second for men, were, however, dominant in Germany until the eighties, to the great profit of Paris, London and Belfast. Then, as the organisation for producing and distributing the goods improved, French underclothing and English collars and cuffs were driven off the market; and the German industry of clothing (*Konfektion*) emerged full grown, retaining, however, even from official and patriotic pens, its distorted French name. Its organisation very rarely took the factory form. Even the middling business or workshop (6–50 hands) was almost unknown in the nineteenth century, and not very common in the twentieth. The outwork system dominated the trades, though there were signs of a movement towards larger workshops and factories in the returns of 1907.

§ 76. Two groups of trades stand out in the history of imperial Germany, not so much because of their size, but because of their great national and international importance and their singularly rapid development. These are the chemical and the electrical groups, the groups which in France were relatively backward (see *ante*, § 65). For these the old Germany had laid a broad and true foundation of scientific knowledge. "Chemical knowledge in its various branches is further advanced than with us," was the opinion of Dr John Bowring in 1840 (see *ante*, § 24). The next thirty years witnessed a further rapid development of chemical and physical knowledge, and of the educational machinery which rendered it available. Leaders of French thought admitted in 1871 that the better educated people had won. England, who had just made elementary education compulsory and had barely begun the reform of her ancient and the creation of her modern universities, might have repeated the verdict of 1840, and might have applied it to some other branches of knowledge. True, an apologist of England could point out that, thanks to the chemical knowledge of a few, to the fortunate juxtaposition in England of salt, coal and iron pyrites, and to English business ability, she was—as a German scholar has admitted—"the real home of the chemical industry." And she remained the only large scale exporter of chemicals throughout the nineteenth century.

For the development of these industries Germany had special geographical advantages. The province of Prussian Saxony is rich in very pure rock salt. At one point, Stassfurt, there lies among the ordinary salt beds an almost unique deposit of potash salts, which are very seldom found free in nature. Similar deposits exist in Thuringia, Hanover, and Alsace; but the last had not been fully developed before 1914, and were in no sense a foundation of the German chemical industry. Down to a late date, although the common salt beds of Stassfurt had long been worked, the potash beds were either unknown or neglected. They were struck in 1852, but only began to be worked systematically in 1860. The sodium chloride, the potassium salts, sulphur which could be extracted from her abundant deposits of iron pyrites, and rich resources in coal and coal tar, gave Germany the raw materials for all the "heavy" and most of the "light" chemical trades. These she proceeded to utilise with an ever-increasing supply of chemical knowledge, industrial organising capacity, and capital. In the early days of the Empire the industries were still on a comparatively small scale. Excluding the retail chemists, whose business belongs really to another category, and the makers of pencils, chalks and matches, but including explosives, the chemical industries in 1882 gave employment to little more than 50,000 men. The basal industry, which prepared the main chemicals in bulk (*Chemische Grossindustrie*), employed only 15,000 workpeople. In 1895 the same industry employed 27,000, and in 1907, 45,000. The numbers employed in the whole industrial group—with the same exclusions—had grown almost threefold in the twenty-five years.

But this is a group in which numbers tell the least part of the story; for few industries benefit more by the large scale production, which marks the modern chemical manufacture. The trades are so complex, that statistical comparisons of output over long periods are not easily made; and in many cases figures are not available. It is possible only to give illustrations of the development. In 1878 the world's output of sulphuric acid is supposed to have been over a million tons. That of Germany was 112,000 tons. In 1907 the German output was 1,402,000 tons. It was almost all consumed at home, half of it in the manufacture of chemical fertilisers (superphosphate). In the ten years 1897–1907 the production of ammonia rose from 84,000 to 287,000 tons. In 1883 Germany raised 152,000 tons of pyrites. In 1912 she raised 262,000 tons and imported more than twice as much. Between 1871 and 1911 common salt production grew from 140,000 tons to 1,400,000 tons; though in 1911 it was still far below that of the United Kingdom (2,100,000) and not much above that of France (1,338,000). Lastly; the output of Germany's peculiar treasure, the Stassfurt crude potassium salts, grew as follows:

1861	2,000 tons	1891	1,371,000 tons
1871	375,000 „	1901	3,535,000 „
1881	906,000 „	1911	9,607,000 „

Potassium salts and other materials for the "heavy" chemical trades were the gift of nature; fine chemicals and dyewares the reward of education and industry. Speaking broadly, the "heavy" chemicals were used to feed the industries and still more the soil of Germany; the fine chemicals and dyewares to strengthen her position in international trade. Although there was an export of the Stassfurt salts, which had risen to over £2,000,000 in 1912, and an export of calcium chloride which in some years had been rather larger, both were of recent growth, and taken together, were much more than outweighed by the import of Chilian nitrate, which had been going on for many years. To the last Germany hardly met her own requirements in sulphuric acid, for which at one time she had been very dependent on England. Her exports of most other rough chemicals exceeded her imports; but the surplus was not large enough to affect her international trade balances appreciably. Dyewares, on the other hand, became, in the twentieth century, one of her chief exports of the second class, the annual value rising from about £5,000,000 in 1908–9 to nearly £10,000,000 in 1913. Yet, even at the highest, they were not 2 per cent. of her total exports; and they were far from equal in value to Great Britain's exports of "heavy" chemicals in 1913.

In its relations to science, capital, and governments, the electrical industry is a typical product of the last two decades of the nineteenth century; and in no country can its characteristics be studied better than in Germany. Electrical manufacture had existed since first the electric telegraph became a practical success, in the forties; but the making of telegraphic appliances, apart from the heavier submarine and other cables, had rarely become a distinct industry. Germany was little interested in submarine cables, and can hardly be said to have had an electrical industry in the sixties and seventies. So far as it existed, it was as a branch of general mechanical engineering. The twenty years 1860–80 saw the inventions and applications which determined its subsequent development. The invention (1861), and the practical adoption (1877), of the telephone widened the field for the existing "telegraphic" branch of the industry. Between these dates came the invention of the dynamo, by Werner von Siemens (1867), and progress in knowledge of how electricity may be transmitted, which enabled Siemens to experiment with electric traction (1879). When the dynamo had been perfected, electrical energy could be generated in any desired quantity; and the remaining problems of its effective transmission over long distances were taken in hand.

In the practical applications of electricity America had always led, and it was American achievement in the seventies which stirred up German enterprise. Specialised factories for the production, first of light, and then of power appliances, sprang up. But the heavy capital requirements for large installations, and the need for powerful commercial organisations to deal with the local authorities, called for businesses of a more general character. Moreover the financial world was now persuaded that electricity was a promising field. The result was the creation of the first large general electrical business in Germany, the German Edison Company, later and better known as the Allgemeine Elektrizitäts-Gesellschaft, the A.E.G. This was in 1883. Lighting installations were rapidly set up. As soon as it was apparent that the thing would work and pay, they began to be taken over by the local authorities. Power transmission came later. After the exhibition at Frankfurt in 1891, at which demonstrations were given of the long distances over which effective transmission was possible, the electrification of street tramways went forward with a rush. The travelling Englishman, in the later nineties, noted how far Central Europe was ahead of his own country in this matter. About the same time, industrial establishments began to appreciate the value of electrical driving.

But when all the towns had got their trams, and the innumerable technical applications of electricity familiar to the twentieth century had not yet become general, the electrical industry—into which capital had flowed like water—found itself in difficulties. Competition became fiercer; prices fell; dividends dwindled; firms collapsed. This was in 1900–2. The cure suggested and adopted was a drawing together of the greater firms to limit competition and, if necessary, production. Very soon (by 1905) three great groups dominated the whole industry—the A.E.G. group, a union of two Berlin concerns; the Siemens and Halske group, a combination of Berlin with Nuremberg; the Felten and Guilleaume group, a combination between Mühlheim and Frankfurt. Next came agreements between the big three, or one might almost say two, since the A.E.G. and the Siemens groups stood far above all others. The firms who specialised on particular electrical appliances, and who had suffered most of all in the crisis owing to their financial weakness, also drew together like their great neighbours into associations and leagues (Kartells).

The figures of the industrial censuses illustrate in a very striking way the swift development of the whole group of electrical industries. In 1882 it had not been thought necessary to arrange for an electrical category in the census at all, the few thousand workpeople concerned being returned under other headings. By 1895 the new electrical category registered 26,000 workpeople. It included the making of generating machinery, telegraphic machinery, lamps and other appliances, and work at generating stations. In 1906–7 the Allgemeine Elektrizitäts-Gesellschaft alone employed 31,000 workpeople, and the whole industry 107,000.

Beyond question, the creation of this industry was the greatest single industrial achievement of modern Germany. The world had before it a new group of scientific and economic problems. In the handling of those problems Germany, now a fully equipped industrial nation, took the lead. She led too in all the specialised applications of electricity during the early years of the current century; electrical furnaces for steelwork and other branches of metallurgy; electrification of railways; electrical driving of agricultural machinery, including even ploughs; and the electrical method of procuring nitrogen from the air. There arose naturally from the existing industries a great wireless industry, though for this development the main credit must not be assigned to her.

Her success was rewarded by a foreign trade in electrical appliances which no other nation could approach. Her great companies were international powers, with extensive diplomatic influence and unstinted support from government. By securing the adoption of their types of generation and transmission, they secured the permanent demand for renewals and extensions from one market after another. Germany, who had no cable industry worth mentioning in the eighties, and an export of cables averaging only £150,000 a year in the early nineties (1891–5), exported £2,500,000 worth of cables in her best year (1908). She sold considerable quantities to the United Kingdom, the home of the cable industry. By 1913, her electrical exports of all kinds, which, in spite of the fluctuations incidental to an industry of this type, had been rising steadily if not continuously, had reached nearly £11,000,000. There was no single electrical machine or appliance of which her imports were of the least significance. In all these developments, the wealth and the concerted action of her great companies had been of the utmost value to her.

§ 77. The success of the movement towards concerted action in the electrical industries opens out an aspect of recent German industrial history to which no attention has yet been given. In discussing the growth of the leading trades since the railway age, opportunities have been taken to illustrate the process of concentration, which was going forward in all. The movement towards concerted action among the businesses thus created, the so-called Kartell movement, remains. The history of the electrical industries is not however really typical. In them we see, first, the creation of a small dominant group of gigantic concerns, and then a measure of agreement as to economic spheres of influence, price policy, and so on between those firms. Competition among businesses leading to consolidation had almost cleared the field of what might be called average firms. But the aim of a typical Kartell was to erect a dam which might check the destructive force of competition, and secure for a large number of businesses some place in the sun. The two tendencies, that towards an ever increasing elimination or absorption of weaker firms, the principle of the American Trust, and that towards the maintenance of a fairly large number of more or less equal firms by means of self-protecting agreements, were both at work in imperial Germany. In 1914 it seemed not unlikely that the latter, the true Kartell movement, might prove to have been a passing phase of German industrial history. But it was a characteristic phase of the years 1880–1910.

Agreements among producers, intended to check the destructive force of competition, have occurred in all times and countries, and have taken many forms. Under modern industrial conditions they naturally occurred first in England. France too had some early examples. In the later nineteenth century, agreements of the Kartell type were fairly common in her iron, steel, and chemical trades. But among the Germans such agreements were more ingeniously elaborate, far more general, and more frankly accepted as part of a rational economic organisation of society than among any other people. Many international agreements also, in the years 1890–1910, were designed and promoted by Germans. Although their experience of the conditions which cause men to desire these things was shorter than that of their neighbours, they had put into the elaboration of them a peculiar patient thoroughness.

Whatever the methods adopted, the two "dominant aims" of the typical Kartell were "that of maintaining prices at fully remunerative levels; and that of mitigating the sharpness of price-fluctuations in regard to the particular products for which the Kartell was responsible[1]." The first Kartells were simple price-fixing agreements, among producers of commodities which were uniform enough in character to make such price-fixing reasonably practicable. They are met with in the sixties among salt works, tin-plate works, and makers of iron rails. There is no difficulty in grading any of these things. The rail Kartell was the upshot of a period of competitive tendering for contracts with government, which had made the production of rails unremunerative. Early in the seventies, bitter competition and overproduction in the alkali industry led to repeated attempts to create a price Kartell. It was made in 1876 but went to pieces next year.

The years of depression which followed the exaggerated trade boom of the early seventies (see *ante*, § 72) brought producers in other trades together to discuss the situation. Industry on a large scale was a new thing in Germany, and still but partially developed. In most trades there were far too many separate producers for common action to be practicable. But in those which were already concentrated into comparatively few hands—such as coal mining and the heavy metallurgical and chemical industries—it was practicable. The very fact that this concentration was recent had made competition more reckless and some limit to it, from the producers' standpoint, infinitely desirable. In the exuberance of victory, and the overconfidence of a young industrialism, the country had engaged more capital in the heavy trades than could find profitable employment. One obvious remedy was to keep out the foreigner.

---

[1] Dr Alfred Marshall, *Industry and Trade* (1919), p. 559, where the whole matter is thoroughly investigated.

So the first result of this drawing together of producers was the tariff agitation of 1877–9 (see *post*, § 78). Having come together, and having got their tariff, they found that it did not fulfil expectations. Prices were falling in all countries; and, even if the foreigner was partially excluded, there might still be more producing capacity than could be employed remuneratively in meeting the needs of the home market.

One thing at least the tariff did. It facilitated national associations for the control of competition, by excluding, up to a fixed point, the unknown and uncontrollable factor of supplies from abroad. In this way it encouraged Kartell making, though it was in no sense its prime cause. That lay in the very nature of competitive industry.

Excluding purely local price agreements, such as were found almost everywhere among brewers for example, only 6 Kartells have been traced to a date before 1870, only 14 to a date before 1877. By the end of the century upwards of 350 had come into existence; but of these many had collapsed. About 275 remained active. Among these active Kartells, 76 had been formed between 1879 and 1885 and 120 between 1885 and 1890. The importance of the eighties, the years of revived protectionism, in the history of the movement is obvious. Because the early eighties were also a time of falling prices and industrial depression, some have argued that the Kartell was a product of distress. So no doubt it was historically. Distress first drove producers to abandon their former isolation. But the years 1888–91 were a time of great trade activity and also of very rapid formation of Kartells. So were the early years of the twentieth century. Evidently the Kartell suited the temper of the German business man in prosperity also.

It is impossible even to enumerate here all the devices adopted by the various Kartells to secure their main objects of keeping prices remunerative and relatively stable. Many Kartells were price agreements and nothing more. Minima were fixed for standard products of the trade, below which members agreed not to sell. But such simple arrangements were seldom sufficient to produce the desired results for any length of time. All the greater Kartells went much further. Price regulation had to be associated with the regulation of production. The first large scale instance of this occurred in 1876-7, when an agreement was made among the Rhenish-Westphalian coal-owners to reduce output by 10 per cent. all round. Subsequent developments in this industry illustrate the evolution of a typical Kartell and the characteristics of Kartell policy.

During the seventies and early eighties, the Westphalian coal-owners repeated several times the experiment of 1876-7. The object was of course to maintain and steady prices; but prices were not made the subject of a regular agreement until 1887. Next it was found convenient to organise common selling arrangements. So in 1890-1, five selling unions, in the form of separate joint stock companies, were created for Westphalian coke, and for Dortmund, Bochum, Essen and Mühlheim coal. The four last united into the Rhenish-Westphalian Coal Syndicate in 1893. Ten years later, the Coke Syndicate and a Briquette Union joined; so 50 per cent. of the coal output of Germany, with a proportionate amount of the output of coke and briquettes, was under unified control. Each pit or company had a certain share of coal-producing capacity assigned to it, according to size, amount of capital invested, and so on. Its output was regulated, in relation to this base line, by the circumstances of the home and foreign markets. All its output, except what was consumed at the pit or in concerns associated with it, for some pits belonged to iron and steel works, was handed over to the syndicate for sale. This exemption of coal used in associated concerns was not part of the original plan, but was a concession extracted by the so-called "mixed" concerns in 1903. The syndicate had various prices; for non-competitive districts; for competitive districts; for foreign markets. Where it enjoyed a practical monopoly, it insisted on long contracts in order to stabilise prices.

As many of the oldest and strongest Kartells were in the metallurgical industries, relations between them and the Rhenish-Westphalian necessitated perpetual negotiation and occasional war. Such were the Pig Iron Syndicate, the Tool Steel Kartell, and the Kartells for rails, wire, half-manufactured steel, steel sheets, and tubes. Large firms with varied resources and output might belong to several Kartells. Special difficulties arose as to the relations of the "pure" coal-pits or steel-works with the "mixed" concerns which were interested in both businesses. In 1903, as has been seen, the syndicate had to give in to the "mixed" concerns, whose strategic position was strong because they hardly needed its assistance. A "mixed" concern had liberties denied to a "pure" concern of either type; it had neither to hand over all its coal at syndicate prices, nor, like a "pure" iron-works, to buy syndicate coke. This stimulated combinations, and tended to defeat one of the nominal objects of the Kartell System—the maintenance of independent businesses.

Meanwhile the Kartells of the steel trades had come together; and in 1904 the Steel Union (*Stahlwerksverband*) had been formed out of the Kartells for half-manufactured steel, girders, rails and sleepers. The union itself undertook the sale of all the rougher goods ("A" class), just as the Rhenish-Westphalian sold coal. It had home and foreign prices, and was in a position to organise "dumping" if desired. "B" goods, wire, pipes, sheets, and the like, were sold by the individual firms, each having an agreed share of whatever total output was considered desirable. By 1911 the union contained thirty steel works, mainly in the west but including two in Silesia. Krupps were only a unit in the great organisation.

Here again one type of friction was partially eliminated and another produced; and everywhere the sufferers were apt to be "pure" concerns. A "pure" rolling-mill, for instance, under the *régime* of the *Stahlwerksverband*, had to buy rough steel at *Verband* prices, and sell in competition with a member of the *Verband* who both made steel and rolled it. Machinery devised to give all a share, seemed to many observers, in the last years of the Empire, to be driving inevitably towards unified control and ownership, as in an American Trust. The Kartells for different commodities in the heavy trades seemed to be only varied aspects of the activities of a few giant concerns.

The Rhenish-Westphalian and the Steel Union illustrate the most important aspects of fully developed Kartell policy. Kartells in other trades did not often go so far; though the two sugar Kartells—raw and refined—had equally intricate histories and policies. Kartells in the chemical industries sometimes had selling organisations of the type introduced by the Rhenish-Westphalian. The alkali works had such an organisation from early in the twentieth century. Many Kartells, on the other hand, remained not far removed from the simplest type of local price agreement. Such were some of the brick-making Kartells. According to the varying needs and technical characteristics of different industries, a Kartell might devote most attention to regulating prices; regulating output; assigning to members their quota of the output; sharing out markets among members; or strengthening their hands when buying raw material. Ostensibly, and as it would appear to a great extent in fact, the Kartell organisation was not used in wage disputes.

Besides the industries already referred to, strong Kartells came into existence at different dates in the paper, distilling, cement, glass, worsted spinning, and shipbuilding industries; also in the transport industries and in various branches of commerce. By 1900 there was hardly a trade which had not its Kartell, strong or weak, from needles, sewing machines, and skates to copper, chloroform, soap, sporting ammunition, sole leather, shoes, flax, hemp, shoddy, dyeing in its many branches and the making of perambulators. Though it was only in trades where grading and price-fixing were relatively easy that the Kartell policy could be carried through to the end, German patience and ingenuity succeeded in applying great parts of it over a much wider field than might have been anticipated—whether for good or evil may be left an open question.

§ 78. That reservation of the home market for the German manufacturer, which cleared the ground for the operations of the Kartells, was the result of Bismarck's throw back to the policy of moderate tariff protection, as carried out under the incomplete Zollverein of the forties (see *ante*, § 23). Political circumstances in the early fifties had checked, and the general trend of European economic thought in the sixties had reversed, the tendency towards a slight increase of the protective barrier for manufactures, which had marked Zollverein policy between 1834 and 1848. In the days of Prussia's political humiliation before Austria, in 1850, it had been the intention of Schwarzenberg to force a way for Austria into the Union. But Austrian industries had been accustomed to a hot-house system of prohibitions and high duties. Therefore it was Prussia's interest to keep the Zollverein's duties low, so as to make Austrian manufacturers unwilling to enter. She strengthened her position by coming to terms with Hanover and Oldenburg in 1851–2. When these treaties became operative (Jan. 1, 1854) the Union touched the North Sea, and Austria remained outside it.

The inclusion of these north-western states increased the free trade element in the counsels of the Zollverein. As yet the north-west was an agricultural and trading country. The north-east, the land of the Junker, was still exporting food. In the south-west, where List's industrial protectionism had always been strong, there was also a powerful agrarian element which did not fear competition and liked cheap tools and cheap clothes. This gave a free trade majority, on a mere balance of interests, apart from the growing belief in free trade among disinterested thinkers and statesmen. It will not be forgotten that relatively free trade had been part of the tradition of government in Prussia longer than in any other country; and in Prussia traditions of government were unusually tenacious, in the absence of effective popular control. Therefore the Zollverein as a whole participated in the commercial treaty policy of the sixties, without many misgivings. Commercial and economic matters were left by Bismarck entirely to his very able colleague, Delbrück, who was a convinced free trader.

The grain duties disappeared in 1865 (see *ante*, § 55). Next year Austria was beaten in the field; and with renewed self-confidence Prussia went her own way. Had Austria won, as her rulers expected she would, it had been her intention to force herself into the Union, or to conclude a union with Germany to the exclusion of Prussia. Prussia victorious, with almost contemptuous tolerance, gave her a very favourable commercial treaty. Some North Germans grumbled because the Zollverein only claimed to be put on the same footing as France and England in the Austrian market, whereas Prussia might have stood out for preferential treatment. But Bismarck had his

political reasons for not pressing hard on Austria; and Delbrück
was not fighting for economic preferences. He was now (1868–
70) embarking on a policy of tariff reduction, independently
of any bargains with his neighbours.

The years 1864–71 saw the inclusion of Schleswig-Holstein
and Alsace-Lorraine in the Zollverein by conquest, and of the
two Mecklenburgs and Lübeck by treaty. Only Hamburg and
Bremen remained outside. Strengthened by the industries of
Alsace-Lorraine, whose competition the German manufacturers
had feared but not much felt in the rich years of the early
seventies, the young Empire seemed to the free traders strong
enough to carry forward its liberal commercial policy. "A
doctrinaire imitation of England," their German critics have
since called it. Delbrück was pressed to get rid of all duties
on iron and machinery. He was not unwilling. In 1873 the
duties on iron itself, shipbuilding materials, and some other
articles were abolished. Those on manufactures of iron were
reduced: they were to disappear on Jan. 1, 1877.

The moment was ill-chosen. In 1873 there began, almost
simultaneously in Vienna and New York, a financial and industrial collapse which was felt throughout the world. Germany
was involved at once. The crisis of financial panic was followed
by years of painful industrial convalescence. Very soon the
leaders of the iron industries came together. The thought of
Jan. 1, 1877 was a constant terror to them. Delbrück resisted
the pressure which they exercised through the Reichstag in
1875; but in 1876 Delbrück resigned "for reasons of health."
Bismarck was inclining towards a tariff on general political
grounds. He was beginning to lean on parties and groups who
were out of sympathy with free trade doctrine, especially the
Centre party, which was strong in the industrial west and the
south-west. Moreover he was preparing to concede a tariff to
the agrarians, whom circumstances were driving into the
protectionist fold; and he was anxious to carry the industrialists
with him. He was now picturing himself and Germany as
having been "the dupes of an honest conviction worthy of the
honourable capacity for dreaming in the German race[1]." The

---

[1] Grant Robertson, *Bismarck*, p. 376.

dream of free trade, he argued with no little force, must not
mislead a country placed between three strong states—Russia,
Austria and France—all of whom were moving, or preparing
to move, away from it. The German Empire must not take
its policy from Manchester.

He did not save the iron duties. His policy was only beginning
to take shape in 1876. They dropped as had been arranged. But
he was ready to listen to the well staged, and quite sincere,
lamentations of the manufacturing interest in 1877–9. Now that
trade was slack, Alsace-Lorraine was making her old German
neighbours most uneasy. While it had been active, she had
enjoyed a double market, because that of France was left open
to her for a time by arrangement. When the arrangement ended,
most of her goods went east. This was a further argument in
favour of the exclusion of alien goods, an argument with which
the Alsatians agreed. They were more thoroughgoing protectionists than the old Germans, having been bred under the
French tariff. These demands of the industrialists received
attention in the tariff which came into force in 1880; though its
most notorious and contentious section was that which re-
imposed duties on corn. The duties on manufactures were in
no case excessive, largely because Bismarck's main interest in
them was financial. He had no wish to kill the import trade.
Probably he was quite sincere in his argument, that protection
to manufactures was only a by-product, though admittedly a
desirable by-product, of his tariff. As the Empire needed funds,
and as customs duties were its chief source of revenue, he was
forced to choose between high duties on a few luxuries, in the
English style, and moderate duties on many things. He chose
the latter, partly because the luxury consuming capacity, and
luxury consuming habits, of different parts of Germany varied
so greatly that a few heavy luxury taxes would press unequally
on different areas, and promote political discontent in the new
Empire. Englishmen, if they recall the Irish case against the
spirit duties, cannot say that he was wrong. If widespread
taxation was financially and politically desirable, there was no
reason why he should not adjust it somewhat to the desires
of the threatened manufacturing interests. It was under

the pressure of arguments of this kind that the tariff took shape.

Complete freedom of entry for manufactures had not been reached before 1879. There were, for example, still duties on most textiles. The duties on the finer cotton yarns and the finer cotton goods were now pushed up, those on commoner qualities remaining unaltered. Duties were wisely kept low on the classes of worsted yarn for which Germany was, and remained, dependent on Yorkshire; although many of them were fine. But, as a rule, the principle of rises on the better class goods was applied in the woollen and other textile industries, just as in cotton. Even the iron duties, for the reimposition of which the outcry had been loudest, were exceedingly moderate. On pig iron the duty was fixed at the level adopted in 1868–70 of 1 mark per 100 kg.—say 10s. a ton. Besides textiles and iron, duties or increased duties were placed on paper, leather, glass and earthenware, rubber and wooden goods, various metal wares, some chemical wares, and many others.

On the whole the manufacturing protectionists secured much less than the agrarians. The latter had been able at the last moment to insist on higher duties than the government had originally proposed. For manufacturers nothing of the kind was done. A small victory over the agrarians was won by the linen industry, which succeeded in defeating a proposed flax duty, while retaining duties on linen yarn and piece goods; but this was an isolated episode.

Nor were the manufacturers able to add much to the tariff barrier during the eighties. Some, who had suffered in foreign markets from the duties on half-manufactured goods, were given in compensation a more thorough control of the home market for the completed articles. Such were the women's dress goods manufacturers, who used English yarn. The cotton spinners, flax spinners, lace makers, makers of embroideries and a few other industrial groups were also favoured. But, in the greater industries, the total increase of duties throughout the eighties was inconsiderable.

The chief raw materials remained free, except oil, tallow and timber, on which the agrarians had required the levy of duties.

In the nineties, the protectionist movement in Western Europe was stimulated by the passing of the McKinley tariff in the U.S.A. (1890–1), and by the continuous building up of tremendous tariff walls about Russia, from 1881 to 1891. The Méline tariff came in 1892; and Germany had to reconsider her position, especially in relation to her commercial treaties. Commercial treaties have often occupied the foreground of German tariff history. It is impossible here to give them the attention which they deserve; but it may be noted that the half political desire to occupy a strong bargaining position, and be able to threaten one's neighbours with economic reprisals, in case of either economic or political differences, contributed both in Germany and in other countries to the elaboration and upward growth of tariffs. A tariff, like a fleet or an army, may take its place in *Machtpolitik*.

The tariff and the Kartells together had succeeded, by 1890, in forcing the German consumer to pay a price above the international market price for a large number of important manufactures. The Kartell organisation facilitated competition abroad, while obviating it at home. The double selling price had become a recognised institution. Germany enjoyed "most favoured nation treatment" in all important markets, including the British Dominions; so she was able in the later eighties to do an increasing export trade with the aid of these special export prices.

It was necessary, in the early nineties, to revise several important groups of commercial treaties. The government of Bismarck's successor, Caprivi, was disposed to pursue a policy of moderation, in spite of the threatening fiscal policies of Germany's most important neighbours. Popular discontent, due to a rising cost of living, was noticeable; and Caprivi's master had started on a course of social conciliation. It was realised that any accentuation of the protective tariff might endanger German export industries—in spite of the two price policy in certain trades—and so lead to emigrations of discontented workpeople. "Germany must export either goods or men" was a catchword of the day. The government decided for goods.

Consequently the treaties were arranged on the basis of a cut in agrarian, and in some industrial, tariffs. Iron duties however were not touched. To help the export of goods, various Kartells developed a policy of private export premiums. In spite however of willingness to come to terms with her neighbours, Germany became involved in a tariff war with Russia (1893), which gave the agrarians an opportunity to press their case once more, for Russia was their great competitor. However, the war was closed by a treaty in 1894, which gave Russia "most favoured nation" treatment for grain, with other advantages. As a result of this and of previous treaties, Germany found herself possessed of a composite tariff system; one set of duties guaranteed by treaty, for a term of years, to certain powers and extended, also by treaty, to all other powers who enjoyed "most favoured nation" treatment; another set for powers such as the United States, with whom no treaty existed.

The treaty rates, as may be supposed, were unpopular in influential circles, both agrarian and industrial. The system which resulted from them was denounced as unscientific and partial. Arguments drawn from the example of other countries were enforced by America's reversion to high protection, by the Dingley tariff of 1897, after Democratic experiment in tariff reduction from 1894 to 1897, and by France's adhesion to the well elaborated protectionism of the Méline tariff. Moreover, near the close of the century, German opinion was stirred by the movement towards imperial preference in the British Empire, and by the dread that it might lead to an imperial tariff.

In 1897, England denounced her treaty with Germany, in order to remove all foundation for the German argument that, so long as the treaty existed, Canada was bound to extend to her preferential tariffs recently conceded to the Mother Country. So the English treaty was gone. In the new century other treaties would again begin to run out. They had mostly been concluded for ten years. It was Germany's business to be ready for all developments.

She set about framing a tariff system more severe, more detailed, and more watertight than she had previously possessed. It was under discussion for a long time, and was not finally adopted until the end of 1902. Even then the government was empowered to delay its application if necessary, in connection with the tariff negotiations still to be carried through. The dominant feature of the new tariff was the high level of the minimum food duties, which were not to be abandoned in any international bargain (see *ante*, § 55). On the industrial side, the general principles adopted were: free raw materials, as before; low duties on goods in the first stage of manufacture, also as before; but an increased scale of duties for every subsequent stage. Thus cotton was to be free; the cotton yarn duties were not raised; but the duties on cotton goods were raised fifty per cent. and more. Absolute freedom for raw material was unattainable, because of the agrarians' demands. Timber was taxed. So was linseed, though cotton seed was admitted free. However, wool was sacrificed to the needs of industry (see *ante*, § 55), and admitted free. So were other textiles and also hides. Clays, ores, coal and most metals in the crude state were free. Iron was the great exception. On it rates were increased at all stages of manufacture. Among the articles, other than raw materials, admitted free for special reasons may be noted many rough chemicals, fertilisers, drain pipes, books, music and everything of the kind, and all shipbuilding material. Agriculture must get its subsidiary requirements cheap; education must on no account be endangered; and not even the interests of the German steel industry must stand between Germany and her future on the seas.

A detailed elaboration of the tariff on manufactures was adopted in order to minimise the indirect results of concessions made by treaty. If articles are lumped together in large groups, "miscellaneous leather goods" or "aluminium wares" perhaps, a concession on one, made to conciliate a foreign government, automatically lowers the duty on all in the group, and that, too, for every state enjoying "most favoured nation" treatment. Thus a concession made, say, to Switzerland on article *a* might open the German market more than was desired to English supplies of article *b*, which chanced to be in the same group. England, it may be added, remained a most favoured nation in the early years of the present century by arrangement, though not by formal treaty. So long as German goods had free access to British markets, a treaty was superfluous; and Germany had had to abandon her attempt to block British imperial preference.

This is not the place to discuss the half economic, half political, history of the commercial negotiations and commercial treaties which followed the adoption of the new tariff. It need only be noted that commercial diplomacy was utilised to bind Austria-Hungary closer to Germany and to secure concessions from Russia. The broad lines of the customs system, as sketched out above, remained unaltered in the critical decade from 1902 to 1912. The German tariff on manufactures was never excessive. It compared favourably, from the point of view of an exporting manufacturer in another country, with that of most great powers. For example, it was calculated in 1904 that the average *ad valorem* equivalent of the import duties levied by Germany, on the principal manufactures exported from the United Kingdom, was 25 per cent. The corresponding figure for Italy was 27; for France 34; for Austria 35; for the United States 73; and for Russia 131. The figures are rough; but they illustrate tolerably well the relative intensity of protective tariffs.

§ 79. Before the March revolution of 1848, neither the state of industrial organisation nor the state of the laws in Germany had encouraged the growth of those labour conditions and labour policies characteristic of the modern world. General "trade freedom" (*Gewerbefreiheit*), that is, free entry into trades, had existed nowhere until 1808, when the French proclaimed it in Jerome Bonaparte's kingdom of Westphalia. It had been introduced two years earlier for some trades, in some provinces of Prussia; it was accepted as a general principle for all Prussia in 1810–11. The Prussia of 1815 included not only "free trade" provinces in the west, but also provinces where the principle had been accepted yet not fully applied, and the recently acquired part of Saxony where compulsory gild organisation remained untouched. Uniform labour laws were delayed for years. When the matter was taken up in 1835, a commission sat for ten years (1835–45) and finally advised the retention of a great deal of official control of industrial life. For purposes of state and police, officially recognised associations of the gild type were most useful. So the Ordinance of 1845, though generally favourable to freedom, specified more than forty trades in which no one was to take an apprentice who was not a qualified member of a gild (*Innung*). For some of the occupations, it should be added, such a regulation would be reasonable in any time or place—chemists, pilots, and the like.

In most other states the policy of the years 1815-45 aimed at the retention of gilds for most handicrafts; the concession of "free trade" only in specified industries; and universal police supervision. Take a Wurtemberg ordinance of 1836. Forty-four trades, including many of the most ordinary, were scheduled as gild trades. Businesses of every kind had to be sanctioned by the local authorities; and no business in any of the scheduled trades would be sanctioned, unless its head had complied with the proper gild rules, *i.e.* was a recognised master. Hanover, where the gild system had been abolished under French influence, went back to it in 1815 and left it almost intact till 1848. Oldenburg re-established it in 1830; and the free towns of Hamburg, Bremen, Lübeck and Frankfurt retained it until 1848.

No strong anti-gild movement existed before 1845 among the workers. This was natural in a land of handicrafts and tiny "businesses." The history of 1848 shows the masters still looking backward to the old order. There had been dearth, unemployment and distress in 1845-7. Here and there capitalism was pressing the master down into a mere outworker, or factory conditions were developing in "free" industries. During the year of revolution, gatherings of master craftsmen often expressed their views. They were apt to demand limitations on the use of steam. At the Hamburg Congress of North German hand-workers, in June, it was argued that only a universal gild system could save Germany from the factory miseries of England and the infection of French Communism. The Congress voted unanimously for the prohibition of "trade freedom," in the constitution of the new Germany for which men were hoping.

The master's right to speak for industry was disputed. First in Berlin and then in Frankfurt, meetings of journeymen (*Gesellen*), or, as they were beginning to call themselves, workmen

(*Arbeiter*), claimed a voice in the settlement, as "the real producers" and "the core of Germany." They were not by any means unconditional friends of "trade freedom." They wanted freedom of migration throughout Germany, a minimum wage, and a twelve hours' day. They wanted representative trades councils and a responsible Labour Minister for all Germany. They wanted to abolish the absolute legal compulsion to belong to a gild, if you were even to practise a trade, which was still quite common outside Prussia, where it was only the taking of apprentices in specified trades that was confined to qualified masters. And they wanted factory owners to be free to hire gild trained journeymen if they liked—such freedom was often denied—because factories might pay better than the qualified masters. On the whole, what they asked for was an easing of the old shoes where they pinched, not a new pair. They were not thinking of general principles or planning a new society. Few of them took any interest in the Communism which Karl Marx, now aged thirty, was just beginning to preach.

Masters' and journeymen's demands for a national industrial code died away with the failure to attain national unity; and they had to be content with such law as the various states chose to give. With the reactionary Prussian law of 1849 the masters were, for a time, very well content. It had an eighteenth century, almost a medieval, flavour. For something like seventy trades, including most ordinary handicrafts, the condition for setting up in business was either membership of a recognised *Innung*, or proof of competence given before a technical commission Government might modify this list of trades at will. The employment of handicraft journeymen in factories was limited, in the interest of the small masters. Shopkeepers might only sell "handicraft wares" if they were themselves qualified masters of the relevant craft—an extraordinarily medieval touch. The sole innovation was the establishment of local trades councils (*Gewerberäte*), to watch over industrial conditions, both in handicraft and factory trades, and to give advice to government. They never became of much importance.

Such legislation helps to explain the persistence of handicraft and small scale industry in modern Germany. True, it did not directly affect many of the more capitalistic industries, whether they were organised on outwork or on factory lines, because they enjoyed "trade freedom." But it must have acted to some extent as a drag on reorganisation in the scheduled industries. It was, however, too reactionary for universal application and, in spite of the excellence of Prussian administration, the system of examination before technical commissions was a failure. So much so that, twelve years later, whole districts could be found in which plenty of houses were being built, though there was no one in the district legally qualified to build them. "Trade freedom" existed in spite of the law.

The legal movement towards freedom was only resumed in the sixties. By that time the Germans stood alone among western peoples in their partial adherence to the system of regulation. English, French, Dutch, Belgians left men free to practise what trade they liked, where they liked, and how they liked. After 1860 a whole series of laws in the various German states led up to a law of the North German Confederation of 1869, on which the later imperial law was based. The old limitations and official tests dropped. Competence was only to be officially tested in the medical trades—chemists, midwives, nurses—and in navigation. Thus the law was modernised and the access to all ordinary trades freed; but not without protests from master craftsmen of the old school.

So rapidly did the successive waves of economic opinion trample on one another in modern Germany, that the law of 1869, the final consecration of individualism, coincided precisely with the foundation at the Eisenach Congress, by Liebknecht and Bebel, of the Social-Democratic Labour party. Government thought it had arranged that the "roaring loom of time" should weave the fashionable European fabric of the sixties; but it was not in control of the *Zeitgeist*; and suddenly in the pattern socialism showed clear. Thirty years earlier, when the word socialism was newly coined, it had been repeated with favour only in a salon or two at Berlin by a few men of letters or learning, and by a handful of wandering journeymen who had learnt it at Paris or in Switzerland. When the democratic movement of 1848 threw up Karl Marx and his little following of Communists, they passed off the scene into exile almost unheeded. There was not yet much in the economic life of Germany on which their doctrine could fasten. Then, in half a generation, modern industrialism gripped the German people. A rich and powerful *bourgeoisie* arose. Socialism became possible, not as a doctrine of intellectual or revolutionary minorities, but as a "mass phenomenon"; and since in no European country was the labouring man better educated, and at the same time divided by a wider social gulf from the "upper" classes, the possible became the actual with astonishing speed.

Nothing showed outwardly during the fifties. Revolutionary leaders were scattered over the earth, in Zürich, London, the United States; and the police took care that no working men's associations should have even the opportunity of considering revolutionary doctrine. The only form of propaganda which was permitted, and that reluctantly, was the cooperative propaganda of Schulze-Delitzsch, who shares with Raiffeisen the honour of starting the German cooperative movement. His first sphere of activity was among the handicraftsmen of his native (Prussian) Saxony. Cooperative credit associations, and cooperative purchase of raw material by cabinet-makers and shoe-makers, were his starting points, in 1849-50. By the sixties his work was bearing fruit, and consumers' retail stores of the familiar English type (*Konsumvereine*) were being added to the earlier cooperative enterprises. Just as his schemes were becoming widely known, they and their founder came into conflict with the first really effective German labour movement, inspired and led by Ferdinand Lassalle.

Lassalle, the son of a Jewish merchant from Breslau, was a man of the world, a scholar, and a democrat of 1848, who cared profoundly for German unity, but for unity—as he once said— *moins les dynasties*. Philosophic and legal studies had led him to take an unfavourable view of the existing political system and the existing relations between "capital" and "labour." Constitutions, he argued at the time of Bismarck's conflict with the young Prussian parliament in 1862-3, should correspond to the realities of economic life. Labour was the rising power in the economic world. The state should give it political freedom and the constitutional position which it deserved, a position which it could never abuse because, being the mass of the people, it could never become a privileged class. These expressions of opinion led to an invitation from a Leipzig Labour Congress to draft the programme for a projected political party. The party was to guard labour interests, in opposition to the *laissez faire* Liberalism of the existing party of Progress (*Fortschrittspartei*). Lassalle's public reply became the profession of faith of the General German Labour Union (*Allgemeine Deutsche Arbeiterverein*) which issued from the Leipzig Congress.

Schulze-Delitzsch cooperation, it was proclaimed, was a mere palliative, not a permanent cure of social evils. These arose from the "brazen law" which, under existing conditions, condemned the workman to a bare subsistence wage, and to exclusion from the benefits of economic progress. So the road to emancipation was to be found by the workman becoming his own employer— cooperative production, in short. As a transitional measure, freely formed workmen's productive associations ought to be subsidised by the state. To bring pressure on the state, workmen must secure the vote. That was their first task. Lassalle's not very novel economic doctrine lay behind all the writings and speeches of his short and stormy career as a political agitator. He died in Switzerland, of wounds received in a duel, on Aug. 31, 1864, leaving behind him a living political movement among German working men, a movement of which statesmen had to take account and by which Marxian socialists profited. It is supposed that his views influenced Bismarck, who knew him and said that he was "one of the cleverest and most agreeable men he ever met," and, through Bismarck, helped to establish universal male suffrage as the basis of the electoral system for the Imperial Reichstag. The party which he had created was captured by Liebknecht and Bebel, five years after his death.

From London, and his seat in the reading room of the British Museum, Marx had denounced Lassalle's contemplated intercourse with the bourgeois state, which to Marx was the unclean thing. No good would be achieved until the "dictatorship of the proletariat" was set up. Nor was Marx very sanguine as to universal suffrage; for he saw the use to which Napoleon III had put it in his *plébiscites*. Nor, again, did he see eye to eye with Lassalle in many matters of doctrine—wage theories and value theories. On that side he was a controversially-minded pedant, convinced of his own infallibility. Lastly, he despised Lassalle's cooperative proposals, just as much as Lassalle despised Schulze-Delitzsch's cooperative achievements.

The year after Lassalle died, Liebknecht, who was working to bring the German labour movement into line with the most advanced section of the International (see *ante*, § 68), converted Bebel, a turner by trade and president of the General German Labour Union. And so, by political manipulation and congress manoeuvres, the Union disappeared; and the Eisenach Congress of 1869 produced the *Sozialdemokratische Arbeiterpartei*, with a purely Marxian confession of faith and a Marxian programme.

§ 80. The growth of the Socialist party in the Reichstag, and Bismarck's long struggle with socialism, are part of the general political history of modern Germany. They are in place here only in their relation to those economic developments which they directly encouraged or retarded. By 1877, socialist candidates had attracted between 9 and 10 per cent. of all the votes polled. Two attacks in that year on the life of the Kaiser, neither the act of a socialist, inflamed public opinion and gave Bismarck his opportunity. His "exceptional law" of 1878, against the socialist party, for a time achieved its purpose. Working-class organisation was interfered with at every point. The party was harried, discouraged and broken up. Socialism was driven underground. Secretly printed journals, meetings under false colours, and the apparatus of conspiracy, became indispensable. The results might have been foreseen. In 1880 the party Congress, which was permitted to meet, voted in favour of attaining communism "by all means." Hitherto the stock phrasing of the vote had been "by all legal means." Next year, when the police allowed working men to organise unions, socialists at once took the lead. Election after election registered Bismarck's failure; and before William II dropped what remained of the exceptional law, with the pilot who had framed it, the socialist vote had grown from 493,000 (1877) to 1,427,000 (1890).

At that time the trade union movement, still regarded with the greatest suspicion, had made little progress. In 1895 even, there were only 269,000 trade unionists reported, in an occupied male industrial population of nearly 8,000,000. For this the long hostility of government and the imperfect industrialisation of Germany were jointly responsible. With industrialism storming forward, and legal obstacles removed, the trade union movement grew; but growth only became rapid after 1901. A total membership of 1,000,000 was first reached in 1902. It had risen to 2,000,000 in 1906; to 3,000,000 in 1909.

With a growth so rapid and recent, the German trade union movement of the early twentieth century was necessarily loose jointed. Territorial and religious divisions had always interfered with cohesion; and in spite of the hard work of the Social Democrats, these had not been overcome. The greater part of the organised wage earners belonged to the "free" unions, which were socialist in tone and were in most cases the work of socialist organisers. Out of a round 3,000,000 trade unionists in 1912, over 2,500,000 were "free." The other important group was that of the Christian unions, which had been founded with the definite object of maintaining the hold of the Church on the workers. They were open both to Protestant and Roman Catholic; but the mass of their members were Catholics. Their total membership in 1912 was only 345,000; but there was one trade at any rate in which they competed on almost equal terms with the free unions. That was mining, in which 118,000 free unionists and 77,000 Christian unionists were reported. Their success among the miners was due to the markedly Catholic character of many parts of the German Rhineland, and to the strength of the Church among the Polish miners, both in Upper Silesia, where they did nearly all the work, and in Westphalia, whither they migrated in considerable numbers.

Besides the free and the Christian unions, there was a small and unimportant group, containing in 1912 just under 110,000 members, of Liberal trade unionists enrolled in the so-called "Hirsch-Duncker" unions. Max Hirsch, who died in 1905, was originally a member of that radical Party of Progress which

Lassalle had derided. As such, he was opposed both to state "interference" and to Social Democracy. His unions took their stand on individualism and self help; but in course of time their platform was knocked from under them by Bismarck's social legislation (see *post*, § 81); and though they remained more or less erect, their teaching no longer carried far. They were strongest among engineers and other skilled metal workers, but were already something of an economic curiosity.

Not every "free" unionist was of necessity an active Social Democrat. There were always far more "free" unionists than there were regular members of the Socialist party. In Berlin, for example, in 1906, there were round about 250,000 "free" unionists; but the "politically organised" Socialists of the city were less than 80,000. Workmen joined the free unions because they were vigorous and efficient. Once they had joined, the vigour and efficiency were no doubt an excellent advertisement for the socialism which their leaders professed; but, as in all such cases, the rank and file cared more for wage rises won or hours shortened than for any politico-economic principles. How far they even voted socialist is unknown; but the Reichstag elections in the principal urban areas suggest that most of them were ready to do so.

Between 1890 and 1910, each of the three main groups of unions developed an elaborate central organisation. The Free Unions had their General Commission; the Christian Unions their General Secretariat; the Hirsch-Duncker Unions their Alliance. Congresses, programmes, propaganda, trade union statistics, a trade union press—none of these things were neglected. Like the economic records of the German Government, those of the organised German workers were obviously the products of a people laborious, thorough, educated, fond of organisation for its own sake, and proud of its organising capacity. The published analyses of expenditure, especially those of the Free Unions, show how much money was devoted to education, agitation, and the press, over and above what was distributed in sick pay, strike pay, unemployment pay, and the other ordinary activities of a trade union.

There is one form of trade union activity, and that perhaps the

most important, which was of slow growth in Germany—
collective bargaining. The fact that most unions had from the
start been offshoots of a great, and in employing circles intensely
unpopular, political party combined with the recent development
of German industrialism, and the marked social cleavage between
the proletariat and the "upper classes," to make successful
collective bargains abnormally difficult of attainment. Employers
justified their natural reluctance to abandon what they described
as the good old personal relationship between master and man,
by reminding themselves how much they, and the state, did for
the workers, under Bismarck's pioneering social legislation of
the eighties. What need was there, moreover, to recognise and
bargain with unions whose activities cut right across all established laws and customs, unions to which a wise government
had assigned no part in the social scheme, which in fact it had
branded as by nature revolutionary and unpatriotic? The men,
on their side, were discouraged by socialistic teaching from
entering into diplomatic relations with a foe who was shortly
destined to be struck down, in the great day of the dictatorship
of the proletariat. With an unrighteous master the slave must
not come to terms, it was said.

Only in one important trade was there a tradition of collective
bargaining running back to the early days of modern industrialism; and this was a trade in which master and man had
at that time stood very near to one another. Printing is the
trade. There had always been piece-work scales among printers.
It is a trade in which they are very necessary; but down to the
fifties the masters had drawn them up. The earliest negotiated
scale covered the Leipzig industry only. From this great
printing centre, joint action among both masters and men
spread outwards. In 1873 the first national scale was agreed on.
After many difficulties it broke down, at the time of a strike
for the nine hours' day, in 1891. Both sides suffered for lack of
a scale during the five succeeding years; so that after its revival
in 1896 the scale was never again allowed to lapse. It became
a model for other German trades, and for the printing trade in
other countries.

Collective bargaining occurred sporadically, during the

seventies and eighties, in various trades allied to printing—type-casting, bookbinding, and so on—and in some other piece-work handicrafts, such as pottery and glove making. In time-work trades it was rare before the late nineties. Even in 1898, there were only 37 negotiated local wage lists for masons. As the figures of trade union membership show, a really widespread system of collective bargains was difficult before the twentieth century. And until 1899, the will to bargain and sign a binding treaty was generally lacking on the men's side. In that year, the collective bargain was for the first time officially recognised as desirable, by a Trade Union Congress at Frankfurt. Five years earlier the fashion in Congress circles had been to call it a cuckoo's egg, laid by liberals in the trade union nest. But now the unions felt stronger, and more able to treat with combinations of employers as equals. Moreover they had wasted their funds in a relatively unproductive strike campaign, between 1895 and 1899, and wanted a period for recuperation.

The change of front may perhaps be traced in part to the decay of pure Marxian dogma among German socialist leaders during the nineties. "Revisionism," the teaching of those who wished to rub off the awkward angles of the official creed and who were not prepared to endorse all Marx's prophesyings, was in the air. In 1899 Edward Bernstein issued his critical *Postulates of Socialism*. The preface is dated from London, and the book is in accord with the less intransigent teaching of English Labour and Fabianism. It reflects also the difficulty of adjusting Marxian doctrine, about the inevitable concentration of capital in fewer hands, to the facts of a country three-quarters of which continued to be owned by peasants. In their rise to the rank of a national party, the Social Democrats were forced to consider the peasant problem; and the more open minds among them frankly admitted, as did Dr David in his *Socialism and Agriculture* (1903), that in agricultural matters Marx was all wrong. And, even although the course of German history was vindicating some of Marx's industrial forecasts triumphantly, such minds could not conceal from themselves the fact that the position of the wage earner was not deteriorating; and Marx had foretold, or at least was believed to have foretold, a growing wretchedness until the day of expropriation and the "abolition of wage slavery."

Trade unionists were not all moulded by, or even interested in, socialist doctrine; far from it. It would be a mistake therefore to overrate the direct results of these doctrinal developments. But at the least they are significant of that more accommodating temper, one of whose manifestations was the growth of collective bargaining. Probably the desire to share in the rapidly growing prosperity of the Empire, round about the turn of the centuries, had much more to do with the new policy than any awkward doubts as to wage doctrine or the coming of the Marxian Day of Judgment. Be that as it may, from the date of a famous building trades bargain for Greater Berlin in June 1899, negotiated wage scales spread rapidly in the older handicrafts. In the twentieth century they spread in the factory industries too. For a few years the leading industrialists stubbornly opposed the movement. Their foremost association, the *Zentralverband Deutscher Industrieller*, denounced the dangers of collective bargaining in 1905. This the men naturally took as a challenge; and a fresh period of strikes and lockouts set in.

After that, the pressure of the unions, the growing desire of the public and of the governments for industrial peace, the arguments of social reformers, and some shifting of opinion among the industrialists themselves, brought about a change. Between 1906 and 1914, the collective bargain was beginning to take a place in German industry, comparable with the place it had begun to take in British industry a whole generation earlier.

§ 81. In the year 1911 there were 13,600,000 people in Germany insured against sickness and invalidity. Of these 327,000 had effected their insurance through societies connected with the *Innungen*, or modernised gilds (see *ante*, § 79). The figures indicate the final result of two legislative efforts of the Bismarckian age—the effort to protect the handicraftsman against some of the dangers of modern industrialism, by adaptation of a medieval institution; and the effort to protect wage earners in general against other dangers, by applying the typically modern method of insurance.

The North German trade law of 1869 had finally set up "trade freedom" in the north. It had swept away all sorts of odd survivals in the minor states. In Mecklenburg, for example, country people were still obliged, in 1868, to grind their corn at the manorial mill, and to buy all beer drunk at marriage-feasts and wakes from the official brewers of the nearest town. Bad trade and growing industrialism, during the seventies, made some conservative thinkers repent of the adoption of this law by the Empire. They wanted to protect the skilled craftsman by giving him special rights and privileges. Bismarck resisted the more thoroughgoing medieval proposals; but he was quite willing to give a little help to the *Innungen*. By a series of laws from 1878 to 1886, "trade freedom" was very appreciably modified in their interests. The avowed objects were to maintain the craftsman's "trade pride"; to strengthen his competitive power by raising the level of technical education and skill; and—with these ends in view—to regulate apprenticeship thoroughly. Restrictions placed upon the employment of apprentices by masters outside the *Innungen*, led to an indirect compulsion to belong to an *Innung*, very near akin to the absolute compulsion of medieval town law.

In the eighties these modern gilds were by no means insignificant. There were over 9000 of them in 1886; and in Berlin, out of 35,000 master craftsmen, 13,000, employing 40,000 journeymen and apprentices, were gildsmen. In 1890, about a quarter of the master craftsmen of the whole Empire were so enrolled; but the majority of them lived east of the Elbe. The main strength of the gilds was naturally in trades which in all countries lie outside the scope of large scale production—butchers, smiths, wheelwrights, cabinet makers, glaziers, plumbers. But, in the eighties, it was hoped that they might maintain craftsmanship in many trades which were subsequently invaded by the factory system, such as tailoring and bootmaking.

During the twenty years from 1890 to 1910, the critical years of German industrialism, the gilds made little headway, though government did its best to help them. In the nineties they were inactive. Of 68 Berlin gilds, in 1895, only 30 ran trade schools;

though the running of a trade school was supposed to be one
of their main objects. They were often poor; and they were
generally very reluctant to spend much money on any but the
most obvious purposes. They were frequently unpopular among
the masters themselves. Yet all this did not prevent their leaders
from asking for wider powers and stricter monopoly. They
ascribed the partial failure to their voluntary character, and
pressed for compulsory membership and compulsory contributions. A law of 1897 met them halfway, by giving local
authorities power to sanction compulsory organisations, but
only among masters who regularly employed journeymen and
apprentices. Within the next seven years, nearly 3000 such
compulsory gilds were sanctioned; and by 1904, the latest
year for which detailed figures are available, nearly half the
gilds of Germany were compulsory.

The figures of that year indicate their final position. Their
total membership was nearly 500,000; and their real homes were
old Prussia, Silesia and Saxony. They had no hold south of the
Main, and no strong hold in the west. It was reckoned that they
included about 50 per cent. of the independent master craftsmen
of Prussia, and from 35–40 per cent. for the whole Empire. They
had done something to maintain the "trade pride" and skill of
their members; but very little to solve the typical industrial
problems of the age; and they were at their strongest where
those problems were present in their least acute form. In no
case did they include any large proportion of the working class.
The 5000 gild members of the Cologne district, and the 27,000
gild members of Berlin, were not the representative workpeople
of those cities.

The craftsman question never interested Bismarck greatly—
not at any rate after his earliest days. Nor was he much interested
in factory legislation of the original English type, that is, the
compulsory improvement of factory conditions, and the regulation of factory hours by the state. Perhaps the Junker's horror
of interference from outside with the affairs of his estate, and
"his" people, made him appreciate the factory owner's point
of view. He feared also that interference between master and
men might encourage industrial strife. After experimenting with

it, he let it slide into the background; with the result that down to the current century Germany was behind England in this work, a work which might have been expected to prove thoroughly congenial to the German administrative mind.

Bismarck neglected it the more readily, because of his conviction that what the modern wage earner most needed, and would most appreciate, was security against the vicissitudes of an increasingly uncertain world. He would have liked to see every German workman insured against sickness, accident, unemployment, and old age. Unemployment insurance he never tackled; but in the other branches of insurance Imperial Germany was the pioneer among nations. Bismarck and his advisers had some foundations to build on. Benefit societies of various sorts were common in the north. In the south, there was a system of parish sick relief for farm servants on the insurance principle. The gilds had their sick and burial clubs. And among the miners of the Harz, an ancient type of benefit society had developed into an insurance scheme to which both the working miner and his employer contributed. But all this did not greatly ease the gigantic labour of creating a national insurance system.

An act imposing on employers liability for expenses arising from all accidents, not due to the workman's fault, had been passed in 1871. The act had led to many disputes; so, when the question of national insurance was taken up, at the close of the decade, it was decided to incorporate accident insurance in the national system.

The system took another decade to complete. Landmarks in its progress are the sick insurance act of 1883; the accident insurance act of 1884; and the old age and invalidity insurance act of 1888. In the first of these acts, an attempt was made to utilise every possible type of existing association which might appeal to any class of insurable persons—benefit societies; gild sick clubs; factory sick clubs. The chief new types created were the local association (*Ortskrankenkasse*) and the communal insurance fund (*Gemeindekrankenversicherung*), the latter being an outgrowth from the south German parish insurance system. These new types eventually predominated. Twenty-eight years later (1911), when the insurance law was codified, they dealt with nearly 9,000,000 out of 13,600,000 insured persons; the local associations alone having 7,200,000 members. Factory associations at that time had 3,400,000 members. So only these three types were really of national importance.

To all these funds and associations both wage earners and employers contributed; and both were given representation on the management. The scheme was at first purely industrial. From Bismarck's day to 1911, however, fresh types of contributors were constantly being added. In this latter year domestic servants, agricultural labourers, and casual workers were compulsorily included for the first time; and an act was passed for insurance of salaried persons (*Angestellte*). The 1911 acts came into force on January 1, 1914.

The burden of accident insurance, under the law of 1884, was to rest upon employers; though during the earlier weeks of disablement through accident it was to be carried by the sickness insurance system. Thus the two systems were linked together. For accident insurance proper, employers were brigaded by trades and districts; and workpeople had no share in control because they made no contribution to the cost.

Like sick insurance, old age insurance was made contributory, master and man each paying half, the state paying the whole during the years of military service. Therefore only people in receipt of regular wages benefited by it. The method of payment adopted was that of cards stamped by the employer, and corresponding wage deductions made by him, as in the English sick insurance scheme. The old age pensions accrued at seventy. They varied in amount from just under 2s. to just over 4s. a week, according to the scale of contribution. The system was managed officially, not through the more or less representative sickness insurance associations.

As might have been anticipated from the date of its creation—during the currency of Bismarck's "exceptional law" against Socialism—and from Bismarck's frank avowal of its aim—to reconcile the working man to existing society and the Empire—the insurance code was not at first welcomed by Socialists. But in the more tolerant atmosphere of the twentieth century's first decade, the undoubted popularity of its principles among working men led most Socialist leaders and writers to confine their criticisms, which were numerous and often pertinent, to questions of scales, ages, and democratic control of the insurance machinery. The principles, they admitted, were "foundation walls," upon which even a Socialist might rightly build.

CHAPTER XII

COMMUNICATIONS COMMERCE AND COMMERCIAL ORGANISATION IN THE RAILWAY AGE

§ 82. The railway system of Western Europe was blocked out, in the more highly developed countries, by 1850. By 1870, its main lines were completed everywhere, even in countries where the start had been late and slow, like Italy and Spain. The Pyrenees had been turned at both ends; the Alps had been pierced at the Mont Cenis, and crossed over the relatively low saddle of the Brenner. Trieste was linked to Vienna, Prague, Dresden and Hamburg. The rails were being pushed far into Switzerland. Plans were in hand for the tunnelling of the St Gothard, where work began in 1872. Already the time was in sight when German coal would be dragged through the Alps to the coalless plains of Lombardy.

From 1870 onwards, the geographical history of railway construction is a local and specialised story. It is the story of a network of ever increasing density, with now and then the completion of some specially significant line, either within the West European economic area like the St Gothard and, much later, the Simplon, or linking that area to eastern points—to Constantinople, Salonica or Vladivostok. In this later period, a country's railway development is gauged not by single lines opened but by the density and efficiency of its whole network, in relation to its area, population, and resources. For the whole period 1850–1910 the table below gives some crude comparative facts. A fine comparison would require, among other things, the amount of single and double track. The figures are those of kilometres of line open for traffic at the various dates. They

	Belgium	France	Germany (1871 area)	Italy	Spain	Holland	Switzerland	United Kingdom
1850	900	3,000	6,000	400	28	176	25	10,500
1870	3,000	17,500	19,500	6,000	5,500	1,400	1,400	24,500
1890	5,000	36,500	43,000	13,000	10,000	2,500	3,000	33,000
1910	8,500	49,500	61,000	17,000	15,000	3,000	4,500	38,000

include some narrow gauge line in all countries and a great deal in Belgium.

The 1850 figures show how little construction had been undertaken at that time outside Belgium, France and Germany. The Austro-Hungarian Empire, however, had 1500 kilometres open. The Russian Empire had only 500. They show, too, the rapid German, and the rather slow French, building of the forties, referred to in an earlier chapter. The 1870 figures indicate with what success the Second Empire had made good the leeway; how Belgium retained her position as the best served country of Europe, in proportion to her size; and how Italy and Spain, Holland and Switzerland, took their places as railway countries. In 1890 France, Germany, Italy and Switzerland have all rather more than doubled their mileage since 1870, and Holland is almost satiated. In the next twenty years Belgium, never losing her position, adds relatively more to her network than any other country; and France falls very little behind Germany in her rate of addition. Spain remains ill-furnished to the end; and Italy makes less progress than might perhaps have been expected after 1890. But in both countries geographical conditions are specially hostile, in Spain the high ungrateful table land, and in Italy the difficult spine of the narrow peninsula and the lack of mineral areas.

§ 83. The doublings of the French and German systems, in the twenty years from 1870 to 1890, were accompanied by important developments in the field of railway policy, developments connected in France with the name of Freycinet and in Germany, like all other important events of those years, with that of Bismarck. Those years also saw a change of policy in Belgium.

There had been constant complaints, during the later years of the Second Empire, that the great companies were reluctant to develop out of the way districts by constructing lines which were not likely to prove remunerative. The government had therefore subsidised a number of small new companies, especially in the west and south-west. It had also authorised the departments to shoulder part of the financial burden of local lines, whether undertaken by local companies or by the great companies. Occasionally, when companies could not be found

XII]   RAILWAY POLICY—FRANCE   341

for particular projects which were considered to be "of public utility," the state itself had started operations, as it had in similar circumstances during the early days of the railroads (see *ante*, § 38).

Like all other imperial institutions, the railway system was saddled by public opinion with part responsibility for the collapse of 1870. Transport had certainly failed; but whether the blame attached to the companies or to the War Office is an open question. Men who had striven to organise national defence, and yet had been forced to accept defeat, naturally concentrated their criticism on defects in the national equipment. A leader, both in defence and criticism, was Gambetta's understudy, the engineer Freycinet. The governments of the early seventies set to work feverishly to improve the railway network. A law of 1875 authorised the construction of 2000 km. of subsidiary lines by the state, leaving the method of working them to be determined later. In spite of the loss of 800 km. of line in the ceded provinces, the amount of line open for traffic had increased, between 1870 and 1875, from 17,500 to nearly 22,000 km.

But many of the smaller companies, authorised between 1865 and 1875, were in difficulties. Some turned to their big neighbours and came to terms with them. The powerful Northern Company absorbed several, without finding it necessary to ask assistance from the state. But parliament was suspicious of the great companies. Grievances as to railway rates were constantly cropping up; and when the Orleans line proposed to imitate the Northern, but asked for a guarantee of interest on the unproductive lines which it intended to take over, permission was refused by the chambers, unless it were accompanied by an amount of state control over rates which the company was not prepared to accept. The upshot was that the state took over 2600 km. of western and south-western lines itself. This was in 1877.

Next year Freycinet, then minister of public works, came forward with his gigantic scheme for the completion of "the national equipment." It was a question not merely of railways, but of canals, harbours, roads and all the machinery of transport.

The original railway project was for 4500 km. of new lines. But the chambers were in a mood of enthusiasm, and the law in its final form provided for no less than 8800 km., a 50 per cent. addition to the network as it had been in 1870. It was not proposed that all the lines should be undertaken at once, or that any of them should necessarily be undertaken by the state; but the pressure of opinion and jealousy of the great companies led to rapid building without their cooperation; and whenever a new company could not be created, or a weak company collapsed, the burden fell on the ministry of public works. By 1882 it was responsible for 16,000 km. of line, either working or under construction, and its financial position was getting desperate; for nearly all its lines were of the non-productive class. Also they were scattered all over the country, mixed up with those of the great companies. Only in the south-west was there a fairly compact block of government lines. Thus the "third network," as the new lines were called, was a most unprofitable proposition.

In 1883 the government cut its losses and came to terms with the companies, by what were known to their critics as the "scoundrelly conventions." The alternative, which had considerable support, would have been the buying out of all the companies, and a complete state system. For the financial operations involved in such a scheme the state was not prepared. There had been a commercial collapse and a sharp fall in revenue during 1882. Money was hard to raise, and the government was glad to be relieved of what has been called the nightmare of having to complete the Freycinet plan single handed. By the "scoundrelly conventions" the companies agreed to take over the greater part of the "third network," finished or unfinished, and incorporate it in their systems. The state retained its block of railway territory lying in the triangle Tours, Nantes, Bordeaux, and linked it to Paris by securing running rights over the lines of the Orleans and Western Companies—an odd and somewhat undignified arrangement for the sovereign Republic. The companies were to find part of the money for the completion of the third network, and were to provide all the rails, rolling stock, and working capital. As none of them except the

Western now needed to draw upon the government guarantee of dividends, which was part of the system worked out under the Second Empire (see *ante*, § 38), they undertook to hasten the repayment of the sums previously advanced by the state, or to set off against these sums expenses which they were now incurring in connection with the third network.

The occasion was taken to simplify the extraordinarily complex system of railway finance. There were no longer, as under the Franqueville agreements of 1859, to be separate accounts and separate bargains with the state for the different "networks." From its single account each company was to pay; *first*, its debenture interest and sinking fund charges; *second*, a dividend limited so long as the company remained in any way indebted to the state. If it did not earn enough to meet these charges, the state guarantee came again into operation. When any company had finally cleared itself of all debt, surplus earnings above the statutory dividend were to be shared between it and the state, as under the Franqueville agreements. Finally, the new conventions were all timed to expire between 1950 and 1960.

When these conventions were negotiated, the termination of the state's liability under the guarantee system was confidently anticipated. But dull trade and falling prices in the late eighties and early nineties drove all the six great companies, except the Northern, back on the guarantee. The P.-L.-M., the strongest company after the Northern, had only a few bad years and needed no assistance after 1895. The Orleans line was self-supporting from 1898; the Eastern, after two good years in 1899–1900 and two rather bad ones in 1901–2, became self-supporting in 1903. In 1904 the Southern followed, and in 1905, for the first time under the Third Republic, repayments from the companies were greater than outgoings under the guarantee scheme. All the while the Western was drawing on the guarantee. In 1908–9 the government decided to exercise its right to buy the line, a right always reserved in the conventions, since there seemed no prospect that the Western would ever repay its debts. Other considerations also came into play. The Western was adjacent to the state system, and its acquisition would bring "the State" into Paris. Nationalisation was a popular word. The Western could be bought cheap, as under the concessions the purchase price was determined by the earnings, and it had never been a good earner.

So the French railway system stood in 1909–14. The two strongest lines were paying well. They had cleared off their debts to the state; and the long deferred day when it would share in their profits seemed to be drawing near. The three weaker lines were, on the balance, in process of paying back their debts, though occasionally, in a bad year, the guarantee came into play. The weakest of all had just become state property, but there had hardly been time to test state management. Nor would an experiment made on this particular system alone have been quite fair to the state.

§ 84. It has been seen that between 1850 and 1870 the construction of state lines in Belgium had ceased. That of private lines had gone forward rapidly; and the state had been engaged in active competition with the companies (see *ante*, § 37), to the detriment of its railway budget and the confusion of railway rates. There was much foreign capital invested in the Belgian railways; and the events of 1870–1, when her neutrality was threatened, brought home to her the political risks of this arrangement. There were also economic disadvantages in leaving the rates to be influenced by foreign directors. So economic and political considerations combined to suggest a reversion to the original policy of government ownership and uniform rates. The reversion was not hurried. For a generation the state continued to buy out private lines as opportunity offered. There were heavy buyings in 1871–3, which more than doubled the state system. By 1880 nearly three-quarters of the main lines were in government hands. But one important company, the West Flanders, serving Bruges, Courtrai, Menin, Ypres and Poperinghe, was only purchased in 1906 and taken over for state working in 1908. The few main lines then remaining in private hands were insignificant, except the Givet-Dinant-Namur-Liège section of the great Meuse valley trunk line which belonged to the Nord Belge Company. The state had been able to reduce and codify rates and charges, to offer excellent facilities, and to make experiments in the cheap carriage of passengers which were studied with interest in all countries. So far as its financial statements can be tested, it appears to have done this at least without loss to the taxpayer. Certainly, in the twentieth century, railway receipts covered interest and sinking fund on the capital expended. Whether there was a small deficit or a small profit on the working expenses was disputed.

Owing to Belgium's position and to the carrying out of the original intention of her state-made railway system—to make of her a great land of transit—special through import and export rates were always prominent in her rate books, especially so after 1890, when the industrial expansion of her neighbours was being rapidly accelerated, and the competition of Antwerp with Rotterdam, Bremen, Hamburg and Havre was becoming keener.

A unique feature of the Belgian system of transport was the network of light railways created after 1880 to meet the needs of the densest population in Europe. They were usually of metre gauge and followed the lines of the roads. Such a system was advocated in the seventies; but as it did not attract the ordinary commercial investor, a special organisation, the National Society for Local Railways, was created to promote them in 1885. It was in close touch with the governments, central and local, which held a large part of its shares. It had no monopoly; but in fact it did most of the work of construction, and that at an amazing pace. In 1888 only 439 km. of these light railways existed. There were 1600 km. in 1898 and 3200 km. in 1908. Nearly 1000 km. were authorised but not built in 1908. They were in hand during the next six years; with the result that the Belgian railway network, which had always been denser than that of any other country, was steadily increasing in relative density, down to 1914. But whether this was all gain is doubtful, in view of the contemporary developments in road traction.

§ 85. The activity of the private companies, which built and worked a great part of the German railways during the fifties and sixties, is one of the most conclusive proofs of the rapid accumulation of capital in Germany during the early railway age. A fast growing population and the decay of rural industries provided the necessary labour. The decade 1865-75 saw the completion of the essential main lines. It was not all due to German thrift. A considerable part of the French war indemnity found its way into railway securities after 1871. "You may say," wrote a German economist in 1903, "that by way of war indemnity France finished off our main railway network for us[1]." Meanwhile the acquisition by Prussia of the state systems of Hanover, Hesse-Cassel and Nassau, and the acquisition by the Empire of over 800 km. of line from the French Eastern Company in Alsace-Lorraine, had raised the whole question of railway ownership. The application by the railway administration in Alsace-Lorraine of an exceedingly simple—for permanent use, an impossibly simple—goods tariff had brought forward the question of reformed railway rates. Rates were necessarily complex and inconsistent, in consequence of the varied policies hitherto pursued by the component parts of the new Empire. It contained not merely imperial lines, state lines, and private lines; but privately-owned lines managed by states and state-owned lines managed by private companies.

Twenty years earlier at least, Bismarck, not yet in office, had played with the notion of a universal state-owned system as a means to German unification. Had he been a dictator in 1871 he would probably have decided at once for imperial ownership, on political, strategic and economic grounds. But it was certain that Bavaria, who had been brought into the Empire with some difficulty, would not sacrifice her railway independence; and during the early seventies free trade and private enterprise economics, still strong in the official and commercial worlds, were an obstacle to nationalisation even in Prussia. He had to content himself for the moment with the creation, in 1873, of an Imperial Railway Office to co-ordinate the construction, equipment, and working of the various systems. It was given private instructions to draft an imperial railway law; but none of its early drafts were discussed in the Reichstag, though one got as far as the Federal Council in 1879. Meanwhile the Prussian government was authorised to offer all lines in its possession for sale to the Empire. But it never offered them.

During the trade depression of the late seventies criticism

---

[1] Sombart. *Die deutsche Volkswirtschaft im Neunzehnten Jahrhundert*, p. 282.

of private railway management grew in unofficial circles. The indemnity had begotten some reckless enterprise, with consequent disappointment and loss. The corn-growing squires of the east grumbled at the "penetration rates," by which Russian grain was moved cheaply over the eastern lines into the heart of the country. A people well educated in military affairs appreciated the strategic argument for state management, especially after the diplomatic rapprochement between France and Russia in 1875–8 had raised the spectre of a war on two fronts. To Bismarck, the rush by railway to the towns was both economically and politically ominous. He hoped, most vainly as it proved, that a more thorough state control might in some way be utilised to keep men on the land and away from urban socialism. Public opinion was now ripening and he decided to act. His working hand was the minister of commerce, von Maybach.

In 1879 the Prussian government bought up 5000 km. of private lines, the property of six strong companies. In 1882 seven companies, with a kilometrage of over 3000, were bought out; in 1884 ten companies with nearly 4000. New concessions to companies for important lines ceased. So the main part of the work was done; though purchases went on for another twenty years, during which twenty-five lesser companies, with a kilometrage of 3400, handed over their property to the state. Many of these lines, like some of the earlier Prussian state lines, ran across non-Prussian territory. Arrangements for joint ownership were in some cases entered into, as when Prussia and Hesse Darmstadt joined in 1896 to buy out the greatest surviving private line in Germany, the Hessian *Ludwigsbahn* nearly 700 km. in length. In every case the Prussian government took over the management, as it did also on several lines where it was not even part-proprietor, such as the Main-Neckar line in Baden.

The results of thirty years' railway buying in Prussia were as follows:

	1879	1909
State lines	5300 km.	37,400 km.
Private lines worked by the State	3900	—
Private lines	9400	2900

The length of all German railways in 1909 was just over 60,000 km. of which 2200 km. was narrow gauge. Besides Prussia's 37,400 km. of state lines, there were 17,000 km. owned by Bavaria and other large states. There were only 3600 km. of private standard gauge lines in all the Empire, and none of the owning companies controlled any route of first-rate importance.

It was not surprising that foreigners constantly spoke of the German state railways, when in fact no such thing existed. The Prussian railway department owned more than two-thirds of the main lines in the Empire. It was the near neighbour of the Imperial Railway Office and, subject to certain rather stubborn differences with Bavaria, was generally able to put its policy through. That policy was, on the whole, a conspicuous success. When lines were bought, provision was regularly made for a sinking fund to pay off the capital burden; and although new construction was constantly adding to the aggregate railway debt, the financial position was always sound. Rates were unified and systematised throughout the Empire; for this was a matter within the competence of the Imperial Office. Hopes for a goods tariff of transparent simplicity, which had been common when the work of nationalising began, had however been disappointed. Crude abuses and inequalities soon disappeared; but year by year, from 1880, the tariff became more complex, as its administrators came to terms with reality. The railways were made subservient to the national economic policy. Special rates for imports, to divert through European traffic from neighbouring countries, and for exports, to help German foreign trade, reintroduced and extended over a very wide field that principle of two or more prices for the same service, according to "what the traffic will bear," which reformers had treated, at one time, as a typical bad product of private ownership. Latterly a very large proportion of the traffic was carried under the "exceptional tariff."

Another promise of the early days was also unfulfilled, but apparently with the consent of those most competent to judge. The state, it had been said, will not aim at profit like a common capitalist. If it has a surplus, it will lower charges or increase facilities. In fact the state made profits and kept them. They had the advantage, from the point of view of the government, that they accrued without parliamentary vote. The public acquiesced because they meant so much less taxation. The service which yielded them was admittedly efficient. Most Germans counted it the most efficient in the world, so that no users of the railways felt that they were being overcharged for an inferior article.

The strategic consequences of Prussian nationalisation and imperial control do not call for discussion. But the rigid military discipline enforced on the railway personnel should be noted. "Post and railway," a German wrote, were "only the civil sections of the army." Their directors, at any rate in Prussia, were not infrequently generals. And there were few facts more significant than that in these two services were placed "three-quarters of a million men who stood stiff at attention when their superior spoke to them[1]." These facts explained in part the excellent method and punctuality of the service. They were responsible also for the complete absence of any railway labour movement, comparable with those which were developing in France and England during the early years of the twentieth century. A four years' war, that was lost, and a political revolution had to come before the Prussian railway-man struck.

§ 86. Far down the railway age, the extent to which railway systems were supplemented by fully developed road systems varied greatly from country to country. The "national" roads of France, that is to say her first-grade highways, amounted to 34,000 km. in 1840. The corresponding roads in all Prussia a year later measured no more than 10,000 km. France was developing her third- and fourth-grade roads between 1840 and 1860, her first-grade roads requiring very little addition throughout the century. Prussia's period of greatest activity in building roads of the national type was from 1845 to 1870. Very little was done in her Eastern provinces until after 1850. Conditions of travel in Prussian Poland during the early fifties resembled those of Western Germany in the Napoleonic age (see *ante*, § 26)

---

[1] Sombart, *Die deutsche Volkswirtschaft im Neunzehnten Jahrhundert*, p. 320.

or of England in the reign of Queen Anne. It took, for instance, over eleven hours for a goods waggon to cover the 25 or 26 English miles between Posen, the capital, and Gnesen. If this was the situation near the capital, that further afield can be imagined. When steam power was coming into use in Poland, boilers despatched from Western Germany were dragged by teams of four and twenty horses; yet the boiler of the fifties was not heavy.

After 1870, the differences in road equipment among the leading nations rapidly diminished; though Italy long remained backward, in spite of the excellence of her road engineers and the incomparable experience which her navvies had acquired at home and abroad. Spain never came into the same economic group as her neighbours. But exact comparisons cannot be made, because of all statistics those of roads are the least satisfactory. There is no standard type even for the first grade; they vary from a Flemish *pavé* to the Brighton road, the Corniche, or the magnificent mountain roads of Norway. For the lower grades, the statistics of individual countries are confused and defective; international comparisons are worthless. But it is probable that what is true of France is approximately true also of Germany and other well developed countries—namely that, by the early eighties, the length of roads of all grades kept in tolerable order was within 10–20 per cent. of the figure reached thirty years later; and that not until the motor-transport age of the twentieth century did standards of grading and surface, on the best roads anywhere, get much beyond those of Telford, Macadam, and the engineers of the first Napoleon.

The late completion of a full road network in Germany is one of the many reasons for the lateness and rapidity of her final industrial development. It illustrates also what has been called the "colonial" character of the economic evolution of at least her eastern provinces (see *ante*, § 39).

On the continent, as in England, the early successes of the railway led to some neglect of canals and river navigation. The active canal building of the Restoration and July Monarchy periods in France ended in 1847, though projects at that time in hand were naturally completed. But, unlike England, France soon resumed work on inland navigation. When the government of Napoleon III turned towards free trade in 1860, it was deemed expedient to give all possible assistance to home industry. Therefore canals and canalised rivers were improved and modernised; but not many important new enterprises were undertaken, except canalisation work on France's chief inland water routes—the Seine, the Marne, and the Yonne. This work continued after 1870, in spite of financial difficulties, and in 1874 the Assembly sanctioned a new canal to join the Saône to the Meuse, the Canal de l'Est.

Freycinet's great programme of "national equipment" in 1878-9 was the starting point for all subsequent developments. Canals were to be standardised into two classes, so as to facilitate through communication without transhipment. Hitherto, as in England, the great variety of canal types had blocked through traffic. Two thousand kilometres of new canals were scheduled for construction; but only a few hundreds were put in hand. In spite of financial obstacles, the standardisation of the first-grade canals went steadily forward, and was almost completed by the end of the century. They were given a minimum depth of 2 metres, and their locks a minimum length of 38·50 metres. The improvement of the rivers went on *pari passu* with that of the canals, and was really more important.

The Freycinet programme resembled the double-tracking of a railway line. Its main results were shown not in the length of canal opened but in the increased traffic carried on canals and canalised rivers. There were 4560 km. of canals open in 1869, and only 4850 in 1900. There were some additions in the twentieth century which brought the figure to nearly 5000; but when 1914 came the chief new enterprise, the Canal of the North, still lay unfinished and dry between Mœuvres and Bourlon Wood. But the (metric) tonnage loaded on to river and canal boats had grown from 21,000,000 in 1886, when the Freycinet programme was still young, to 29,500,000 in 1896; 34,100,000 in 1906; and 42,000,000 in 1913. Nearly three-quarters of this tonnage, in 1913, was made up of coal and building materials other than timber. Rather more than a tenth was agricultural produce and foodstuffs. Not much more than a thirtieth was manufactures. The figures bring out the classes of traffic for which water transport seems best fitted.

Few of the older canals did more than a local business, in the twentieth century, in spite of Freycinet. The Canal du Midi, at which Arthur Young marvelled, was almost deserted. The Rhone-Rhine was not much better; but then its terminus was in hostile hands. The Canal du Centre, from the upper Loire to the Saône, and the new Canal de l'Est (Saône-Meuse) carried a fair traffic. But the bulk of all the water carriage of France was on the Seine, its tributaries and its ancillary canals including the Marne-Rhine, and on the canals which link the Oise to the northern coal-fields and the rivers of Flanders.

It is useful to put side by side the growth of traffic on waterways and railways, during the period of French industrial expansion from 1890 to 1913. They are given below in tonkilometres, *i.e.* the number of tons carried for one kilometre; one ton carried five kilometres, and five tons carried one kilometre, being both entered as five.

Ton-kilometres carried, in millions.

	1890	1895	1900	1905	1910	1913
Waterways ...	322	377	467	509	520	618
Railways ...	1170	1290	1616	1770	2200	2590

The waterways, it will be seen, gained on the railways a little down to 1905; but for the whole period rail traffic, tested in this way, grew faster than water traffic. This, although the state, in order to provide cheap water carriage, was losing on the waterways every year and was not getting a penny of interest on more than £60,000,000 spent on them since 1820. The waterways were doubtless valuable to France. But whether this heavy subsidising of water transport was, properly speaking, remunerative, whether the money might not have been spent to greater advantage on land transport, is a matter for debate.

Germany also spent freely on water transport in the imperial age. As in France, it had been neglected while the first railway net was being woven; but towards 1880 it began to receive attention and thereafter money was not spared. Some of the greatest enterprises were primarily or partly strategic. Primarily strategic was the Kaiser Wilhelm (Kiel) canal; which, in spite of its excellent position, did not become an important international highway down to 1914, though it did something to revive the trade of old Baltic towns such as Lübeck. Somewhat less strategic was the great Dortmund-Emden canal, through which ships of 900 tons were eventually to pass from the lower Rhine to tide-water, without crossing Dutch territory. The main canal was opened in 1901; but the final link with the Rhine was only put in hand in 1906 and finished after 1914. The heavy traffic on the main canal from the start indicated the real economic value of a waterway for the coal and iron of West-phalia to the ports of the north; but strategic considerations were very present to the minds of its promoters.

At the end of the imperial age the canals proper in Germany amounted to about 2600 km. against nearly 5000 km. in France[1]. *Per contra*, Germany had nearly twice as much canalised or fully navigable river as France; and as all her greater rivers, except the Weser, rise outside her borders or flow from Germany into other countries, they act as international highways.

Before 1870 most of the river basins of Germany had been linked together by canal. Just as in France, the main problem of the later nineteenth century was how to increase the efficiency rather than the length of the waterways, above all of the Rhine and the Elbe which united carried more than half the water borne trade of Germany, and of the Elbe-Oder-Vistula cross connections on the north German plain. How brilliantly the engineering problem was solved the figures of inland ships and cargoes make clear. In 1877 cargoes of 800 tons could ascend the Rhine up to Mannheim; in 1905 cargoes of 2000 tons. In 1877 cargoes of 4-500 tons could ascend the Elbe to Magdeburg; in 1905 cargoes of 1300 tons. In 1877, 80 tons was the maximum cargo on the Ems; in 1905 cargoes of 900 tons could get through from the Ems to Dortmund. The average canal boat cargo coming into Berlin in 1878 was 70 tons; in 1905 it was 190 tons. Or again, in 1887 there were 600 boats or barges of more than

---

[1] These figures are very rough, as none of the terms, canal, river, navigable, are exact. From the German figures are omitted the "moor canals," which are comparable with our fen district main drains.

400 tons at work on the inland waterways; fifteen years later there were nearly 4000, and of these 1200 were upwards of 800 tons.

In spite of this revolution in water transport, the available figures suggest that in the twentieth century the railways were at least holding their own as bulk carriers of goods. A careful calculation, in which water and land transport were reduced to ton-kilometres, showed that in 1875 the inland waterways carried 21 per cent. and in 1895 22 per cent. of all the traffic of Germany, a slight loss by the railways. For later years so exact a comparison has not been made; but the gross tonnage figures of goods carried by rail and by water, irrespective of distance, in the year 1910 were—railways, 401,000,000 tons; waterways, 77,000,000 tons. This gives the waterways just over 16 per cent. of the gross traffic. No doubt the percentage would be higher in ton-kilometres, as the average journey by water tends to be long; but the analogy of France suggests that it would not be more than 20[1]. It may be noted that, in 1910, in Germany, 23,000,000 tons of coal and coke were moved by water and 155,000,000 tons by rail; in France 11,000,000 tons by water and 45,000,000 tons by rail. There is no commodity better fitted for water carriage, except perhaps building material. Even of building material the French railways carried twice as much as the waterways.

German waterways were run at a loss while German railways made large profits. The greatest German authority on the economics of transport was decidedly of opinion, in 1900, that the technical superiority of waterways had not been demonstrated. He regarded the imperial canal policy as simply "a method by which the national revenue may be sacrificed to the claims of certain business and agrarian interests[2]." He was thinking of the eastern squires and the Westphalian coal and iron magnates, who got their water transport cheap at the expense of the state and of the general trading and travelling public who furnished railway profits.

[1] For France both sets of figures are available. In 1913 the railway gross traffic figures were five times those of the waterways; the ton-kilometre figures just over four times, as given above, p. 352.

[2] Gustav Cohn, Zur Politik des Deutschen...Verwaltungswesens, p. 293.

Although the rivers of Germany are first rate international highways, they carried, even when fully developed in the twentieth century, only about a quarter of her foreign trade. Had Russia kept pace with her in the development of waterways, as Austria-Hungary very nearly did, the figures would have been somewhat, but perhaps not greatly, different. Of 76,000,000 tons of imports in 1911, 22,000,000 tons came in river or canal boats. More than a quarter of this was iron ore brought from French Lorraine, or up the Rhine through Holland from overseas. Nearly a quarter was grain and seeds, coming both from east and west, but mainly from the east. More than a tenth was timber, mostly floated down the Russian rivers in summer. Of 67,000,000 tons of exports, only 15,000,000 tons went by the rivers. Over 9,000,000 tons of this was coal, and nearly 2,000,000 tons iron and steel.

The sustained supremacy of the railway in modern continental commerce cannot be better illustrated than by Germany's coal exports. There was every possible facility for export by water, and the water borne export trade in one case at least, that of Holland, was gigantic. By water, coal can be moved without breaking bulk. Yet in 1911 nearly twice as much coal left Germany by rail as by river. It went to all her neighbours; and every year between half a million and a million tons traversed Switzerland and crossed the Alps into Italy, aided it is true by special rates on the St Gothard line.

§ 87. In earlier chapters, the French and German mercantile navies, since the age of steam began, have been examined from the standpoint of the shipbuilding industry (see *ante*, §§ 62 and 72). It remains to examine them in relation to other navies and to the development of the world's trade since 1850. The table on page 356 gives the overseas mercantile tonnage of the chief seafaring nations at four critical dates.

France's inferiority in tonnage to Norway at the last; her inferiority in steamer tonnage to Italy; and the revival of shipowning in Holland since 1900 are the outstanding facts; other than the familiar predominance of the United Kingdom, weakness of the United States, and swift rise of Germany.

France, as has been seen (see *ante*, § 62), was specially un-

Total mercantile tonnage and steam tonnage (s.).

		1850	1870	1900	1910–12[1]
United Kingdom	{	3,565,000	5,691,000	9,304,000	11,700,000
	s.	168,000	1,113,000	7,208,000	10,700,000
United States ...	{	1,586,000	1,517,000	827,000	928,000
	s.	45,000	193,000	341,000	618,000
France	{	688,000	1,072,000	1,038,000	1,463,000
	s.	14,000	154,000	528,000	838,000
Germany ...	{	—	982,000	1,942,000	3,000,000
	s.		82,000	1,348,000	2,500,000
Holland... ...	{	293,000	390,000	347,000	565,000
	s.	3,000	19,000	268,000	523,000
Norway... ...	{	298,000	1,023,000	1,508,000	1,526,000
	s.		14,000	505,000	896,000
Italy	{	—	1,012,000	945,000	1,107,000
	s.		32,000	377,000	945,000

fortunate because the modern age of ocean steam began during her difficult decade, 1870–80. As a result of her failure to take rank as a steamship owner quickly, she lost her best chance of profiting by the most decisive event in the maritime history of the later nineteenth century, the opening of the Suez canal in 1869. Yet the canal was French in conception and execution. England, through her diplomatists, who remembered Napoleon's Asiatic projects, had opposed it to the end. Leading English statesmen had prophesied that it would benefit primarily, if not exclusively, the Levantine and Mediterranean peoples; though Sir Charles Dilke foresaw in 1867 that, "even if it proved a complete success," France "would only find that she had spent millions on digging a canal for England's use[2]." Seven years after it was opened, the British government became the principal shareholder, as a result of Disraeli's opportune purchase of the Khedive's very large holding. Throughout the rest of the century, it was used mainly by English ships, and its use hastened the victory of the iron or steel built screw steamers for whose construction England was particularly well equipped.

The disappointment of Suez was followed for France by the tragedy of Panama. Men had dreamt of a Panama canal since the days of Cortez. Von Humboldt had traced alternative routes in the first decade of the nineteenth century. That company

---

[1] The figures are not all available for the same year. They come from the return Cd. 329 of 1902 and the German Statistisches Jahrbuch, 1913, p. 46.
[2] Greater Britain, p. 569.

promoting King, William I of Holland, had made a company
for this also; but it collapsed in 1830. Goethe had prophesied
in 1827 that the United States would be forced to make it, and
eight years later the United States Senate had ordered a report
on it to be drawn up. Louis Napoleon had written a pamphlet
about it while in prison at Ham; England had safeguarded her
possible interests in it by the Clayton-Bulwer treaty of 1850
with the United States. In 1855 an American company had made
the first Panama railway—the quickest route to California before
the opening of the Union Pacific in 1869. A few years later
America again took up the canal project. But France began the
work with de Lesseps' *Compagnie universelle du canal inter-
océanique de Panama* in 1881. It was one of her many acts of
economic self assertion after 1870. Unexpected engineering
difficulties, yellow fever, and dishonest finance brought the
company to bankruptcy in 1889. *Panamiste* became a term
of contempt in France; and the building of the canal was left
to the twentieth century and to the United States, who bought
off England diplomatically by the Hay-Pauncefote treaty in
1901.

Had the French company completed its task, there can be
little doubt that the history of Suez would have been repeated,
with America in place of England. The conditions of French
trade and French shipping made it in the highest degree unlikely that any large share of traffic on the Panama route could
have fallen into French hands. France's true overseas interests
lay nearer home, in her rapidly growing North African Empire.
The conditions of her shipping were such, that even the acquisition in this period of important new colonial dominions
east of Suez, in Further India and Madagascar, did not drive
very many French ships through the Suez canal; and the Panama
canal led only to a few French Pacific islands. France did not use
Californian fruits. She was doing her best to keep out Californian wheat. Certainly California did not need her wines.
The nitrate and guano of Chile, which she did use, were shipped
in tramp steamers, of which she possessed very few. And her
liners, for passengers and the more valuable cargoes, were hardly
in a position to compete for non-French traffic with the old

established lines of the United Kingdom and the rapidly growing lines of Germany.

Attempts to create French transatlantic lines had been made before 1850, but they had not succeeded. In 1851, just before the railway was completed from Paris to Marseilles, the company of the *Messageries Maritimes* was founded, in the first instance for the Mediterranean trade. It was followed by Atlantic lines which were eventually successful, such as the *Compagnie Trans-atlantique* based on Havre. But, excellent as the best of these lines were, they did little but French business. This is not surprising when it is borne in mind that during the steam age, *i.e.* since about 1870, the proportion of France's business carried in French bottoms declined seriously. During the decade 1874–83, nearly a third of the loaded tonnage entering and three-sevenths of the loaded tonnage leaving French ports was French. In the decade 1904–13, of the entering tonnage not a quarter and of the leaving tonnage not a third was French. It was thus unlikely that much French shipping would compete for non-French trade on the ocean routes.

The contrast with Germany, by the end of the nineteenth century, was overwhelming. Between 1880 and 1890, Germany's steam fleet passed that of France. By 1900 it was more than two and a half times, by 1910 three times, as great. Some check had been placed upon German development, down to the early eighties, by the fact that Hamburg and Bremen were not yet fully absorbed into the body of the Empire. The two great Hanse towns had stipulated in 1871 that they should retain their fiscal autonomy. The customs boundaries of Germany lay outside them; and there was friction between them and their neighbours, and between them and the central government. Finally, in 1882–5, first Hamburg and then Bremen came to terms. They were allowed to retain "free harbours," from which, as from bonded warehouses, goods could be re-exported without coming under the hands of the customs authorities. As an earnest of goodwill the Empire contributed generously to the necessary expenditure; and the ports were laid out afresh on modern lines. Yet twice again, between 1887 and 1900, Hamburg had to increase her harbours. Bremen grew no less rapidly.

In 1880 Hamburg owned a steam fleet of 99,000 tons and Bremen one of 59,000. Twenty years later they owned, Hamburg, 746,000, and Bremen, 375,000; and that was only a beginning. The figures were doubled by 1914. When the negotiations for customs union with the Empire were in progress, there were only four important steamship lines in Hamburg and one in Bremen. By the end of the century the numbers were twelve and four; but far more important than the growth of separate lines was the increase in power of the two greatest, the *Hamburg-Amerika* and the *Nord-Deutscher Lloyd*. Route after route of the ocean trade was invaded by the two companies. Already in 1888 the N.D.L. started regular sailings to Australian waters; and by the twentieth century there was no sea where the German flag was unknown. For the first time since the age of steam, there existed a merchant navy which could compare itself with that of England without appearing ridiculous. In point of quality comparison was far from ridiculous.

§ 88. In an earlier chapter (see *ante*, § 29) some illustrations were given of the relatively unimportant part played by foreign commerce in the economic life of most European nations during the first half of the nineteenth century. Almost everything that has been said in subsequent chapters about agriculture or industry might serve to illustrate the way in which this situation changed, with the advent of modern means of communication. France dependent for one third of her coal; Germany dependent for thirteen-fourteenths of her wool; England dependent for four-fifths of her wheat; all three dependent for the whole of their cotton, rubber, jute, rice, and for almost all their mineral oils, tin and copper, are illustrations which need not be multiplied.

And yet most countries except England had aimed at as much self-sufficiency as circumstances would permit. France had been so far successful that her imports, measured in money— a defective measure but the only one available—had not increased by much more than 50 per cent. in the thirty years from 1880-3 to 1910-13; though they had grown fourfold between 1850-3 and 1880-3, when she was emerging from her earlier self-sufficiency and modifying her old restrictive policy (see *ante*, § 67). Her exports, in the fifties and sixties, tended to exceed

her imports; she was sending capital abroad heavily for the
first time. She continued to do so while she was paying the
indemnity of 1871; but, from 1876 onwards, her established
position as a creditor nation gave her a permanently "unfavourable" balance of trade, although she had to deduct from the
surplus of goods which represented the yield of her foreign
investments the considerable sums due, chiefly, to England who
carried for her.

Germany followed in France's footsteps as she became richer.
During the eighties her trade balance was still generally
"favourable." She was beginning to invest abroad. She had
not been doing so long enough to receive a large flow of goods
as interest and profit on these investments. Other nations still
did more carrying for her than she did for them. Towards
the end of the eighties the balance began to turn. In the nineties
it was regularly "unfavourable"; in the next decade it was more
"unfavourable" than that of France. When first the balance
turned, opinion in Germany became uneasy. A permanent
surplus of imports seems so unwholesome to the natural man,
that much persuasion is required to convince him that it is, or
at least may be, a sign of prosperity. At the great national stock-
taking in which Germany indulged, when the century which
had seen her unification closed, the matter was fully debated.
Economists explained that the Empire was not buying more than
it could pay for, but was gathering in the fruits of its enterprise
and thrift, the interest on its investments and the profits of its
ships. In time the public became accustomed to this new position
as a creditor nation, like France or England, or like Holland, who,
thanks to her shipping and her ancient colonial investments,
had enjoyed an "unfavourable" balance almost all through the
nineteenth century.

The industrial and populous nations, however strong their
agriculture and however thorough their policy of agrarian
protection, all imported foodstuffs heavily. France, it is true,
succeeded, in the early years of the twentieth century, in keeping
her expenditure on foreign food of all kinds rather below what
it had been in either of the preceding decades. But France's
population was almost stationary. Germany, with a population

whose growth had not begun to slacken, had a food bill which
grew steadily after 1890, even when world food prices were
falling. The combined effects of protection and falling world
prices, in the eighties, had kept the annual expenditure below
what it had been in the late seventies; but with 1890 the rise
was resumed. In the eighties Germany spent £40–50,000,000
a year on imported food, including live animals; in the nineties
£70–80,000,000. By 1910 the figure stood at £130,000,000, and
in 1912 it reached £160,000,000. That year the United Kingdom,
the country whose purchases of foreign food were the greatest,
spent £260,000,000 for a population less by one-third than that
of Germany. France, whose expenditure under this head had
begun to rise again in 1910, spent rather over £70,000,000 for
a population less by two-fifths than that of Germany.

The United Kingdom's dependence was greater than the
mere figures would indicate, because of the position of her wheat
supplies. In all three cases, there was in the imports a considerable amount of "luxurious," *i.e.* not absolutely essential,
food and drink. Had France increased the acreage yield of her
crops so successfully as Germany (cf. § 46 and § 56, *ante*) her
bill for imported food would have been reduced. On the other
hand, had her industries grown like those of Germany it might
well have been increased. When all allowances have been made
and all possibilities considered, it is clear that England's position
was, in its broad outlines, the normal one for a modern European
industrial people with a growing population. She reached it
first because she was first industrialised. Even in the United
States, the total imports and exports of foodstuffs almost
balanced one another between 1910 and 1914, though the
imports included an abnormally large proportion of semi-
luxuries.

From 1914 war inflicted on Europe most of Malthus' "positive
checks" to population in their most terrible forms. But population statistics before 1914 suggested the working of his "preventive checks." A few people thought that France might not
long remain alone in that "stationary state" which English
economists of the mid-nineteenth century, with the fear of
Malthus still strong upon them, had hoped for and praised.

It had been the aim of those nations who, unlike England, tried to regulate the character of their imports, to take all that they could in the form of industrial raw materials, including, where necessary, fuel. France's permanent fuel shortage and Germany's swift industrial development had swollen this group of imports, until by 1910–12, for France it was approaching, and for Germany it had exceeded, the corresponding group in the United Kingdom. Germany also, it will be recalled, was a buyer of English coal. In her case too the group of industrial materials contains some half-manufactured goods which are excluded from the English group. It about doubled in value between 1880 and 1900, in a time of falling prices, and more than doubled again between 1900 and 1910–12, in a time of rising prices. The comparison between the three countries, in the last age of industrial expansion since 1890, is necessarily rough, but it is worth making. It is as follows:

Imports of industrial materials.

	Average for the years		
	1891–2	1901–2	1911–2
	£	£	£
United Kingdom	127,000,000	158,000,000	237,000,000
France ...	92,000,000	112,000,000	184,000,000
Germany ...	83,000,000	123,000,000	274,000,000

Here the great and growing dependence of the industrial nations on international commerce is again illustrated. The fact that the groups are not composed in precisely the same way in each case does not impair the value of the comparison from this point of view. With the exploitation of tropical and sub-tropical lands, and the growth of raw material producing communities in the southern hemisphere, every decade saw fresh industries arise which could not maintain their vigour for a year if the steady flow of goods across the oceans were interrupted. The world had become a single market and there was hardly a commodity which had not its world price.

§ 89. The laying of the first successful oceanic cables in the sixties, which very nearly coincided in point of time with the completion of the Suez canal and of the Union Pacific railway, had been the starting point for the age of world prices. Very rapidly, between 1866 and 1876, the main ocean cables were laid—almost entirely by England and the United States. It was really an English enterprise. The nations of Western Europe took a very small part in it, and the United States only a subordinate part. So late as the beginning of the twentieth century, more than three-fifths of the ocean cables were British owned; and although other countries, and in particular Germany, participated more in the work of cable laying during the twentieth century, the overwhelming predominance of the British Empire was never challenged.

The first ocean cables were all laid by private companies; and down to 1914 private ownership of cables remained the rule, although the United Kingdom had taken over the inland telegraph system in 1869. On the continent, the telegraph had been regarded from the first as a matter for the state. In France it was so declared by law (1851); in Prussia state ownership was taken for granted without any law. By 1875 the various telegraph systems of the German states were amalgamated under the imperial post office. Fourteen years later the German government initiated state control of international cables, by the purchase of the lines from the island of Borkum to Lowestoft and from Greetsiel (north of Emden) to Valentia. In 1891 it initiated state laying of cables, by an arrangement with England for a second line from Borkum to the east coast. But in 1913, out of 516,000 kilometres of sea cables on the earth, only 94,000 km. belonged to governments; and of these the various governments of the British Empire owned nearly a third. Out of 422,000 km. of privately owned cables, 250,000 km. were the property of companies whose headquarters were in London. Companies domiciled in Germany owned 36,000 km., and companies domiciled in Paris 52,000 km. Almost all the rest belonged to companies domiciled in New York.

On land the West European state telegraph network had become exceedingly dense. In proportion to population, Switzerland made the most use of her telegraph system; though France was hardly behind her. But the telephone had for many purposes superseded the telegraph. In telephone work Germany led the way for all Europe, including Great Britain. It was a natural result of her powerful electrical industry. Effective development began in the early eighties, of course in the hands of the state. Within thirty years, there were sent daily more than three times as many telephonic messages in Germany alone as telegraphic messages in all the world. Exact comparisons between Germany and England cannot be made, because the collection and issue of statistics was not part of the business of the National Telephone Company; but there can be little doubt of the superiority of the German system in the early twentieth century. Between Germany and any other great continental country there was no comparison, though Denmark, Switzerland, Holland and Scandinavia were all exceedingly well provided with telephones. In 1912 Germany had nearly three times the telephone mileage of France, and more than five times as much single line. She had more than four times as many installations, and her people spoke over the telephone nearly seven times as much. So far will statistics carry, in a matter rather intractable for the statistician. They mark the contrast between a country with many, and a country with few, dense, interlocked industrial and commercial areas.

§ 90. All the going to and fro, the buying and selling, insuring and speculating, loading and unloading, warehousing and retailing, telegraphing and telephoning—in short all the commerce, in its widest sense, absorbed a growing proportion of the population in every country. As a rule each fresh means of communication, though at first it seemed to threaten its predecessors with extinction, after a time added to their vigour and to the number of those who lived by them. Railways might kill posting on the old main roads; but for many years they greatly increased posting in out of the way districts; and they stimulated road transport continuously. The telegraph did not kill the letter post, nor even the telephone the telegraph. Every means of communication stimulated trade. Census statistics of those occupied in commerce do not go far enough back on a uniform basis to make comparisons possible, decade by decade, for any important country from 1840 or 1850 to 1910. But there are the very detailed figures of the German census of occupations, for the twenty-five years 1882–1907, which are undoubtedly typical of the general movement; though the pace may not have been so rapid at earlier dates or in other countries.

For both intercensal periods, 1882–95 and 1895–1907, the commercial group of the population (*Handel und Verkehr*) grew faster than any other. Than any other group of occupied persons, that is; for with Germany's rise in wealth the fastest growth of all was that of the group "unoccupied persons of private means." This class and its dependents more than doubled in the twenty-five years, thanks to the economic surpluses which but for commerce would not have existed. The figures for all the classes are:

Occupations, persons engaged in them and their dependents.

	1882	1895	1907
Agriculture and forestry	19,225,000	18,501,000	17,681,000
Industry	16,058,000	20,253,000	26,387,000
Trade and transport	4,531,000	5,967,000	8,278,000
Public service and professions	2,223,000	2,835,000	3,407,000
Personal services (not domestic)	319,000	382,000	447,000
Casual ("variable") labour	620,000	504,000	346,000
Independent means	2,246,000	3,327,000	5,175,000

In 1882 the people engaged in trade and transport, with their dependents, were almost exactly one-tenth of the whole population; in 1895 they were more than a ninth; in 1907 considerably more than an eighth.

The trade and transport group had five main divisions— trade, insurance, post and railway, other transport industries, and hotel and inn-keeping; the first being as large as all the rest put together. Much the most rapid growth in the twenty-five years was in the second group, insurance. Its membership, though not great absolutely, had increased more than fivefold during these years in which the principle of insurance was being applied, not only individually, as hitherto, against fire and flood and death and sickness and "the act of God or the King's enemies" at sea, but also nationally against the risks that threaten whole social classes.

Next to insurance in rate of growth came the post and railway group. Among other things, this growth reflects the creation of the telephone service. The innkeepers' group and the general trade group grew at about the same pace; in each the number of those actually engaged in the occupations rather more than doubled in the twenty-five years. The slowest growth was that in "other transport industries." Between 1882 and 1895 this class grew very little; but in the next twelve years it grew 60 per cent. In the first period, labour was being saved on road and water transport, by the spread of the railways and the use of larger vessels for inland navigation. In the second, the completion of the electric tramways, followed by the beginnings of motor traffic, led to a swift increase of employment. The general trade group grew uniformly in both periods, as might be expected. Unfortunately the complexity of modern trade made it impossible to retain the old Prussian statistical distinction between the "great trader," who had no shop, and the mere retailer, a distinction which was used in an earlier chapter to illustrate the insignificant part played by the true merchant in the life of Prussia before 1845 (see *ante*, § 29). Therefore the growth in the number of the "great traders," and of those employed in "great trade," must remain unmeasured; it need not for that be the less vividly pictured.

One reason for the abandonment of the old statistical group was no doubt the blurring of the lines of division between "great trade" and "great industry," on the one hand, and "great trade" and retail trade, on the other. Early in the nineteenth century there was no serious risk of confusing merchants with manufacturers. Even in the third quarter of the century, merchant and manufacturer were normally distinct types; but with the growth of great businesses, syndicates, and Kartells, the distinction often disappeared, especially in the metal and engineering industries, but not in them only. This was so in all countries. A firm of Paris motor car manufacturers, the Allgemeine Elektrizitäts-Gesellschaft, or Messrs J. and P. Coats managed their own merchanting. On the other hand the retailer, who was normally a humble person before 1850, had acquired in some cases a new dignity, with the outward spread from Paris of the great shops and stores, which were one of the most characteristic commercial products of the period from 1850 to 1890.

§ 91. The first generation of great Parisian shops mostly

sprang from the little shops of mercers and spicers which came down from the Middle Ages. Before 1830, there was a mercer's shop near the flower market where M. Parissot sold needles and thread and calico and tape. His sign was the *Belle Jardinière*. Between 1830 and 1850, M. Parissot built up a business in ready made clothing—beginning with blouses and working suits for different trades. His shop absorbed five-and-twenty adjacent houses; and when he handed over the business to a relative in 1856 his capital was estimated at 3,000,000 francs. A greater man was Aristide Boucicaut who, in 1852, went into partnership at the *Bon Marché*, a mercer's shop in the Rue du Bac. Boucicaut decided to sell good stuff cheap. He marked the price on his wares instead of bargaining over it as was the custom. He paid his employees by a commission on sales and he understood advertisement. After twenty-five years his business, now become very miscellaneous, had a turnover of 67,000,000 francs. By 1893, Boucicaut having long been dead, the turnover was 150,000,000 francs.

In 1855 two young mercers' shopmen, with a friend who had a shop of his own and had saved 100,000 francs, set up in a newly finished block of buildings in the Rue de Rivoli. They called their establishment the *Louvre*. Like its predecessors it was to be a *magasin de nouveautés*. The struggle was long and hazardous. Even in the seventies the business was not very large; but it made headway; was always adding fresh "lines," and at the end of the century was second only to the *Bon Marché*. All these shops and others of the same class, like the *Printemps* and the *Samaritaine*, were in the line of descent from the mercers. Their original clients were women: their methods were founded mainly on a knowledge of women's economic psychology.

The great shops descended from those of the spicers succeeded because, like their contemporaries the early cooperative stores in England, they decided to stop the petty dishonesty and adulteration which prevailed in the retail food trade of the forties. About 1840, a certain M. Bonnerot began to make a modest fortune, because he gave fair measure and took small profits on a quick turnover. His fellow spicers were furious at this unfair competition. He was followed by M. Potin, who added to these commercial maxims that of good quality. If necessary, he maintained quality by mixing or making his wares himself. Potin died prematurely in 1871, after having established the reputation of his business by singular public spirit shown during the siege of Paris, when he refused to "profiteer." After his death the firm went into manufacturing on a large scale. It made Champagne at Epernay and "French plums" in the valley of the Garonne. It had a chemical laboratory at its Paris factory. When he began making cocoa, Potin had declared that a spicer ought to be a chemist. This was novel doctrine at the time; but the firm kept it in mind.

Not much attention has been given by historians to shop-keeping origins of this kind. Yet they are at least as significant as many industrial or commercial episodes in eighteenth and nineteenth century history which have been fully discussed. Fortunately we know about Paris[1] and Paris led the way. The Parissots and the Potins had their imitators in every important town. The first is heard of in Berlin in 1850[2].

Paris was imitated by Germany in another matter connected with distribution, the organisation of her food markets. The Paris *Halles* have a continuous history stretching back to the reign of Philip Augustus. Originally they were a food market of the primitive type, in which townsmen bought from peasants. As the city grew, a smaller proportion of the townsfolk attended market, and often the dealer took the place of the grower. Dealers, shopkeepers, and food hawkers came in between producer and consumer long before the nineteenth century. When the *Halles Centrales* were modernised in 1851, they were already the head-quarters of the wholesale trade in foodstuffs; a function to which they were more and more restricted in subsequent years. They were to Paris what Smithfield, Billingsgate and Covent Garden were to London, only—in the fifties—better managed. Besides them Paris had various local retail markets.

Other French towns followed the lead of Paris and built central market halls, where both wholesale and retail dealings could be carried on. Metz and Strasbourg possessed such halls

---

[1] Thanks principally to the Vicomte d'Avenel, *Le Mécanisme de la Vie Moderne.*

[2] Hermann Gerson: he sold 20,000 mantles. S. von Waltershausen, *op. cit.* p. 142.

while still French. In 1871 almost every German town had a food market or markets of the old sort, where producer and consumer met and bargained. So had small towns often in 1910; "in many regions selling is for the most part done by the producer himself," wrote a German economist in that year[1]. But in large towns food supply conditions had begun to approximate to those of Paris before 1860. The markets continued, but the market personnel began to change. Buying at market by consumers declined; and with the widening gap between them and producers, the quality of the goods sold was said to have deteriorated. It probably did. The erection of central market halls, after the French pattern, was intended to check some of the abuses of the retail shop system, by giving such consumers as desired it a chance to purchase nearer the source, and to secure a more regular and abundant supply of foodstuffs. Frankfurt was the first large town to build a central market hall, in 1879. It was followed by many other towns, and the results, thirty years later, were believed to have justified the movement. As in some English towns, where the municipal market hall has been adopted, wholesale and retail transactions often went on side by side, the poorer inhabitants of the central districts preferring the markets to the shops. Indeed, in Germany, the shop system for ordinary perishable foodstuffs never became so general as in England. For example, when Berlin organised its food markets in 1886, it created a Central Market Hall on the lines of the Parisian *Halles Centrales* for wholesale dealings, and no less than twelve local halls for the retail trade.

There is no better illustration of the changes which were occurring in the commercial system of central Europe, after the decade 1840–50, than that furnished by the history of the German yearly markets and fairs (see *ante*, § 29). In the largest towns the yearly markets had given way before the shop and all-the-year-round trading by 1835–40. "A great part of the inhabitants," said a contemporary, "hardly even notices that a yearly market is being held[2]." But he added that "lower down the urban scale," the yearly markets retained their old importance,

---

[1] K. Rathgen, in Conrad's *Handwörterbuch*, VI, 596.
[2] J. C. Hoffmann (1841), quoted by Rathgen, VI, 595.

and that in the small towns their importance was even growing. After the railway age, and more particularly after 1870, the yearly market sank, slowly and almost without record, from its old position. No longer the occasion on which people of all ranks, in all but the greatest towns, laid in their stocks of clothing materials, utensils and miscellaneous luxuries, it became more and more a fête day for peasants, who poured in to country towns to buy "fairings" and cheap luxuries—damaged or unfashionable goods for the most part. In towns of the second rank it came to occupy the position which it held already in 1841 in those of the first. It retained its importance, however, in some northern and eastern provinces, as a distributing centre for the wares of local handicraftsmen—shoemakers and saddlers and potters—who could sell for cash to the consumer in the ancient way. In Pomerania, Mecklenburg, Posen and Silesia "market shoemaking" was still vigorous at the end of the nineteenth century; and it was dying hard so far west as Thuringia.

The great fairs, in 1830–40, had been essentially meeting places for two groups of traders, not for trader and consumer. To them the traders brought their wares, as they had ever since the Middle Ages. The most westerly of the great fairs, that of Frankfurt-on-Main, was the first to decline. It was losing ground in the eighteenth century. The most easterly, Frankfurt-on-Oder, did a growing business down to 1855, but probably not a growing share of all the wholesale business done in the east. Leipzig, the great central fair, was still growing in the sixties; although more than thirty years earlier it was officially reported that it had ceased to be the clearing house for the trade of mid-Europe, because traders were dealing with one another direct all the year round, not waiting to meet and deal at fair times. Evidently the growth was absolute only, not relative to the general mass of trading. Moreover, from the decade 1850–60, the whole character of the business at the fairs was beginning to change. Men met to exchange not goods in bulk but samples. It became more convenient to despatch the goods direct, as wanted, than to drag them to the fairs. And of course the goods of those "heavy" trades, which were characteristic of the later nineteenth century, could never go to the fairs at all.

By the end of the century this sample trading had become the rule at Leipzig, for pottery and glass, light metal goods, fancy goods, hardware and toys. There remained something of the old fair business in leather and furs, articles which had become more important than any others before 1885. But even furs and leather were bought and sold as often out of fair time as in it. Sample trading, having conquered the old trades, was applied to new ones. Leipzig developed a sample fair for bicycles and motor cars. But, by the twentieth century, even the Leipzig fairs in their new form, the only fairs which retained any vitality, had become mainly local in character. Few traders from the west visited them and foreign goods were less and less seen. Within their limits they did useful work; but the main streams of trade had long since been diverted into other channels.

§ 92. In their later developments, the fairs had not much to do with the staple articles of modern commerce. Leather is to some extent an exception; but leather has never become standardised for market dealings so thoroughly as cotton or wheat. The method of dealing by sample was, however, both a tribute to the uniformity of modern machine made goods, and an approach to the type of dealing which is connected with exchanges for staple articles, rather than with fairs. No article can be handled on a modern exchange (*bourse* or *Börse*) unless it is at the least able to be sold by sample, like tea or wool. The commodities fitted for the perfect exchange are those which are so uniform that they can be bought and sold unhandled and unseen. That is why, in all countries, stocks and shares became the first subjects for exchange dealings of the type which subsequently extended to many classes of produce, to coal, metals, and some half manufactured goods like pig iron or yarn. In the perfect exchange, the commodity dealt in may be bought and sold not only unseen, but when the seller does not yet possess it, nor the buyer necessarily wish to use it. That is the "market in futures," *marché à terme*, *Termingeschäft*, in which the dealer seeks to take advantage of price changes, not between places but between times, changes anticipated at the close of specified periods, such as the "settlements" of the English Stock Exchange.

Holland had possessed an elaborate exchange system early

in the eighteenth century. There were organised markets for bills and for stocks and shares; but besides these there were "future" dealings in all kinds of articles for which, as a contemporary says (in 1722), it was possible to fix some standard average quality as a basis for the transactions[1]. Half-developed stock exchanges existed at that time also in London and Paris. Indeed the Paris stock exchange was organised with its officially recognised brokers, or *parquet*, and its unofficial brokers, or *coulisse*, very much as it still is, by a royal ordinance of 1724.

In eighteenth century Germany neither type of exchange dealings had made much progress; though there was a little stock and share dealing in Hamburg and Vienna before 1750, and some officially recognised bill broking in Berlin.

The collapse of Holland during the great wars had driven some of her financial business to Frankfurt; and, in the age of international borrowing which followed the wars, stock exchange technique was acclimatised for Germany in Frankfurt. This was during the decade 1820–30. During the railway age the now familiar sequence of stock exchange speculation, boom, and collapse was seen also in Berlin. France and England, not to mention Holland and Belgium, had had earlier, though intermittent, experience of all this. Its occurrence in Berlin illustrates the eastward spread of that most highly organised type of market or exchange, upon which other exchanges were more or less consciously modelled.

Stages in the development of produce, mineral and metal exchanges are not easily traced, because records are scarce. Now and then a definite date can be given, a date for instance at which some standard type of goods was formally adopted by the traders of a particular market, as a basis for "future" transactions. Thus the futures market for coffee was organised at Havre in 1882. Similar organisation followed in Hamburg, Antwerp, London, Marseilles, Amsterdam, and Rotterdam. But in such cases it is probable that informal transactions in futures long preceded the official organisation. The Dutch markets for colonial produce, as we know, were highly organised in the eighteenth century; and so soon as Holland had recovered her

[1] Sombart (*Moderne Kapitalismus*, 3rd ed., II, 500) argues that these were not true "futures" markets.

commercial independence, after 1815, she began to rebuild her commercial machinery. The market for American cotton developed in its modern form at Liverpool between 1841 and 1876[1]. Liverpool was followed by Havre, and Havre by Hamburg and by Bremen, where a cotton exchange was organised to include both Bremen dealers and up-country spinners in 1886. Other outstanding cotton markets towards the end of the century were Antwerp, Dunkirk, Marseilles, Genoa and Venice.

Commodities like coffee and cotton, for which all Europe was entirely dependent on imports, naturally acquired specialised markets early. Grain and flour followed, as the continental nations became partially dependent on imports, and adopted the trading methods of Chicago, London and Liverpool, during the eighties. Sugar is a case in which the specialised market was based on an export trade. In England an overseas commodity with port markets, on the continent it acquired inland markets near the producing areas. It is easily graded and standardised. So we find the Paris sugar market, in the last decade of the nineteenth century, provided with machinery for dealings in futures, and often the scene of wild speculation. The leading German sugar exchange was that of Magdeburg; the leading Austrian exchange that of Prague; but in neither place were future dealings ever organised.

These dealings, together with similar dealings on the stock exchanges, and the opportunities which they provide for speculation by persons not furnished with technical knowledge, were severely criticised in Germany, as they came into prominence during the eighties and early nineties. Finally, in 1896, government took up the whole question of exchange law. In no part of the continent were stock and produce exchanges a series of private self-governing associations as in England. Either the French system of officially recognised brokers, or some more thorough system of state oversight, had always existed. In several of the leading continental trading cities, there was not a group of exchanges separately organised and housed; but a great exchange where business of many kinds was con-

---

[1] 1841, formation of the Cotton Brokers' Association; 1876, of the Cotton Clearing House.

ducted, with perhaps a few subsidiary institutions. This was, for example, the position in Hamburg. Even in Paris, transactions were considerably more concentrated than in London. Such concentration facilitated official supervision. But, until 1896, supervision had nowhere gone the length of proscribing certain classes of business.

This was what the German law did. It forbade the prevalent type of "future" dealings in grain, flour, and flour mill products, and in certain classes of securities. It attempted to limit, as was believed in the public interest, the establishment or maintenance of other such markets, and the admission to them of unqualified persons. No new "futures" market was to be officially sanctioned, until the relevant groups of traders and manufacturers had been fully consulted; and no one was to be admitted to such a market who had not established, by his position in the commercial world, his "fitness" for the business. Futures contracts in which both parties were not "fit to deal in futures" (*börsentermingeschäftsfähig*) were not to be legally binding.

The law killed, as it was intended to kill, the existing organisation of future dealings in grain at Berlin, Mannheim and other centres. Buying and selling for future delivery did not cease; but a heavy blow was struck at the Berlin grain trade. There was a struggle between the brokers and government over the general question of control; and in the long run not all the contemplated measures of control were applied. Apparently amateur speculation was checked; but whether this particular measure of protection for fools was worth the general interference with the self-determination of the commercial world has often been called in question. More than ten years later Germans were pointing, with generous appreciation, to the self-determining exchanges of England and their successful careers[1].

While in Germany control over exchanges was being tightened, in France the old law, as revised under the Empire, remained substantially unaltered; though there was a tendency to ease the sharp division between the *parquet* and the *coulisse* on the

---

[1] Ehrenberg in Conrad's *Handwörterbuch*, III, 196 (1909). See also Flux, *Economic Journal* (1900), p. 245. The law was modified in 1908, but still showed hostility to "futures." S. von Waltershausen, *op. cit.* p. 522.

stock exchanges. Produce exchanges, though requiring official sanction, were but little interfered with. An attempt made in the chamber of deputies, during 1898, to secure the adoption of an exchange law like that of Germany failed. No country had more organised futures markets than France. She went further than England, having, for example, a market for "tops" (combed wool) at Roubaix which had no equivalent in Bradford. Paris had a futures market for alcohol (commercial spirit), which also had no English equivalent. This, however, was because England was not an important producer. Alcohol producing and exporting countries regularly developed such markets, for alcohol is easily standardised. There was one at Hamburg and another at Buda-Pest.

Holland and Belgium also, where exchanges were free and no special exchange law existed, took advantage of their position as transit lands to provide facilities for specialised dealings in the maximum number of commodities passing into Europe by way of Amsterdam, Rotterdam and Antwerp. A specialised exchange did not necessarily carry with it a futures market in the technical sense, as the case of Roubaix and Bradford shows; but there was a universal tendency, in the late nineteenth century, for such markets to grow up wherever it was possible to hit on a standard average quality of the commodity dealt in. So it had been found in Holland nearly two centuries earlier. And as the whole tendency of production in the last age was towards uniformity and standardisation, both in materials and in manufactures, the field for the *marché à terme* was always growing. Its commercial, and still more its social, utility might be disputed. Its growth is referred to here because it was a representative development of that period of rapid transport and specialised trading; of delicately poised and ever shifting world prices; of massed demand and massed supply, in which the trader journeying with his goods to the fair was not easily found, even at Nijni Novgorod—for there, too, trading by sample was growing up—but had to be sought out in Kabul and Kashgar, where the railway had not yet arrived.

CHAPTER XIII

MONEY BANKING AND INVESTMENT,
1850–1914

§ 93. Three times over, in the half century from 1850 to
1900, the monetary balance of Europe quivered as the precious
metals were poured into it in unexpected quantity and un-
anticipated proportions. The same kind of thing had happened
before; but never so often or with so much violence in so short
a time. Before the Californian and Australian gold discoveries
of 1848–51, there had been no important event in gold or silver
production since the gold output of Brazil had reached its
maximum, between 1740 and 1760. In those twenty years Brazil
added some forty millions sterling to the world's stock of gold.
After that her output slackened. So did the silver output of
South America after 1810. In neither case was increase or
decline marked enough to upset the relative values of the two
metals or the level of prices measured in either of them. For
a century and a half before 1850 the ratio of silver to gold, in
the open markets of Europe, had never fallen so low as 14 oz.
of silver for 1 oz. of gold, and had only once or twice, in very
exceptional circumstances, risen so high as 16 : 1. It is not
surprising that something like 15 : 1 should have come to be
regarded as a natural and inevitable ratio.

The decline in American gold supplies was more than counter-
balanced, after 1830, by an increased output from alluvial deposits in the Urals and Siberia; but even so the world's output
for the six years 1841–7 was only £5–6,000,000 a year. Then
came Placerville and Bendigo, and an average annual world
output of some £28,000,000 during the fifties, excluding Chinese
and other supplies which had no effect in Europe. From this
high water mark there was a slow decline to just over £20,000,000
a year in 1881–5.

Silver production had been at its lowest, for the nineteenth
century, in the decade 1821–30. After that there was a slow

increase down to the sixties. In 1865–6 the available annual world output was just over 1,000,000 kilograms; say £8,000,000 measured in gold. Ten years later the output had been doubled; and it continued to grow, with few and occasional setbacks, until it was at its maximum, upwards of 7,000,000 kilograms, in 1911–13. Long before that the old price of approximately 5s. an ounce, corresponding to a ratio with gold of about 15 : 1, had collapsed. The silver of these forty years came from all over the world—Nevada, Mexico, South America, Broken Hill; above all, latterly, from Mexico. The huge increase in output was due as much to fresh metallurgical methods as to the discovery of new lodes.

Meanwhile the third great disturbance had occurred; the Witwatersrand had been opened up, and the methods of the Rand had been applied in Western Australia, the western states of America, and wherever else gold bearing reefs could be found. The company with a huge capital and plant had replaced the digger. For the first time in history gold mining had become an industry rather than an adventure. By an odd chance, the early years of the industrial age coincided with a short-lived adventure of the old sort; the rush of placer miners to the Klondyke in 1897. The new epoch may be roughly dated from 1890, when the annual output of the world (as already defined) stood at about £23,000,000. From that point it rose to over £63,000,000 in 1899, the year of the outbreak of the Boer War. It was back at this level, and beyond it, in 1903. By 1912 it had risen to over £90,000,000, of which nearly a half came from South Africa, nearly a quarter from the United States, and an eighth from Australia. South Africa alone was producing almost as much gold in a year as Brazil in her best days had produced in twenty.

The Californian and Australian discoveries had not sufficed to upset the market ratio between silver and gold. For several years before 1848 the ratio had been rather high, almost 16 : 1. The flood of gold drove up prices and drove down the ratio, in the next ten years, to nearly 15 : 1, but not lower. In a prospering Europe, more gold was absorbed in the arts, so soon as it became a little more plentiful. England was a steady buyer both for industrial and for currency purposes. In 1852–3 she minted over £20,000,000 of gold. The French monetary system, and its allied systems, absorbed gold readily (see *ante*, § 31). Napoleons replaced five franc pieces; the Bank of France improved its gold reserve; and the only inconvenience of the relative dearness of silver was that the government was sometimes criticised for not providing enough small silver change.

By 1867–70 the gold output had slackened; the silver output had increased; and the ratio was again rising. It passed 16 : 1 in 1874; and thereafter went on rising almost without interruption, barely affected by the gold flood of the later nineties, to a maximum of almost 40 : 1 in 1902. The revival of the Transvaal gold output in that year drove it down a little, but it was back at nearly 40 : 1 in 1909; though it went down to 30 : 1 in 1906 and to 34 : 1 in 1912. In terms of English money, the price of silver, which before the great disturbances had fluctuated gently about 5s. an ounce, fluctuated violently in the twentieth century between 2s. and 2s. 6d. These are yearly averages; the limits for day to day fluctuations were several pence wider.

This revolution in the relative values of the two metals was by no means all a matter of supply. Monetary policy, in Europe and out of it, was a decisive factor on the side of demand. Briefly put, every civilised country in the world except China had abandoned silver as standard money by 1905. Germany led the way. The fifties and sixties had seen no important changes in monetary policy; although an international monetary congress held at Paris in 1867 voted almost unanimously for the gold standard. Holland had gone over to the single silver standard in 1847 (see *ante*, § 31). In 1857 the leading German states had arranged with Austria-Hungary a mint convention which contemplated permanent silver standard currencies for all the signatories. The United States in the sixties was mostly using greenbacks; but the bimetallic theory of her currency (see *ante*, § 31) was unchanged, although gold had come into much more general use during the fifties. Then came the decision of the young German Empire to use her war indemnity to help the establishment of a gold currency. The coinage of silver ceased in 1872: the law which pointed to the final adoption of a gold standard was passed in 1873; and in 1874 the calling in of silver began—at a time of slackening gold output and increasing silver output in the world at large. The United States had just stopped coining silver dollars. Not only was an important currency demand for silver stopped, but already in 1873 silver from the German currencies was being sold on the London market.

Thereafter things moved rapidly. Holland, crushed in between a gold using England and a gold using Germany, could not maintain a silver standard, when silver prices were falling fast. She stopped the coinage of standard silver in 1874 and never resumed it. How she finally took up gold need not be explained here. More important was the action of the franc-using nations, the Latin Union as they had been called since France, Belgium, Switzerland and Italy had agreed, in Dec. 1865, to regulate their currencies jointly. By this agreement only the five franc piece was recognised as full standard silver money, in which debts to any amount might be paid. Alarmed by the situation of 1872–3, the signatory powers agreed in Jan. 1874 to limit their coinage of five franc pieces—thereby robbing silver of its standard character, since if a metal is to be really a currency standard it must be freely coined[1]. Four years later they stopped minting standard silver altogether; and from that time onwards France and her colleagues enjoyed the so-called "lame" standard, silver being nominally legal tender, kept in considerable quantities in the banks, but neither freely coined nor much used in ordinary transactions.

Western Europe's main currency demands for silver thus ceased during the seventies, when the ratio to gold was still under 19 : 1. The later currency history of the two metals is part of world history, its most important chapters being American, Indian and Japanese. After 1880 Western Europe made no important change.

But Europe talked a great deal about making changes, and incessantly criticised the gold standard to which she was turning. This was because her turning to gold coincided with a world-wide fall in prices measured in gold. From 1873 to 1896 the general trend of international prices was steadily down. In

---

[1] Or at least freely bought by the government.

England, a good test case because of her gold standard her world-wide trade and her open market, commodity prices had fallen by 1896 between 36 and 40 per cent. below the average level of the decade 1867–77; and considerably more than that below the maximum reached in 1873. This great price fall was a most complex phenomenon. There would have been a fall from the post-war boom prices of 1873, even if conditions of production and transport had remained uniform and no change had been made in currencies. For many, if not for most, commodities the time and labour saving revolutions in production, and still more in transport, which occurred between 1873 and 1890, would have reduced prices on the European markets, had there been no post war boom and no currency changes. The currency changes cannot be measured only in terms of the precious metals. While the world was turning to gold it was also turning more and more to credit documents based on gold—notes, bills, cheques. But, however these various forces might act, intensifying or neutralising one another, the argument which said—had Europe taken as its standard money some commodity or commodities less rare than gold, then the price fall might not have occurred or might have been less; this argument, so far as it went, was sound. It generally took the form of an argument in favour of the retention, in France, or the introduction, into England, of bimetallism. Make both metals standard, by international agreement, it was said, and you will at once check the disastrous fall in silver and the continuous melancholy sagging of general prices measured in standard money.

There were many aspects of the bimetallic movement. The difficulty of maintaining satisfactory exchange relations between Europe and the silver-using East, during the period of the great depreciation of silver, was a matter of great concern to England. But as the argument from the eastern trade usually ran that India was undercutting Europe, because her labour was paid in the now depreciated silver, and so was driving world prices down, it is fair to say that the European price fall was the mother of the argument. If the Witwatersrand and the cyanide process of recovering gold from the crushings had been known a dozen years earlier, much subtle economic thinking on currency matters, many public discussions, and several government inquiries might never have occurred.

For no sooner did prices trend upwards again, as they did after 1896, than bimetallic propaganda and discussion abruptly stopped all the world over. And the price rise, which continued down to 1914, was certainly connected with the unprecedented gold output of those years. There were complicating causes, just as there had been in the great fall. Some of the new lands were filling up. The prairies of the American middle west were beginning to need either manure or a rotation rest from wheat crops—hence dearer wheat. Waste of accessible forests and neglect of replanting in some countries were driving up timber prices. The world was showing a marked inability to keep its cotton growing area up to its requirements, or to increase its head of sheep as fast as its demand for clothes; and so on. The extension of banking facilities and the decline in hoarding—among the French peasants for instance—were supplying additional purchasing power, independently of any increase in the world's stock of coined gold. But it is again impossible to believe that the very large addition to that stock, which took place after 1896, was not the main factor in the rise which seemed so great a matter to the world of 1910-14. It was during this last period of rising prices that Russia, Japan and some other countries finally adopted the gold standard, and that India linked her silver currency to gold. But these additional demands for gold were insufficient even to check the price rise, so prolific was the Rand, and so steady the growth in the ratio of credit documents to cash in the world's trade.

If the English price level of 1871 be called 100, the changes just referred to would be represented numerically as follows[1]:

1873	111	1896	61
1883	82	1903	69
1893	68	1913	85

§ 94. It is said that the precious metals cannot of themselves produce prosperity. But they certainly promote activity. They fire the imagination; and even economic progress needs the

---

[1] This is Sauerbeck's Index Number. His base line (100) was the average of prices for 1867–77, with which the price level in 1871 happens to coincide.

fired imagination, not merely the grasping hand and the patient bowed back. Man labours and contrives and invents to get gold. When he has got it, the price rise which normally follows stimulates all kinds of enterprise. There is usually plenty of waste in the getting. There may be more waste in the resultant enterprise. An age of rising prices is not necessarily an age of prosperity. But it is at least possible that the stimulus which gold getting administers, though admittedly irrational, involves a real, and not merely an apparent, addition to the world's wealth. There might have been fewer useful activities and fewer useful things without it.

Perhaps—to fit all this to history—the inventions and the railways of the twenties, thirties and forties, and the free commercial laws which followed the Revolution of 1848, would have produced the great industrial and commercial activity of the Second Empire in France and of the age of Bismarck's rise in Germany, had there been no flow of gold into Europe, accompanied by rising prices, in the early fifties. Or again, perhaps the still more marked activity of the years after 1895–6 throughout Europe may have been all due to electrical invention, chemical progress, better nourished peoples, more rational social laws, and the like. The Witwatersrand may have had no real part in it. But it is not unlikely that the opening up of California, Australia and South Africa, to get at the gold, stimulated economic energies which might otherwise have lain dormant, or might not have been employed to equal advantage; and that the resulting price rise did the same.

The immediate stimulus of the new gold in the fifties was obvious, especially in the fields of banking and finance. England was the country primarily affected. There was an enormous demand for exports and a great increase in the gold reserve of the Bank of England. But France, and Europe generally, were in a similar if less advantageous position. French exports were in great demand, not only at the diggings, where they drank champagne in buckets, but in England where profits and wages were high. For six or seven years France had a "favourable" trade balance, a surplus of ordinary commodity exports over ordinary commodity imports. She took the difference in gold.

Gold arrivals coincided with the restoration of confidence in the business world, after the troubles of 1848. The commercial mechanism of the continent had been so shaken that some sound investments had fallen 50 per cent. in value. People had hidden away their cash or invested it in England or America. The luxury shops of Paris had emptied. With the establishment of Louis Napoleon as president, and then as emperor, confidence revived. The new government was eager to pose as a dispenser of prosperity, a careful guardian of the French inheritance; and it had every opportunity to do so. The Bank of France, which had come through the Revolution with added prestige (see *ante*, § 32), had large, and now growing, gold reserves. Everyone was willing to lend. The Bank was discounting at 3 per cent.; and promoters saw their opportunity to float new schemes.

Government also seized the occasion to reduce the rate of interest on the 5 per cent. Rentes to $4\frac{1}{2}$ per cent. and to press forward the railway programme which had been held up for years (see *ante*, § 38). It began rebuilding Paris. And it sanctioned two great financial enterprises of European importance, the *Crédit foncier* and the *Crédit mobilier*. The former was, in effect, a national mortgage bank to make advances on the security of land to peasants and townsmen. It was planned by the economist Wolowski, who had studied Prussian agrarian mortgage institutions (*Landschaften*), which went back to Frederick the Great. The latter was partly modelled on the Belgian *Société Générale* (see *ante*, § 32). Its aims were wide and ambitious, but it is best described as a national company to promote and control industrial joint stock enterprises: it was planned and directed by the Jewish *haute finance*, Isaac Pereire and his brother, Eichthal, Salvador, Oppenheim. Its history was short and not entirely creditable. It helped to float or finance French and Spanish railways, to build the Rue de Rivoli, to extend the harbours and make the gas company at Marseilles, and to create the Transatlantic Shipping Company (see *ante*, § 87). Finally, having got into difficulties, it collapsed, after the Bank of France had refused to come to its assistance unless its leading men, the brothers Pereire, resigned. But, although it failed, it was

a forerunner of all later "industrial banking," and in particular
of the close associations with industry of the great banks of
imperial Germany (see *post*, § 96)[1].

The *Crédit foncier*, on the other hand, remains an important
part of French financial organisation. It was meant to help the
conservative landowning classes, great and small, upon whose
industry and support the Second Empire relied. It was also
empowered to make loans to communes for public purposes.
To start operations it was given a subsidy of 10,000,000 francs;
so that its first loans might be made at reasonable rates. It was
allowed to receive a certain amount of money on deposit; and
these deposits it might invest in treasury bills or in discounted
commercial bills. But it was hardly a bank in the English sense.
For years it had a monopoly of mortgage operations, except in
so far as these were carried on not by companies but by individuals. Under the Third Republic it lost its legal monopoly;
but as no other large company ever specialised in mortgage
operations, it retained, in the words of its secretary, "very
nearly...a practical monopoly" in 1908, when its aggregate
business was about 4,000,000,000 francs[2]. No assistance had
been received from the state since the initial subsidy of 1852.
Its useful, if somewhat limited, operations had not given all the
credit which the French cultivator could employ with advantage;
so that there was room enough for the cooperative credit movement of the late nineteenth century, and for the official *Crédit
agricole*, initiated in 1900, through which money provided gratis
by the Bank of France at the time of a renewal of its charter in
1897 (see *ante*, § 48) was to be lent for agricultural development
by regional banks (*caisses régionales*) in the departments.

The two French *Crédits* are merely conspicuous samples from
a long list of credit institutions set up between 1850 and 1857,
while the gold fever was working. Germany perhaps went
further and faster than France, because she had less experience.

---

[1] It was reorganised in 1871 and existed obscurely till 1902. It "must not
be confused with an existing bank of similar name and excellent reputation."
Fisk, *French Public Finance* (1922), p. 286.

[2] This statement, and other bankers' statements quoted below, come from
the volume of *Interviews on...Banking and Currency*, issued by the American
National Monetary Commission in 1910.

Her laws were only now in course of adjustment, so as to admit the easy creation of companies and the free use of credit instruments. She was not distracted during those years, nor were her savings diverted into non-industrial channels, by war. France was. So Germany could plunge into speculation with ignorance and a single mind. The absence of uniform law, and the relaxation of official control outside Prussia, made it easy to find domiciles even for very speculative undertakings. Joint stock, note-issuing, and "business," *i.e.* company promoting, banks were started freely, especially in the smaller states— Darmstadt, Weimar, Brunswick, Gotha, Gera. Even Prussia, whose national bank had been founded to keep note-issue under official control (see *ante*, § 32), was drawn into the stream and sanctioned large joint stock banks of issue in Cologne, Magdeburg, Danzig, Königsberg and Posen. They were, however, well regulated, which some of the others were not, the Darmstadt Bank in particular having a very wild career. In 1856 came the Vienna *Kreditanstalt*, another omnibus development company, like the *Crédit mobilier* but built on sounder lines. Everywhere the new credit institutions gave generous help to industry. Germany's true industrial revolution was just beginning. In Saxony, Westphalia and the Rhineland, said a contemporary, "tall chimneys grew like mushrooms[1]."

In Belgium and Holland joint stock banking was well developed before 1848. No new principles were required. The Dutch Bank retained its monopoly of note-issue, and the quarrels of the *Société Générale* and the *Banque de Belgique* (see *ante*, § 32) were closed by the creation, in 1850, of a new central institution, the *Banque Nationale*, to which were transferred the note-issuing powers of the other two. The *Banque Nationale* was no omnibus institution, but a well regulated central bank, with limited functions, to which the government entrusted its funds.

§ 95. The world-wide commercial crisis of 1857, in which the first age of gold fever ended, swept away many of its financial and industrial creations; but most of the greater banks and all the national banks stood firm. Holland and Belgium, the most experienced countries, probably suffered least. The Bank of

[1] M. Wirth, *Geschichte der Handelskrisen*, p. 309.

France fulfilled its task as the flywheel of the financial machine. It continued to discount—at a price—when confidence was badly shaken; and it helped to clear off the financial wreckage. This same year its charter was renewed for another thirty years. It was allowed to issue notes of 50 francs to meet the needs of trade—hitherto 200 franc notes had been the lowest allowed— and its capital was doubled. In return, government took a loan on easy terms and arranged that, as from 1867, it could order the opening of new branches of the Bank where required. Under this clause twenty-five additional branches were opened between 1873 and 1877.

The Bank was thus made more really national than ever before. As France had not developed, and never did develop, the cheque system on English lines, its position as the sole issuer of paper money added both to its prestige and to its real strength. In the sixties, it had a short struggle with the Bank of Savoy, which enjoyed note-issuing rights when Savoy was ceded to France and wished to extend the use of its notes into old France; but agreement was reached in 1864, the Bank of Savoy selling its rights of issue.

A year earlier there had been opened at Lyons a joint stock bank without note-issuing rights, which took the name of the *Crédit Lyonnais*. Its founder, M. Henri Germain, presided over the Board of Directors until his death in 1905. For a year or two it did business only in the south-eastern departments; but in 1865 it started an office in Paris, which became its head office under the Third Republic. Not often in French history, economic or general, has a provincial institution invaded the capital in this way and then grown, as the *Crédit Lyonnais* ultimately grew, into an institution of national importance. This it did by an early and extensive development of branch banking. Branches were opened, during the last quarter of the century, in every considerable industrial centre. There were 214 in 1898 and 266 in 1908. Of the 266 no less than 54 were in Paris, so completely had the Lyons concern become metropolitan. It still held its general meetings at Lyons, even though M. Germain was dead. Throughout, its business had been banking proper, though not quite of the English sort. Deposit and discount were its main functions; it also made loans against securities and short loans on the Stock Exchange. Like most French banks, it sold new industrial and commercial bonds (debentures) on commission to the investing public. As a rule it did not touch the riskier business of ordinary shares.

While the *Lyonnais* and a few institutions of the same type, such as the *Crédit Industriel* and the *Société Générale*, were providing banking facilities throughout France, the position of the Bank of France was in no way impaired. Its most severe trial came in 1870-1. A moratorium for bills of exchange was declared; cash payments were suspended; Bank notes were made legal tender, and 20 franc notes authorised. In the difficult years of indemnity payment, 10 and even 5 franc notes were authorised and the legal maximum note-issue was repeatedly increased. But no sooner was the indemnity paid (1873) than the Bank's gold reserve grew quickly. Cash payment was fully restored on January 1, 1878, the smaller notes having been redeemed before that date. With expanding trade however, the note circulation was as large in 1883 as it had been in 1873; but the cash reserve had more than doubled. During the relative gold shortage of the eighties an increase of the gold reserve was difficult, and as silver was still legal tender the silver reserves often exceeded the reserves of gold. But after 1890 advantage was taken of the new flood of gold to build up an immense reserve and cut down the useless accumulation of silver. In 1890 there was almost exactly £50,000,000 of gold and £50,000,000 of silver, taking the silver at its nominal value. By 1913 the gold stood at £134,000,000 and the silver at a nominal £25,000,000. Against this was a note circulation of £32,000,000 in 1890 and £227,000,000 in 1913. The proportion of cash to notes at both dates was notable.

It was desirable for cash reserves to be strong and note circulation large, *firstly* because the French, not having the cheque habit, were great users of notes and coin, and *secondly* because the French commercial and banking system was to an unusual degree dependent on the central institution. Bill discounting always played the leading part in banking properly so-called. The Bank of France had a special obligation laid upon it from the start (see *ante*, § 32) to help traders by discounting small bills. This obligation was retained and extended. In 1895, with a view to democratising credit, the Bank was obliged to handle bills of 5 francs; and from that time forward the small bill business grew continuously. It is only necessary to picture an attempt to discount a 4s. bill at the Bank of England, or at any other English bank, to realise the gap in banking practice between the two nations. Even in 1906–7 the average bill discounted by the Bank of France was under £30. At the same date one other large bank had an average of £24, a second an average of £20. They worked an even smaller public than the Bank of France, though they only took bills of the 4s. class for collection, not for discount. They got in the money for their clients.

The predominance of discount business was illustrated by the activities of France's oldest credit institution, the *Comptoir d'Escompte*, which specialised in this line. Down to about 1887–90, when it went through a crisis and had to suspend payments (1889), it had worked with only two or three branches; but from that date it adopted the branch system, pushing out and discounting bills from little provincial places which the Bank of France would not or could not handle.

For the Bank of France was not entirely master of its own development. Continuing the policy of 1857, the government had obliged it to open in every departmental town. Not all of these were good commercial centres. It was not indeed limited to these centres, but they formed a large part of its 120–130 regular branches (*succursales*) in the twentieth century. After 1898 it was pursuing a vigorous popular policy, extending its branches, opening deposit accounts for all comers and simplifying its formalities. Thus it was increasing its direct dealings with the commercial world, but it had not covered all the ground. Hitherto those dealings had been largely indirect. Nothing illustrates better the dependence of all other banking institutions on the Bank of France and the great part played by discount in French banking than the huge business of rediscounting with the Bank of France which the other banks had always carried on. Instead of holding much cash or keeping a full account at the Bank, ordinary banks relied on rediscount to bring them as much cash as they wanted at any desired moment; for, to quote a modern French banker, "no one ever complained that the Bank of France would not discount a normal bill presented by a proper person." It was this liability to be called upon to rediscount practically for all France which made the Bank tenacious, as some thought unduly tenacious, of its reserves in notes and gold.

Besides the Bank, the great joint stock banks, and the other credit establishments referred to, France, under the Third Republic, contained a number of local private banks which however were of little importance after 1890, a few local joint stock banks without branches and a few larger concerns with branches, such as the *Crédit du Nord*. There was also a group of so-called business banks, which did not try to attract deposits from the public, although they received money on deposit from the companies whose flotation was their main concern. They were in the direct line of descent from the *Crédit mobilier*. The oldest, the *Banque de Paris et des Pays Bas*, was a fusion carried through in 1872 of a Paris bank founded under the Empire and an Amsterdam bank. Its only other branches were in Brussels and Geneva, as its work was confined to great centres. Like every French bank it did some discounting, but this was a subsidiary business. Two other central banks of the same class, the *Union Parisienne* and the *Banque Française*, were established after 1895 during the period of industrial expansion and company promotion which coincided with the price rise that followed the inflow of the South African gold.

§ 96. During the years 1866–72, when the German Empire was in the making, the young German banking system was loose-jointed and sprawling. In the first place there were thirty-three banks with the right of note-issue. Twenty-five of these had come into existence between 1850 and 1871; four, including the Prussian Bank (see *ante*, § 32), between 1846 and 1850; four only, and they unimportant, before 1846. There were a number of mortgage-banks and other institutions for giving credit on the security of land, one or two being of considerable antiquity, like the "Knightly" Credit Institute of Brandenburg, which

Frederick had set up to finance his Junkers in 1777. From the same decade (1772) dated that curious organisation the Prussian *Seehandlung*, started to promote industry and foreign trade and provided with funds by the king, but become in course of time an institution whose main business was to finance Prussian loans, though it still actually owned a few industrial concerns. There was one fairly old established business bank without rights of note-issue, the *Schaafhausenscher Bankverein* of 1848. There was another group of about six business banks of various types dating from the age of company promotion in the early fifties, of which the notorious Darmstadt Bank of 1853 and the Discount Bank (*Diskontogesellschaft*) of 1856 were the most important. To these were added in the days of the war and the indemnity the *Deutsche Bank* of 1870, the *Dresdener Bank* of 1872 and many others, some whose lives were to be short, some who played an important part throughout the imperial age. Lastly there were many groups of private bankers, mainly Jewish, strongest in the free cities and in Berlin.

From this raw and variegated banking system there grew in the next generation a system which, although it never became absolutely simple and uniform, was dominated by one great central bank of issue, the *Reichsbank*, and by a group of powerful business banks, of which the *Deutsche*, the *Dresdener*, the *Diskontogesellschaft* and the *Darmstädter* were the most powerful; though by 1906 more than twenty others had capitals of £1,000,000 and upwards. In no country had the alliance of banking and industry been closer. "In Germany," said Herr Schuster of the *Dresdener Bank* in 1908, "our banks are largely responsible for the development of the Empire, having fostered and built up its industries. It is from 1871 that our real development dates, and it is since that year our great banks have been organised." "To them, more than to any other agency," he added with pardonable complacency, "may be credited the splendid results thus far realised." If his historical summary was not literally accurate, it was accurate in substance. The greatest banks were creations of the imperial age, and the pre-imperial foundations had attained greatness under the Empire.

German bankers in 1908 were not less well satisfied with the

Reichsbank than they were with their own institutions. They leant on it and trusted it absolutely. The director of a great private house (Bleichröder's) expressed his absolute confidence in it, adding "that in his judgment the organisation...could not be materially improved." A director of the *Deutsche Bank* said it was "their strength, the great strength of their financial system." He added, much as a French banker might have done in speaking of the Bank of France, that under this system "the question of their own cash reserve was of secondary importance, as they could at all times convert their holdings of commercial paper into cash at the *Reichsbank*."

The *Reichsbank* was built upon the Prussian Bank of 1847 and its charter was a law of March 1875. Government's first care in organising it was the control of the note-issue throughout the country. Of the thirty-three banks with rights of issue existing at that time, ten enjoyed the right only from year to year. The ten were all Prussian; for Prussia had never whole heartedly abandoned the idea of centralised issue on which the Prussian Bank had been founded. Ten others had charters timed to expire before 1900. In a few cases the charters ran to 1952, 1953 or 1956, and two or three were unlimited. There could therefore hardly be a question of summary centralisation of issue for all Germany. But conditions of issue were made onerous, so that the right ceased to be very attractive. No issuing bank might accept bills of exchange, or buy or sell goods or securities ahead for itself or for a customer: it could not issue notes below 100 marks ($£5$): and all its transactions had to be given the greatest publicity. No new bank of issue could be created save by imperial law. Every bank, including the *Reichsbank*, was given a maximum figure for its uncovered note-issue, *i.e.* the issue against which cash need not be held. If it exceeded this maximum it paid a 5 per cent. tax on the excess. The uncovered maximum for all banks together was £19,000,000, of which no less than £12,500,000 went to the *Reichsbank*. Another £2,000,000 went to Bavarian and Saxon banks which had to be handled gently for political reasons.

This was the starting point. Provision was made, as in Peel's English Bank Act, for transfer of issuing rights to the central

institution. At once the other banks of issue began to take
advantage of this provision. Issue regulated as theirs was had
no great chance of profit and they were excluded from certain
very lucrative lines of trade. The buying and selling of securities
through banks was already common: eventually it became the
regular practice in Germany. By 1908 the *Deutsche Bank* alone
required fifty members of the stock exchange to do this business
for it. The limitation on acceptance was almost equally troublesome. So no less than fourteen of the thirty-three surrendered
their right of issue in 1876; another followed next year. By
1897 only seven retained it. Ten years later only four remained,
all semi-national—one each for Bavaria, Wurtemberg, Baden
and Saxony. They were little heard of outside Germany and
their aggregate note circulation was £7,000,000. At that time
the *Reichsbank* note circulation, covered and uncovered, was
about £100,000,000. In 1912 out of a total circulation of nearly
£134,000,000, nearly £126,000,000 were *Reichsbank* notes. For
practical purposes centralised issue had been secured.

The second function of the *Reichsbank* as originally conceived
was to carry the main cash reserve for the Empire. In the late
seventies that reserve stood at £25–30,000,000; in the late
eighties at £40–45,000,000. Thereafter it grew slowly until
1902; then more rapidly, gold being more plentiful. In 1910–13
it averaged about £60,000,000. Originally a large part of this
cash reserve had been silver. The proportion of gold steadily
increased, just as in France, although for a series of years it
never got beyond an average of about 75 per cent.; but whereas
in the early years much the greater part of the silver consisted
of the old standard thalers, which had been passing out of
circulation since the adoption of the gold standard, in the
twentieth century it was predominantly marks and other small
change. The gold standard was in full working order thanks to
the Transvaal supplies.

Thirdly, the *Reichsbank* was to provide banking facilities
for the whole Empire, making no distinction of persons or of
places. The government took powers to order the setting up of
additional branches where needed. But the bank did not require
pressure. In thirty years it had opened nearly 100 head branches

and about 4000 sub-branches reporting to their respective head branches; so that every place of any importance had its branch. This was most necessary, for one of the bank's chief activities was the transfer of cash from place to place for all who asked, not merely for its own customers, at very cheap rates. The system prevented the growth of the cheque habit and was considered in Germany superior to transfer by cheque.

As part of its duty to the public the bank was prepared to discount bills as low as 10 marks; but more than half its discounting latterly was for bankers not for traders. Further, with a view to formal equality among its clients, it decided in 1896 to abandon the practice followed hitherto, in imitation of the Bank of England, of discounting "prime" bills at specially favourable rates. There was to be one rate for all, small and great. On the same principle it was prepared to consider applications for loans or discounts from anyone, whether he kept an account with it or not. But in view of these various obligations its lowest rates were normally higher than those of other banks.

Meanwhile the non-issuing banks had developed in the closest association with the industrial development of the imperial age. Owing to Germany's backward financial organisation during the third quarter of the nineteenth century, they had from the start done a far more miscellaneous business than that of the typical contemporary bank in England. The avowed object of the *Deutsche Bank*, on its foundation in 1870, was "to foster...commercial relations between Germany and other countries." The banks undertook every kind of credit operation —advances on personal security, advances against goods, discount, assistance in company flotation. Credits to industrial concerns, at first short, became longer and longer until they amounted almost to partnerships. Industrialists sat on the directorates of banks and—much more important—bankers tended to control the policy of industry. All these developments were most conspicuous in the great outburst of industrial activity during the twenty years that ended with 1914; but they were the natural outcome of forces at work since the age of bank and company promotion of the early fifties[1].

[1] For German banks see Marshall, *Industry and Trade*, pp. 341, 566, etc.

In the twentieth century the greater banks had their recognised industrial areas, so to speak. The *Dresdener Bank*, for instance, was "recognised as representing the Krupp interest" and was sure to be engaged financially in any Krupp project. The *Deutsche* had special interests, among other places, in Turkey, so "business emanating from that source was expected to and naturally did go to the *Deutsche Bank.*" Banks had the widest discretion as to their investment. They could finance industrial schemes singly; but more often, in the later years, they did so by syndicates of banks. An illustration will best explain the process. "A company has been formed," said Herr Schuster of the *Dresdener* in 1908, "to build a cable line from German West Africa to Brazil....They have come to us and asked us to finance the proposition. We...are forming a syndicate consisting of nine or ten other banks and bankers, each participant having an equal interest." So the risks were spread.

It need hardly be noted, in view of this close association between the banks and industry, that the Kartell movement was to a great extent the work of the banks. Their instinct was to shield from competition industrial concerns with whose interests theirs was involved; hence their activity as "dykebuilders" in the Kartell age. On the other hand, some of the giant businesses which were tending latterly to break down the Kartell dykes (see *ante*, § 77) might themselves be strong enough to dispense with bank aid and defy bank policy. Whatever may have been their position in the years 1850–75, they were quite capable of standing alone in 1900–14.

An interesting feature of the great business banks in this later period was the comparatively small number of their branches. Unlike the English joint stock banks, neither the *Deutsche* nor the *Dresdener*, for example, made any effort to reach the small country towns, though of course they had branches in the great trading centres. To some extent they reached smaller places by controlling the stock of local banks, just as they controlled industrial enterprises, but this development was relatively insignificant from the ordinary banking point of view, though the controlled banks "undertook nothing of importance" without the controller's approval. The big concerns were not interested in local deposit banking. They "did not care for that class of business" they said.

Control and absorption were proceeding fast after 1900; but still a great part of the smaller local business was done by local banks, with the assistance of the very numerous branches of the *Reichsbank*. Indeed down to 1907 the number of banks at least nominally independent was still growing, new foundations keeping pace with absorptions. There had been 71 banks in in 1883; 94 in 1895; 143 in 1906. In 1907 there were 144. These are the so-called "credit" banks, *i.e.* the ordinary joint stock commercial deposit banks, excluding land banks and note-issuing banks on the one hand and the various cooperative organisations on the other. The tendency was rather for the great banks to absorb or control other great banks, and so extend their power in the chief commercial and industrial centres, than for all the minor local institutions to lose their individuality as in England. To these surviving local banks must be added the private banks of which no statistics are available. But such facts do not appreciably modify the statement already made—that the *Reichsbank* and the small group of powerful business banks dominated the German banking world.

§ 97. Much has been said of the company-promoting activities of the modern West European bank. It remains to trace the evolution of the various types of company pro-moted, and their application to different classes of commer-cial and industrial enterprise, since the railway age and the political upheavals of 1848. First used for foreign trade, next for banks, waterworks, canals, railways and other public utility companies, the true joint stock company (*société anonyme*) had been used but little for industrial enterprises before 1848, except in Belgium. In France official formalities and delays made its use difficult. The very absence of this official supervision had commended the sleeping partnership with share capital (*société en commandite sur actions*) to the more speculative class of business *entrepreneur*; while the cautious French investor, in spite of hard experience in the thirties and forties, seems long to have believed that the unlimited personal liability of the *gérants* in a *société en commandite* (see *ante*, § 33) gave him a measure of security against wild trading which the more impersonal type of company would not provide.

Belgium was again the first country to make extensive use of the *société anonyme* in the golden years after 1850. In 1850 she had about 120 such companies. When the crisis of 1857 broke out there were 200. So successfully was the crisis handled that not many *sociétés anonymes* failed: by the end of 1860 their number had risen to 263.

All this time, and indeed right down to 1865, the *société anonyme* remained rare in France. It was still confined to railways and large public utility companies. A year in which more than twenty such companies were started was exceptional. However an important step was taken in 1857, when Belgian limited companies were given free access to France for all purposes of business, and another in 1862 when the same concession was made to English companies. Meanwhile (in 1856) the *société en commandite sur actions*, the typical speculative instrument of the forties and of what may be called the *Crédit mobilier* age in the fifties, had been put under stricter control. The result was a handicap to French enterprise, which had not a free hand either with the older or the newer type of company; for every *société anonyme* still required individual official authorisation. Noting the experience of Belgium and England, the French investing public was becoming less shy of the principle of limited liability and less tolerant of handicaps on profit making. The government of Napoleon III therefore, after experiments with a hybrid type of company in 1863, decided in 1867-8 to do away with the individual authorisation for the *société anonyme*, except for life insurance companies and a few other selected classes, while introducing into the law some safeguards against abuse of the principle of limited liability which it was free for any *société anonyme* to adopt. The response was immediate. In 1867 nine "authorised" *sociétés anonymes* and from 70 to 80 of the hybrid type had been founded. Next year the newly founded *sociétés anonymes* numbered 191, in 1869, 200, and in 1870, 223.

The *société en commandite sur actions* remained however a recognised form of French business organisation. Further, the law of 1868 had made provision for so-called "cooperative" companies. These were small concerns in which the total amount of capital was variable, not fixed from time to time as in an ordinary joint stock company. But by 1877–8 the annual output of *sociétés anonymes* greatly exceeded that of the other two types of share issuing companies combined, while the capital invested per company was enormously greater for the *société anonyme*. It had become the representative type of organisation for all large commercial and industrial operations. From that time forward the annual creations of *sociétés anonymes* became an ordinary test of business activity or depression. There was, for example, a low output of companies during the difficult years of falling prices and growing international competition from 1883 to 1890. The average was not much over 300 a year. After 1891, and still more after 1895—in the period of what was called in an earlier chapter the real French industrial revolution (see *ante*, § 61)—the annual figure rose fast, to over 500 in 1896 and to over 1000 in 1899. Then came a few years of relative stagnation, with an annual output of 600–700 companies; followed, from 1906, by a final outburst of activity in company promotion, which drove the figure again above 1000 in 1907 and to an average of about 1500 in 1910–12. Contrast this with the 25 *sociétés anonymes* per annum of 1840–65, or with what seemed the remarkable figure of 200 in 1869.

The contrasts in Germany were, as might be expected, much more marked; but they cannot be so clearly traced for lack of an equally long and accurate series of statistics. Before 1850 no German state except the Hanse towns, which had adopted and eased the French Commercial Code, and Prussia had made any general legal provision for the establishment of joint stock companies. Prussia's action had only been taken recently, by a law of 1843 based on the French Code. This implied "authorisation" for each company; though the conditions on which authorisation might be procured were standardised. Elsewhere in Germany every company was a distinct and separate creation with a law of its own. Companies were therefore few. Down to the sixties, only in Hamburg and Bremen could a company come into existence by merely complying with the law without also securing individual authorisation from government; though most states had passed company laws in the fifties. Not until 1870-2 was a series of laws passed which freed companies from the necessity for "authorisation" throughout Germany and laid down general rules for their establishment and conduct. The limited liability of the shareholder was an essential part of the original German law; in other countries, though the limited liability type of company eventually prevailed, the company laws had made provision for other types. A series of German imperial laws, of which the most important were those of 1884 and 1897, attacked the abuses of flotation and management to which the ordinary limited company is liable. In the end Germany had a stricter, and from some points of view a better, joint stock company law than any other great country. But it was so elaborate and the procedure of promotion was so open that this form of organisation was not well suited to small or confidential enterprises. Moreover there was a strong objection to the rapid growth of speculation in industrial and commercial securities, during the eighties and nineties, an objection which finally produced the German Exchange Law of 1896 (see ante, § 92). It was therefore decided, in 1892, to create a new type of company which should embody the principle of limited liability and yet not provide masses of marketable shares. The new type was intended to meet those needs of comparatively small businesses which were met, somewhat awkwardly, in England by the private joint stock limited company, whose shares never came on the market. A strong argument in favour of the new type was that the existing law, with its insistence on publicity, gave foreign competitors too "free an insight into the foundation and management of the concern," as a German economist put it[1]. Simpler forms, greater privacy, far fewer shareholders, together with the absence of a mass of shares marketable among the general public, differentiated the new "company with limited liability" (*Gesellschaft mit beschränkter Haftung*) from the older "joint stock company" (*Aktiengesellschaft*), which also had limited liability.

No uniform German figures either of the annual creations

---

[1] E. Rosenthal in Conrad's *Handwörterbuch*, IV, 707.

of companies or of the numbers existing at any one time are available for the sixties and seventies. The total number of joint stock companies (*Aktiengesellschaften*) existing in 1886–7 is put at 2100, or not 50 per cent. more than the annual creations in France twenty-five years later. In 1896 the figure was 3700; in 1906, 5100; in 1912, 5400. But, whereas the paid-up capital of the 2100 companies of 1886–7 was £244,000,000, that of the 5400 companies of 1912 was £857,000,000. These figures, it should be noted, contain a small number of companies of the *société en commandite sur actions* type; but in 1906 this type was only 2 per cent. of the whole. As the average capitalisation (over £100,000 in 1886–7 and nearly £160,000 in 1912) suggests, we have here the great businesses of Germany only. Of the 5100 companies existing in 1906, nearly 500 were banks and other credit institutions; over 500 were engineering concerns; nearly 500 again were shipping, railway, tramway and other transport companies; nearly 300 were coal and iron businesses; over 900 were in the food and drink trades—mainly breweries.

Meanwhile the lesser businesses had rapidly adopted the new legal form of the "company with limited liability." But for this, the size of the average joint stock company might very well have declined, as the need for some kind of joint stock enterprise touched wider circles of trade. During the first year after the passing of the law (*i.e.* in 1893) nearly 200 of the new companies were created. By 1907 there were over 9000, and in 1909, 16,500. They were being created by thousands every year. Their average capitalisation was just over £11,000, a sufficient indication of the class of business which made use of them. They were much used in commerce, wholesale and retail, and in every branch of industry. Nearly a third were, in the widest sense, commercial. A ninth were connected with engineering and instrument making; a tenth with quarrying, brickmaking, and cement; an eleventh with the food and drink industries; the remainder with other industrial groups.

It is worth noting that, to the end of the period, joint stock organisation in any of its forms was far less common either in Germany or in France than in the United Kingdom. If to the German "companies with limited liability" are added the true joint stock companies and the few companies of the *société en commandite sur actions* type, the total for the year 1909 is, in round figures, 22,000. For France figures are not available for any year after 1898. At that time there were 6300 companies of all sorts including the railway companies. Owing to the active company promotion of the early twentieth century, it is possible that this number had doubled by 1909. The United Kingdom in 1909 contained 46,000 limited companies under the companies acts, exclusive of the railway companies, of statutory companies other than railways and of the chartered companies for imperial development.

Comparisons of the amounts of capital invested in the three countries are difficult and unsatisfactory, as the returns are not compiled on the same basis and Germany had no large privately owned railways. But, excluding railways, the amount was un-doubtedly very much greater in the United Kingdom than in either Germany or France.

Such rough figures must not be pressed; but they help to suggest the extent to which the three leading nations of Europe had come to rely on associated and, to a great extent, anonymous capital in the conduct of their industry and commerce. In each case the mass of this capital existed as transferable and freely marketable shares, the sign and symbol of the age in which ultimate legal ownership of mine or factory, warehouse or steam-ship line, might be spread in minute fragments over a country, or even over the commercial world, divorced from the manage-ment and the labour which earned for it its yearly increments of wealth. This dispersion of ownership and this divorce had gone furthest in the United Kingdom. But Germany was hastening after her; for in the decade before 1914 the capital invested in German companies was increasing absolutely as fast and rela-tively much faster than that invested in the companies of the United Kingdom.

§ 98. The latest company age completed that economic inter-locking of the nations the beginnings of which were pointed out in a previous chapter (see *ante*, § 35). Not merely were the nations buying from and selling to one another on a scale alto-gether unprecedented; not only was it possible for the United

Kingdom to import four-fifths of her wheat, France a third of her coal, and Germany nearly all of her wool; but, owing to the easy transfer and movement of the joint stock share, the various nations had become part owners of one another's resources to an extraordinary degree. Companies with their main domicile in one country had manufacturing establishments, affiliated companies, "interests" of one kind or another, in a neighbouring country; or it might be in nearly all neighbouring and in many remote countries. There had grown up too, chiefly since the industrial and commercial revival of the nineties, a variety of international agreements between more or less independent concerns almost as important as the international spread of the daughter-companies of great industrial firms. These agreements were akin to the Kartell agreements of Germany (see *ante*, § 77). They were the result, that is, of attempts to dam back the destructive forces of international competition. There were divisions of the markets or the trade routes of the world between groups of producers or of carriers. There were, in some cases, international price-fixing agreements among producers. Beyond and behind particular businesses and trades stood banking concerns, financial groups, even individuals of uncommon power and range, who—very largely owing to the universal prevalence of the joint stock company—could influence economic life, and with it politics and the fate of nations, throughout the inhabited world. Illustrations from the commercial vicissitudes and commercial crises of the period since 1857 are not necessary to prove the economic interdependence of the nations. Every aspect of their modern history illustrates it. Some of them might specialise on the "peaceful penetration" of their neighbours, but penetration, if unequal, was mutual. With the railway and the telegraph the world had become one market. With the spread of a fairly uniform company law and of a uniform commercial practice, it was tending to become a single economic organism.

EPILOGUE

§ 99. At the end of any economic survey of history, it is right to stop and ask—and what had the developments of this time and these places done for the common man? The answer cannot be in terms of happiness, for which the economist has no measuring rod. And it cannot be precise, whatever the terms. Still, it can be attempted.

The representative common man of France and Germany in 1815 was a peasant. By 1914 he was not; but in both countries the peasants were much the largest single economic group, and in France very much the largest. In 1815 the French peasant was recently freed from a most distasteful system of land tenure and from a thoroughly bad system of taxation and government. He had taken a step forward in opportunities for economic well-being such as can only be taken at long intervals in the history of any social group. But, except in favoured districts, he still lived very hard and worked unceasingly. In spite of his work he was not yet entirely free of the spectre that had followed him all through the ages—that of famine in years of harvest failure and dearth.

If the nineteenth century had done nothing else, it would deserve credit for having first reduced and then, it may fairly be said, removed the age-long dread of famine from the peasants and people of Western Europe. Whether its methods were the wisest for the future is not the question. The thing done stands to its account. It was so well done that people almost forgot the risks which of old had been daily realities. Old France, as the Vicomte d'Avenel once pointed out, had a whole string of proverbs about bread. The France of 1894–1914 had forgotten them. You no longer praised a man by saying he was "as good as good bread," because it no longer seemed a high compliment. You no longer talked of the "black bread of adversity," because black bread was not made in France. The most unfortunate Frenchman ate the white wheaten bread that was served to princes in the middle ages, and ate it freely. Besides his abund-

ance of good bread, the average Frenchman during the second
half of the nineteenth century increased his consumption of
wine and potatoes by fifty per cent.; his consumption of meat,
beer and cider by a hundred per cent.; his consumption of
spirits by two hundred per cent.; his consumption of sugar and
coffee by three hundred per cent.[1]
The improvement in dietary had been equally great for the
German peasant, and the average German. He ate rye bread,
which had almost disappeared from France; but otherwise his
position was similar. Between 1860 and 1900, for example, the
consumption of meat per head in Germany increased nearly a
hundred and thirty per cent.[2] Moreover the German peasant
had, in numberless cases, acquired his full freedom and his
land since 1815. That the land reforms had been accompanied
by a certain crushing down of men in the social scale, and that
the peasant of the east in 1914, was often miserable enough,
judged by absolute standards, must not be allowed to hide the
far more miserable position from which he had been raised. The
"hapless missing link between a beast of burden and a man"
had become at least human. It was no longer likely that a
traveller in the east would see a woman in the fields, in October,
working in an old open coat, a skirt, and nothing else, a sight
possible in the years before emancipation[3].

In both countries the peasant dressed better—very much
better. All through the century woollen clothing had been
driving out linen (see *ante*, § 21), and leather boots sabots or bare
feet. The sabot was not extinct; nor for that matter was the clog
in Lancashire. Both had their value and the clog was not a symbol
of poverty. The sabot had been. Where it survived, it generally
survived for reasons of use.

Both countries had their agricultural labourers, some of
whom were not to be envied; but no class had been created to
inherit the struggle and the wretchedness of the less fortunate
peasants and wage earners of 1815. The peasant had not risen

[1] These are d'Avenel's figures for the years 1840–95, *Le Mécanisme de la
vie moderne*, pp. 157–8.
[2] Further figures are given in S. von Waltershausen, *op. cit.* pp. 372–3.
[3] Knapp, *Die Bauern-Befreiung*, etc., I, 79.

on another man's shoulders, except perhaps in so far as he and his wage-earning cousin left the meanest tasks of all to migrants from outside, Poles, Italians, Spaniards, as the case might be (see *ante*, §§ 43 and 54). These people also lived better than their grandfathers had lived, so far as one knows.

Whether either the true peasant or the rural wage earner of 1914 did a lighter day's work than the men who had seen Napoleon ride by their fields, anywhere from Poland to Spain, is unknown. Those who have watched the peasant on his land often doubt whether a heavier day's work is possible. It is even likely that he does more than his grandfather, just because he does it all for himself. Of the labourer it is still harder to speak. Organised specialists, like the French woodmen or vineyard workers, had won for themselves by collective action hours and conditions of work certainly better than those of their predecessors. The farm servant, living in, on the other hand, either in France or Germany, might do as hard a day's work as ever; although the conditions of his housing had probably improved a little, impossible as that may appear to anyone who knows what they are sometimes like.

In so far as the urban wage earner had become the representative man in either country, he shared the better bread, the more abundant meat, the beer, the sugar, the coffee, the woollen clothes, the leather boots, and the other material advantages of the average Frenchman or German. Comparisons with the life of his grandfather are harder for him than for the peasant, just because his grandfather as often as not had been a peasant or half a peasant. To many outside judges the life of a workman at Krupp's in 1914 may seem less attractive, even economically, than that of the peasant-ironworkers of Siegerland in the forties (see *ante*, § 20). Looking at the economic considerations only, John Stuart Mill's doubt, expressed in 1847, comes to mind—"hitherto it is questionable if all the mechanical inventions yet made have lightened the day's toil of any human being. They have enabled a greater population to live the same life of drudgery and imprisonment[1]." All that can be said with certainty is that Krupp's workman had a command over necessaries and

---

[1] *Principles of Political Economy*, Pt IV, Ch. 6.

simple luxuries, much greater, probably very much greater, than
that of the Siegerland peasant-ironworker; that, in the second
half of the century, mechanical inventions had often tended to
lighten toil; and that, towards the end of the century, there was
everywhere a movement for a shorter working day. England
led the way. In France and Germany, however, the movement
had not got far before 1914. Factory law in 1900 contemplated
a maximum week's work for women of 60 hours in France and
of 65 in Germany. The French law of that year (see *ante*, § 69)
cut the men's day to ten hours, when they worked in the same
places as women. There was also a tendency, outside factories
proper, to reduce the more exacting forms of work (*e.g.* on
locomotives) to 10 hours. But in 1906 France still needed a
law to secure a weekly day of rest for all. So long had it taken
her to rectify what she lost when she swept away ecclesiastical
high days and holy days. *La semaine anglaise*, *i.e.* the Satur-
day half-holiday, was still an ideal.

Germany revised her Industrial Code in 1908. Rules about
hours of work were still confined to women, for whom the
maximum was fixed at 60, subject to numerous exceptions.
Men's working days at that time varied greatly. Many years
before, the building trades, where organisation was good, had
adopted a ten hours' day. Ten hours was also the rule in over
60 per cent. of the factories in Prussia. It may therefore be
taken as the typical German day for wage earners.

Considering that the working day of the Parisian mason or
carpenter in 1848 was eleven hours and that of the French day
workman in the provinces twelve, it might appear that, even in
the current century, legislation and collective action had not
done much more than cancel that lengthening of the standard
day's work which in all countries had been one of the first
consequences of mechanical invention and the harnessing of
men to machines. If, as is possible, the intensity of work
balanced any reduction in duration, Mill's saying might remain
approximately true of the machine workers of France and
Germany in 1914. With the important qualification that a body
of workpeople better nourished and clothed were more capable
of intensive work without suffering.

That the factory worker of 1914 was in both countries economically far better off than he had been, say, in 1847-60, is however beyond question. And a comparison between factory conditions and outdoor day labouring conditions is not quite satisfactory. Perhaps, among a mass of difficult and more or less inconclusive comparisons, the fairest for the whole century would be that between the factory worker of 1914 and the industrial outworker of 1815—hand loom weaver of Lyons, garret craftsman of Paris, or cutler of Solingen. Here the decision would be far more decisively in favour of the conditions of 1914. The outworker had not a standard day. He often worked incredibly long hours, as the hand loom weavers of the Cambrésis did even in the present century (see *ante*, § 64). Very probably he drank bad well water. His home, where he worked, was no doubt far less sanitary than the home or the factory of the man of 1914. His standard of food and clothing was far lower. His expectation of life was far less. Innumerable material comforts and conveniences which were easily within reach of his successor were for him quite unattainable.

"Never," wrote d'Avenel in 1896, "never has this French people of ours been so happy as it is to-day, and never has it believed itself more to be pitied. Its grievances have grown with its comfort; and in proportion as its condition became better it deemed it worse. The mark of this century, favoured among all the centuries, is to be dissatisfied with itself." Precisely as he wrote, prices everywhere began to move slowly up (see *ante*, § 93), to the permanent annoyance of persons with fixed incomes and the temporary annoyance of wage earners who failed to get their earnings adjusted to new conditions. So the early twentieth century was rather more dissatisfied with itself and with rather better reason. There was some evidence, in the years 1901–14, of a slight deterioration in standards of living—not, of course, as compared with 1815, 1845 or 1875, but as compared with the favoured nineties. "Natural" causes connected with price movements were not entirely responsible. The policies of the armed peace and economic self-sufficiency had to be paid for both in France and Germany. German economists admitted that, with an equal expenditure, an English workman was better fed than a German. And English specialists noted, in the ten years before the war, that German rags were not quite so good as they used to be. This is a sure test; for prosperous nations and classes throw away their clothes early. The best rags on the market are American and Canadian; the worst Italian and Greek.

So some people said, and others believed, that "the rich were getting richer and the poor poorer." It is possible that there was a widening gap between, not "the rich" and "the poor,"— terms with no definite meaning—but between specified groups of the richest and the average wage earner. And "the poor" were getting poorer in the sense that some wage earners found that their incomes did not go so far as they used to—and so struck hard and swiftly for more. Whether the gap was wider than it had been a century earlier may be questioned; but no decision either way is possible. No doubt, when prices rise from a monetary cause, gain comes first to dealers and *entrepreneurs*. But when all has been said, it is impossible to argue that the solid economic gains which the average hand worker had made during the great peace of the nineteenth century were seriously threatened. A purely historical conclusion this, which involves no blessing and no cursing of the social system of Europe in the first decade of the twentieth century.

INDEX

Aachen, 90, 94, 293
Accise, 98
Africa, South, 377, 382; South West,
   394
Agricola, 140
Agricultural Societies, French, 181–2,
   184–5
Agriculture, Alpine, 7; Flemish and
   Dutch, 9, 29; open-field, 7–9,
   29, 164, 202 sqq.; specialised,
   173 sqq.
— freedom of and the Revolution,
   11
— machinery and, 168 sqq.
— progress of, French, 21 sqq.,
   177; German, 47 sqq., 202
   sqq., 209, 214 sqq.
— tariffs and, 212–4
Aisne, the, 106; Dep. of, 9, 16, 17
Alais, 145, 234
Algeria, ores of, 239
Allgemeine Elektricitäts Gesellschaft
   (A. E. G.), 307, 308, 366
Allier, Dep. of, 191–2
Alpes Maritimes, Dep. of, 173
Alps, 7, 12, 29, 107, 166–7, 339, 355
Alsace, agriculture of, 9, 22, 29, 33,
   203, 219; cession of, 237; cotton
   industry of, 64–6, 245 sqq., 297;
   peasants of, 2; roads of, 106; 153,
   155, 242, 293, 298, 301, 304, 316–7,
   346
America, *see* United States; South,
   133, 136, 376–7
Amiens, 64, 66, 249; Abbey of St
   John of, 17
Amsterdam, bank of, 122; finance
   and trade of, 123, 135, 372, 375,
   389
Andrézieux, 143
Angers, 8
Angoulême, 8
Anjou, 15, 255
Anne, Queen, 350
Antwerp, 114, 135–6, 140, 248, 264,
   345, 372–3, 375
Anzin, Coy. of, 56, 140, 237
Apprenticeship, 83, 85, 289, 334–5
Arabia, 114
Archimedean screw, the, 112
Ardennes, 29, 30, 149

Argonne, 149
Arkwright, 55, 68
Armentières, 66
Arnim, 39
Artois, 9, 16, 17
Arts and Crafts, museums of, 54, 55,
   87
Asiatic Coy., 130
Assignats, 19, 138
Augé-Laribé, quoted, 159, 172
Augsburg, 82, 101
Australia, 67, 377, 382
Austria, 31, 42, 116, 154, 174, 282,
   292, 295, 297, 315, 317, 322, 355,
   378
Auvergne, 8, 15, 147, 240
Avenel, Vicomte d', quoted, 368,
   402–3, 406
Avesnes, 250
Aveyron, Dep. of, 60
Avignon, 147, 165

Bac, rue du, 367
Baden, agrarian reforms in, 42,
   agriculture of, 29, 219; industrial
   experiment in, 86; railways in,
   153, 347; 49, 392
Bakunin, 270
Bamberg, 100, 109
Banfield, T. C., quoted, 30, 88–9, 101
Bank, of Amsterdam, 122; of England,
   121, 137, 382; of France, 121,
   125 sqq., 137, 188, 378, 383 sqq.;
   of Germany, 390 sqq.; of the
   Netherlands, 123; of Prussia, 122,
   128, 389, 391; of Savoy, 386; of
   the United States, 136
Banking, Belgian, 127–8, 131–2,
   136, 385; Dutch, 122, 127, 385;
   French, 125 sqq., 383 sqq.; Ger-
   man, 128–9, 384 sqq.; Swiss, 123,
   129
Banque de Paris et des Pays Bas, 389
Banque Française, 389
Barbary, 113
Barberet, 271
Baring Bros., 133
Bar-le-duc, 173
Bar-sur-Seine, 23
Basel, 123, 154
Basses Alpes, Dep. of, 22

Bastiat, F., 74
Bauernlegen, policy of, 36–7, 39, 43, 198
Bauernschutz, policy of, 36, 42, 228
Bavaria, agrarian policy of, 36, 46, 49, 195, 197–8; agriculture of, 219; banks in, 392; industry in, 83–4; railways in, 150, 153; roads in, 100, 108; and the Zollverein, 99
Bayreuth, 296
Beaucaire, 145
Beauce, 16
Bebel, 325, 327–8
Beet, *see* Sugar beet
Belfast, 116, 291, 303
Belgium, agriculture of, 177; banking in, 127–8, 131–2, 136, 385; currency of, 125; company law of, 130–2; early industrialisation of, 56–7, 116, 135; prosperity of, 123; railways of, 140 sqq., 344–5; trade of, 114
Belle Jardinière, 367
Belleville, 241
Belt, 110
Bendigo, 376
Berlin, coal of, 283; fields of, 32; industries of, 86–8, 94, 293, 300, 307, 334–5; population of, 87; railways from, 152, 154; shopping in, 118; telegraph at, 156–7; University of, 47; 226, 323, 330, 353, 369, 372–4
Bern, 129
Bernstein, 332
Berri, 8, 15, 158
Bessemer, 236, 284
Béthune, 56, 233
Béziers, 104
Biddle, Mr, of U.S.A., 137
Bilbao, 239, 284
Billingsgate, 368
Bimetallism, 123 sqq., 379 sqq.
Birmingham, 54
Birth-rate, 280
Biscay coast, 8, 11
Bismarck, 39, 50, 83, 196, 211, 230–1, 314 sqq., 326–8, 330–1, 335–6, 337, 346–7, 382
Black Country, 90
Black Forest, 34, 96, 118, 300–1
Black Prince, 115
Blanc, Louis, 266 sqq.
Blanqui, 268–9, 270
Blanzy, 234
Bleichröder, 391
Blockade, continental, 87, 111
Bochum, 312
Boer War, 377

Bohemia, 30, 31, 34
Boiler Makers' Union, 286
Bonaparte, Jerome, 322
Bon Marché, 367
Bonn, 89, 154
Bonnerot, M., 367
Boot-making, French, 70; German, 301–2, 370
Bordeaux, size of, 53; agriculture of district, 163, 173, 190; trade of, 115, 119; 80–1, 126, 145, 154, 342
Borsig, 91
Boucicaut, Aristide, 367
Boulton and Watt, 54
Bounties, 244, 264
Bourbonnais, the, 15, 191
Bourbons, the, 14, 67, 71, 105, 266
Bourges, 145
Bourgin, G. and H., quoted, 78, 81
Bourlon Wood, 351
Bourses du Travail, 274 sqq.
Bowring, Dr, quoted, 101–3, 303
Bradford, 249, 375
Braine-le-Comte, 141
Brandenburg, canals in, 107; co-operation in, 225; Electors of, 37; village life in, 41, 83; 389
Brassey, Thomas, 134
Brazil, gold of, 376–7, 394; 298
Bremen, gilds of, 323; industries of, 86, 295; shipbuilding at, 286; trade of, 113, 117, 282, 297, 358–9, 373; 154, 345
Brenner, the, 339
Breslau, 31, 152, 296, 326
Brest, 145–6, 154
Briand, M., 275
Bridgewater, Duke of, 104
Briey, 237, 239
Brighton Road, 350
Brindley, 104
British Museum, 327
Brittany, agrarian life of, 7, 11, 15, 23, 119, 173
Broken Hill, 377
Bromberg, 154
Bruges, 141, 344
Brunel, 156
Brunswick, 50, 153, 199, 203, 385
Brussels, 140–1, 389
Buda-Pest, 375
Building Trade, 75–6, 79, 275
Burg, 90
Burgundians, 7
Burgundy, agrarian life of, 15, 18, 160, 165, 173, 186
By-industries, of German peasants, 89, 92–3, 95–6, 299 sqq.

Cables, submarine, 157, 363
Calais, 50, 110, 147, 154
Calico printing, 63, 64, 94
California, 357, 382
Calvados, Dep. of, 16
Camargue, the, 167
Cambrai and Cambrésis, the, 104, 250, 255, 406
Cambridgeshire, 216
Canada, 320
Canals and waterways, French, 104–6, 350 sqq.; Flemish, 107; German, 107, 352 sqq.
Cape of Good Hope, 292–3
Capital, blind, 133, 136
Capitalism, as old as civilization, 2; slow growth in Germany, 85 sqq.; and French agriculture, 192 sqq.; and the Commune of 1871, 271
Caprivi, 211–2, 319
Carcassonne, 67
Cardiff, 282
Carding machinery, 55, 68
Carpathians, 34
Carpentras, 185
Cassel, 99, 100, 154
Cateau, Le, 67–8, 249
Cenis, Mont, 105, 150, 339
Cens payers, 13, 14, 38
Centre, canal du, 352
Chalons-sur-Marne, 119, 147
Chalons-sur-Saône, 147
Champagne, 21, 23, 191
Channel, the, 11
Chappe, Claude, 156
Chaptal, quoted, 55, 56, 233
Charleroi, 141
Chartres, 119, 146
Châtellerault, 241
Chemical industry, English, 256; French, 256–7; German, 303 sqq.
Chemistry, 54, 69, 103
Chemnitz, 282, 296
Cher, Dep. of, 190
Cheshire, 256
Chevalier, M., quoted, 107, 109
Chicago, 113, 373
Chile, 357
China, 378
Class warfare, 275
Clayton-Bulwer Treaty, 357
Clermont, 8
Cleves, 30, 52
Clock-making, 80, 96
Cloth, finishing, 63; shoddy, 67, 250; union, 67
Clothing trades, German, 302–3
Clyde, 244
Coal mining, Belgian, 57, 240–1;

French, 56, 233 sqq.; German, 89, 91, 234, 280 sqq.; trade, 115, 234, 281–3
Coats, J. and P., 366
Cobden, 74, 178, 246, 260
Coblenz, 156
Coburgs, 100
Cockerill, Wm., 58
Coffee trade, 114
Cognac, 119
Cohn, G., quoted, 354
Collective bargains, 331–3
Cologne, 90, 140, 154, 223, 335, 385
Combination law, French, 76, 269
Comices, 184, 185
Commentry, 237
Commercial classes, growth of, 364 sqq.
Commons and Common Rights, French, 11–12, 27, 166 sq.; German, 40, 48, 201 sqq.
Commune, of 1871, 270–1, 303
Communism, 324
Communist Manifesto, 268
Compagnie Transatlantique, 358
Compagnonnage, 76–81, 270, 275
Comptoir d'Escompte, 388
Concentration, industrial, 61, 71, 90, 258 sqq., 277, 281, 287–9, 301
Confédération Générale du Travail (C. G. T.), 274 sqq.
Conflans, 237
Conservatoire des Arts et Métiers, 54–5, 87–8
Considérant, V., 268
Constantinople, 339
Cooperation, French, 183 sqq.; German, 221 sqq., 326 sqq.
Corbie, Abbey of, 17
Corniche road, 350
Corn trade, 10, 113, 119, 181–2, 209
Corporations de Métiers, see Gilds
Cortez, 356
Côte d'Or, Dep. of, 190
Cotentin, the, 7
Cotton industry, French, 64–5, 245 sqq.; German, 93–4, 295 sqq.; trade, 135–6
Courland, 113
Courrières, 233
Courtrai, 141, 344
Covent Garden, 368
Cracow, 154
Crédit, agricole, 384; du Nord, 389; foncier, 383–4; industriel, 387; Lyonnais, 386–7; mobilier, 127, 383 sqq.
Creusot, le, 54, 59–60, 62, 134, 234, 236–7

Crimean War, 4
Crises, commercial, 135 sqq., 316, 385–6, 401
Crompton, 55
Cromwell, Oliver, 230
Crops, yield of, 27, 177, 213, 218–20
Cugnot, 242
Currencies, 121, 123, 125, 376 sqq.
Customs, *see* Tariffs
Customs Union, proposed Franco-Belgian, 74; *and see* Zollverein
Cutlery industry, French, 240–1; German, 288–9

Dairy industry, 174, 226
Dalmatia, 105
Danzig, corn trade of, 50, 113, 212; 34, 154, 385
Daracq, 242
Darmstadt, 385, 390
Dauban, quoted, 271
Dauphiné, 22, 167
David, Dr, quoted, 332
Dawson, W. H., quoted, 207
Decazeville, 60
Delbrück, 315–6
Delescluze, 270
Delisle, quoted, 6, 158
Denain, 60, 237
Denmark, agrarian development of, 32, 41, 178, 185, 219, 226, 272; 111, 364
Desandrouin, the Vicomte, 56
Deutsche Bank, 390 sqq.
Devoir mutuel, 77
Dieppe, 64
Dieterici, quoted, 85, 95
Dietrich, 237
Dijon, 145–6
Dilke, Sir Charles, quoted, 356
Dingley Tariff, 320
Diskontogesellschaft, the, 390
Disraeli, 356
Distilleries, 51; cooperative, 226
Domesday Book, 62
Dortmund, 312, 353
Douai, 9
Doubs, Dep. of, 185
Douglas, machine maker, 55
Dover, 157
Dresden, 151, 154, 339
Dresdener Bank, 390
Dufaud, M., of Grossource, 60
Dundee, 116
Dunkirk, 256, 264, 373
Dürer, 82
Durham, cattle, 25; miners, 273; coal, 239
Düsseldorf, agrarian frontier near, 30, 31; 151–2, 154

Dyeing, 92, 99

East (Est), canal of, 351–2; Railway Coy. of, 147–8, 343, 346
Economists, Congress of, in 1847, 74
Education, agricultural, in Germany, 216; and German industry, 103; in Polish Prussia, 229
Ehrenberg, quoted, 374
Eichthal, 383
Eiffel, M., works of, 241
Eiffel, the, agriculture in, 30
Eisenach Congress, 325, 328
Elbe, as division of East and West Germany, 30, 31, 39, 46; navigation of, 353–5; tolls on, 109; 33, 35, 100, 110, 199, 200, 216, 280
Elberfeld, 93–4, 151–2, 293, 298
Elbeuf, 67, 251
Electrical industries, 257, 306 sqq.
Electricity and industry, 235, 254, 289
Emancipation of the peasantry, *see* Peasants
Emden, 130, 353
Emigration, German, 208, 279
Ems, 29, 353
English Historical Review, quoted, 113
Entrepôt trade, 114
Epéhy, 250
Epernay, 368
Epinal, 246
Erzgebirge, 300–1
Essen, 91, 312
Estrées, 250
Eure, Dep. of, 16
Eure-et-Loir, Dep. of, 16
Evreux, 64, 67, 251
Exchange (*Bourse, Börse*), development of modern type, 371 sqq.; laws about, 398
Exhibitions, industrial, 54

Fabianism, 332
Factories, 2, 65, 70, 194, 246 sqq., 288; *and see* Concentration, industrial
Factory legislation, 335–6, 405
Fairs, 117 sqq., 369 sqq.
Fallowing, 8, 9, 23–4, 175–6, 218
Farming, *see* Tenant farming
Felten and Guilleaume, Messrs, 307
Fields, rearrangement of, 201–3; *and see* Agriculture
Finance, *haute internationale*, 122
Fischer, P. D., quoted, 157
Flanders, 9, 16, 18, 24–5, 26–7, 29, 107

Flax, growing, 10, 51, 255; industry, 69, 92, 95, 255, 289 sqq.; trade, 113
Flux, A. W., quoted, 374
Fontainebleau, 76
Foreign trade, balance of, 360–1; growth of, 114–5, 115–6, 359 sqq.
Forest colonies, German, 34, 204
Forests, 12, 40, 167, 200–1
Fortschrittspartei (Party of Progress), 327, 329
Fourchambault, 60, 237
Fourier, 266
Fourmies, 250
Fraisans, 237
Franche Comté, 14, 186, 237
Frankfurt-a-M., banking and finance of, 123, 133, 372; gilds of, 323; fair of, 99, 117, 369–70; 100, 153, 223, 246, 307, 332
Frankfurt-a-O., 117, 152, 154, 370
Franqueville conventions, the, 148, 343
Frederick the Great, 42–3, 47, 51, 85, 130, 383, 390
Frederick William IV, 152
Freiburg, 298
French Revolution, of 1789, 1, 6, 9, 10–12, 14–5, 17–8, 28, 37, 71, 80, 121, 184; of 1830, 105, 131; of 1848, 15, 24, 70, 137
Freycinet, 341 sqq., 351
Friendly Societies, 78
Frisia, 33
Fruitières, 187
Fulling mills, 68
Fürth, 151
Futures, dealings in, 371 sqq.

Galicia, 90
Gambetta, 341
Gard, Dep. of, 234
Garonne, 7, 8, 106, 160, 368
Gas, 69
Gaudin, 124
Gauss, 157
Gelders, 30, 52
Gemeindekrankenversicherung, 336
General German Labour Union, the, 327–8
Geneva, 7, 123, 389
Genoa, 373
Genossenschaftswesen, 203–4
George III, King, 50
Germain, M. H., 386
Gesell, see Journeyman
Gesindeordnung, the, 205
Gewanne, 31
Gewerbefreiheit, 322 sqq.

Gewerbe Institut, the, 87, 91, 102
Ghent, 141
Gilds, 76, 83–5, 289, 322 sqq., 333–5
Givet (-Dinant-Namur-Liège railway line), 344
Gnesen, 350
Goethe, 357
Gold, discoveries and influence of, 123–4, 376 sqq., 381–2; standard, 123–4, 378 sqq.
Gotha, 100, 385
Gothein, quoted, 96
Goths, 7
Göttingen, 156, 157
Greetsiel, 363
Gros fermiers, 17
Grossmann, quoted, 203
Grossource, 60
Guesde, Jules, 272, 274
Guienne, 15
Guillaumot, quoted, 144
Guise, 249
Guizot, 74

Hainault, 57–8
Halle, 154
Halles centrales, 368
Ham, 357
Hamburg, gilds of, 323; industries of, 86; shipbuilding at, 286; trade of, 113, 135–6, 282; 100, 109, 117, 154, 226, 261, 339, 345, 358–9, 372–5
Hamburg-Amerika line, 359
Hamm, official's walk to, 108
Handicraft, 84–5, 301
Handloom Weavers' Commission, Report of, quoted, 59
Haniel, Huyssen and Jacobi, works of, 91
Hanover, agrarian life of, 36, 50, 199; railway policy of, 153, 346; and the Zollverein, 99, 100, 315; 154, 155, 293, 304
Hanse towns, 87, 100, 111, 114, 125, 132, 287, 358, 397
Harburg, 154
Hardenberg, 44
Hargicourt, 250
Harkort, Fritz, 150
Harvests, bad, of the '40's, 137; of 1878–9, 180, 267
Harz Mts., mines of, 89, 336
Haute-Garonne, Dep. of, 172
Havre, 75, 114, 126, 136, 144–5, 154, 244, 248, 264, 345, 358, 372–3
Hayange, 236–7
Hazebrouck, 9
Heilmann, invention of, 68, 232, 249

Hemp-spinning, 69, 92
Hesse, 99, 153, 155, 225-6, 346-7
Hildesheim, 216
Hirsch-Duncker Unions, 329-30
Hof, 296
Hoffmann, J. C., quoted, 369
Holden, invention of, 249
Holdings, size of, 164 sqq., 198, 207 sqq., 227 sqq.
Holland, agrarian life of, 29, 30, 33, 177, 225; banking in, 122, 127; company law of, 130; currency of, 125, 379; trade of, 59, 114, 116, 130, 133, 245, 355, 360, 371-2
Holstein, 100, 225
Homeworkers, 86
Hope Bros., 123, 133
Hottinguer and Co., 137
Humboldt, 356
Huntley and Palmer, 183
Hydro-electric development, 235

Ile de France, 9, 16, 17, 21
Immigrants, agricultural, 168 sqq., 206 sqq.
Implements, agricultural, 26, 52
Inclosure, in France, 6, 7; in Germany, 32; in Denmark, 32; in Hanover, 50; in Low Countries, 29; in Prussia, 48; in Schleswig-Holstein, 50; in Sweden, 32
Industrial census, the German, 287
— concentration, see Concentration, industrial
— Revolution, 53, 71, 279
Industrialism, 56, 233, 238, 265, 278 sqq., 326
Innung, see Gild
Insurance, 333, 336 sqq., 365
Interdependence of nations, 135 sqq., 209-10, 262-3, 400-1
International, the, 270-1, 328
International trade, see Foreign trade
Interviews on Banking and Currency, quoted, 384
Investment habit, 132 sqq.
Ireland, 2, 137, 201, 223, 255, 292
Iron industry, see Metallurgy
— ores, 237-9, 283-4; pig, output of, 283
Isère, Dep. of, 56
Italy, 2, 104, 110, 130, 179, 252-3, 322, 339-40, 350, 355

Jackson, President, 136
Jacquard, his loom, 55, 69, 232
James, Master, his children, 80
Japan, 253, 381
Jaurès, quoted, 271

Jena, battle of, 43, 87, 122
Jews, 123, 223, 383
Joint Stock enterprise, 130 sqq., 395 sqq.
Joseph II, Emperor, 42
Journeyman, the, 79 85, 289, 323
July Monarchy, 106, 350
Jung, Messrs, 95
Junker, 35-6, 47, 50, 197, 199, 200, 204, 206, 219-20, 315, 335, 390
Jura, 12, 167, 184

Kabul, 375
Kartells, 307, 309 sqq., 319-20, 394, 401
Kashgar, 375
Kay, 55
Keynes, J. M., quoted, 284
Kiel, 157, 353
Klondyke, 377
Knapp, G. F., quoted, 41, 196, 403
Königsberg, 154, 385
Köthen, 152
Krefeld, 93 sqq., 298-9
Krupp's, 91, 394, 404

Laboulaye, C., quoted, 70
Labour, see Compagnonnage, Factory laws, Socialism, Trade Unions, Wage labour, Working day
Labour law, 76 sqq., 324-5
Labourers, agricultural, 17-8, 39, 45-6, 162 sqq., 204 sqq., 227 sqq., 403
Lafayette, 25
Laibach, 154-5
Lamartine, 144, 146
Lancashire, 65, 71, 245, 256, 273, 286, 297, 403
Landes, the, 8, 11, 167, 191-2
Landownership, French, 18 sqq., 160 sqq.; German, 198 sqq.
Langensalza, 100
Langres, 240
Languedoc, 104, 190
Laon, 17
Lardner, D., quoted, 141, 157
Lassalle, Ferdinand, 326 sqq., 330
Latin Union, 379
Lausitz, 293
Lavergne, L. G. de, quoted, 8, 107, 158
Leather industry, 70
Lebeau, 141
Leblanc, 54
Leeds, 54, 116
Lehrling, see Apprenticeship
Leipzig, bank of, 129; fair of, 99, 117, 370-1; 99, 151, 154, 156-7, 327, 331

Lens, 56, 233–4
L'Escarpelle, 233
Lesseps, 134, 357
Levallois-Perret, 241
Levant, 110, 252
Levasseur, quoted, 73–4, 120, 258
Levine, quoted, 77
Libau, 113
Liebig, Justus von, 52, 216
Liebknecht, 325, 327
Liège, 57, 58, 140–2
Lignite, 280–2
Lille, 53, 64–7, 126, 233, 242–3, 246–8
Limoges, 8
Limosin, 15
Lincoln Wolds, 216
Linen industry, 64, 255, 289 sqq.
List, Friedrich, 101, 151, 315
Liverpool, 54, 136, 143, 261, 373
Liverpool's Act, 121
Livestock, 176, 220
Livret, the, 77
Locomotive building, 242–3
Lodève, 67
Loir-et-Cher, Dep. of, 16, 185
Loire, 7, 15, 56, 106, 143, 234, 352
— Dep. of, 78
Loiret, Dep. of, 16
Lombardy, 339
London, 32, 67, 114, 135–6, 173, 185, 264, 269, 293, 303, 326, 363, 372–3
Longwy, 237, 239
Loos, 233–4
Lorraine, 14, 22, 237, 284, 286, 301, 316–7, 346
Louis XIV, 104
— XV, 105
— XVI, 16, 22, 25, 104
— Philippe, 73, 75, 77, 105, 134, 156, 260, 267
Loutchisky, J., quoted, 16
Louvain, 141–2
Louviers, 67, 251
Louvre, 367
Lowestoft, 363
Lübeck, 316, 323, 353
Ludwig of Bavaria, 150
Lüneburg Heath, 50
Luther, 32, 96
Luxembourg Commission, see Workers' Commission
Luxemburg, 280–1, 283–4, 286
Lyons, 23, 53, 55–6, 64, 69, 82, 119, 126, 143–5, 253–4, 267, 298
Lys, the, 106

Maassen. 97, 99
Macadam, 350

Machine making, 55, 87, 242
Machinery, agricultural, 26, 52, 168, 170 sqq.; textile, 61–2, 65–6
McKinley Tariff, 319
Madagascar, 357
Magdeburg, 100, 109, 151–2, 154, 216, 353, 373
Main, 33, 34, 109, 153–4, 347
Maine, 15, 21, 255
Mainmortables, 14
Mainz, 109, 154
Malines, 140–1
Malthus, 280, 361
Manby, Wilson and Co., 60, 134
Manchester, 54, 143, 317
Mannheim, 110, 353, 374
Manteuffel, 196
Marche, La, 15
Market, yearly (Jahrmarkt), 117, 369–70; halls, 368–9
Marne, 25, 106, 240, 351–2
Marseilles, 53, 110, 126, 144, 358, 372–3, 383
Marsh Colonies, 34, 204, 207, 225
Marshall, Dr A., quoted, 310, 393
Martin, 238
Martin Saint Léon, quoted, 79
Marx, Karl, 268, 270, 324, 325, 327
Mason, funeral of a, 80
Maybach, von, 347
Mazamet, 67, 251
Mazzini, 270
Mecklenburg, agrarian life of, 34, 37, 198, 200, 206, 219, 225; currency of, 125; gilds in, 334; industry of, 83, 370; steamers of, 111; and the Zollverein, 100; 316
Mediterranean lands, agrarian life of, 7
Meiningen, 100, 300
Meitzen, quoted, 35, 52
Méline Tariff, 182, 247, 263–4, 320
Memel, 98
Menin, 344
Merchant, evolution of the, 116
Meredith, H. O., quoted, 258
Merino sheep, 25, 51, 66, 115
Messageries maritimes, 358
Metallurgy, Belgian, 58; French, 59–61, 235 sqq.; German, 89 sqq., 102, 283 sqq.
Métayers, 14–16, 19, 21, 161, 191–2, 199
Metz, 237, 368
Meurthe et Moselle, Dep. of, 239
Meuse, 58, 344, 351
Mexico, 134, 377
Middleman, 70, 85, 86, 192 sqq.
Middlesbrough, 239, 244, 284

Mill, J. S., quoted, 15, 404
Millerand, M., 275
Minette ore, 237
Mirabeau, 121, 144
Mississippi Scheme, 132
Mœuvres, 351
Moltke, 155
Money, purchasing power of, 138 sq., 379 sqq.
Mons, 57, 141
Monte Cristo, Count of, 156
Montmartre, 268
Mosel, 33, 107, 207, 237
Motz, 97, 150
Moyeuvre, 237
Mühlheim, 307, 312
Mulhouse, 65, 145, 242, 245
Mun, Thomas, quoted, 113
München-Gladbach, 293, 295
Munich, 153-4
Münster, 108

Nail-making, machinery for, 70
Namur, 58, 141
Nancy, 145
Nantes, 53, 126, 145, 342
Napoleon I, 1, 4, 9, 20, 24-5, 60, 65, 71, 79, 104, 270, 350, 356, 404; his Codes, 3, 76-7, 130, 397
— III, 184, 260-1, 269, 327, 351, 357, 383, 396
Nassau, 346
National debts, 121-2
— Telephone Coy., 364
Navigation Laws, English, 111-12; French, 261 sqq.
Navvies, British, 134
Neckar, the, 33, 34
Necker, 123
Neuvilly, 250
Neuwied, 223
Nevada, 377
Nevernois, 15
Nevers, 8, 60
New York, 135, 157, 316, 363
Newcomen, 56
Niederbronn, 237
Nièvre, Dep. of, 190
Nijni-Novgorod, 117, 375
Nîmes, 27, 190
Noel, O., quoted, 72
Nogent, 240-1
Nord, Dep. of, 16, 54, 56, 64 sqq., 233-4
— Canal, 351
— Railway Coy., 147 sqq., 341 sqq.
— Belge Railway Coy., 344
Nord-Deutscher Lloyd, 359

Nördlingen, 108
Normandy, agrarian life in, 16, 18, 19, 21, 23; industries of, 64, 66, 67, 247-8, 251; population in, 160
Norway, 111, 350
Notre Dame de Paris, 76
Nova Scotia, 112
Nuremberg, 31, 82, 84, 102, 118, 151, 300, 307

Oberhausen, 91
Odenwald, the, 34
Oder, the, 35, 280, 353
Odessa, 73
Oettingen, 108
Oidium fungus, 178
Oise, Dep. of, 9, 16, 17
— the, 106
Oldenburg, cooperation in, 225-6; gilds of, 323; 100, 315
Open-field agriculture, 7, 29 sqq., 48-9, 164, 214-6
Oppenheim, 383
Orleans, 10, 15, 126
— Railway Coy., 147, 341 sqq.
Ortskrankenkasse, 336
Ostend, 141
Oudet, M., 185
Ourcq, 25
Out work, 63-4, 86, 240, 288, 297, 301-3, 406
Owen, Robert, 268

Palatinate, 84, 302
Panama Canal, 356-8
Panhard, 242
Paper money, 19, 122
Paris, agriculture near, 9, 13, 18, 24-5, 162-3, 191; food of, 16, 119; gas light in, 69; growth of, 53, 82, 119; industries of, 68, 70-1, 240-2, 267; quays of, 105; railways from, 144 sqq., 342; shops of, 120, 367-8; 124, 135, 269, 303, 325, 358, 363, 372-5, 378, 406
P.-L.-M. Railway Coy., 147 sqq., 343 sqq.
Pariset, quoted, 253
Parissot, M., 367
Parmentier, and potatoes, 22
Parthenay, 23
Partsch, quoted, 282
Pas de Calais, Dep. of, 16, 17, 25, 56, 233-4
Peasant, agricultural backwardness of, 6, 26, 178, 219-20
— by-industries of, 89, 92-3, 95-6, 299 sqq.
— emancipation of, in Austria, 42;

in Denmark, 41; in France, 1, 8, 13 sqq.; in Germany, 37 sqq., 41 sqq., 195 sqq., 215; in Savoy, 41; in Russia, 2

Peasant, material progress of in 19th century, 402–3; *and see* Agriculture, Cooperation, Crops, Machinery

Peddlers, 86, 118–9

Peel, Sir Robert, 140, 260, 391

Percheron horse, 25

Père la Chaise, 271

Pereire, Emile and Isaac, 144, 383–4

Petersburg, 110, 156

Petin Gaudet and Co., 237

Philip Augustus, King, 368

Photography, 69

Phylloxera, 178–9, 184

Picardy, 9, 16–7, 66

Pirmasens, 301

Placerville, 376

Plymouth, 156

Poitiers, 23

Poitou, 240

Poland, 35, 90, 99, 109, 404

Pomerania, 34, 48, 52, 151, 228, 291, 370

Pont-à-Mousson, 237

Ponts et chaussées, 105

Poor Law, English, 45

Poperinghe, 344

Population, agricultural, French, 167–9; German, 204 sqq., 208–9

— European, growth of, 5, 361

— German, before 19th century, 32

— urban and rural, French, 159–60, 232; German, 82, 278–9

Porter, G. R., quoted, 91, 110, 209

Portsmouth, 156

Posen (and Polish provinces of Prussia), 31, 41, 44, 97, 108–9, 152, 154, 195, 228 sqq., 291, 349–50, 370, 385

Potato, 22–3, 51, 137, 175, 177–8, 213, 217–8

Potin, M., 367–8

Potsdam, 151

Pouyer-Quertier, M., 261

Prague, 31, 151, 154, 339, 373

Price fluctuations, *see* Money, purchasing power of

Printemps, the, 367

Printing trades, 331

Proudhon, 266, 273

Provence, 14, 15, 19, 22

Prussia, agrarian life of, 1, 31, 41 sqq., 49, 195 sqq., 225, 228; bank-

ing in, 122, 385, 391; canals of, 107; gilds of, 83–, 322 sqq.; railway policy of, 151–2, 346 sqq.; roads of, 108–9, 349; tariff of, 97 sqq.; textile industries of, 93–4, 289 sqq.; traders' statistics in, 117, 366; steamers of, 111; 34, 132, 278, 292, 315, 335, 363, 405

Pyrenees, agrarian life of, 7–8, 12–13, 167, 190; 61, 145–6, 339

Raiffeisen, F. W., 221 sqq., 326

Railways and Railway Policy, Belgian, 140 sqq., 344–5; English, 140; French, 143 sqq., 340 sqq.; German, 150 sqq., 345 sqq.

— comparison of development in eight European countries, 339–40

— economic effects of, 28, 52, 81, 155–6, 158, 215, 280, 283

— versus waterways, 352, 354

Rambouillet, 13, 25

Rathgen, K., quoted, 369

Reichsbank, see Bank, of Germany

Reims, 25, 67, 68, 119, 249 sqq.

Renault, 242

Rennes, 146

Restoration period, French, 20, 25, 72–3, 77, 80, 105–6, 130, 184, 260, 350

Reuss-Gera, 293, 385

Reuss-Greiz, 293

Revisionism, 332

Reybaud, quoted, 75

Rhenish Provinces (and Rhine valley), agriculture in, 29, 33, 46, 49, 52, 89, 203, 225; industries of, 88, 90, 93–4, 288; 97, 329, 385

Rhenish-Westphalian Coal Syndicate, 312 sqq.

Rhine, 30, 88, 99, 105, 106, 150, 152, 280, 283, 352; navigation of, 109–10, 353–5

Rhone, 26, 56, 106, 143, 252, 255, 352

— Dep. of, 23, 75

Riesengebirge, 31

Riga, 113

Rittergut, 35–6, 215–6

Rittergutsbesitzer, see Junker

Rive de Gier, 237

Rivoli, rue de, 367, 383

Roads, Dutch and Flemish, 107, 350; French, 104 sqq., 349–50; German, 88, 107 sqq., 349–50; Italian, 104, 107; Norwegian, 350

Roanne, 56, 246
Robertson, Grant, quoted, 316
Robespierre, 270
Roer coal-field, 90, 280
Rogier, M., 141
Romans, agriculture of, 8, 26; law of, 11; roads of, 104, 107
Rome, fall of, 2, 4
Rosenthal, E., quoted, 398
Rotation of crops, 8, 10, 24, 175 sqq., 217 sqq.
Rothschilds, 123, 133
Rotterdam, 264, 345, 372, 375
Roubaix, 54, 65–6, 67–8, 248 sqq., 375
Rouen, 53, 64, 71, 119, 144–5, 185, 246
Rousillon, 25
Ruhr coal-field, 90, 280, 282–3
Ruhrort, 91
Rumania, 210
Runan, 23
Russia, 2, 19, 40, 59, 99, 137, 174, 264, 317, 320, 322, 347, 355, 381

Saar coal-field, 88, 91, 238, 280, 282, 286
Sachs, Hans, 82
Sadowa, 4, 281
St Denis, 64, 241
St Dié, 246
St Etienne, 54, 56, 72, 143, 237, 254, 259
St Gallen, 129
St Germain, 144
St Gothard, 107, 123, 339, 355
St Just, 270
St Martin's Hall, 270
St Omer, 104, 233–4
St Python, 250
St Quentin, 104, 248, 250
St Simon, 266
St Trond, 141
Salonica, 339
Salvador, 383
Samaritaine, the, 367
Sambre, 58
Saône, 119, 351–2
Sardinia, 125
Sauerbeck, quoted, 381
Savoy, 41, 168, 184, 386
Saxony, coal-field of, 280, 282; co-operation in, 225, 326; gilds of, 84, 322; industries of, 88, 94; population of, 278; sugar production in, 51, 217; wool of, 50, 292; and the Zollverein, 99, 117; 30, 34, 98, 292, 301, 304, 385, 392
Scandinavia, 29, 116, 364

Schaafhausenscher Bankverein, 390
Scheldt, 9, 56, 58, 106
Schleswig-Holstein, 30, 32, 50, 225, 316
Schlumberger, 242
Schmoller, G., quoted, 1, 290
Schneider and Coy., 60, 237
Schulze-Delitzsch, 221, 326–8
Schuster, 390
Schwarzburg-Sondershausen, 99
Schwarzenberg, 314
Scutching mills, 64
Sedan, 67, 251, 260
Seehandlung, 390
Séguin, Marc, 242
Seine, the, 15, 29, 55, 109, 119, 351–2
Seine-et-Marne, Dep. of, 190
Seine-et-Oise, Dep. of, 24
Self-sufficiency, policy of, 113, 209, 359–60, 406
Septimer pass, 107
Seraing, 58, 62, 91
Seven Years' War, 130
Sewing machine, 70
Sheep, decline of, 176, 220
Sheffield, 54, 90, 288
Shipbuilding, iron, 112; steel, 243–5, 286–7; wooden, 112, 244
Shops, evolution of, 117 sqq., 303, 366 sqq.
Siberia, 376
Sicily, 113
Sieg and Siegerland, 89, 283, 404
Siemens, Werner von, 157, 236; and Halske, 307
Silesia, coal of, 89, 90, 280, 282; iron of, 286; linen of, 118; Poles in, 231, 329; spinners of, 95; weavers of, 92; wool of, 292–3; 31, 34, 51, 152, 154, 335, 370
Silk industry, French, 64, 69, 252 sqq.; German, 93–4, 298–9
Silkworm, 26, 252
Silver standard, 123 sqq., 376 sqq.
Simplon, 105, 339
Slavs, 30 sqq., 169, 206
Smith, Adam, 70–1, 88, 132
Smithfield, 368
Smithianismus, see Smith, Adam
Socialism, French, 265 sqq., 276–7; German, 325 sqq., 337
Société générale, the, 127–8, 131–2, 136, 383
Solesmes, 250
Solferino, 4
Solingen, 89–90, 102, 288–9, 406
Sologne, la triste, 165
Solomon, his children, 79
Sombart, W., quoted, 346, 349

Somme, 106, 256; Dep. of, 16, 17, 25
Sound, the, 110
South Sea Bubble, 130
Southern (Sud) Railway Coy., 147–8, 343 sqq.
Spain, 130, 134, 176, 179, 286, 339–40, 404
Spice trade, 114
Spinning, by hand, 64, 69, 87, 94–5, 291, 296; by machinery, 55, 65, 68–9, 248
Splügen pass, 107
Stahlwerksverband, 313–4
Stassfurt, 256, 304–5
Steam-engine, 62–3, 66, 68, 88–9, 239–40, 259
Steamers, 110–2, 243–5, 286, 358–9
Steel industries, *see* Bessemer, Iron ore, Martin, Metallurgy, Ship-building, Thomas
Stein, 83
Stephenson, 156
Sterkerade, 91
Stettin, 34, 129, 152, 154, 286
Stieringen-Wendel, 237
Stockholm, 110
Strasbourg, 145, 147, 368
Strikes, 78, 190 sqq., 275, 333, 407
Stuttgart, 296
Sud-Est, Union du, 186
Suez Canal, 134, 253, 356–7, 362
Sugar beet (growth and industry), 25–6, 51, 69–70, 87, 177, 181, 194, 216–7
— trade, 114
Sweden, 32, 58, 90, 111
Switzerland, banking in, 123, 129; capitalism in, 2, 86; coal trade of, 282; company laws of, 130; currency of, 125; railways in, 339; 110, 116, 174, 235, 299, 321, 325, 327, 355, 363
Syndicalism, 273–6
Syndicates, agricultural, in France, 185 sqq.; labour, *see* Trade Unions; industrial, *see* Kartells

Tanivray, M., 185
Tapestry weaving, 63
Tarare, 75, 246–8
Tariffs, French, and agriculture, 179 sqq.; and industry, 71–5, 180 sqq., 251 sqq., 260 sqq.; and shipping, 245
— German, and agriculture, 210 sqq.; and industry, 314 sqq.
— Prussian, 97 sqq.
Tarn, Dep. of, 23
Telegraph, 156–7, 306, 363–4

Telephone, 306, 363–4
Telford, 350
Tenant farming, French, 15–18, 161 sqq.; German, 199, 207
Termonde, 141
Terre Noire Coy., 237
Teschen, 98, 154
Thaer, Albrecht, 47–8, 50–1
Theilbau, 199
Thernaux, M., at the sign of *Bonhomme Richard*, 120
Thiers, Adolphe, 111, 144, 261–2
— town of, 240
Thionville, 236–7
Thirty Years' War, 36
Thomas and Gilchrist, invention of, 237–8, 284
Thuringia, 34, 95, 98, 100, 118, 152, 304
Timber trade, 113
Tirlemont, 141
Tobacco trade, 114
Tonnage, growth of in various countries, 112, 355–6
Toulouse, 53, 126, 145, 172
Tour de France, the, 79
Tourcoing, 65, 66, 248
Tours, 8, 144–5–6, 342
Town growth, 32–3, 53–4, 82–3
Trade Unions, French, 77–8, 189 sqq.; German, 329 sqq.
Transvaal, 378
Treaties, commercial, 260 sqq., 319 sqq.
Treitschke, quoted, 100, 150, 155–6, 280
Trèves, 107
Trieste, 154, 339
Trust, American, 309
Tudors, 36
Tuileries, 267
Turkey, 114, 298
Turgot, 22
Turnips, 24

Union Pacific Railway, 362
Union Parisienne, 389
United States, bank of, 136; carrying trade of, 112; emigration to, 208; tariffs of, 251–2, 264; 114, 181, 233, 285–6, 319–20, 326, 357, 363, 377–8
Ural Mts., 376

Vaine pâture, 13
Valenciennes, 9, 56–7, 65, 144–5, 233
Valentia, 363
Vandals, 7
Vandervelde, quoted, 127

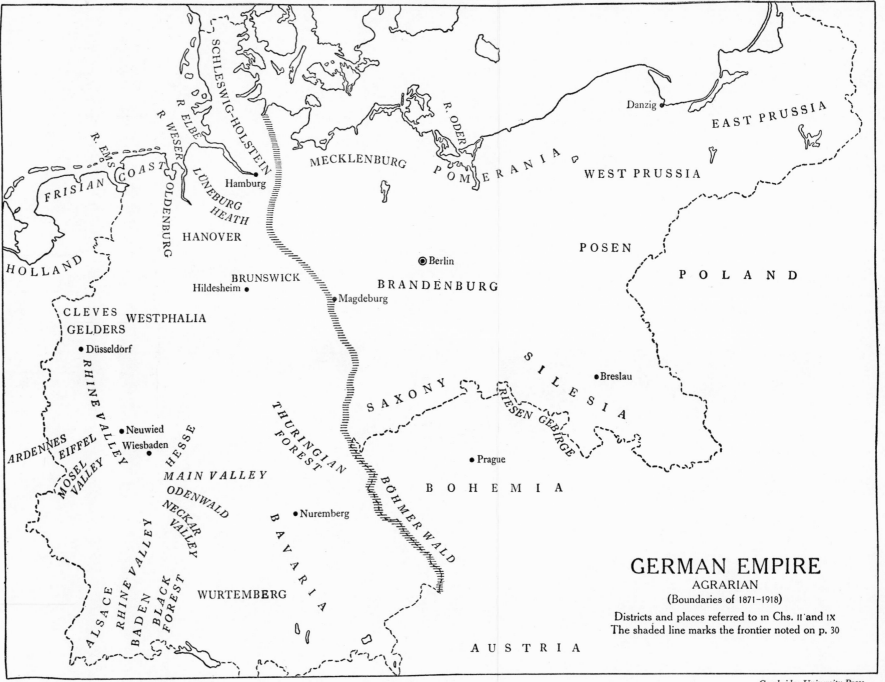

GERMAN EMPIRE
AGRARIAN
(Boundaries of 1871-1918)

Districts and places referred to in Chs. II and IX
The shaded line marks the frontier noted on p. 30